HERBERT CORRESPONDENCE

HERBERT CORRESPONDENCE

THE SIXTEENTH AND SEVENTEENTH CENTURY LETTERS OF THE HERBERTS OF CHIRBURY, POWIS CASTLE AND DOLGUOG, FORMERLY AT POWIS CASTLE IN MONTGOMERYSHIRE

Edited by

W. J. SMITH, M.A.

BOARD OF CELTIC STUDIES, UNIVERSITY OF WALES
HISTORY AND LAW SERIES, NO. XXI

CARDIFF: UNIVERSITY OF WALES PRESS
DUBLIN: IRISH MANUSCRIPTS COMMISSION
1963

MADE IN GREAT BRITAIN

Printed by

R. H. JOHNS LIMITED

NEWPORT · MON.

PREFACE

IT was as long ago as 1953 that I first began the preparation of this Calendar, in my capacity as Researcher in Welsh History to the Board of Celtic Studies of the University of Wales. When I left the University's service a year later I continued the work as an independent editor. By the beginning of 1956 the volume was virtually complete, and was on the point of going to the Press when I learned from the Deputy Keeper of the Public Records, Mr. D. L. (now Sir David) Evans, that the Earl of Powis had recently deposited with the Historical Manuscripts Commission a large body of letters and papers of the Herbert family. These proved on examination to be complementary to those which I had just finished calendaring (and which had been deposited in the National Library of Wales by the late Lord Powis some twenty years earlier). These were, in fact, no more nor less than two halves of the same group of archives. The History and Law Committee of the Board of Celtic Studies were of one mind with myself in the view that, even at this late stage, the Calendar should be re-cast and these newly-discovered papers incorporated into it. They were accordingly deposited for some years in the Berkshire Record Office, where I could conveniently work upon them, and eventually transferred to the National Library of Wales in 1959.

Since about half of the letters and papers calendared in this volume relate to the Irish estates of the Herbert family, the Irish Manuscripts Commission agreed at an early stage to co-operate with the University of Wales in publishing this volume, which accordingly appears as a joint publication of the two bodies. Because of the discovery of the additional material in 1956, and because since 1954 all the work upon this Calendar has had to be done in my spare time, the Commission have had to wait far longer than originally anticipated for the completed work. I am grateful to them for their forbearance.

Throughout this period I have been fortunate in being able to draw upon the knowledge and experience of Dr. J. G. Simms in all my problems arising in the field of Irish history, and my debt to him is very great. I have received similar help in matters of Welsh history from my former colleagues at the National Library of Wales, in particular from Mr. E. D. Jones (now the National Librarian), Mr. G. M. Griffiths, and Dr. B. G. Charles. Dr. Simms, in addition to the repeated help he gave me at earlier stages, has read the completed work in proof for the Irish Manuscripts Commission, and Professor A. H. Dodd has done the same for the Board of Celtic Studies. I am grateful to them both for the suggestions they made, which I have adopted. But, naturally, neither of them bears any responsibility for the mistakes which this work will inevitably be found to contain. I have received help on particular points from many others, acknowledgment of which will be found on the appropriate pages. To all these I should like to express my thanks. It gives me especial pleasure, lastly, to be able to record the particular debt of gratitude which I owe to Dr. Elwyn Davies, Secretary to the Board of Celtic Studies and to the University of Wales Press, for the constant, patient and expert guidance which he has given me throughout.

W.J.S.

Reading,
December 1962

INTRODUCTION

The letters printed in this volume constitute all the sixteenth and the greater part of the seventeenth century correspondence among the vast accumulation of Herbert family records formerly preserved at Powis Castle, near Welshpool, in Montgomeryshire, and now deposited in the National Library of Wales at Aberystwyth, partly by the 4th Earl of Powis in 1933 and 1937, and partly by the present Earl in 1959. But these letters, though part of the Powis Castle archives, were not, for the most part, the correspondence of the family whose seat the castle then was. More than three-quarters of them were written by or to members of another Herbert family, the Herberts of Montgomery—better known by their peerage title of Herbert of Chirbury.[1] A third important, though much smaller, group of letters comes from the Herberts of Dolguog (a *plas* not far from Machynlleth, Montgomeryshire). This family was an offshoot of the Montgomery Herberts that was later reconnected to the parent stock by a marriage that brought it half the estates with, in due course, a re-creation of the Herbert of Chirbury peerage. There are also groups of letters that belonged originally to other families whose relationship to one or other of these three main Herbert lines is (with rare exception) well-established.

Much of the most substantial and important of these non-Herbert accessions is that which came in consequence of the marriage of Francis Herbert of Dolguog to Dorothy, daughter and heiress of John Oldbury, merchant, of Broad Street, London. It contains, in addition to family letters and papers, John Oldbury's business correspondence and commercial documents (invoices, bills of lading, insurance policies, and the like) from 1678 to about 1700, and includes also his letter-book, in which are copies of about three hundred and fifty letters outwards between 1669 and 1690, many addressed to agents, ships' masters, and merchants in foreign ports.

These several groups of manuscripts travelled their separate converging routes to Powis Castle, as inheritance or marriage, merging estates and uniting mansions under the same ownership, transferred, at the same time, ownership of family records. Muniments of title passed, of necessity, with the estates. But the letters and other papers must often have come to their successive new owners incidentally, with the houses and furniture in which they happened to be stored. Neither the exact descents nor the precise movements of these letters can now readily be established. But it may be presumed that by the year 1748 the process of amalgamation had

[1] Chirbury is three miles north east of Montgomery, over the border in Shropshire. Philip Herbert, brother of the 3rd Earl of Pembroke, had been created Earl of Montgomery in 1605, and this is no doubt why, when Sir Edward Herbert of Montgomery, the philosopher, already Baron Herbert of Castle Island in the Irish peerage, was in 1629 given a place in the English peerage, he took his title from his near-by manor of Chirbury.

reached the stage at which the then Lord Herbert of Chirbury—Henry Arthur Herbert, son of Francis Herbert of Dolguog and Dorothy Oldbury, 1st Lord Herbert of the third creation—had become the actual possessor of all the separate groups of letters already mentioned except one—that of the Herberts of Powis Castle itself. In that year the last Marquess of Powis died childless, bequeathing his estates to this Lord Herbert, who was thereupon immediately created Earl of Powis. Three years later he made this union of families total and final by marrying the sole daughter and heiress of the late Marquess's only brother.

But although this new Earl of Powis thus united in himself the ownership of all these family archives, it does not follow that they were immediately brought together under one roof at Powis Castle. Just when this happened is not known. They are now completely merged into one series, and there is every indication that they have been so for a considerable time. Nevertheless, throughout the letters and personal papers—these together form the class within the *Powis Castle Collection* known as the *Powis Castle Correspondence*—there remain many signs of the former distinct identities of the several family groups. These groups have fortunately never been merged deliberately and thoroughly into one chronological (or other) sequence—indeed, there is no attempt at any chronological arrangement—but are intermixed in a haphazard and half-hearted way that can most probably be attributed to frequent consultation and handling over a long period. In short, the *Correspondence* is rather like an inadequately-shuffled pack of cards—a run (perhaps short, perhaps long) from one family suit, a solitary letter from the next, two or three from a third, and so on.

This volume begins with the earliest document in the *Correspondence* and continues, in chronological sequence, to three different *termini* in the 1690's, a separate, convenient, one for each of the three main Herbert lines. The Powis Castle letters proper end with the death of the 1st Marquess of Powis in 1696. Those of the Herbert of Chirbury family end with the death of Henry, the 4th Lord Herbert (and the last of the first creation) in 1691. And those of the Herberts of Dolguog end with the death some time in the early 1690s of Richard Herbert (brother-in-law to the 3rd and 4th Lords Herbert of Chirbury and grandfather of Henry Arthur, 1st Lord Herbert of Chirbury of the third creation). The Oldbury letters and papers are entirely omitted, not because they are less worthy of publication, but principally because they are so different in character and, many of them, in form, that they would be ill-served by any effort to bring them into the framework of this volume.

There was no love lost, and virtually no communication, between the Catholic Herberts of Powis Castle and the Protestant Herberts of Montgomery, and their respective letters therefore fall naturally into two entirely distinct sequences.[1] The Dolguog Herberts, on the other hand,

[1] The Montgomery Herberts themselves remained obstinately Catholic for a time. Sir Edward Herbert, grandfather of the 1st Lord Herbert of Chirbury, was a Catholic at least until late in his life. The 1st Lord Herbert's own indifference to religion is well known, however, and the generalization expressed above is certainly true of the whole of the seventeenth century.

were always on friendly, and often intimate, terms with the members of their senior line the Lords Herbert of Chirbury; in fact a substantial part of the small group of Dolguog letters included in this Calendar consists of correspondence with the Montgomery family. These two groups have therefore, for convenience, been merged. Thus the calendar consists of two parts: The first (by far the smaller) contains the letters of the Herberts of Powis Castle, the Lords Powis and later the Marquess of Powis. The second contains, in one chronological sequence, the letters of the Herberts of Montgomery, later the Lords Herbert of Chirbury, and those of the Herberts of Dolguog (also, of course, later Lords Herbert of Chirbury, though not within the time-span of this volume). This second part contains, also, under their own proper dates, the second most important of the 'foreign' groups—a small batch of letters of the Fox family of Bromfield, near Ludlow, inherited by the Dolguog Herberts. An Appendix, similarly divided, lists those documents which have not been calendared (either because they are too trivial or too defective, or because they can be adequately dealt with by a brief listing).

The essential history, over most of the relevant period, of the principal Herbert families, including those chiefly concerned here, is available in *The Complete Peerage*, and less comprehensively elsewhere. Biographies of a number of their more prominent members are at hand in *The Dictionary of National Biography*. One, Edward, 1st Lord Herbert of Chirbury, whose correspondence makes a not unimportant contribution to this work, is well known, especially through his famous autobiography.[1] No attempt will be made, by way of introduction to this volume, to write a history of the Herbert families, for that would be too large and complex a task. Certainly no attempt will be made to re-write the life of the 1st Lord Herbert (however overdue that work of scholarship might be). Nevertheless, some brief reminder of the facts of the common ancestry of these Herbert families, of their relationship to one another, and of their 'pre-peerage' history in particular, may be useful to those who have occasion to use this Calendar.

Sir William ap Thomas, who died in 1466, was the common ancestor of all the Herbert families with whom we are here concerned. His predecessors had been small Monmouthshire gentry of little estate. He himself was steward of the lordships of Usk and Caerleon under Richard, Duke of York, and was knighted in 1426. He became lord of Raglan by purchase from James, Lord Berkeley, who was his stepson. Raglan had previously belonged to Sir John Bluet of Daglingworth, Gloucestershire, whose daughter and heiress had been the wife of Sir James de Berkeley, Lord Berkeley's father, before she took Sir William ap Thomas as her second husband.

By a second wife Sir William was the father of two eminent sons, William Herbert, created Earl of Pembroke in 1468, and Sir Richard Herbert of Coldbrook, near Abergavenny. These two brothers were beheaded together in 1469 after being captured by Lancastrian rebels at

[1] *The Autobiography of Edward, Lord Herbert of Chirbury*, ed. Sidney Lee. 2nd, ed. revised, 8vo, London, n.d. (1907).

the Battle of Edgecote. Before their descendants are referred to something must be said about their surname, Herbert. Their father, Sir William ap Thomas, is called "Sir William Herbert" in a number of works,[1] but there seems to be no evidence that he or his forebears used the name or were known by it. His eldest son, the later Earl of Pembroke, was, however, apparently using it in his father's lifetime, and refers in his will to a brother as "Thomas Herbert" and also to a "John Herbert" who is obviously a near relation. It seems probable that the name was assumed, for use as a family surname, in the English style, a little before 1460. It is natural enough that a Welsh family living on the borders of England, and seeing itself to be rising rapidly in the world, should want to exchange the Welsh system of patronymics, varying from generation to generation, for a fixed family name. But why they chose the name Herbert remains unexplained. A pedigree from a certain Herbert Fitzroy, said to be an illegitimate son of Henry I, is contained in an alleged commission purporting to have been issued by Edward IV for the purpose alike of ascertaining the newly created Earl of Pembroke's ancestors and of fixing his surname. But this commission was considered by Lewis Dwnn to be a forgery.[2]

Of Sir William ap Thomas's two sons, the elder, William, Earl of Pembroke, was ancestor, through his illegitimate son Richard Herbert, Gentleman Usher to Henry VII, of the later Earls of Pembroke and of Montgomery, and of the Barons, Earls, and Marquesses of Powis. Another son, Sir George Herbert of St. Julian's, Monmouthshire (who must be assumed to be illegitimate also, or he would have succeeded to the Earldom of Huntingdon), was great-grandfather of Sir William Herbert, the Irish 'undertaker' of Queen Elizabeth's day, whose daughter and heiress carried her father's considerable Irish estate, as well as his Monmouthshire lands, to her husband, the 1st Lord Herbert of Chirbury.

The other son, Sir Richard Herbert of Coldbook, was ancestor, in the senior line, of the Herberts of Coldbrook, but they have little or no part in these letters. There is one point only in their pedigree where we need to look more closely. William Herbert of Coldbrook, fifth in descent from Sir Richard, had a younger son John whose son Mathew Herbert, of Crickhowell,[3] was the father of a Thomas Herbert who became servant to Richard, 2nd Lord Herbert of Chirbury, went to Ireland as steward of his patron's estates in co. Kerry, and founded the family of Herbert of Muckross in that county.

It is the descendants of Sir Richard Herbert's younger son, Sir Richard Herbert of Montgomery, that mainly concern us. This Sir Richard Herbert (who died in 1539) had the post of receiver of forfeited York and Mortimer estates under Charles Somerset, Earl of Worcester, steward of the royal manors of Montgomery, Kerry, and Cydewain, and Constable

[1] E.g., Lee's *Autobiography of Lord Herbert* (in the Genealogical Table, pp. 168-169).
[2] G.E.C., *Complete Peerage*, 1st ed., 1887-1898, Vol. VI, p. 212.
[3] In a manuscript pedigree of the Herbert family ("The Genealogy of the Family of Herbert and all its numerous Branches . . .") in the Public Record Office of Ireland in Dublin, he is described as rector of Crickhowell. I am indebted to the Deputy Keeper for a photostat copy of this pedigree.

of Montgomery Castle.[1] His son, Sir Edward Herbert, became himself Constable of the castle, having already obtained, in 1553, the lordship of Chirbury. He was a courtier, being one of the Squires of the Body to Queen Elizabeth, and a soldier of distinction. In Montgomeryshire his power and influence were great; he was Sheriff three times, was *Custos Rotulorum*, and regularly represented the county in Parliament between 1553 and 1588.[2] Sir Edward died, an old man of eighty, in 1593, to be followed only three years later by his eldest son, Richard Herbert, the father of the 1st Lord Herbert of Chirbury, of George Herbert, the equally famous divine, and of Sir Henry Herbert, who held the post of Master of the Revels under both Charleses.

We are now on familiar ground, well documented in the standard works of reference, and very little need be said at this point about the successive Lords Herbert of Chirbury. Richard, the 2nd Lord, succeeded his father in 1648, but survived him only seven years. His two sons, Edward and Henry, then followed him in succession as 3rd and 4th Lords, dying respectively in 1678 and 1691, when the titles became extinct.

In 1694 the Herbert of Chirbury barony (but not the Castle Island title) was re-created for Henry Herbert of Ribbesford, near Bewdley, Worcestershire, the son of Sir Henry Herbert, the Master of the Revels. When his son, another Henry, died without issue in 1738 the title became again extinct. It was created again, for the third time, in 1743. On this occasion it was necessary, to discover the appropriate grantee, to go back beyond the 1st Lord and his brothers to his elder uncle, Mathew Herbert of Dolguog, the new Lord Herbert of Chirbury being Henry Arthur Herbert, fourth in descent from Mathew. This descent from the 1st Lord Herbert's uncle had been reinforced by the marriage of Richard Herbert, Henry Arthur's grandfather and Mathew Herbert's grandson, to Florentia, one of the sisters of the 3rd and 4th Lords Herbert. It is this Henry Arthur Herbert who, in 1748, became Earl of Powis in the manner already described.[3]

What it is necessary to say of the Powis Castle Herberts, by way of general introduction, is more quickly told. The Earldom of Pembroke conferred upon Sir William ap Thomas's elder son was surrendered by the latter's son, at Edward IV's request, in exchange for the Earldom of Huntingdon. There being no Earl of Pembroke in 1551, the title was revived in favour of the 1st Earl's grandson (through his illegitimate offspring, Richard Herbert[4]) Sir William Herbert, President of the Council of Wales, and Master of the Horse. This Earl of Pembroke's second son, Sir Edward Herbert, bought Red Castle (as Powis Castle was then called), together with the Lordship of Powys, in 1587 from Edward Grey, whose family had been lords of Powys for several generations. Sir Edward died in 1595. He was succeeded by his son, Sir William Herbert, who in

[1] *Y Bywgraffiadur Cymreig hyd* 1940, article on "Herbert (Teulu), Trefaldwyn . . . etc." by Prof. A. H. Dodd, pp. 326 ff.

[2] *Ibid.* and *List of Sheriffs for England and Wales*, Public Record Office.

[3] *Supra*, p. 2

[4] *Supra*, p. 4 He is often called "Sir" Richard Herbert "of Ewyas", but as to this see Richard Symonds' *Diary of the Marches of the Royal Army during the Great Civil War*, ed. C. E. Long, Camden Society, 1859, p. 237, and G. E. C., *Complete Peerage*, 1st ed., Vol. VI, p. 216, and the revised edition (1910-1959), Vol. X, p. 405.

1629 was created Baron Powis. He, with his son Percy Herbert, 2nd Lord Powis, and his grandson, William Herbert, 3rd Lord Powis, 1st Earl of Powis in 1674, and 1st Marquess of Powis in 1687, are the members of the family whose letters make up Part I of this Calendar.

The inter-relationships of these various branches of the Herbert family are set out in the pedigree table at the end of the volume; this is intended to illustrate also, as far as possible, the Herberts' connections with other prominent families.

The fewness of the letters of the Powis Castle Herberts is in striking contrast to the remarkably full muster left by their neighbours and kinsmen of Montgomery. So many chance events can bring about the loss or destruction of archives that there is little point in hoping to explain this difference. It may well be, however, that the slenderness of Part I of this Calendar has something to do with the fact that the Powis Castle Herberts were and remained a Catholic family—looked upon, in fact, as among the principal leaders of the Roman Catholic section of the nation. In consequence they were, during most of this period, an object of suspicion to the authorities, and subject to search and surveillance in times of tension—no inducement to committing things to paper, or to keeping letters or records longer than necessary.

Although few, these letters are fairly well spaced between 1624 and 1696 (ignoring the three earlier ones of the Derbyshire FitzHerberts), and they throw valuable light upon the family's concerns and activities at a number of points. The short series of the Civil War period is particularly useful, especially as they relate largely to Sir Percy Herbert, 2nd Lord Powis, about whom little has been written. They touch upon the bitter quarrel between him and his father, arising (ostensibly, at least) from accusations of disloyalty on Sir Percy's part towards the King, and upon Sir Percy's exile abroad (being regarded as an enemy by both sides).

To come to the family's domestic concerns, two stewards, one in the 1630's and the other in the 1670's, found it necessary to defend their actions (in each case, curiously enough, to the Lady Powis of the day) at considerable length.[1] On the second occasion we have two such letters from the steward, sandwiching the draft of Lady Powis's reply to the first. The value of correspondence like this, surveying (albeit in partisan spirit) almost the whole range of the steward's work, is obvious. The Powis Castle ladies have a surprisingly large place in this correspondence, and it is clear that Elizabeth Craven and Elizabeth Somerset, the wives of the 2nd and 3rd Lords Powis, were both women of strong character, and played an influential role in the managing of their husbands' affairs.

The Herbert of Montgomery letters begin (after a solitary chance survival of the 1550's) in 1567 with a remarkable group of twenty-two letters and documents dealing with the setting up, near the mouth of the River Dovey in central Wales, of an installation for the purpose of distilling salt from sea water. These are the papers of Edward (later Sir Edward) Herbert, grandfather of the 1st Lord Herbert of Chirbury. Being both the chief local magnate and well known to the great men about the Court who were behind this salt-making venture, it is natural

[1] Nos. 5 and 21-23. This and future references in this form are to the letters in this volume.

that he should have been deeply concerned in it himself. It is clear that his drive, organizing ability, and commanding influence were much relied on; indeed, it is more than likely that it was he who first suggested Cors Fochno, on the south side of the Dovey, as a spot possessing the special physical characteristics necessary for the making of salt by the method intended to be used.

The first embassy to France of Sir Edward Herbert the grandson (later Lord Herbert of Chirbury), from 1619 to 1621, has left in these Powis Castle archives, now in the National Library of Wales, some slight trace in the form of a dozen documents (eight of them calendared and four of them listed in the Appendix). There is nothing at all from his second embassy, from 1622 to 1624. These few ambassadorial papers are, however, by no means the whole story. They are a mere remnant, the papers of this nature (except these few which were obviously overlooked) having been extracted many years ago and bound into volumes which are now in the Public Record Office.[1]

Lord Herbert's wife, in right of whom he held the Kerry estate that she inherited from her father, Sir William Herbert the 'undertaker', died in October 1634, and very soon after that date the letters reveal a breach between Lord Herbert and his eldest son, Richard, over the possession of this estate. Lord Herbert claimed to hold it after his wife's death by the tenure known as the courtesy of England. Richard claimed it as his mother's heir, apparently alleging, on certain technical grounds, that his father had forfeited his right to be a tenant by the courtesy.[2] It is difficult to know just how deep this breach went. It was not quickly patched up—they were still actively trying to frustrate one another's designs five years later—and the quarrel was then a public one, at least in the sense that Lord Herbert was openly accusing his son, at the end of 1639, in a petition to the Lord Deputy of Ireland.[3] But although the bone of contention was no trifle, one never gets the impression that the quarrel was a passionate one. It seems probable that Richard was seeking to assert himself and to gain some measure of control over the inheritance that would, in any case, be his in due course, rather than actually to deprive his father of a large part of his annual income. If any rancour was left it did not prevent Lord Herbert using to the full what influence he had with Parliament on his son's behalf during the last year of his life.

As Lord Herbert had sat on the fence with a fair measure of success during the Civil War, it is not surprising that the letters of that period contain little or nothing bearing upon the conduct of military affairs (although there is a detailed account of the Battle of Julianstown in

[1] The ambassadorial papers are not all that has been separated from the Powis Castle papers and placed in the Public Record Office. I understand that there are thirteen volumes, of which the following details have been supplied to me, *viz*, 1-6, Correspondence of Sir Edw. Herbert as Ambassador in France, 1619-1624; 7 and 8, General correspondence, 1568-1772; 9, Historical papers, Henry VIII-1692; 10, Letters and papers of Sir Edw. Herbert, 1615-1639; 11, Herbert papers, miscellaneous, 1568-1735; 12, Parliamentary diary, 1640-1641; and 13, Notes of proceedings against the Earl of Strafford, 1641. The P.R.O. Class number is 30/53. I am grateful to Mr. E. K. Timings for this information.

[2] Nos. 127 and 135.

[3] No. 155.

Ireland in November 1641).[1] But the surrender (or seizure) of Montgomery Castle, and its subsequent demolition by order of Parliament, are well documented. Lord Herbert's own accounts and justifications of his conduct are not lacking, and his detailed estimates of his losses in the wars are so copious as to be tedious.

With the Restoration the new regime was faced with the problem of public safety, and the instruments relied upon were the well-tried ones of lords lieutenants, deputy lieutenants, constables high and petty, and the militia. Richard Herbert of Dolguog was a justice and a deputy lieutenant, and he, to our great good fortune, had copied into a paper-bound booklet all or part of the correspondence sent to him in those capacities by the Earl of Carbery, who was both President of the Council of Wales and Lord Lieutenant of North and of South Wales. These missives were frequently accompanied by copies of the original commands received by Lord Carbery himself, and these too were duly transcribed into Herbert's letter-book. The whole group presents a useful picture of the extent and the strength of the opposition in Wales to the return of the former dynasty and constitution, as it was seen through the eyes of those responsible for the task of containing or if necessary suppressing it. It is clear that that opposition was not regarded as negligible.

In the last thirty years of the Herbert of Chirbury section of the Calendar there are several short series of letters which have particular interest, e.g., those of Henry Herbert, the future 4th Lord, as a captain in the army, and those relating to the *quo warranto* proceedings against the borough of Montgomery in the reign of James II. But undoubtedly the main strength of this part of the correspondence is the extraordinarily full picture that it gives of the management of the Herbert estates in Ireland. This is, indeed, the principal sustained strength of the whole correspondence of this family, beginning with a letter of 1589 of Sir William Herbert's[2] (a letter not directly concerned with his own estates, but one in which he discusses, in the most incisive manner, the steps necessary to secure the general welfare, as he saw it, of the whole province of Munster).

Out of the forfeited estates of the Earl of Desmond, Sir William had been granted a seigniory known variously as the lordship of the Castle of the Island of Kerry, the lordship of Mounteagle Loyal, or, more familiarly, as the lordship of Castle Island. It comprised the upper valley of the River Maine, lying in the centre of co. Kerry, east of Tralee and Castlemaine. Lord Herbert claimed in 1647 that before the wars it had been worth £1,200 yearly,[3] and in 1683 the then Lord Herbert's agent gave the same figure as the total of its rent-roll.[4] However much we may discount the former statement, the context in the latter case suggests that the figure should be regarded as a reliable one, and that, although presumably not the precise sum, it was intended to be accurate to within £25 or so. Naturally, the estate never brought its absentee master anything like that amount. This last-mentioned estimate puts the

[1] No. 167.
[2] No. 85.
[3] Nos. 201 and 202.
[4] No. 503.

regular necessary expenses—the crown rent, the salary of a resident agent, administrative expenses, and the cost of remitting the net revenue to England—at about £175 per annum. No allowance is made for unpaid rents, vacant lands, or the cost of law-suits. But then 1683 was a time of peace and relative prosperity, and it is not impossible that at this period substantially the whole of the rent was being collected.[1] At other times, however, in periods of economic distress or political unrest, rents would be in arrears, holdings would be untenanted, and long-drawn-out law-suits would swell the debit side of the agent's account. For some years during and after the rising of 1641 the income from the Irish estate ceased altogether.[2] But quite apart from that exceptional period, it seems unlikely that over the years the actual income accruing to the proprietor, in Montgomery or London, would have exceeded three-quarters of the gross value, and was possibly much less.[3]

For a time, under the 1st Lord Herbert, the Irish estate was leased, the tenant being Sir Thomas Roper (created Viscount Baltinglass in 1627) as the first of three lives. It is not possible to infer all the terms of the lease from the correspondence,[4] but it would seem that Roper was to have out of the lands £500 a year clear,[5] which must surely mean that he had paid a very heavy fine on entering (probably something in the region of £5,000). The lease was made in the sixth year of James I, i.e., between March 1608 and March 1609. This is the very time when Sir Edward Herbert (as he was then) was arranging his affairs (by no means seeing eye to eye with his wife in the process) and preparing to go abroad on a belated 'grand tour'. He says, in his *Life*, that he left his wife with the rents of all her father's lands, reserving his own for his brothers' and sisters' portions and his own charges abroad.[6] But it seems a fair inference, from the incomplete evidence available, that in fact he left her estates charged with the very considerable clear profit that Roper, as lessee, was to take. And it is difficult to resist the conclusion that this transaction was entered into at this time precisely for the purpose of raising, by way of a fine (in effect an advance payment of Lady Herbert's rents), several thousand pounds in ready cash to help meet the extraordinary expense of living and travelling on the Continent, in no mean style, for the ensuing two years. Lady Baltinglass, the last survivor of the three lives of the lease, died in January 1640, when the demise came to an end and the lands returned to Lord Herbert; it is clear that he had been exercising an increasing degree of control over them since Baltinglass himself had died three years earlier.

[1] The 1st Lord Herbert asserted that his Irish rents were better paid than his English ones (No. 200). It may be worth noting that an anonymous description of co. Kildare in this same year, 1683, describes the native Irish as "good tenants, selling all of any value to pay their rents" (Dr. Edward MacLysaght's *Irish Life in the Seventeenth Century*, 2nd ed., Cork and Oxford, 1950, p. 316, quoting Trinity College, Dublin, MS. No. I.1.2).

[2] The lands were in possession of the Earl of Glamorgan in 1647 (No. 202).

[3] Precise answers to this question and many others may lie in the vast mass of *Powis Castle MSS.* (other than the *Correspondence* here calendared) in the National Library of Wales, now in process of being catalogued.

[4] Some valuable details will be found in No. 135.

[5] No. 119.

[6] Lee, *Autobiography of Lord Herbert*, pp. 46-7.

Although in 1644 Lord Muskerry reported that the Castle Island estate had 'no way tasted the miseries of war',[1] co. Kerry suffered heavily in the Cromwellian conquest, so that by 1653 the 2nd Lord Herbert was told by his distant relation Colonel (later Sir) Thomas Herbert, then a Parliamentary official in Ireland,[2] that such had been the devastation that he would need to send over a new colony.[3] This re-plantation, which was carried out under the supervision of another Thomas Herbert who has already been referred to,[4] Lord Herbert's servant, can be traced, though with many lacunae, in the correspondence.

Persuading Lord Baltinglass to deal with the estate in a manner which safeguarded his landlord's interest as well as his own had been the problem before the wars. Now the problem was the management of the seigniory as its immediate lord, either by residence or through agents. Residence seems to have been deliberately resorted to only once, although it is possible that when the 3rd Lord Herbert went over and made a short stay in 1659, he may have intended to remain much longer.[5] When Lord Herbert did go to Kerry in 1672 with the avowed intention of living there 'for some years',[6] he did so not because he thought the estate needed his presence, but because the war with Holland made it difficult to get his rents remitted to him in England, and partly also as a measure of economy, intending, as he said, to live off the Irish estate and devote his English and Welsh revenues to paying off his debts. In fact, on this occasion also he stayed only a matter of months.[7]

Thomas Herbert was only the first of a long succession of agents employed in Castle Island between the re-colonization after the wars and the end of the first line of Lords Herbert in 1691. It is not surprising that this correspondence illustrates—perhaps too fully—the obvious difficulties of running a great estate from a distance, and from across a stormy sea at that. Agents all too often turned out to be (in the eyes of their employers) dilatory, extravagant, or self-seeking; there was constant backbiting between them and the principal tenants; and other servants who might be deputed from time to time to concern themselves in the management of the estates were almost invariably resented bitterly. While none of this may be particularly interesting in general (although individual cases often are), it is occasionally instructive to observe the absentee landlords' periodic attempts to evade the perennial difficulties by deliberately choosing men of substance, or, at the other extreme, mere dependents, or occasionally joining two in commission—according to the way the lessons of recent experience were interpreted.

Thomas Herbert, a distant kinsman, but not, apparently, one of any great wealth or position, went over with the heavy responsibility of re-establishing his master as landlord and seignior after a period of chaos

[1] No. 170.
[2] See note to No. 222.
[3] No. 225.
[4] *Supra*, p. 4
[5] Nos. 262 and 263. Lord Herbert went over in February, but may have felt obliged to return soon by rapidly developing events in England. Before the summer was out he was back home and actively engaged in Booth's rising.
[6] No. 364.
[7] Nos. 355-370.

and collapse. This task he accomplished. Yet within three years we find him regarded as completely untrustworthy, and the new Lord Herbert on the point of hurrying over to secure possession of his lands and muniments.[1] This pother, however, blew over, and Herbert remained agent till early 1663. The story of the shifts and failures of the following two years may be read in Lord Herbert's letter of March 1665 to Sir Arthur Denny.[2] This was a period in which servants sent over *ad hoc*, a relation (William Browne, Lord Herbert's brother-in-law), and 'small' men on the spot (an Irish tenant and the parson of the Castle Island parishes) were employed. Surprisingly, Thomas Herbert was in charge again in 1671,[3] while in 1672-3 Lord Herbert himself was in residence.

By 1675 Herbert was using the services of a ruined Radnorshire gentleman, Captain Thomas Browne, who seems to have left his homeland heavily in debt.[4] A year later he was replaced, having converted £700 of Lord Herbert's rents to his own uses—in short, "the basest fellow on the face of the earth".[5] Herbert took this lesson immediately to heart, and appointed in Browne's place a well-to-do Anglo-Irish squire worth not far short of what Herbert himself received from Castle Island lordship—John Blennerhassett of Ballyseedy.[6] This arrangement seems to have worked well enough until the new agent fell ill and died at the end of 1677. Lord Herbert lived only another year, and it was some time before his brother and successor, Captain Henry Herbert, placed the estate in the hands of a regular agent. A Welsh servant, Roger Jones, was sent across on Blennerhassett's death, and he was in charge again in 1681. Meanwhile offers from men who were perhaps in the chapman class were ignored, and the agency was placed in the hands of a certain Charles Mason (who in 1665 had apparently been a servant or tenant of Sir Arthur Denny's[7]), though he was not left to act without a good deal of assistance from Jones and the Reverend Samuel Wilson, rector of Castle Island.

The 4th Lord eventually picked upon a man of similar standing to Blennerhassett: Edward Kenney of Cullen, brother-in-law to Thomas Herbert the former agent. He did not always give satisfaction, and in 1684 Herbert was looking (without success) for someone of an entirely different type to put in charge—neither a local gentleman, nor a relation, nor one of his trusted servants, but an English 'man of business' to be recruited especially for the position.[8] Kenney's task was a difficult one. He had to handle the business of the short-lived Commission for the Remedy of Defective Titles of 1684, which aroused an anguish of uncertainty and indecision in Lord Herbert as to whether the title to part of his lands was or was not open to question, and whether he might lose more by making public his doubts than he might gain by seizing this

[1] No. 250.
[2] No. 313.
[3] No. 347.
[4] No. 382; Lord Herbert calls him "cousin" and Browne signs himself "kinsman" (No. 427), so he may have been related to Herbert's brother-in-law William Browne.
[5] No. 388
[6] No. 386; Blennerhassett was, incidentally, Thomas Browne's father-in-law.
[7] No. 313.
[8] Nos. 525 and 526.

opportunity of securing renewed confirmation of his ownership, and which produced over a short period a remarkable volume of conflicting and often acrimonious correspondence. The following year Lord Herbert sent over one of his senior and most trusted servants, Humphrey Owen or Owens (later Bailiff of Montgomery), not to replace Kenney, but armed with power to enquire into all his lordship's affairs in Ireland.[1] By 1687 Owen had supplanted Kenney as agent,[2] and he remained responsible for the management of the estates until 1689.

Not the least disconcerting of Kenney's duties had been that of assisting at the partial dismemberment of the lordship by a substantial sale at the end of 1683 or early in 1684 to Patrick (later Sir Patrick) Trant. While no precise statement emerges as to the extent or location of the lands sold, it seems, from a letter of Lord Herbert's to Samuel Wilson,[3] that they constituted the south-eastern part of the seigniory—they were probably substantially those comprised in the third table in Kenney's melancholy letter of 9th July 1683.[4] If that is the case, they were worth at that time approximately £300 a year, or about a quarter of the whole lordship by value.

The insecurity of land tenure in seventeenth-century Ireland is well known. Being rich and influential, and ready and able to defend themselves to the last in the courts, the Herberts probably lost little or no land to rival claimants after the estate came back into possession on the expiry of the lease to Baltinglass (although land was no doubt lost before and during the term of that lease). Conflicting titles arose from many causes, the root of the trouble being, of course, the successive forfeitures of rebels' lands and subsequent grant to others. Uncertainty could arise from doubt as to whether particular lands were ever properly forfeited in the first place; from the vagueness of many patents as to what lands were comprehended in them; from the tenderness of the law in matters of real property, which allowed even royal patents to be questioned on a number of grounds; from the opportunities for fraud which arose in times of war and commotion; and, not least, from lack of records with which to correct genuine defects of memory. In any seigniory in Ireland at this period there were lands which could be attacked with colourable rival titles, and the lordship of Castle Island was no exception. No attempt can be made here to examine and analyze the numerous law-suits which are a recurring theme throughout the correspondence. But it will not be amiss to refer, by way of illustration, to two incidents touching upon the title to one particular property in the seigniory, namely, Ballymacadam, a townland in Castle Island parish.

When the issue whether or not to take advantage of the Commission for the Remedy of Defective Titles was being debated in 1684, Ballymacadam was one of the lands in question. Edward Kenney, in justification of his view that a patent within the terms of the Commission was necessary, advanced an exposition of the case which effectively convinced Lord Herbert's servant and sage adviser, Robert Griffith. "None of

[1] No. 589.
[2] Nos. 628 and 631.
[3] No. 511.
[4] No. 503.

those lands were Lord Herbert's before the Rebellion," said Kenney, "but when the spoils were dividing Mr. Thomas Herbert, then agent, thought his employer should put in for a share, and so put up some old pretended title, and interest being made and the people not so curious, those lands were adjudged . . . to Lord Herbert".[1] There can hardly be any doubt that Kenney believed these to be the true facts of the case. Yet referring back to an earlier period we shall find how wrong he was. In 1635, when Castle Island in common with other plantation lordships was still being attacked by 'pretenders' on the grounds that their ancestors were in possession of the lands claimed at the time of Desmond's revolt, we find that Ballymacadam was being sued for on these grounds, though clearly at that time in possession of Lord Herbert as part of his seigniory; it may be added, incidentally, that Francis Lloyd, Lord Herbert's servant then in Dublin, admitted that the land was not in the inquisition of attainder.[2]

It remains only to say some necessary words about the style of this Calendar and the conventions adopted in it. The Calendar is a full one; it is intended to reproduce all that is in the original except what is common form or repetitive, but, of course, in as abbreviated a manner as is possible. Conciseness, however, has not been achieved in the same way as a précis-writer achieves it. The letters have not been re-written. The method consists rather of condensation, so that the language is still essentially that of the originals.[3] All editorial interpolations have been placed within square brackets. The editor has followed the principle that it is not for him to exclude from the calendar version any part of the original letter on the grounds that the information it contains seems trifling, of restricted interest, or obscure. In short, this Calendar is intended to be not so much a guide to the original documents as a practical substitute for them except in those cases where nothing short of the full and exact text will serve.

The references to the originals, which appear at the end of each calendared letter, on the right, are of two types. Letters distinguished by a simple number are in the *Correspondence* section of the earlier deposits (those made in 1933 and 1937) of the *Powis Castle Collection*. Those distinguished by a reference of the form "HM2.9/46" or "HM2.23/81" (to take two examples) are in the 1959 deposit, a group known until then as *Herbert MSS Series II*. This group consists of one bound volume and a number of bundles, the documents within each volume or bundle being serially numbered. Thus "HM2.23/81" means document 81 in bundle 23. "HM2.9/46" means document 46 in the solitary volume, which bears the inscription "IX". The bundles are numbered serially after the volume, i.e., from 10 onwards, so that the numbers 1 to 8 are not found in this series.[4]

[1] No. 558.
[2] No. 131.
[3] All texts have been transposed into the third person, in accordance with a decision of the History and Law Committee of the Board of Celtic Studies in 1951 when the policy of preparing calendars such as this was first put into operation.
[4] Numbers 1 to 8 are the first eight volumes of that part of this group which was abstracted and placed in the Public Record Office (see p. 7 *supra*).

The original spelling has been retained for all personal and place names, and of course, for actual quotations; but superscript abbreviations and symbols reproducable only by the use of record type have been extended, while the thorn (as in "ye") has been replaced in all cases by "th". Enclosures mentioned in the texts of letters should be assumed to be missing unless the contrary is indicated.

The editor's footnotes are intended as a convenience to the reader, by answering some of the questions that will come to his mind in perusing the text. It is hoped that they will not often be wearisome to him by telling him what he already knows or what is to him obvious. They are selective in the sense that they are restricted to those questions which the editor finds himself able to answer, either as a consequence of some degree of familiarity with the whole correspondence, or because he has himself found it necessary to search out the answers in order to understand the text. But a great many points that the editor would like to be able to explain and to understand more fully himself remain obscure. This is due simply to the fact that the task of searching for the answers to all these questions would have turned this volume into a life's work. At the same time, inability to explain everything that needs to be explained has not seemed to the editor to be a sound reason for refraining from giving what information he can.

THE CALENDAR

PART I

HERBERT
OF
POWIS CASTLE

HERBERT CORRESPONDENCE

[1613–17]

1. MARTHA FITZHERBERT TO MR. THO. BAMFORD AT LANGLEY.

On Friday came a messenger from Mr. Rowland Eyre of Hassop to tell her that Lady Shrewsbury has sent to the tenants of Padleis to demand their rents; today is the day of payment. He advises her to send two servants to countermand it and [order] that they pay to none but Nordens. Would not be wanting in anything that may do her or her son good. Eyre says he knows not what is done concerning his son Adam, but she doubts that. What would he have her do? 395a.

The writer was the widow of Anthony Fitzherbert of Norbury, Derbyshire, who died in 1613. Sir Ralph Winwood, mentioned in the reply (the next letter), was abroad until 1613 and died in 1617. It is difficult to say how this and the following two letters came to Powis Castle; it is possible they came into the hands of Lady Shrewsbury and were eventually carried home by Mary, daughter of the 2nd Lord Powis, when she was widowed by the death of her husband, George, Lord Talbot, son of the 10th Earl of Shrewsbury.

[1613–17]

2. THO. BAMFORD TO [MARTHA FITZHERBERT]. *Written on the dorse of No. 1.*

If there had been a stir of kindness in Mr. Addam Eire, upon his "avoydance" by Lady Shresbury he might have done "us" great good. Because the court awarded an injunction against him for possession upon their bringing into court one moiety of the £240, he presumed of the other £120 from "you", and so gave out, which caused Mr. Nordens to exhibit a bill against him . . . upon Beecher's statute, so that Mrs. Vernon may plead her release. . . . She having a moiety of the land, if she does not bring in £120, as Lady Shresbury has, she will not find such favour. Lady Shresbury and Sir Raphe Wynwood have obtained order to stay the filing of Mr. Norden's *liberate* of the statute; there may be matter in the order that may breed opinion against Mr. Norden of contempt. The tenants would not pay to her if put to it, then more ill would be done than good. Mr. Dyott would advise her to try them, but not so the writer. So soon as Mr. Rowland Eire has answered there will be a motion for Mr. Norden by Mr. [? Watter] and Mr. Dyott. Mr. Littleboy follows it diligently. 395.

[? c. 1615]

3. JOHN FITZHERBERT TO MRS. MARTHA FITZHERBERT.

"Good mother". There was due to him last Michaelmas £100 of his wife's portion. Humbly entreats that he may receive it upon Saturday where she pleases. Desires answer by this bearer. 308.

1623/4

4. Charles Pryce to Lady Herbert.

"Sweete Madam". Knows she loves her husband, and he them both, so well that he durst not be the author of [ill] news. Thought it better to hold her in expectation of her husband's return than to thrust her into fear. It was not her husband's will it should be revealed to her too hastily, still hoping, by mastering his malady, to [avoid] causeless fear. Will not tell her in what case her husband was. God be praised, he is now well recovered and will be at the heels of this bringer—they will not adventure him in this unseasonable time till he have five or six days' confirmation of his strength. Service to her sister and brothers. Sir Percie is in a place where he wanted no comfort but them.

Lloydiarth,
2 January. 327.

[? c. 1635]

5. ————— to [? Lady Powis]. *Contemporary copy.*

Is troubled with what he hears of her last night. Has his being (under God) only by their bounty; owes thanks to neither friend nor kinsman for help in feeding his children. Charged with neglect in his duty and the foul sin of "ingratuity", he stands in doubt whether he cleared himself. Desires to satisfy "your La'p" concerning Lewys Gwyn's lease; did not tender his suit, he being "my sisters" servant. Gwyn desired a lease of enclosures held (as he said) by adversaries paying little rent, he to pay three times as much. Did not say 20s. was all it was worth; did but say where the law lay. Jo[h]n Price was suitor for a lease thereof. Did not expect a reward—Gwyn said "my Mr." had promised him a lease three times and three times denied to seal, and that he would never ask more.

Is charged that he insinuates with the country and neglects his master's good. Never lost him one penny he could get with a safe conscience. Hopes there is no hurt to his master though (being a poor man) he carries himself mildly. If he did otherwise it would quickly be laid to his charge. What should his master get if he called a poor man a knave . . . ? Is charged that his master's perquisites decreased through his neglect. That cannot be unless he conceals presentments and leaves them unextracted. If they be not presented, what can he do? Those formerly presented for enclosures have taken leases or pay yearly rent, having compounded with Sir Jo[h]n H. All enclosures now are presented though not a quarter of six hoops "seednes". If they enclose no more (as they do not except they compound before) how can they be presented?

Is charged that there are no improvements within the lordship. Knows of no "tilles" not discovered and questioned within Powys. All belonging to the lord have been searched for narrowly this forty years. Would deserve small thanks if he persuaded his master to question any that have not been questioned. Is charged with negligence in soliciting suits; never lost one. Was not privy to Roberts' suit before he was sent to Mr. Tournour to declare upon the lease. There was no proof for Roberts against sixty years' possession but Moris Powell's oath and his wife's that he held by lease from his father in right of Lady Herbert.

Sir Jo[h]n Bridgman, to save the credit of the cause, took it from them to see whether "my Mr." could find any record for his title; Sir Jo[h]n chided the writer for bringing such a case. Since, there is found but a lease by the Queen to Richard Broughton, esq., of Broughton, who was never in possession by it, which is therefore nothing worth. If any solicitor recover with that evidence, "respecte me as my adversarys desire".

Is charged to love their enemies. Solicited against his own kinsmen, as Lord Churbury, Baronet Price (whom he indicted at Llanidlos before the whole county), Edward Price, Mathew Price, and others his kinsmen. His master is angry that he settles not the rents of assize. In Krenion it is known where it was wanting, and everywhere else but Uchkoed—and that [requires] an old extract from [former] bailiffs there, for the rent of assize there is certain, and the customs uncertain, as ox money, castle money, etc., which were added to the rent of assize (also accounted rent of assize were 12s. 8d. for Mivore Frith, out of Llantything Mill, Mivore Mill, etc.). His master is angry he does not make certain that is paid. But they may discover more—if they indent an extract with a jury they debar future discovery. Thomas Calcot, John Calcot, and others have promised old extracts.

That his children are proud. . . . Cannot help it if they be not bred as they ought. Used as sharp correction as any father in this parish, but in vain, for when he corrected their mother would cherish. She is subject to faults, especially stubborn self-will, but she [denies] disrespect to his master or her ladyship. His own misbehaviour was but by inducement of that treacherous cheat . . . whom all the world thinks not fit for the entertainment he has in her house. Begs to be respected as her honest servant, not defamed by her unworthy guest. Must live by his service, and desires to retain his credit. Such detractors take his means, for he can get but a poor living by his hands. Yet God will provide. . . . Will never forget to pray for them. *HM* 2.23/80.

"Mr. Tournour" is no doubt Timothy Turner (the name is spelt in various ways), King's Solicitor in the Court of the Marches from 1627 to 1637, and later Chief Justice of Chester; Sir John Bridgman was himself Chief Justice at this time. The writer of this letter seems to be Lord Powis's steward.

1636

6. ———— TO ————.

"My worthy good Lord". He, his wife, etc., are in good health, but the bill coming out [now] declares there are dead of the plague in this city and suburbs this week 650 persons. Mr. Perry has been at his daughter's house in Essex, and his wife out of town this month, leaving her maid to look to the house. The house is guarded to the best of their powers; have had in [a] mastiff or other dog this eight weeks. On Monday night some rogues that have haunted the house robbed the coach of the boots and both the curtains. Three days before a knight's coach was likewise robbed. It is not through any defect in them, for they sit up late and rise early to prevent a mischief, and yet this ill-chance is come by reason the house is so noted. [Letters may be] delivered to Mr. Miller.

8 September. 474.

1639/40

7. WILLM. WHITMORE TO [? LADY ELIZABETH HERBERT].

Sends "your Ladyshipp" by his master's order both Pipwell and Henden accounts, which he entreats her to peruse and rectify if she finds error. And if they have committed any in paying Lord Powis it shall be set straight next half year ; it seems she paid him some money in the country. They had thought to set all straight when he received his last annuity of £150. His master is still troubled with his old infirmity in his eye. "My Lord" being out of town, he has delivered her letter.

London,
8 February.

Endorsed: "This Sr H. did returne answer on the receyt dated 12 March 1639 wherein he wrot 30.l. was pd. to much for the year past in my Uncle Ed['s] Annuytie". 359.

1645/6

8. SIR PERCY HERBERT'S PETITION TO THE COMMITTEE OF LORDS AND COMMONS FOR SEQUESTRATION. *Contemporary copy.*

Lately appealed for discharging of sequestration of a third of his estate, the whole being sequestered for some supposed delinquency. They referred it to the committee to whom sequestration was made to examine and certify, and if no other cause than recusancy appeared to allow him a third according to the ordinance. Attended the committees where the greater part of his estate lies, who have certified the state of the case. Prays they will consider it, and if no delinquency appears than he by his counsel now present or otherwise can clear, that they will allow him one full third and arrearages during sequestration.

Notes at foot, afterwards deleted: To have counsel and the certificate from Hendon Committee ready ; only stay for a day to [? hear] it with instructions from counsel. Many other things "which I hould not fitt to present in [? respect] danger . . ."

Endorsed: 29 January 1645. *HM*2.12/38a.

1645/6

9. THE COMMITTEE OF SEQUESTRATION FOR MIDDLESEX TO [THE COMMITTEE OF LORDS AND COMMONS FOR SEQUESTRATION]. *Contemporary copy.*

Received their order of 3 December to certify the cause of sequestration on the estate of Sir Percy Herbert. The ground thereof arose as well from the annexed orders of the House of Commons as for his absenting himself, and (as they are informed) he victualled a castle in Wales and maintained it against Parliament. Have no other matter of sequestration against him recusancy excepted.

Spiller House,
13 February.

William Roberts
Richard Downton
Thomas Swalons

Edw. Markham
Thomas Fowler
John Morris

Marginal note: ". . . both labour and tyme to gitt it of them . . . They have had the estat soe long they thinke none would have looked after it."

The orders: 29 January "1645". That Sir Percy Herbert be sent for as a delinquent. *Marginal note*: Sir Percy did appear.

29 April 1642. That the Sergeant-at-Arms bring in Sir Percy Herbert and that Sjt. Wyld and Mr. Grimston draw a charge against him.

Hen. Elsing
Cler. Parl., Com. D.

Marginal note: No charge against him, and such a general charge not sufficient for seizure or sequestration. Hopes it will be . . . (*illegible*) . . . before long. *HM*2. 12/38b.

Wm. Roberts and Thos. Fowler are presumably Sir. Wm. Roberts of Willesden and Sir Thos. Fowler, bart., of Islington, respectively. Spiller House remains (despite help and advice from Miss E. D. Mercer, County Archivist of Middlesex, for which I am grateful) unidentified; it may be a town house of Sir Henry Spiller of Laleham, an imprisoned royalist. The year given for the first order, 1645, is an error for 1640/41.

[? 1647]

10. DAME ELIZABETH HERBERT'S PETITION TO THE KING. *Draft*.

Her husband in the beginning of [these] troubles was committed by the Commons, and continued under restraint about eighteen months upon accusation that he had a command in Wales from His Majesty or Marquess Worcest[er]. Having put in bail of £20,000 he repaired into Montgom[er]yshire, to Powys Castle, his dwelling-house, which at his own charge he began to fortify, and raised and trained soldiers, but was interrupted by his father Lord Powis, who possessed himself of the soldiers' arms, alleging he had forfeited his commission. Shortly after, her husband was commanded by His Majesty to Oxford, where articles were preferred against him (some no less than treason). After much attendance he obtained to know his accuser, to his sad amazement. But he was certified His Majesty did not credit them; some might be disproved by his royal knowledge and [by] Secretary Nicholas when His Majesty was at Shrewsburie.

After long attendance without prosecution, he petitioned to be restored to his castle, but was [told] his father would prosecute, who then possessed himself more and more of the castle, to her husband's great prejudice in goods, rents, [etc.], and now to the loss of the castle and all his estate there (and His Majesty has lost a strong fort and the contributions there).

Her husband is become deeply indebted, and his whole revenue taken (being at present under the power of Parliament), and he, as she believes, travelled beyond sea by His Majesty's licence, having left her without subsistence or means to return him supplies.

Therefore beseeches (for enabling her to support herself and supply her husband) leave, not to give to His Majesty's enemies, but to take from them such of their means, now detained, as they can procure by composition or otherwise—not attempting anything therein [without] His Majesty's leave.

Endorsed: Corrected by Mr. Palmer. *HM*2.12/39.

According to a printed sheet, *The State of the Case of Sir Percy Herbert . . . submitted to . . . Parliament* (No. 35 in Bundle 12), he was summoned to Oxford in 1643, obliged to follow the King to Gloucester, and there took the opportunity afforded by the approach of the Earl of Essex to leave the royal camp and go home, retiring to the Low Countries a year later (in September 1644). "Mr. Palmer" is possibly Geoffrey (later Sir Geoffrey) Palmer, a barrister and a close adherent of the court.

1647

11. [Lady Herbert] to Sir Percy [Herbert]. *Contemporary copy; last page only.*

. . . Whether he thinks it fitter to be sent for or come of his own accord with a pass. "Enterchange your mynd" to Mr. Knarsb. (who is in the country) whom she will acquaint with his letter. Makes apology to her brother, also to "your selfe whoe are a suffitient stranger", for the rude entertainment he will find here. "And soe deare hart farewell, and lett us pray for a happie meeting".

Added: His friends much hope to see him. Has left Will Knarsb. to his [own] father's directions; Sir Percy should send for him. And in the interim, for [her brother's] maintenance, and discharge of Sir Percy's own passage and decrements (understands "somewhat must needs be remayninge"), it will be convenient to assign what Sir Percy has made use of all this time for these purposes. Doubts not but at their meeting they will find sufficient for temperate minds and to pay Sir Percy's debts—hers shall not trouble any "if that I live and the tymes waxe not worse".

Endorsed: "Answeare to Sr Percys letter in 11 Au. 1647" (*the day and month are obscure*). *HM*2.23/4.

Sir Percy was brotherless, so the reference here must be to one of Lady Herbert's own three brothers—William, Lord Craven of Hampsted Marshall; John, Lord Craven of Ryton; or Thomas Craven.

[1648]

12. [Lady Herbert] to [Sir Percy Herbert]. *Draft.*

"Sweett H." He performed not his promise of writing when he came to Parrice by her brother (without distinction now—"God will protect us"—hopes the other is lost but for a time) who writes that [Sir Percy] will make haste to be with her. Mr. Knarsb. is here. Will send him to London when occasion serves; he would write thence often to [Sir Percy] if assured his letters were received. "Your Daughter is well, whoe . . . prayes for your . . . speedie returne . . . with her bro." Has not written to Will, but sends him her blessing—her letters procure none from him. Has been much troubled in repairing decays; now has set up part of "our ruined building brought from Poole". Robert Lynor, an innkeeper, has a grant to keep the other part. Fears her work cannot be finished so soon as she hopes to see him here. Builds not for delight but necessity, that he may have a spare room ten yards long to turn in, and a chamber for their son, with other necessary offices. Almost everyone now desires to seem his friend. Desires he may receive content in his own country, hoping he will prepare lightly to regard those cross accidents and alterations that cannot be avoided. In his content will consist her happiness . . . . *HM*2.23/78a.

Lady Herbert now felt that she had, in effect, only one brother—William, the eldest—hence she could refer to him "without distinction". The second brother, John, Lord Craven of Ryton, had died very early in 1648; the third, Thomas—of whom little is known—must be the one who was "lost". There are figures in brackets at intervals throughout this draft, presumbly indicating the places of insertions on a separate sheet now missing.

[1648]

13. [Lady Herbert] to [Sir Percy Herbert]. *Draft.*

"Sw. Heart". Received her heart's content in his letter and the relation from [their] son. But upon second consideration her heart became as lead, supposing if any comfort might be hers from her brother's decease she should have had "a touch theire of". Had confident hopes given her of what she prayed for; now trembles to enquire more. Frames herself to be contented with God's will, and let this scene pass.

Has been providing ever since June with haste, hoping to see him here by the end of the three years and her design finished. But materials, workmen, and carriage have been scarce. Has a bargelading of coals to entertain the relation of adventures since his absence and the "large perticulers" of his travels; but not as yet one chimney to put them in. That may quickly be done, but other matters she cannot bring to decency before seeing him.

Her brother gives her hopes of seeing him, with [Sir Percy], before Christmas. [Understands] it is thought convenient by her brother that their son be detained to complete him in manly exercises. He should not be over-long detained, that he may have a year before he comes to twenty-one to understand his own country and affairs.

Encloses copy of the certificate of his estate. His servants that had the managing under the committee can testify that, contributions [etc.] deducted, she received not (*blank*). Expects some friend will compound if he desires, or rent it. Knows of no more preparations but a certificate from the committee at the castle: That in subduing the country neither [Sir Percy] nor any under him opposed them—no, not in the taking of his castle.

Marginal note: The "snake in lurke" if need be is N.B.'s relation in "theire" custody—little to the purpose, [Sir Percy] being a prisoner.

*HM*2.23/78b.

Lady Herbert's elder brother, Lord Craven of Hampsted Marshall, who was seeing to her son's "manly exercises", was well fitted to do so, being a soldier of repute.

1648

14. Tho. Warberton, Tho. Pownall, Tho. Robinson, and Richard Willcoxon to [? the Chairman of the Committee for Compounding]. *Contemporary copy.*

"May it please your honour". Received his order of 1 March with Mr. Bradshaw's report in the case of Sherington Talbott, esq., trustee for the Earl of Shrewsb., by virtue of an indenture 20 July, 17 *Car.*, by the

Earl to the said S. Talbot and one Jo. Liggon of divers messuages and lands for the said Earl in cos. Salope, Chester, Wigoron., Berks., Devon, and Derbie for twenty-one years, first for £400 per annum to the Earl for his wife's and children's maintenance, next for £4,150 of the Earl's debts in the schedule annexed to the report, next for £6,000 for portions for his two eldest daughters by a former wife, and the remainder to the Earl. Have received information the Earl's estate is of the yearly value of £7,842 10s., so that besides the £300 to be yearly paid by His Honour's order to the Earl and the £4,150 [for] debts, there should yearly grow due to the Common Wealth about £3,000 per annum. If it go to raising £6,000 portion for the daughters, £4,000 thereof belonging to the State for their recusancy, the State must receive much prejudice unless all the estate in every county be proportionably charged with the Earl's £300, the £4,150 debts, and £2,000 as a third of the daughters' portions.

Humbly certify that the lordship of Dunham in this hundred of Edisburie, co. Chester, with other lands in this and other counties, were in January, 14 *Car.*, three years before the deed of trust, granted by the Earl at the marriage of his son G., Lord Talbott, with the daughter of Sir P. Herbert, now Lady Talb., for assuring to her £1,000 per annum jointure. The deputy lieutenants for this county ordered 25 June 1646 that she, being a recusant, should have the third of her jointure out of the lands in this county, which has ever since been paid, and is still earnestly required by her agents. Desire further directions.

Weverham,
3 August. 375.

John Bradshaw (the regicide) was solicitor to the Sequestration Committee.

[? 1648–55]

15. [Lord] Powis to Mr. Juckes. *Contemporary copy.*

How he has been used by his son and the latter's wife is well known. They utterly deny to pay his rent since he came hither except he seals what acquittance his son pleases. He is to take this notice that he pay no more of his rent to her. All Powis is liable to his rent, as she will not deny. Means to drive away and distrain all the goods he can find upon Powis where they have any rents. Will not starve if he can help it. Has been patient this long. If he please, he may acquaint her with the writer's resolution—does nothing but what is legal. Did not expect this requittal for his kindness to his son. Has not one penny to make provision to his house and supply necessities for his own use.

The Poole,
27 October.

True copy of so much as concerns prohibition of payment of rent.
Witnesses: Fra. Thomlenson Hugh Jones

*HM*2.23/81.

[c. 1650–54]

16. Wm. Habington to ————.

Acquainted Lady Palmer with his desire to pay the money upon safe acquittance from cousin Eleanor Vaughan. This is very acceptable.

But her ladyship with passion resents that deduction is made, without her privity, for which she is highly offended with her daughter—which she would have known to "both your nearest frends above", that her daughter's expenses may be better regulated. She has prepared a place to set out the money, and promises it shall not lie upon his hands. The want of being well understood is the "originall" of all distrusts. She therefore tells him: His bond is in Sir James Palmer's hands, ready to be delivered up upon payment, and Eleanor Vaughan is prepared at an hour's warning to receive it; he may deduct what he has parted with or stands engaged for.

Lloydyarth,
9 November. *HM*2.23/79.

There is an account of the writer in *The Dictionary of National Biography*. Lady Palmer, wife of Sir James Palmer and a daughter of the 1st Lord Powis, was the mother of Eleanor Vaughan by her first husband, Sir Robert Vaughan of Llwydiarth.

1654

17. A. BELSON TO LADY HERBERT AT BUTTINGTON. LEAVE AT THE PHEASANT IN SHOOSBRY TO BE SENT.

Whereas a marriage is intended between Mr. William Herbert and Lady Elizabeth Somersett, and Mr. Humfry Wilde has undertaken for the performance of all things to be performed [by] Sir Percy Herbert, by commission from Viscount Mountague the writer undertakes that the Viscount shall upon request give security out of his estate for raising Lady Elizabeth's portion.

Endorsed: 9 May. *HM*2.21/5.

Lord Montagu was the bride-to-be's uncle by marriage.

[c. 1655]

18. DEPOSITION AS TO THE TITLE TO LLWYDIARTH *Copy or draft.*

Herbert Vaughan, esq., was sequestered in 1644 for being a commissioner of array by the Committee for Sequestration in co. Mountgom[er]y, whose estate in cos. Mountgom[er]y, Denbigh, and Merrionith was reputed to be £2,500. And so much as was not received by Herbert Vaughan was collected by the Committee the same year. In 1645 Mr. Edward Vaughan, pretending to be a friend to Parliament, and having many friends in the Committee, procured an order to be tenant of the estate, paying the full value (it being all in the hands of tenants except the demesne of Lloydyard, which was in 1644 managed by agents of the Committee). One of the Committee added a proviso to the order that the Committee of Lords and Commons for Sequestration approve the same. By virtue of which order Mr. Vaughan possessed himself of the estate.

Some friends of Herbert Vaughan moved the Committee of Lords and Commons that Mr. Edward Vaughan might not be tenant to the estate, in regard he claimed a title thereto, and so gain possession to the prejudice of Herbert Vaughan. The Committee ordered he should deliver up possession and not be tenant. Several orders to the same effect were procured by Herbert Vaughan's friends, but Edward Vaughan refused obedience. One order was directed to the Committee [of

Montgomeryshire] to use the forces then in the land to remove him out of possession; orders were issued to Col. Mytton, Commander-in-Chief in Northwales, to that end. But Edward Vaughan having erected a garrison upon or near the estate—as he pretended, for King and Parliament—the place being strong, and therein many men, arms, and ammunition, [neither] the commander-in-chief nor the Committee were willing to hazard the few forces they had against one that pretended himself a friend, it being in the heat of the war. He enjoyed the estate about five years till Herbert Vaughan died. Cannot tell whether the Committee's agents distrained upon any of the tenants by virtue of the aforesaid orders; if they received any of the rent during that time it was inconsiderable.

Mr. Vaughan was questioned for the rent at Haberdashers' [Hall]. What judgement was obtained against him for the then Commonwealth . . . (*unfinished*). Heard Mr. Rice Vaughan obtained judgement against him for about £8,000. Mr. Vaughan in his defence endeavoured to prove it was not in possession of Herbert Vaughan when sequestered. But it is as clear as the sun that [it] was, and that it was sequestered as Herbert Vaughan's estate . . . . *HM*2.12/37.

There is no indication of the deponent's identity. Edward Vaughan, of Glanllyn, had been active for Parliament since 1643 at least; in 1646 he seems to have been the principal member of the Committee of Accounts for Montgomeryshire, his high-handedness obliging the county Committee to report him to the Committee of Accounts for the Whole Kingdom (*Cal. of State Papers*, *Domestic*, 1625-1649, p. 647, and 1645-1647, pp. 441, 461, and 491). His title to Llwydiarth seems to spring from his marriage to Mary Purcell, daughter (and probably heiress) to Herbert Vaughan's sister Eleanor, wife of John Purcell of Nantcribau; Herbert Vaughan himself died without issue.

1668

19. [Lord] Powis to Sir Mathew Price at Newtowne Hall.

Repines that he cannot, till Mr. James's return from London, [know] whether he can in this circumstance serve him; having given him, as belongs to his place, disposal of the places for keeping all the courts. After James's coming (about a fortnight hence) he will be resolved, and then Sir Mathew shall command him.

As for delivery up of the lands, he long since expected Sir Mathew should have had the deeds; thinks it cannot be done but upon the sealing the writings. Will readily execute what is thought fit if he please to discourse it with this bearer.

Powis Castle,
30 November.

His wife's service; and his respects to Sir Mathew's lady.

*HM*2.23/10.

James's place in the Powis household is discussed in Nos. 21-23.

1670

20. [Lord] Powis to Sir Mathew Price, bart., at Newtowne Hall.

An unexpected accident has put him upon some necessity for a present supply of money; is constrained to desire he would pay in what arrears he can conveniently for Beander rents. Hughes', this bearer's, receipt will be as if under the writer's own hand. And if he please they will settle the past account at the same time Mr. Serjeant Jones can be at leisure to perfect the other businesses. And, as the writer engaged, Sir Mathew may then either continue this yearly payment or buy it off, as he judges most for his convenience.

Powis Castle,
9 May. *HM*2.23/11.

Mr. Serjeant Jones is presumably the Thomas Jones who became Chief Justice of the Common Pleas.

[1671]

21. [WALTER JAMES] TO [LADY POWIS]. *Contemporary copy.*

Upon stating his account there may be question whether the money paid him and employed for his own use be not satisfaction sufficient for his seven years' service; presents these considerations [as to] the justness of what he expects. She may consider his beneficial employments when he first took her employment, and perhaps his quality and vocation . . . and how her service increased. Can give no other proof of the greatness of his [former] employment than the vote of his country. Never heard that any nobleman gave so great a salary as what he got. Truly, his profession, which cost so much, was ill bestowed to deserve no more than an ordinary person. It is well known that before the King's restoration he was a considerable gainer by his profession; but to his great grief had some that spent inconsiderately.

Shortly after the restoration he had £80 per annum from her father to act in his affairs, which with what he had, and an increase of employment by the access of her father's was a considerable fortune, and all in his own country. When her father's employment ended he came to Buttington as promised to advise in her affairs. Found cousin Vaughan at the castle; told him he resolved to take employment abroad, hoping to take from his domestics their unreasonable dependency on his "gettinge", and desired him to offer his service to her (one of the chiefest members of the family he and his ancestors had dependancy upon). Was told she accepted, but would be at a certainty what he expected; could not give a rate, but his cousin said he should have £50 for a year's trial. Told him his clerk got so much, but yet he would accept of it on trial that year. . . . Thus he was entertained. Employed that year in surveying—the service was easy. Next year troubles and suits increased. Held out the next, but coming from Oxford term he resolved that Christmas to depart (but did not make it public) and had letters from several to undertake considerable employments. But before he took his journey for Southwales "my lord" came to his chamber with £40 as a gratuity. This made him alter his resolution, being by this precedent confident he should for every year have such satisfaction. Businesses doubled and trebled. Now, having spent almost seven years in her service without any certainty than what was for the first year concluded, he requests a quietus and her determination whether he deserves more, or [that he may] in love and favour at Christmas depart. If frustrated of his expectation he returns honest but old and poor, having lost his acquaintance, practice, his time of gaining knowledge by reading [etc.], and without penny in purse or owing. Yet has occasion to pray for her, for storms of "crosses" and temptations so tossed him that his soul was in danger of shipwreck had he not anchored at her blessed haven.

When she chooses another to succeed him, he advises a Welshman, a Catholic if she can, well read and practical in the law, and knowing how to set and supervise all inferior officers; otherwise she will be put to the charge of many officers.

Appended, in the same hand, are answers to hypothetical objections to the foregoing, one being: Why did he make no mention of his expectations? *Ans.* Presumed he would have what he merited. Would have been accounted an "uncivill griper" if then, when he was the only person that knew the secrets and intrigues concerning the suits depending, he should depart unless he had his demand; had he left he might have been rewarded by her enemies.

Is sure the lawyers, attorneys, and clerks exclaim against him; they were more used and had more money when there was less business. The tenants say he is severe. Others who detained her rights curse him. What service he has done may appear in the accounts and rentrolls. Made no use of his profession but in her service. Relinquished to others duties due to him. Received £2 or £3 for leases, and spent it in her service—she may remember that most of his country expenses were defrayed by such money, received by discoveries, etc.

Further appended in the same hand: Things in London and England to be looked after this term: 1. The defendent in Chapman's business being dead, a suit must be prepared against the survivor, or composition made. 2. Abell's fine must be prepared—something ticklish, the heirs being beyond seas. . . . 3. A fine of £70 in Hendon must be disputed—Mr. Sawyer undertakes to settle it by compounding or a regular way of law. 4. Stating of new fines next court in Hendon and Owndles is of consequence—time of payment, by custom, begins when the fine is set. 5. The clerk's accounts to be cleared. Suits concerning encroachers may be done by direction. 6. The house in London, if she resolves not to live in it this year, must be exposed to be set. 7. Will prepare bills against [such] as shall not compound before return of the writs.

*HM*2.23/83.

Lord Powis's steward at this time was Walter James, and he is clearly the "Mr. James" of the letter that follows this and the writer of this and No. 23.

[16]71

22. [Lady Powis] to Mr. James. *Draft.*

Desirous to appear just, she answers in writing. As to the beneficial employments he was in when he undertook "ours", she is ignorant what they were. Had she known he did himself a prejudice she would not have received his offer. Doubts not his gains were more when at home, "an universall practiser"—if one may call gains what obliges one to spend as much as is got. . . . He never had a more universal respect paid him than here. Has endeavoured he should have all conveniences, in sickness or health, that she can afford herself.

As to his meriting a more than ordinary salary, is not £50 a year "and in the house" such? Does not count her sister Talbot's actions any precedent, or she would give more to her servants than she is worth. It might be objected that sister Talbot gave £500 to a waiting-woman that served her but two years, and other things not to be intimated. . . . Knows of none but Will Knas. that ever had such wages with so little reason (though that was made up between Lady Powis and sister [Talbot] as doing the business of both). Instead may be instanced Lord Northumberland to Mr. Gee, Lord Craven to Sir John Baber and Sir Edmond Farrier who preceded him, cousin Thom. Whitmore, and others. Almost all the noblemen of England, men who have double and treble "our" estates, give £100 a year to their chief officer, [living] out of the house and [having] no other conveniences. Never heard that her grandfather gave so much. And Mr. Jenner, who formerly lived in this house, a lawyer by profession and a practiser, and a Justice of Peace in his own country, had but £30 per annum besides the making of the leases (and made at least 300 in Kedewen, some yet extant, though the unhappy times made them not very advantageous), and James's not having that profit was his own act.

As for the advantage [in] the rent-rolls and accounts since James's coming, she weighs [rather] the care and goodwill with which it was done. [Against] the profit he must put expenses both of law and stays in London upon that account, which perhaps turn the balance. But what is done with kindness and goodwill ought to be acknowledged in the same manner. Knows not why James should suspect "my Lord" or the writer could not find a fit time for a gratification as well as the end of his second year. Has her hands tied by the construction "my Lords" action met, which it seems was thought by James to be out of fear lest they lose the advantage of his continuing in that employment. Confesses it to be great, yet will never desire it with his prejudice. Therefore if the certain salary agreed, with his own diet, his man's, horses, and all other advantages, with expenses when abroad upon their occasions, do not give satisfaction, she must submit to the misfortune of losing James's company. . . .

Must desire two things: That he will finish the suits begun, since none that come after will know upon what reasons and notions they were undertaken; and that he perform his promise when he first came, of "making my Lord perfaitly knowing" in his own affairs, which she most insisted upon, and would be glad herself to be partaker [thereof]. Supposes it cannot be done in three months, but perhaps may be in another year. Truly, a quarter's warning will be given by the meanest servant in the house, and cannot be sufficient to find a person [of] so many qualities. . . . Besides, so many businesses ready this term at London require his presence, or [are] to be laid aside with "our" prejudice.

This accident confirms her opinion of the inconstancy of human things. Had persuaded herself, if James had as much kindness for her as she has for him, they should never have parted, especially upon so slight an interest. But [would not] hinder his future good, therefore submits to whatever he resolves. . . . As for what he has done for Sir John Gifford or sister Talbot, she confesses herself his debtor, and hopes not to die without making satisfaction.

Endorsed: Answer to Mr. James when he went into Herefordshire, Mic. '71. *HM*2.23/13.

"Sister Talbot" is Mary, daughter of the 2nd Lord Powis, and widow of George Talbot, eldest son of John, Earl of Shrewsbury. The "Lady Powis" mentioned is, of course, the dowager—Mary Talbot's mother. This "Will Knas." must be the "Will Knarsb." of Nos. 11 and 12, more than twenty years earlier. "Mr. Jenner" may well be Sir Thomas Jenner, later Justice of the Common Pleas, while "Mr. Gee" is presumably Sir Orlando Gee, Registrar of the Court of Admiralty. "Cousin Thom. Whitmore" is Sir Thomas Whitmore of Apley—the dowager Lady Powis's mother was a Whitmore.

[1671]

23. [WALTER JAMES] TO [LADY POWIS].

Confesses himself a great debtor for her care and respect toward him in sickness and health; yet in all his indispositions he needed more help than he "required", and defrayed the charge, unless in possets and suchlike. She named several who acted under noble persons and had not such salaries; truly, those were rather commissioners than labourers (as he was) and found a way which got them more than he would had he the opportunity. . . . Is sorry he is blamed for not taking the benefit of making of leases; left it by her direction to ease her of Hughes's wages.

Finds the advantages brought by his endeavours esteemed inconsiderable. The riding charges in the country commonly brought a recompense—if he spent five shillings, he made a discovery of five shillings per annum for ever, more if looked unto. The London charges have been much, but unavoidable in maintenance of suits with those he need not name, and, since, by occasion of her English estate, which was improved so much as it needed not a complaint. . . .

Knows not how to deny her desires. But to stay till all the suits begun have ended perhaps must be during his life. The suits begun by him, if none else can prosecute them, [may] be so stopped that his lordship shall not be damnified with costs. . . . The instructions he had any other may have; the writings remain. As for notice of his going, he supposes none is requisite in any of his condition. . . . Is sorry he should be deemed of those who must give a quarter's warning. Never denied to give his lordship or any for him instructions concerning the estate—often desired him to find a person capable to take them. . . .

She seems to esteem Lady Talbott's and Sir John's business an increase of business upon him. He does not; it was long managed by others, and he expected to have the burthen. Thanks God he overcame all journeys and difficulties; it was the blessing God has for her and hers enabled [him] to go through all he did, considering his age and undertakings.

Resolved never to act for any in this way but her, and never depart her service while they lived both. . . . Riches or honour could not tempt him to desert his friend. . . . But having lived thus seven years, and having children unprovided for, he found nothing to do it but his real estate, which he designed to the heir. The £50 per annum which is supposed a full desert found but necessaries in the employment he was in. Therefore it was better to fare harder and put up a little store for the children. This made him alter his intention. Perhaps his children will never be the richer, yet the world will be satisfied with his endeavours. Will deliver all his charge in London to whom she appoints this term, and after Christmas will deliver all his charge here.

That she may know he has no other end than the preferment of his children, he makes this proposition: Will serve her while they both live for £50 per annum if, for a gratification for the time past and to come, she will, when she finds occasion, bestow on his son Water an annuity or farm for life, or let a farm to him with such abatement as countervails the gratification of the writer's service past and to come, saving only £40 which he must use himself.

[? October].

Endorsed: Mr. James's second paper. *HM*2.23/14.

[1667–1682]

24. ————— TO [LADY POWIS]. *Contemporary copy.*

She is desired to let the Marquess of Worcester know that she has seen a bond of £220 principal dated 7 December 1653, due from her father to John Handson, bound together with him Sir Ralph Blackstone, baronet, whom out of respect to her father they did not molest in his lifetime; which if the Marquess her brother will satisfy, it will be a great charity for the poor mission of the discalced Carmelites. *HM*2.24/3.

[16]79

25. R. SMITH TO MR. RICHARD HUGHES.

This is done with "my Lord and Ladyes" privity, unknown to all the world. Hughes must own it as his own orders, and receive the money . . . and send [some]one to put "him" in possession. "They will here pull his eyes out". Hughes may seem to admire to Evan Griffies that the writer sets it so cheap. Will wait upon him if he can get a pass. . . . Service from his wife.

18 May.

Endorsed: Millner of Green Halls mill . . . 415.

Since Richard Hughes was Lord Powis's servant, "my lord and lady" are presumably Lord and Lady Powis, though the former was a prisoner in the Tower at this time, a victim of the Popish Plot scare. Green Hall is near Llanfyllin, Montgomeryshire.

[16]79/80

26. JO. THOMAS TO MR. RICH. HUGHES AT POWYS CASTELL.

Was with the now Lord of Powis in behalf of the bearer, Dd. Moris, after the decease of his father, about having the reversion of a lease upon one summer house, land, etc., in Keven y Llys. Mr. James promised it to the sister and her husband, the terre-tenants. His lordship promised the bearer that if he did not have it during his sister's life, afterwards, being his father's heir, he should have it.

9 March. 8.

A summer house here means an upland house, used while the sheep and cattle were at summer pasture in the hills.

[16]85/6

27. Cha. Morgan to Mr. Richd. Hughes at Powis Castle.

Waited on Lord Powis for a year's rent for the manors of Mountgom[er]y *et al.* and £72 7s. 1½d. arrears, who directed him to send to Hughes for it. Desires he take course for payment to the writer for Lord Danby's use (whose receivers Mr. Auditor Tuder and the writer are for all his rents in Wales). "Your . . . Country man".

Coursiters' Alley,
6 February.

Direct to him at "the Aud'rs Office for Wales" next to the Maidenhead in Cursitors' Alley. 425.

Thomas Tudor was Auditor of Wales. Cursitor's Alley is now Cursitor Street, Chancery Lane.

[16]86

28. Cha. Morgan to Mr. Richard Hughes at Powis Castle or his house in Poole.

Desires to see him before he leaves this country, and that he would give him meeting at Mr. Bevis Lloyd's at Llanymonith [by] Thursday. There is a great arrear upon the lordships of Mountgom[er]y, Kerry, and Kedewen—two or three years. Prays him bring money and settle the matter.

Bodvach,
16 October. 427.

Bevis Lloyd's house was at Llanymynech (half-way between Welshpool and Oswestry).

[16]86

29. Richard Hughes to Charles Morgan, esq., at Mr. Tydder's office in Cursitors' Alley, London.

He may direct such as can give acquittance to call here for two years' rent. Desires to know what the clerk of the peace's yearly allowance has been at the audit; Morgan conceived it might be about 24s. May justly require it from such as have detained it from him for seven years past. "Your Countryman . . ."

Po. Castle,
5 November. 429.

1687

30. William Blathwayt to Lord Montgomry.

The General Officers having appointed to meet at ten in the morning on Friday the 25th of this instant November at the Great Room in the Horse Guards concerning allowance of medicaments to His Majesty's forces, His Majesty thinks fit that the colonels now in town be present.

*HM*2.26/2.

Blathwayt was Secretary at War. Lord Montgomery was colonel of a regiment of foot for a short period in 1687 and 1688.

1688

31. [LORD] CARINGTON TO MR. HUES AT POWIS CASTLE.

Troubles him with the particular of the estate the writer's lady recommended to him to enquire after.

28 May. 770.

Lady Carrington was Lord Powis's daughter. The particular is the next document in the bundle, a rent-roll and survey of the manor and farm of Acton Burnell, Acton Pigot, Ruckley and Langley, Burrington, Rusbury, and East Wall.

[16]88

32. RICHD. HUGHES TO LORD CARINGTON. *Holograph copy.*

Received his with the particular, but is sorry that he is altogether a stranger to that concern. Never was upon the place, nor is he acquainted with any of the tenants. May not therefore [give] a true estimate, but if he pleases he will make the best enquiry and view he can.

30 May. 773.

1688

33. [LORD] CARINGTON TO MR. HUGHES AT HIS HOUSE AT POOLE.

Must yet renew his request. Questions not but the tenants will give what information he thinks requisite. So respects the candour of Sir Edward Smyth that he has not the least suspicion of the particular, only in prudence cannot omit enquiry. . . . Desires him, where a tenant has anything considerable, to see his lease, but his chief desire is to know if the value in gross answers the particular. His, his wife's, and his sister's service to Lord and Lady Mountgomery. . . .

Wotton,
4 June. *Armorial seal* 772.

The Complete Peerage (Vol. X, p. 649) dates Lord Montgomery's marriage "*circa* 1695", but this letter and No. 33 are evidence of a much earlier marriage.

1688

34. [LORD MONTGOMERY] TO THE MARQUESS OF POWIS AT POWIS HOUSE, LINCOLNE'S INN FIELDS, LONDON.

"My Lord". Is glad to hear the young prince comes on so well; is in no apprehension for him because God appears to take care of him. Has been solicitous in obeying his commands about the trial of Mountgomery. Sent immediately to Major Lloyd, Mr. Foxe, and Mr. Wood, and discoursed Mr. Kinaston (who is here), and they all promised secrecy. Told them, though it were his lordship's concerns as lord of the manor, it would be a fatal blow to the King's concerns in all the neighbouring countries if his *quo warranto* took no effect. Told them it would not become his lordship to appear in it, but the King's counsel would manage it in the King's name. Begs him to represent the consequences to the King's attorney. Though a small place, few corporations have more gentry, and few places in this "subject" are of greater consequence to the King. Hopes he will take care to have a good solicitor. Mr. Hughes says Edmund Price is employed in it. Moses

Reynolds was bred up under Hodson, and therefore Mr. Hughes suspects he is a creature of Mr. Ireland. Is so bold as to give another caution—to have a care of Sir W. Williams, who underhand does all he can for Mountgomery. William Morgan, bailiff of Mountgomery, was deputy to Sir John Morgan, the King's steward in Radnorshire; supposes he does not continue as Lord Powis's deputy for the same county. Mr. Foxe could not come but promised to go to Mr. Layton of Watlesburough and send an account. [Suggests] he puts off settling the jurymen till then. Here are the persons recommended by Major Lloyd and Mr. Kinaston, who believe they can answer for most:

Protestants:

Phippe Prince of Holly Cross, esq.	? what hundred.
Timothy Wareing of the Isle, gent. Tho. Gough of the Marsh, gent. Basill Wood of the White Abbey, gent.	Ford hundred.
Richard Lloyd of Ford, gent., receiver to L[ord] Craven for "the ii Towns".	
Thomas Lloyd of Osbaston, gent. Edward Payne of Maesbrooke, gent. [? John *torn*] Lloyd of Melurley, gent. Andrew Thomas of Edgerley, gent.	Osestry h[undred].
John Edwards of Nesse, jr., gent. Arthur Chambres of Burleton, gent. Tho. Barns of the Low, gent.	Pimhill h[undred].

Catholics:

Walter Blunt, bart.	? whether he will be in the country.
Edward Smith, bart.	" " " " " " " "
Thomas Ireland of Albrighton, esq.	Pimhill.
Thomas Berington of Mote Hall, esq.	Ford.
Henry Fox of the Hurst, esq.	Ford.
Tho. Lacon of Linley, esq.	?
Edward Hunt of Morton, esq.	Osestry.
Edward Lloyd of Melverley, esq.	Osestry.
Basill Brooke of Madeley, [esq]r.	?
John Purcell of Madeley, [esq].	?

By next post he shall have a further account from Mr. Foxe. Supposes Mr. Ireland's interest may get some. Edmund Lloyd, now in London, can give full information of the Mountgomery business; he will be wanted here to manage it—beseeches him to get him down with all speed. If he will show this to Mr. Ireland he may rectify any mistake.

"Your . . . dutyfull . . . sonne".

Powis Castle,
24 June.

419.

Lord Powis was Steward of the Royal Manors in Radnorshire and several other counties. Lord Craven's "ii Towns" are perhaps the "eleven towns" of Ruyton-of-the-Eleven-Towns, a Craven manor. The defence of Montgomery's privileges is referred to in a number of letters in Part II (Nos. 608 ff.).

1688/9

35. The Prince of Orange's Order for Lord Montgomery.

Whereas Lady Montgomery [states] that there have been quartered at her house in Wales since a week before Christmas one Mr. Mason, an ensign, and twelve private soldiers of Ludlow Castle; that Mr. Devereux has seized divers horses belonging to Lord Montgomery, and that neighbours have entered upon his said "horse" [*recte* house] and carried away a considerable quantity of furniture: Being desirous to preserve the peace of the kingdom and the property of every private man, he hereby commands that Ensign Mason and the soldiers return to Ludlow, that Mr. Devereux and others restore the horses, and that the Justices of the Peace make strict search after the goods and cause them to be restored. G. H. Prince d'Orange.

St. James's,
19 January.

Endorsed: True copy. *HM*2.15/5.

Despite the endorsement this has every appearance of being an original—perhaps a second original supplied to Lady Montgomery for her protection. Mr. Devereux is probably Price Devereux of Vaynor, later 9th Viscount Hereford.

1689

36. Ralph Mylott to Mr. Richard Hughes at Welsh Poole.

His lordship will give answer concerning Madam Palmer next post. Was this day at the Bell in Wood Street to enquire for Wm. Lloyd or the cheeses and what else he brought up, but understood at the arrival of the horses [that] there was nothing. His lordship desires he be very diligent in enquiring after those goods delivered to Lloyd. He should speak to Mr. Fox's mother, who is supposed to have the management of his estate, and have that sum he took a note of for Mr. Rigmaton's use; also give account of Mr. Gilbert's affairs; not forgetting when Wm. Pugh [and] Wm. Lloyd come to town. Will endeavour to look after receiving the moneys.

10 October. *HM*2.23/59.

[16]89

37. John Evans to Mr. Richard Hughes at Welch Poole.

Lately waited on Lord Montgom[er]y in London, who promised to send Hughes instructions touching payment of the fee-farm rent due to the Marquis of Carm[ar]then for the manors of Mountgom[er]y, Kerry, and Kadawen. Encloses a letter from his lord. Hughes has good authority to gather these as well as other his lord's rents, but if he thinks it necessary the writer come and distrain, he must be paid for his journey. He should have the money returned to Sir Tho. Fowles, a goldsmith by Temple Bar—will allow for the charge. Or he may order it to be brought by the writer's friend Mr. Jervis, now in Hughes's town. Is here about a concern. The account is underwritten.

Kilsane,
5 November.

Arrears: Mich. '87, £72 7s. 1½d. Anno '88, £144 16s. 8¾d. Anno '89, £144 16s. 8¾d.

Notes at foot: Paid by E. W. for a bull, £3. Paid of this to Mr. Jno. Evans, £144 16s. 8¾d. 22 January 89/90. Paid more £100, 30 June '90.

Endorsed: Lord Danbye's demand. . . . 424.

1689

38. RALPH MYLOTT TO MR. HUGHES.

This day "my Ld." was admitted to bail. Service to Mr. Aubins and his family, Mrs. Toler, etc.

7 November. *HM*2.23/60.

"My Lord" is Lord Montgomery.

1689

39. [LORD] MOUNTGOMERY TO MR. RICHARD HEWS AT HIS HOUSE AT WELCH POOLE.

Prays him (if convenient) to get ready £31 10s. for Mr. John Lloyd of the Chancery Office by the middle of next month (he being to pay a sum of moneys in "your parts" then).

14 November. *Armorial seal* *HM*2.23/61.

1689

40. RALPH MYLOTT TO MR. HUGHES.

"My Ld.", being busy tonight, will answer by the next. His lordship being for some time in debt to Mr. Jo[h]n Lloyd of the Six Clerks' Office, has given him a bill for £31 10s. to be paid about the middle of next month. He is to satisfy it if he can. Received his by David, with Mr. Gilbert's account; did not answer, to save charges.

London,
14 November. *HM*2.23/62.

[16]89

41. RALPH MYLOTT TO MR. RICHARD HUGHES AT WELSH POOLE.

Encloses a quom[inus] against Lloyd. "My Ld." designs to answer his letters next post. Desired Mr. Aubins to call upon Hughes for the 30s. received for Mr. Gilberts—has an opportunity of receiving such a sum here upon his account. Service to all friends. Hopes shortly to see him.

17 December. *HM*2.23/63.

Lloyd was a carrier who seems to have embezzled some of Lord Montgomery's goods. For a letter from him, giving his own version of what happened, see No. 58.

1689/90

42. RALPH MYLOTT TO MR. RICHARD HUGHES AT WELSH POOLE.

"My Ld." is busy this night; he says that to return the moneys as Hughes proposes will do very well. As for setting the land, his lordship would have him do it, for he has no thoughts of coming down. Encloses a quom[inus] "speciall", returnable the last day of term, as he wrote for.

London,
17 January. *Monogram seal* *HM*2.23/64.

1689/90

43. Ralph Mylott to Mr. Richard Hughes at Welsh Poole.

His lordship is, by visits and other business, this post disappointed of [writing]. If the man in Sallopp can, for less than the goods are worth, retrieve any of them, Hughes is to "give it him"; or, if he will, for a sum certain, come to London and perform what he proposes, he is to bargain with him. Otherwise they are in a prospect of taking Lloyd, if he is to be had. By the next he shall have fuller directions from his lordship.

19 January. *Seal of a crest* *HM*2.23/58.

1689/90

44. Ralph Mylott to Mr. Richard Hughes at . . . . Welsh Poole.

"My Lord", having business tonight, cannot write. He is desired by next post to give account in whose regiment Lloyd the carrier is, who his colonel and captain are; when his lordship does not doubt to have him secured.

4 February. *Armorial seal* *HM*2.23/65.

1690

45. Ral. Mylott to Mr. Richard Hughes at Welsh Poole.

The party his lordship proposed to speak to concerning the excise, who has an interest with the Commissioners, is out of town, and his lordship would not attempt a thing he could not be assured of. But he thinks it will come to nothing. As for the tax being assessed double, the like is done here. But the commissioners—being acquainted the property is invested in trustees for payment of debts, and the tenant[s] warned not to pay at their peril, the assessment being wrong[ly] laid as against Lord Powis—are at a stand, and will levy only 3s. per £. If they do, he should let them distrain, and take a course with them that distrain. He is desired to get Judge Mathwes or some "Lyer" [? lawyer] he can trust to acquaint the commissioners that to act otherwise is contrary to law. He may have speedily an affidavit before a Master of Chancery if it will be of service.

London,
3 April.

Addition by Lord Montgomery: Sorry he has not time to write. Desires him to pay Nan Warburton's sister £5.

Armorial seal *HM*2.23/66.

"Judge Mathwes" is no doubt John Mathewes, who had been Second Justice of North Wales between 1687 and 1689, and was Chamberlain of cos. Denbigh and Montgomery. Anne Warburton, daughter of Sir Peter Warburton, bart., of Arley, Cheshire, had two sisters.

[? 1689–90]

46. The Earl of Dunbarton's and the Earl of Dover's Petition to the King. *Contemporary copy.*

All houses, sheds, and everything erected upon His Majesty's highways, streets, and common passages are encroachments and common nuisances, and all vaults and cellars under the same are trespasses punishable by fine or imprisonment or both. Pray his grant of the premises for fifty-one years, the first year gratis for their charge and trouble, and reserving to His Majesty [there]after such share as he thinks fit. *HM*2.15/18.

There are two possible dates for this petition. George Douglas was created Earl of Dunbarton in 1675; John Carey, 2nd Earl of Dover, died in 1677. It is thus possible that it belongs to those intervening years. Douglas and Carey, however, are an ill-assorted pair, and—unreal though such a petition seems in the circumstances—the date suggested at the head has more to be said for it. The Earl of Dunbarton was a member of James II's *émigré* court, and so for a time was Henry Jermyn, whom James created Earl of Dover in 1689—they were, in fact, Lord and Gentleman of the Bedchamber respectively. Lord Powis was, of course, their fellow-exile. Jermyn submitted to William III after the Battle of the Boyne in 1690.

1690

47. John Evans to Mr. Richard Hughes at Poole.

He wrote that he would return, for the lordships the Marquess of Powis holds from the Crown, the rent payable to the Marquess of Carm[ar]then. It was not performed, and the writer is much blamed; [may] be out of the employ for not doing his duty. Has a regard to Hughes's condition and the humour of the times, but must look to himself. Desires the money here or any part of Cardigan shire; will meet where he appoints. Otherwise he should send a bill to be paid in London. The account is underwritten. Has as much veneration for the noble family Hughes has dependency upon . . . but [cannot stay] longer for the rent. Will defray the charges of his messenger with the money. Had letters these three last posts from his lord's own hands requiring him to do his duty. Their audit begins at Carm[ar]then on 17 October, whence he must go for London and have money and accounts ready. If Hughes wants assistance distraining he will send those fit, Hughes paying them moderate allowance.

Kilsane,
13 September.

'87, £72 8s. 4½d. '88, '89, and '90, £144 16s. 8¾d. each. Received £144 16s. 8¾d. 433.

[late 17th C.]

48. J. Edwards to Mr. Richard Hughes at Mountgom[er]y.

"Cozen Hughes". Lady Herbert desires she be admitted to lay her year's rent due to Lord Powis under the same circumstances as the arrears of "my Lord".

Lymore,
24 August. 434.

1691

49. [LORD MONTGOMERY] TO MR. RICHARD HUGHES AT HIS HOUSE AT WELCHPOOLE.

His eyes being recovered, he answers Hughes's of the 23rd. A replication was put in to the plea concerning the manor of Hendon. Yesterday a rejoinder was filed, so it will probably come to issue this term. Questions not but the trustees will carry it by the justness of the thing. Approves his proceedings. Thinks distresses very convenient if they may be done with what assistance he can get in the country. But it is too hazardous to be at a great charge to send down persons when a verdict is daily expected. As for J.J., if the person named be in danger of his life, why cannot he swear the peace against him and have him bound over to good behaviour?

As for "Aas" coming down, it is a mere jest—he cannot stir hence during term; what forgeries and lies knaves invent to carry on their roguery. The great person likewise, whosoever he be, can have no thoughts of coming down—no great man about a king can be spared in time of Parliament.

The mills and weir must be taken care of. Nothing is so secure as that lordship; Mr. Noel's title is as clear as the sun—[is sure] he will allow it in the accounts. If the trees to be planted are of a right bigness he would be sorry to lose a year's growth.

If Mr. Haywood brings a bill from the writer for £100 and Hughes cannot raise so much, he should get [it] of Mr. Vaughan or somebody's steward that wants it in London, and draw a bill upon the writer—will not dispose of the money. Supposes Mr. Vaughan may be at Shrewsbury by Friday. Prays him visit Myl. with his service. His sister Montaigu desires him to speak with Mr. Price concerning payment of the money she lent his son, which he promised the writer's mother he would repay.

31 October. *HM*2.23/72.

Lord Montgomery's sister Mary was the wife of Francis, 4th Viscount Montagu.

[16]92

50. JOHN EVANS TO MR. RICHARD HUGHES AT POOLE OR RED CASTLE.

Had a letter from Lord Carm[ar]then to levy by distress all rents three months [over]due. Cannot forbear the half year's rent without his lord's particular order, which Hughes may procure if he thinks fit. Will be for London about Christmas. Meantime prays him order the money to be paid Mr. Wotton, or send Mr. [? Jervis] with it. If he does not hear in a fortnight he must send men to distrain, which he would be loath to do, for he has not been wanting to assist to get Hughes's due. Hears the Marquess of Powys is at Red Castle; sends his humble duty. Prays speedy [answer] by way of London or Llanbadarne.

Llanbadarne Vawr,
19 September. 435.

Wotton was a London goldsmith. The Marquess himself could hardly have been to Powis Castle; Evans no doubt meant Lord Montgomery.

[16]92

51. [RICHARD HUGHES] TO MR. EVANS. *Draft.*

Received his from Llanbadarn. Mr. Millett will settle the account at London in Christmas—£72 8s. 4½d., half a year's rent; the money[s] are already paid here in the country. Evans promised to send the writer's note.

Sent to Mr. Rees Thomas by Mr. Jarvis a copy of the indictment in which he, Mr. Howells, the writer, and two more are the indicted. It were well Thomas might take the legal course besides, for the great abuse he received. Owen Hodson makes account that the mare taken paid his chief-rent of £3 0s. 6d. Mr. Chettwind knows of "your" proceedings at the sessions; they are people that will swear sufficiently . . . (*Breaks off unfinished*).

2 December. 436.

[16]92

52. [RICHARD HUGHES] TO MR. EVANS. *Draft.*

Finds by his of the 7th he has not received the letter sent by London post directed to Killsane, that he had paid a half year's rent . . . the bill lodged with Mr. Millett. Cannot regulate the half year in dispute, being but an agent, and [it] transacted before his time. Will see whether Mr. Millett can discourse with any that knows of it. Is glad Mr. Rees Thomas minds a little to be remedied in the abuse he received; he and others were violently aimed at by one Owen Hodson with pikes and afterwards indicted for a pretended riot. A fine country to raise money in [in] several places to this very day. Must the mare taken from Owen Hodson pay Mr. Thomas his fees, as fit such a man should be put to pay? Then his chief-rent of above £3 will be unpaid, and who will distrain for it that loves his life?

Vron Green,
11 December. 437.

1693

53. JOHN EVANS TO MR. RICHARD HUGHES AT POOLE OR ELSEWHERE.

Entreats him to send by a safe hand the year's rent due to the Marquis of Carm[ar]then for Lord Powis's manors, or a bill that he may send to London. Must make up his accounts and pay the money by 6 January. Has been very ill with doctors in Carm[ar]then, but is now come home. Hopes all things well and that they are "all quiett with Rogues".

Kilsane,
18 December. 430.

1693/4

54. JOHN EVANS TO MR. RICHARD HUGHES AT POOLE OR ELSEWHERE.

Wrote by a "purpose messenger" who had not the happiness of seeing him. Sends again to desire a bill to pay Mr. Wotton, the writer's goldsmith in London, or that he send hither in a week's time the money due from Lord Powys's estate in Hughes's own management. Will not demand them again but by distress, and will send such a one as will not take a "bafle". He owes a year's rent. He knows the writer is dunned for the money. Service to his lady, though unknown to him. Has his old bills for him.

Kilsane,
13 February. 432.

[16]93/4

55. R. H. TO MR. EVANS. *Draft.*

Received his of the 13th. Designs to return to Evans's goldsmith what money he can shortly. Has seldom received such letters. He well knows the obligation of that payment lies not upon the writer. Prays by London post what papers Evans has that belong to the writer, matters having been settled with Mr. Millett.

18 February. 431.

1694

56. JAMES II'S INSTRUCTIONS TO HIS SUPPORTERS. *Contemporary copy.*

That all parties join to hinder and explode all excises in Parliament. That money be delayed as long as possible and appropriated. That the Bank be "pushed of", and that [they] join with the goldsmiths to break it. That our "most Considerable Friends the Church of England Men Unravell this years Administration by Sea and Land" and enquire into the vast sums carried out of the land and misapplied to the design of Parliament. That if votes for money be carried, "Our friends" lodge them upon voluntary acts and projects. . . . Is extremely satisfied in his secretaries, Lord Midleton and Mr. Carryll. . . .

That all parties unite to set forth the miseries of his kingdoms and the oppression they labour under. . . . Is convinced of the Most Christian King's zeal for his speedy restoration, of which his friends shall be timely advised by such of the nobility and gentry as he more particularly trusts. . . . Conjures his loyal subjects not to rise or embody themselves without direction first had by such noblemen and gentry. . . .

That enquiry be made concerning the management of the navy and those who advised sending it into the Straits [to] winter, by which it was exposed to ruin. . . . That such popular bills be pressed as [it] is supposed the P. of O. will not pass. Or what else his friends upon the place judge for his service. James R.

3 December.

Minutes for the Present Conjuncture: 1. To join to advance Mr. F———o to the Speaker's chair. 2. To press the reasonableness of the quota vote in the last parliament and insist on it as a national interest. 3. To stir up Lords and Commons to assert the hereditary rights of the Crown in opposition to any new projects for its settlement. 4. To labour friends in both Houses to renew complaints against those who received bribes and pensions to pervert justice and betray their country. 5. To persuade friends in Parliament to call in the base coin. . . . 6. To enquire into the state of the navy, the decay of trade, the insupportable losses of merchants, and to redress these and other grievances. . . .

Folded and sealed but unaddressed. *HM*2.15/12.

Paul Foley was appointed Speaker very soon after; it is presumably he who is meant here.

1695

57. RAL. MYLOTT TO MR. RICHD. HUGHES AT WELSH POOL.

Acquainted Sir Edmd. Wiseman (who is proposed to be sheriff of London) of Hughes's kindness to wait upon his son. Credit must not be given to all the stories of Count Rochford alias Ealiston. The writer's master desires Hughes to write to Mr. Tho. Sanders to be satisfied with the performance of the articles agreed by him and Mr. Brian Hind, and to accept Mr. Miles and Mr. Anthony Harrod for security for payment, and not insist on particular security for every article; and that Mr. Hind be restored to possession of his house, goods, and land; and if Mr. Ralph Mylott comes down, to take his instructions in this; and that [he send] the writer a letter that he may have authority. Has written to Mr. Sanders. Prays him tell John Lloyd that his master has given him leave to go to Holywell when he has a mind for three or four days.

2 July. 447.

"Ealiston" is Zuylestein, William Henry Nassau de Zuylestein being the newly-created Earl of Rochford.

[16]95/6

58. WILLM. LLOYD, LATE CARRIER, TO [LORD MONTGOMERY].

His lordship's goods that William Rodgears of Hamarsmeth had were several candlesticks and bowls gilt . . . silver tankards, a chafing dish, forks and spoons, etc., in all about 43 lbs. box and all—all plate, nothing else—the box wrapt in canvas. [While] his lordship was in custody the writer delivered them by persuasion of his porter to Rodgears, to be delivered up when he sent for them. Went by coach to Hamarsmethe to Rodgers's house; his man came purposely to see the delivery of them. His desire only was to know really whose goods they were, and to detain them till he had settled accounts with his lordship, and to know whether he would atone the Marquess's bill. . . . Owns that the £200 his lordship lent him in his necessity was a great kindness. Remained indebted to him £60, for which he gave his bond to Mr. Hubbard. Had no ill desire. Thought the plate safe till called for, though Rodgears would have persuaded him to keep them, saying they were traitor's goods.

At that time one of his gangs of packhorses were stopped on the road by reason of his debts. Was forced to abscond, and when he came up to London his porter Ralph Kellet was dead and his servants all gone. Sent to Rodgers a penny post letter to come; he refused. Sent to his old servant to come to him at Mr. Baules in Bell Yard or Alley, near Temple Bar. Sent to Rodgars to come and bring the goods, who came and owned he had melted them down and sold them, saying the writer or his child should have all, "I not thinkinge but hee might goke upon mee". Within a few days his servant, that was evidence in the thing, was removed. . . . Sent letters still to him to deliver the plate. He answered he was a stranger to the thing. Having no evidence, he did not [tell] his lordship. Now within six weeks his old man found him; then made his lordship's secretary acquainted with the thing, and has been at the charge to take him. Hopes his lordship will proceed in it; is mighty low in the world, and has not wherewith to do it.

For the £60 due, he hopes he will take his bond to pay within five or six years, and at least abate half. If he pays everyone half what he owes, he will not have £10 to maintain his wife and her children. The rest of his creditors are willing. Or if his lordship or any friend will lend him £20 he will give his wife's fortune in security—her annuity is £10 a year till the death of Lady Bridges of Sallop (now 68 and under several distempers) when a living of £100 a year falls to his wife's younger brother, he paying her £500. Now his wife is at age he can sell or give it. . . . Refers all to him. If he could do more he would, by reason his father, brothers, and himself all their lifetimes have been servants to his family. It will pay no one keeping him here. . . .

White Friars,
8 March.

Wrote to Rodgers and "swettned him and soward him, and all would not doe, but hathe bult howseis withe the plate". *HM*2.23/70.

It will be noticed that Lloyd writes from refuge—the notorious Alsatia.

1696

59. Ral. Mylott to Mr. Richd. Hughes at Welsh Poole.

Received his doleful letter; sends one more melancholy. All Lord Powis's estate real and personal except Powis House is granted to Zuliston, now Lord Rochford; it is passed all the seals. He is in possession of Hendon and has begun to let leases; believes the same is with Pipwell. Is of the opinion the Welsh estate will follow, for the Attorney-General has given notice they will move for a trial next term. They propose to try it by a Middx. jury, believing the ancient Britons have no kindness for the Dutch. Hughes is desired to come to London with speed to settle accounts and help manage the trial, being a trustee and knowing all the proceedings there. The trial will be in the King's own, but they also bring a bill against Mr. Noell in Lord Rochford's name to bring him to account what he has received to the discharge of his mortgage, and to pay the rest off. Has not seen J.J. nor none of them. Is almost wearied off his legs, and longs to see him.

16 May. *HM*2.23/69.

PART II

HERBERT OF MONTGOMERY
AND
HERBERT OF DOLGUOG

[1554–9]

60. ——————— TO [? EDWARD HERBERT OF MONTGOMERY]. *Part only.*

. . . her grange of Gwernogo in co. Mountgom[er]y a little before the death of the said king; *item*, if the assurance pass on the grange only, which is well known and meared and lies in the township of Gwernogo, and yet not the twentieth part of the town. Further, he is to understand that Lord Williams and those that claim under him occupy divers tenements in the townships of Hopton, Wynhayllion, Keven y Berren, Kaellebar Yssa, and Gwenrewe in co. Mountgom[er]y and one tenement in Brompton, co. Salope. 802C.

This is a mere isolated fragment. The date range assigned is that of Sir John Williams's tenure of his barony as Baron Williams de Thame.

1566/7

61. JOH. TRE[VOR] TO MR. EDWARD HARBART, ESQ. *Torn.*

A thousand thanks, for himself and for his master. Encloses a letter to cousin Jankyn Gowyn, that he should declare to Herbert his offer of [an] end with the writer. (*A very defective passage about money paid or due to Mr. Hudson, Johnes, etc.*) Mr. Gowyn knows what sums he has sent and what remains, but if Herbert can cause him to send up between [now] and the beginning of next term £60, the writer will stay his suits. Otherwise he prays him declare the writer more busy than he is, that he [ma]y have time to understand [h]ow commodious the manor of Generglyne is for salt makers, and whether thereby the writer may . . . by Herbert's means . . . those things he does at present "shiwet at"—getting £60 and time to understand whether there is any good to be done at Gowyn's wife's manor of Generglyn. (*Another passage, largely unintelligible*). Commendations to Mrs. Harbart, Mr. Sheriff . . . "my good sheryffe . . . last yere", and Mr. . . . M[ere]dayphe ap Owen W. . . .

B. . . . ke . . . est,
16 February. 794.

"Jankyn Gowyn" is Jenkin Gwyn, Surveyor of North Wales.

1566/7

62. W. WIGHTMAN TO MR. [EDWARD] HERBERT.

The Lord Keeper, the Duke of Norff., the Lords Pembroke and Leycestre, Mr. Secretary, and others their co-partners in the saltworks have determined upon certain houses to be erected this year . . . one in Cardigan or Meryoneth shire near Dovy, where the herring fishing is, and have committed the whole trust thereof to Herbert and the writer. Is to deliver to him by way of prest £50. Has to give attendance here and cannot accompany him about the work till May.

He must provide a frame of timber to make a house, 120 ft. by 21 ft., the posts not above 6 ft. high, the walls of twig and loam or some such, with thatch of reed, fern, or straw; the roof to have a louver from end to end to "avoyde" the smoke and the reek of the salt waters therein to be boiled. Also brick or stone sufficient to make furnaces for ten pickle pans 10 ft. by 7 ft. and two salt pans, round or square, 15 ft. over, and loam or horse-dung for setting the same if lime be chargeable. He must fell eight hundred wain-loads of wood and make it into "handesoome" billets. For the placing of the work he will receive instructions by Mr. Xpofer, a German, who will repair to him before the last of this month. The work must be set upon a salt marsh near the deepest sea he can find and distant from fresh springs or rivers a mile and a half at least. The marsh must be such that the sea may be taken into it every high tide, first received into a store pond 15 yds. by 10 yds., which may be drained at low tide [after] foul weather. Between this and the house must be twelve or fifteen acres of marsh cut into ponds 20 or 24 ft. square and ½ ft. deep, to be filled from the store pond, [the water] to lie a time and be enriched by the sun and then let by sluice into another pond joining hard to the house called a saver pond, 30 ft. by 15 ft. and 6 ft. deep, with a house or hovel over it, thatched [against] rains and mists. The water is to be drawn by a sweep and bucket out of this pond, as the dyers and brewers upon Thames use, and conveyed by troughs into the pickle pans, there to be boiled till it will bear a new-laid egg or an amber bead. After boiling the pickle must eftsoons be put into coolers of oaken board, 3 ft. broad and 10 ins. deep, standing all along the outside of the house to seaward and covered from rain; thence conveyed by troughs into the salt pans and boiled to salt. A house must be made, 20 ft. square at least, [by] the long house, to keep the salt in, walls and floor on the inner side boarded.

Of many other matters he must receive instructions of Mr. Xpofer, the most perfect man in that art. . . . What rent he agrees for with the owner of the ground shall be justly answered. Above all, the work should be ready by 1 May. It is all one to do it with many hands quickly and with few hands slowly; but loss of time is great loss to the partners. (*A passage about wages follows, too torn to be intelligible.*) The work [? will] yield one hundred bushels of salt, London measure, every twenty-four hours. For the "vent" of the salt he must devise all means he can to utter it by water or land. (*Another badly torn passage follows.*) As soon as he can have the pans made they shall be sent out of Suss[ex] to Dovye.

London,
18 February.

775.

The writer is William Wightman, Receiver of South Wales. "Mr. Xpofer" is Christopher Schutz, a German expert, who had a grant in 1565, with William Humfry, a Paymaster of the Mint, to search and smelt minerals in England and Ireland (*Cal. of State Papers, Domestic*, 1547-80, p. 259).

1566/7

63. Pet. Osborne and W. Wightman to Mr. Edward Herbert of Mountgomerye, esq.

His letters of 14 March came on the 19th. They perceive the little time Mr. Christopher had with him and the unaptness of the tide to make trial of the water. It grieves them that there is such loss of time. Pray him go forward with the frame. Pray his advice how to get the pans thither. Cast pans "frame not" in Sussex; are driven to trust to plate pans. Will have ten for pickle and two great salt pans—six or seven wain-loads if they go by land to Bristowe or Shrewsbury. Mean to prove whether they can be carried by water into Sussex and [thence] by the Lord Deputy's carriage by sea to Dovye; but ask his opinion for the more "handesoomenes". Mean to send the salt pans in quarters and the pickle pans in halves, and a smith shall come to set them together—he shall also be a salt maker. Have great hope of that work for its conveniency and the certainty of "vent". Mr. Christopher's notes must be observed as certain grounds—his skill is answerable to his honesty; are glad Herbert's opinion of him concurs. Their new devices for furnaces "take no place" yet; must stick to the old. If Mr. Chr[i]stopher hits upon a better they will procure him the reward he desires.

London,
21 March.

Addition by Osborne: In Mr. Wightman's absence he has written to Mr. Christofer of a device to have leaden pans, if lead may be gotten conveniently at Bristow or elsewhere about; and how to help the sandiness of the ground. "Comends" to brother Fowler and his w[ife].

Ivy Lane,
22 March.

Thinks Mr. Christopher is at Bristowe. 776.

Osborne had been Keeper of the Privy Purse to Edward VI (see *Dictionary of National Biography*, *s.n.*). The Lord Deputy, Sir Henry Sidney, had large estates in Sussex, and was, of course, President of the Council of Wales. William Fowler of Harnage Grange, Shropshire, married Mary, daughter of Dr. John Blythe, first Regius Professor of Physic at Cambridge, while Osborne married her sister Anne.

[1567]

64. CRISTOFFE[R] SCHUTZ TO MR. EDWARD HARBORD AT MUNGUMBERY.
A mixture of German and English

Trusts he and Mrs. Herbord are in health. Received his of 26 March and therein perceived "wo" this place will serve for making "Sale . . .", which will be "tzarsable". Will tell nothing until he has answer from London [from] Mr. Asbhorn, "w'ch ei dunck wol be shueretlj"; has written him [as to] how he likes the samples. [When] he knows "wadt de thue Indentt to thue" he will go speedily forwards.

Drutherun,
28 March. 778.

I translate the passage in quotation marks in the last sentence as "what the two intend to do", referring presumably to Osborne and Wightman. It is not easy to identify the place from which Schutz was writing; since he was at Chepstow in April and wrote later from Tintern (see Nos. 65 and 75) this might be Dyffryn, near Newport, where Wentlloog Level might have provided a suitable site for the salt-works he was proposing to erect in that district.

[1567]

65. [EDWARD HERBERT] TO MR. WIGHTMAN "AND OTHERS". *Draft.*

Received his of 22 March by the hands of a servant of Mr. Justice Throckm[or]ton this 4 April. Sent to Mr. Christopher on the 5th to

Chepstow for his speedy coming over. Encloses copy of his answer. It is a great grief to him that Mr. Christopher does not accomplish the lords' pleasure and Wightman's desire. As for Christopher's doubts at his being with the writer at the sea side, he was answered fully by letters before Easter. Sent the ninety-three men of good skill for levelling the ground, "advoiding" the fresh water from the pans, and bringing the sea. 777.

1567

66. Joh. Trevor to Mr. Edward Harbart, esq. *Part only.*

. . . which was due to "hym" for the moiety of the fee for the Surveyorship of North Walles, and this is all the writer received. Leaves other debts which Mr. Gowyn owes him by bargains between them. Has not written any sum but such as the writer paid as surety for him or took up and made himself debtor for, taking his bond. And by this account Gowyn rests more in his debt than he and all his tenants at the Brere Dew shall be able to pay upon a day's warning. Yet let Mr. Gowyn send up in May £60 upon a reckoning, as money lent to Herbert, and the writer will stay all matters till he comes this summer to the country. . . . Touching Herbert's own matter, the writer rides [now] as far as [? Dovere], and at his return will do therein as though it were his own. Has no more news than he wrote yesterday. Hopes he will procure the money of Mr. Gowyn—must pay £680 [*or* £740] for himself and his friends.

10 April. 802A.

The amount in the last sentence is written "Diij^{lx}" or "Diiij^{lx}".

[? 1567]

67. Articles for the Salt Works.

Articles to be well considered before beginning the making of salt: 1. It is necessary to bring in the water from the sea level to the ground where the writer thought the work should stand. 2. The saver pit must be at least 5 ft. deep under water level, and "close" that no fresh water may come to it. 3. A square pan shall be made 4 ft. and a "hanful" deep, hard beaten on bottom and sides; sea water must be put half an inch high to try how the ground will hold it, and what it will consume in a day and a night, and the water remaining shall be sent to the writer. 4. Send also a little of the "mene" sea water, whereof he may make a subtle assay to see what it will hold. Provide to bring the fresh water from the back side, where the work shall stand.

On the dorse in another hand: Make one pit 4 ft. square . . . (*substantially as 3 above*). Get "one with a yeurne that cuthye ther burnyng turffe" to make shallow pits, and for the deep pit workmen with a spade. 792.

It is not known who the writer was; the hands are new ones. A handful is the same as a hand in measuring horses, four inches. "Yeurne" is perhaps iron—an iron for cutting peat.

1567

68. PET. OSBORNE AND W. WIGHTMAN TO MR. EDWARD HERBERT OF MOUNTGOM[ER]Y, ESQ., AT DOVYE OR AB[ER]USTWITH, OR TO SUCH AS HE HAS APPOINTED TO THE ERECTIONS OF THE SALT WORKS THEREABOUTS.

They send by this bearer, Thoms. Wilson, master of a good hoy, the *Christopher*, of London, the parcels hereafter mentioned and in his bill of lading. Pray him discharge the vessel with all speed and give friendly entertainment to the master and his company. He is agreed with for the freight. The smiths, salt maker, and other ministers, if not al[ready] come, will not be long. And the writer, Willm. Wightman, will [keep] his time there with Herbert. Trusts to find everything in good forwardness.

London,
3 May.

12 pans with their furniture; 50 double plates for setting up and mending them, a barrel of nails to set the pans together; 50 staples to rivet into the pans and 50 hooks to support the same; a barrel of pitch and one of tar to close the joints of the saver pound and the coolers; 2 barrels of tarras; 1 barrel of powder called "cacke" to stop the running of the pans, being mixed with white of egg, rye flour, and "East"; 70 ft. of cast pipe and 6 copper corks; [40 ells of "sowltwitche" that the pans are lapped in *deleted*]; half a hundred of solder to mend the pipes and solder [in] the corks; a piece of cast pipe, 12 ft.—the 2 pieces of cast pipe weigh seven hundred p[ound] weight at [112] lbs. the hundredweight; a barrel of plaster of Paris to stop the running of the pans if the other will not serve; 6 sides of plate for the pans t[o be] left upon; a bar of cross-bow steel to make the smiths' tools; 2 smiths' hammers. Herbert must provide a forge and anvil. 780.

"Cacke" is perhaps cauk, i.e., calc-spar; "sowltwitche" is soutage (canvas). The number of pounds in the hundredweight is supplied from the previous document, No. 779, which is a contemporary copy of most of this letter.

1567

69. PET. OSBORNE TO MR. EDWARD HERBERT OF MONGOM[ER]YE, ESQ.

Tomorrow by four in the morning the pans and other stuff for Wales shall be laden and the ship will set forward the day after. He may tell Mr. Wightman he has not heard from Christofer nor of the lords' letters to the latter. Their old house in Suff. is working "on Suff Syde". The other will be within seven days, likewise the old works in Kent. Their house in Sussex is raised and toward thatching; the pans for it go hence on Tuesday. Hears nothing of Southampton, nor of Mounte from the north. He should provide that his pickle pans fill when they waste the "frenche" away with "whott luke warme" water. . . . Reserves the rest to Mr. Wightman, whose Harrow family and London friends are in health.

Ivy Lane,
11 May. 781.

A certain John Mount had recently set up salt works at Blyth, Northumberland;

one of his letters to Cecil was dated from Southampton (*Cal. of State Papers, Domestic*, 1547-80, pp. 274 and 282). "Frenche" is perhaps french salt, or bay salt, produced by natural evaporation. Wightman lived at Harrow-on-the-Hill.

1567

70. W. WIGHTMAN TO MR. EDWARD HERBERT OF MOUNTGOMERYE.

Received answer from Mr. Christopher, who cannot be at Mountgomerye before Wednesday in Whitsun week. He must leave word at his house that Christopher should come to Dovye, and appoint him a guide. This slackness will alter their determination for their meeting. Would like to hear from him at Carm[ar]ffen. Perceives Mr. Christopher comes not very willingly to these matters—his appointment with the writer was to be at Dovye on Tuesday in Whitsun week.

Brecknocke, pressed towards Carm[ar]then,
12 May. 782.

[? 1567]

71. REMEMBRANCES BETWEEN MR. WIGHTMA[N] AND MR. HERBERT TOUCHING THE SALT-WORK.

Mr. Herbert is to provide with all speed two boats or barges for carriage of fuel and salt. The frame must be brought down, and the stone and loam, and horse-dung to mingle with the loam for setting the furnaces. Mr. Herbert is to make so many bars of iron as Mr. Christopher thinks meet; they must be "just" for the furnaces. The roof to have louvers. . . . There must be provision of all kind of nails for lathing, boarding, and planking the house, etc. The houses for keeping the salt will be best each end of the long house. The pickle pans to be in the midst of the house, and at each end a salt pan. The houses for keeping salt must be so close and staunch as may defend all weather, wind, and sand—beware of drift sand. The work must be walled round with the turf and stone from the pits. A "whilewaght" to make carts and wheelbarrows must be had. The workmen from London to be provided for by Mr. Harb[e]rt, and touching their wages he shall receive order from Mr. Osborne and the writer. The pans, etc., that come from London must be dry-housed, and great sleds 11 ft. by 8 ft. made to draw them from Dyvy to the work. They must be landed this side the water of Dyvy towards the work. Spades, shovels, and mattocks must be in great plenty.

Endorsed : . . . Touching the salt work at Dyvy. 790.

The reference to landing "this side of Dovey" seems to confirm that the salt works were on the south side of the estuary, presumably somewhere on the edge of Cors Fochno. This is the view also of Mr. W. J. Lewis, who used these letters as the basis of his article "A Welsh Salt-Making Venture of the Sixteenth Century" (*The National Library of Wales Journal*, Vol. VIII, No. 4, Winter 1954), and whose assistance on a number of points I take this opportunity of acknowledging. It will be recalled that earlier, in No. 61, John Trevor had referred to Geneu'rglyn (in which parish Cors Fochno lies) in connection with salt-making.

1567

72. ARTICLES MOVED TO BUCKHOLT AND HIS COMPANY ON BEHALF OF THE LORDS THE PARTNERS OF THE SALT WORKS IN ENGLAND AND IRELANDE. *Contemporary copy.*

1. Whether they can sever the fresh water from the salt that comes out of the sea without fire. 2. What quantity of fresh water they can take from every cwt. of salt water. 3. After the fresh is severed, what quantity of salt every hundred shall hold. 4. How many months in the year they will work. 5. What quantity of salt shall every "Qoorke" yield every twenty-four hours. 6. How many works they mean to erect to serve the realm of Englande. 7. At what price they shall be able to make a bushel of salt. 8. Whether their salt shall be as strong and good as any refined salt of Holland and Zelande. 9. Whether they will [use] only sea water, and not bay salt refined. 10. What number of workmen they will occupy at every works. 11. Whether they will use houses, ponds, pits, and pans, as the lords' works do. 12. Whether their works may not be set up at the lords' houses new-erected, to save charges. 13. What quantity of the £16,000 they will discharge the lords of, and what [clear] yearly profit the lords shall have 14. Whether they will deal both for Englande and Yrelande. 15. Whether they will make sufficient to serve both England and Yreland, and in how many years. 16. How many works they will erect in one year, and when they will begin.

15 May.

Endorsed: . . . Buckeld and his company. 783.

Buckholt is twice mentioned—first as "Mr. Buckholt" and then as "the Lord of Buckholte"—in *Cal. of State Papers, Domestic*, 1547-80, as soliciting and holding a grant to operate salt works (pp. 251 and 296).

1567

73. ROBERT PURSELL TO MR. EDWARDE HERBERT OF MOUNTGOMERYE, ESQ.

These two smiths, sent by Mr. Osborne, are agreed to have for their day's wages, Michaell Millard 20d. and Willm. Laycrofte 18d. They entered into wages this day. Has paid them a month's wages. Paid Thoms. Justice, bricklayer, 26s. 8d. for him and his man, and Raef Eaton, salt maker, 13s. 4d., part payment of their wages. Has sent by the salt make[r] two great amber stones to try his pickle with. The bricklayer can certify him how to use the tarras, and the smith how the plaster of Paris shall be used to stop the running of the pans.

London,
26 May. 784.

1567

74. "REMEMBRANCE FOR SALTE . . ."

Except the water be enriched in "fieldes" the quantity of salt will not rise so much from "th'only" sea water, nor be brought to salt with so small charge. If the riches of the water be sought [by] sharp boiling and force of fire, the water [? may] be overboiled to the destruction of the salt. For remedy of which, as soon as the pickle will bear an egg it must be let into a cooling "back" till cold, then put into the salt pan and given a fast f[ire?], whereby the salt will come in great . . . (*torn*) . . . and be more merchantable than if small.

8 July. 785.

[1567]

75. CRISTOFFER SCHUTZ TO MR. EDWAR HERBERTT, ESQ., AT MUNGU.

Franncs Tongain came yesterday from the writer's men at Maychuntley, where there are many hindrances. Foremost, they desire to have more of their own countrymen, without whom they can do nothing. Because of the water they have met with the work must go day and night. Not being at present provided of strangers to satisfy their turn, he thinks it convenient to take them away from thence until the spring. Mr. Wighteman will be at Aberdovy on 22 October and desired the writer to meet him there, which he is not able to do because of his great businesses here and hereabouts—is about to build another house, and is charged with a great many workmen. Prays them excuse him and consider his great charge [by] his whole company and co-partners to bring his work to a final end. Trusts to repair to him afore Christmas. Is very glad of the good success in the salt works; understands by the bearer all is far forward. Has no news from London but that the lords of Anwerppe are taken prisoners and Spaniards inhabit their houses. King Phillippe is still looked for there. Four men were burnt in the said town, anabaptists as was reported to the common people, and when they were suffering four drums were stricken up that none might hear their confession. Commendations to Mrs. Herb[er]t and all his children, household, and friends.

Tynterne,
1 October. 786.

Fortunately only the signature is in Schutz's own hand.

1567

76. JOH. TREVOR TO MR. EDWARD HARBART, ESQ.

[Thanks] him and Mrs. Harbart for his entertainment. Received his by this bearer, cousin Morgan, touching the controversy between the latter and the writer's brother. Thought good for the time not to enter in the title for the house and lands, but to stay till his brother will be at the hearing. Also thought it fit cousin Morgan should not return home without some money to bear his charges till the matter is heard before Herbert and the writer. And if it appears that Morgan has the better title, he shall have four old angels to bear him holy company homewards, and the lands also. Will write again within two days with his servant, whom he sends to his cousin Mr. Jankyn Gowyn.

21 October.

Perceives that by Herbert's help cousin Morgan is become purchaser of lands near him, towards which if he wants 40s. he prays Herbert undertake for it and the writer will see it paid. 787.

1567

77. W. Wightman to Mr. Edwarde Herbert, Sheriff of co. Mowntgomerie.

Since his last they have had little ado touching the salt. This very evening there is come to Mr. Osbourne and him two strangers out of Holland, Peter Bryet and Xpofer de Braye, who offer certain devices. For aught they can perceive the whole feat rests in a number of field pits, well made, in wind and sun and warm, dry weather—which when God sends they have little need of help. He shall know of any conclusion. Meantime he should proceed with his boat. Is busy about Herbert's benefice; they will have the preferment of the farm at worst—Mr. Gardiner has so promised and begins to yield in the rest. The news is very strange out of Fraunce. The Prince of Coondye this day sevennight overthrew all the French king's power. The Constable was slain three weeks past. In this the King's brother [the] Duke of Anjeowe, the Constable's eldest son Duke Maumreansye, the Duke Monpensier, the Marshal Brysack, the Marshal Sansack, M. de Vilbone, M. de Ville Vyle, M. de Bourdillion, and almost all the nobility were taken prisoner; Marshal Danvyle, the Constable's second son, the Duke Destampes, and many others slain. The King's power is reported to have been 30,000 foot and 5,000 horse, put to flight; the Prince's company were little above 4,000 foot and 1,500 horse. The sequel will breed great alterations in Fraunce. This is God's work to pluck down the proud and set up the simple. At the coming of the Court hither Herbert shall be the first to hear.

London,
6 December. 788.

This account relates to the Battle of St. Denis, fought on 10 November.

[? 1567/8]

78. Thomas Beapell to Mr. Edward Harbar at Mongoumbry.

Hearty thanks for the gentleness he has received at his hands, and especially for his letters to Londone in the writer's behalf. Desires him to write again to Mr. Whitheman and other friends there, otherwise "whe" shall be able to do nothing. When Mr. Rysseabeddar and the writer came first to Loundon the judge of the Admiralty meant to show them great extremity; but when he heard from "me Lordes" steward, by the "meayne" of Herbert's letter, they found him very reasonable. Mr. Whithman and Dr. Allvrye travailed very much in their quarrel; desires him give them thanks and write them again, for he means to be at Loundon again this term for the same matter.

Has sent him 125 lbs. of "spekys" and bolts for the "bellinge" of Herbert's "Lauthetear" at 3¼d. the pound (33s. 10d.), which he shall receive of John Abeven up Roberts. Of the same man he shall receive

1½ cwts. 16 lbs. of "peyche" at 8s. the cwt. (13s. 3d.). And of the same he shall receive 20 lbs. of "okecom", cost 20d. So the whole is 48s. 9d. Has sent him a box of marmalade by John Abeven. Promised to send him ship-carpenters, but cannot get any to come if he got £100 by the sending of them. The ship-carpenter Herbert spoke to [at] the Borthe was contented to come but none would go with him. Means to be in Brestaw on the 25th and there will do his "dylygeynce" to get ship-carpenters. Will be content to receive his money in London of Mr. Whythman.

Bearnystabell,
19 January. 312.

"Dr. Allvrye" may be Dr. William Aubrey, the famous civilian; Herbert may well have formed acquaintance with him when they were at St. Quentin together ten years earlier, and according to Churchyard (writing nearly twenty years later) he had a house in the Welsh Marches, at Brecon (*The Worthiness of Wales*, 1776 ed., p. 70). It seems that the ship that Herbert was building was to be called *Laughter*.

[? 1567/8]

79. ARTICLES TOUCHING THE SALT-WORK. *Part only.*

Item. The said lords and co-partners are pleased for a time only to accept the fourth part of the clear profits, the other three parts remaining to the merchants towards their charges and the satisfaction of Fraunces Bartie, whom the merchants shall satisfy of all sums the lords and co-partners are bound to pay him. And after he is paid, the merchants shall of the first clear profits pay to the lords and co-partners £4,500 by them already defrayed about the said works. After which the houses, pans, [etc.] shall remain and be to the said merchants, and the moiety of the profits thenceforth shall be equally divided between them and the lords and co-partners. The merchants to be bound before the feast of the Birth of Our Lord yearly to make true account and payment. [*Marginal note:* The partition altered thus—9s. of the £ to Bertye, 6s. 8d. to the merchants, 4s. 4d. to the lords; and after Bartye paid, equal partition.] If the Queen does not resume the privilege before the twenty years, she stands not chargeable with payment of the £25,000; but if she do resume, the £25,000 is to be equally divided between the lords and merchants, so far forth as the merchants have satisfied Fraunces Bartye and paid the £4,500.

The lords agree to the liberty the merchants require to refuse the bargain at the year's end if they do their uttermost during the next summer to bring the works to perfection, and make refusal in writing, and yield up the privilege before 1 December, with the salt-houses, etc. . . . The merchants to pay the fourth part of the clear profits of this year to the lords and co-partners before Christmas next. If the merchants do not make refusal, they are bound to set up as many more houses, pans, etc., as within two years after next summer . . . shall furnish the realm of Englande; and after the other two years as many more as shall furnish both the realms of England and Irelonde. The lords are contented with the letting out of any of the salt-houses by consent of four of them and four of the merchants.

The lords request a determined answer before the [last *deleted*] day of this present month of January. [Finally, the merchants are contented the lords and co-partners shall appoint one honest man at every house to keep reckoning how the profits arise, and make certificate monthly. *Deleted.*] 791.

In July 1565 Francis Bertie, an Antwerper and a London merchant, was granted the exclusive privilege of making white salt for twenty years (*Cal. of State Papers, Domestic*, 1547-80, p. 255). The reference to "the moiety of the profits" in the first paragraph is puzzling; one can only conclude that it is an error.

1567/8

80. W. Wightman to Mr. Edward Herbert, esq., Sheriff of Mountgom[er]ye.

Being yesterday at the Court with "my Lord" when he wrote to Herbert touching Lord Graye's man, his lordship complained much that he had so often written in that and received no answer and the party unsatisfied; he instructed him to write to Herbert in every point as he wrote himself—which being without purpose, the writer refers Herbert thereto. It behoves him not only to agree to the request, for it seems just, but also to answer "my Lord", who is "throughelye" angry. Said it was meet every sheriff should make his own gaoler; he answered that good and sufficient bonds might suffice, that letters patent were not to be so obstinately resisted, and that Herbert was like to hear more of it.

London,
13 March. 789.

1568

81. John Wen[e]r to Mr. Edward Herbert, esq., Sheriff of co. Mountgom[er]y.

Encloses a "perfect inotroccon" of the lordship. He prayed the writer to procure some trusty friend to travel it with the mare. If it be his pleasure, in this or any other matter, before going to London, to come in with the writer, he [asks] knowledge by this bearer. Commendations to Herbert's mother and "my master your wife".

Strayngworth,
7 October.

Prays him see this forward [in] London. 793.

1569

82. Pet. Osborne and W. Wightman to Mr. Edwarde Herbert of Mountgomerye, esq.

Mr. Bryet and the rest of the merchants with whom the lords dealt for the salt works are now to tender account. And because they allege they are to pay the profits upon sale of the salts which heretofore they provided, he should, notwithstanding former letters, permit them or their factors to make sale to their most profit, but the money to be paid to

Herbert, whereby it may be answerable to the lords or the merchants as the case fall out. They complain grievously of the wilful spoil of above a hundred barrels of salt by weather through measuring it in the open fields ; also of the sale of it, which they say is required to be at 2s. 6d. the barrel by Herbert, whereas they can sell for 4s. Cannot believe these reports, but pray to be advertised at large. Pray that the merchants' factors be courteously used and made privy to all things.

Ivy Lane,
3 August.

Pray him deliver the merchants' factor reasonable money for his charges. 795.

1587

83. [SIR] WILLIAM HERBERT TO MR. MATHEWE HERB[ER]T OF COLDBROOKE, ESQ.

Lord Pembrooke has appointed him his Lieutenant within this county together with cousin Thomas Morgan of Machen ; and, understanding his employments into Irelande, has licensed him to substitute some gentleman in his stead. Chooses him. What they are to do Thom[a]s Morgan and he sufficiently know ; notwithstanding, lays down a few notes :

First, to muster and enrol all able men. Secondly, to divide them into bands of 100, 200, or 300, according to discretion. Thirdly, to appoint captains and charge [each] to appoint his lieutenant, ensign, sergeant, corporals, and drum—these he must have for training his men, but if any band be commanded to march the captain must provide a godly minister, a "painefull" clerk, an honest and expert surgeon, and a careful harbinger. Fourthly, see that all arms, as well for the body of the shire, wherewith every man is charged (that have £10 in goods or £5 in lands, according to the statute 4 and 5 Phil. and Mar.), and the common arms of every township, be in readiness and produced to the musters ; whereby a great number of their men will be armed. They must arm the tallest and strongest with corslets and pikes, the least and lowest with calivers and "hargabuts", the middle sort with coats of plate and blackbills or bows and arrows.

Fifthly, train the men one day every month—which consists of four points : marching, turning, retiring, and observing an order in fight (to which belongs skill in using their weapons). Sixthly, when the day of training is past to deliver back the armour ; the armour of the shire to the place appointed, that of particular persons to the owners, that of townships to those appointed—whereof indentures ought to be drawn, one to remain with the Clerk of the Peace. Seventhly, to give in charge that this armour, etc., be brought again for the next training ; that meantime what is amiss be amended and what is well be maintained, at the country's, private men's, and townships' charge [respectively]. Eighthly, if any be disobedient they are to commit him to the gaol until the Lord Lieutenant's pleasure be known. . . .

That these things be more readily done they must confer with the Justices of every division. Touching the writer's own division : Has delivered the note of armour, etc., of the hundred of Caldicot to Sir Charles Som[er]set; will leave that of the hundred of Uske with brother Morgan; and that of the hundred of Wenllog shall remain with cousin Thomas Morgan of Machen. With these also are notes of their names that are appointed for the service in Irland if need be—seventeen men out of every of these hundreds, and £50 is rated upon every hundred towards their furniture. The money is already cessed, collected, and delivered to the high collectors, whom they must "presently" charge to provide armour, according to the Lord Lieutenant's letters; wherein they ought to take special care, for he directs it as Lord President and Lord Lieutenant. They are to understand from the Lord Lieutenant what to do touching the armour of the body of the shire, which is in "marvelous evill plight", whereof he has advertised his lordship.

Lastly, prays him to supply the writer's place in the Custos-ship Rotulorum; makes him his substitute. He should send for the Clerk of the Peace to charge him that his year-rolls be perfectly made in parchment, and in the roll of this year this letter be word by word enrolled.

St. Julians,
13 April. *HM*2.9/43.

"Brother Morgan" is Edward Morgan of Llantarnam, Sir William's brother-in-law.

"1597" [*recte* 1587]

84. [The Privy Council] to the Earl of Pembrok. *Contemporary copy.*

The Queen, being informed of great preparations in Spaine for a mighty army with a navy to come speedily to the[se] seas, and having causes to doubt of some attempt against her dominions, has thought it necessary her whole realm forthwith be guarded with such strength as God has given; and [that] her Lieutenant-General over Wales and Marches be hereof advertised. And that he without delay consider former directions for putting the [forces] under his charge in strength, and cause all heretofore mustered to be in readiness; and if any be dead or departed, to appoint new sufficient persons. And though he will not have time for general musters, he should cause view to be made in all the hundreds of the shire—where he cannot be personally, by men of credit and understanding. Because she would be satisfied what account she may make of the forces of her subjects, horse and foot, her express commandment is that he forthwith certify the numbers of all forces furnished and able to serve, and who their captains and petty-captains, making distinction of their weapons. She wills that all forces be ready to march with all furniture upon an hour's warning. . . .

He has by letters certified [how] he provided for execution of their last orders, but for some parts has made no answer. Hope this summer he has had more care to see the execution [thereof]. Require answer now, and of any other things meet for them to understand.

The Court at Richmond,
9 October.

Chr. Hatton, Canc.
H. Derby
Fra. Knollys

W. Burghley
Ch. Howard
Fra. Walsingham
J. Wolley

A. Ashley

*HM*2.9/44.

[early 1589]

85. [SIR WILLIAM HERBERT] TO [? THE LORD DEPUTY OF IRELAND]. *Draft.*

"Sith it is [my lorde deputyes *deleted*] youre lordships pleasure" to stay the writer's journey to England, he craves the following, that he may in Ireland do Her Majesty better service : 1. That the *concordatum* or general law of oblivion be interpreted the best way for the multitude, and stand firm and assured. 2. Whereas injuries and exactions throughout Mounster have been done by Sir Edwarde Denie's soldiers and others his lordship gave direction to, that the Vice-President and Council there see them severely punished and the parties satisfied, with caution that the like be not committed hereafter. 3. That the writer have authority to muster, order into bands, govern, and direct the forces of Kery and Desmond. 4. That if occasion be he may have a hundred Englishmen there in pay, for to rely wholly upon the Irish stands with little judgement [and] less safety. 5. That the Earl of Glinkarr's base son and base brother, with four and twenty kerns whom he will name, being their followers, be employed either in Wulster or sent to serve under Sir Thom. Norris, for which they have been suitors to the writer. 6. That such freeholders and others that claim their lands by descent within the country of Desmond, and have within this twelve months been put off the same, be restored, unless the lands have been found by office for the Queen. 7. That Oswilivan Moore, brother-in-law to Florence mk Carty, be put in safe keeping, and that a "custodiam" of Castlelogh and lands pertaining, now in mortgage with Finin mk Carty, be granted the writer till Her Majesty's pleasure touching Finin be known. 8. That the Knight of Kerye's son and brother be put in safe keeping, [and one Jhames Stach of Clanmorice *inserted and then deleted*], and pledges taken of MakCarty Reoghf, Sir Owen Oswilivan, and Cormak mk Diermond, lord of Muskry. 9. That he be given authority upon occasion urgent and necessary to commit to safe keeping within these countries of Kery and Desmond those suspected or contemptuous and disobedient, and to execute martial law if need be upon great cause.

Endorsed: Sir Wm. Herbert's propositions. . . . 801.

Sir Thomas Norris received his knighthood only in December 1588, while Herbert left Ireland in the spring of 1589. Florence (or Fineen) MacCarthy—they are one and the same—was at this time a prisoner in the Tower of London in consequence of his marriage to the daughter and only surviving legitimate offspring of the Earl of Glencar or Clancarthy, MacCarthy Mor. Castle Lough was a principal seat and fortress of MacCarthy Mor. Sir William Herbert's interest in it is shown by the following extract from a letter which he wrote to Walsingham on 27th December 1588, viz, ". . . For that I mean to take 6000 akers within the countye of Kerrye and am desirous to have oother 6000 akers in . . . Desmonde, after the Earl of Glincarr's death, I beseatch your . . . furtherance to Her Majesty, that I may thear have Castle Logh [etc., etc.]" (*Life and Letters of Florence MacCarthy*, p. 54). The Earl of Clancarthy's base son, Donnell MacCarthy, is well known, but I have found no other mention of his base brother. O'Sullivan Mor—Sir Owen O'Sullivan—was married to Florence MacCarthy's sister, Julia, daughter of Donough MacCarthy Reagh. He is not the same as the Sir Owen O'Sullivan mentioned later in the letter; this is O'Sullivan Bere. The hereditary Knight of Kerry at the time was John FitzGerald of Rathanan. Cormac MacDermod MacCarthy, lord of Muskerry, was father of the 1st Viscount Muskerry. The "MakCarty Reoghf" referred to is Sir Owen MacCarthy, lord of Carbery.

1592

86. GIL. JONES TO MR. RICHARD HERBERT, ESQ., AT WALCOTT.

He and Mr. Baldwyn made further search in the records in the Tower touching Redg's daughter's tenure, but find nothing more to do him good, saving that they find the hundred annexed to the custody of the castle of Mountgom[er]y by special suit made by one that had the custody, alleging it had been so time out of mind. Has drawn a case whereof he has acquainted Mr. Neweporte, Herbert's brother-in-law. They are determined this week to retain Mr. Cooke and send down his opinion. Wishes him meantime to stay proceedings. Mr. Willm. Corbett of Lighe has obtained grant of the wardship of the child if it fall out to be the Queen's—he and the feodary were in the Tower to search for records but met with no more than the writer has copies or notes [of].

London,
14 May.

Endorsed in an 18th C. hand: Gil. Jones's . . . relating to Chirbury.

796.

"Mr. Cooke" is presumably the future Sir Edward Coke. The feodary was an officer of the Court of Wards and Liveries.

1594

87. THO. WIGMOR TO CHARLES FOXE, ESQ., AT BROMFYLDE. *Torn.*

Has obtained a wa[rrant for a] buck of this season to be taken of [Fox for the] Justice of Eyre within Okeley Par[k. . . . His] request is that he may . . . find when he sends for [it]. . . . Also that he will in favour reserve for the writer a "frindely" buck, which he will shortly send for. Prays him take notice of this his warrant lest some other procure a like and come before him, and the writer be disappointed. Well wishing to him and his bedfellow.

Shobdon,
2 July. 797.

Fox was father-in-law to Mathew Herbert of Dolguog.

1596

88. Q. ELIZABETH TO SIR WILLIAM RUSSELL, DEPUTY OF IRELAND, THE CHANCELLOR, AND THE REST OF THE COUNCIL. *Copy, 17th C.*

Upon the suit of Lady Florence Herberte, widow, and Mary, her daughter, being moved to take commiseration of their estate, Her Majesty has information from the Privy Council that where[as] they directed letters by her commandment for redress, answer was returned that their order cannot sufficiently warrant the passing of what is required. Therefore, where[as] she heretofore granted to William Herberte, knight, the seigniory of the Island of Kerry, and by reason of a survey taken in his absence, and divers parcels recovered by the Irishry and clergy, Lady Herberte and her daughter are charged with a rent far exceeding the acres they possess: Hereby wills and authorizes, according to the Privy Council's letters of 4 July 1594, a new survey at their charge, and that letters patent be renewed to the heir in such sort that the heirs general be not defeated, and that abatement be made for such lands as shall be found wanting or evicted. Further, if there be any lands escheated adjoining the seigniory not yet granted to undertakers, a grant is to be made to them, in the usual form of passing those lands, of so much as they like to accept of, to be added upon the new survey.

The Palace of Westm[in]ster, 10 December. Under the Signet

Endorsed: Upon reading this, the year Sir Thomas Norris was Lord Justice, it was ordered that Sir Wm. Herbert's heirs pay £100 a year until it be measured.

In rotulo patent. Cancellarie Hibernie, 20 *April,* 39 *Eliz. per me:* Jacob. Newman, *cler.*, Anthonio Sentleger, *milit.*

Enrolled in the Council book: Pa. Foxe. *Cop. vera ex:* Fr. Lloyd.

798.

The copyist, Francis Lloyd, was Lord Herbert's agent in Dublin in the 1630's and '40's.

1597

89. Petition of John Hollis, gent., agent for Mary Herberte, to Sir Thomas Norris, Lord Justice of Irelande, and the rest of the Council. *Copy,* 17*th C.*

Where[as] the Queen directed letters on behalf of the said Mary for a new survey of the seigniory of the Island of Keirie, formerly granted by patent to Sir William Herberte, for an abatement of rent for lands evicted and supposed to be in the patent (where there is not so much by half), and new letters patent, as appointed by Her Majesty's said letters dated 10 December 1596; he beseeches that they direct the drawing up of the commission of survey, etc., and instal the rents at a favourable abatement till the truth be known, otherwise the tenants will depart and leave all waste.

Endorsed: 12 November 1597. Ordered that Mary Herberte shall yearly pay to Her Majesty for the rent of the said seigniory £100 as for this last year, until the seigniory be measured. . . .

Tho. Norris
Nicho. Welch Anthony Sent Leger
and others of the Council

Cop. vera: Fr. Lloyde.

799.

[? 1599]

90. Edward Morgan to [Mary Herbert].

Is right glad it has pleased God to perfect her match in so good a place. Had not said so much in approving cousin Herbert of Cowlbrook's motion thereof had he not thought it fittest for her, whose parents left [it] in speech at their deceases, especially her father [in his] will. And although she has not yet, he hopes the young gentleman her husband will not fail in thankfulness for her frank bestowing of herself and hers on him. They should endeavour to preserve and increase the love so well begun between them. Although it takes first hold in regard of the gifts of nature or fortune, yet modesty and the gifts of the mind are the only means to preserve it. Will not trouble her with more, but must entreat her not to suffer herself or her husband to be carried by informations to dislike and turn off her father's and mother's old servants, especially if told they have wronged them by words or letter to the writer, as he is told by Nedd Morgan and Willm. Gunter. The last never wrote word to him touching Mr. Herbert; the other ever commended his person and behaviour and seemed sorry that she, by means of some about her, gave him so cold entertainment at his coming to her. Hopes she will inherit her parents' discreet proceedings.

"Your lovyng Uncle". 761.

The writer is Edward Morgan of Llantarnam.

1600

91. The Privy Council to [? the Sheriff of co. Montgomery].
Contemporary copy.

Her Majesty being informed of the sudden raising of the prices of corn, has commanded speedy course, that the markets may be served and prices brought down to reasonable rates. Cannot impute these prices (after so great plenty as this last year) but to the greedy disposition in the corn-masters and causeless doubts of unseasonable weather. Have caused orders to be set down for the service of the markets and restraining of badgers, regrators, etc., which he is to see executed. Where it is suggested this dearth comes by reason great quantity has been transported out of the realm, it is a malicious slander, for long since Her Majesty [forbad it]. That her Majesty may be informed of his proceedings, they look to have a certificate from such as take pains in this charitable work . . . wherein such may be forborne as buy corn to the intent to sell it—severe course [should] be taken against such, and those that countenance them. These letters are to be openly read, that Her Majesty's care for the poor and bringing down of excessive prices be known to all.

Thomas Egerton

The Court at Greenewyche, 1 June.

T. Buckhurst, W. Knollys, J. Fortescue
Nottingham, Ro. Cecyll, Jo. Poph[a]m

*HM*2.9/46.

A printed copy of the orders referred to is listed as No. 22 in the Appendix.

[c. 1600–1610]

92. I[sabella] Foxe to her daughter [Margaret] Herbert at Dolgiogge.

[Margaret's] sister is delivered of a girl on Twelfth Even; was sent for that morning to Burwey. The christening is Sunday, Lady Lewknor and cousin Foxe of Ludforde godmothers and Mr. Harley godfather. [Margaret] disappointed her sister of her christening stuff; they hoped Meredith [would have] brought it down. They sent Ales Paul[m]er before the writer was up to have her write in haste to W. Bauldewine for his stuff, whom she fears will not be found on this sudden, "and then we ar all shamed". Her sister trusted she would send it, else she had sent a messenger to Harvi[n]gto[n].

Sent her yarn to the weavers. The weaving will be dear enough. The bottoms were two stone two pound "by oure weight". Gave a charge to lay it to seven broad yards and a half. Was busy for the wassail when the warper came; found afterwards she laid it to six broad yards and a half, "he" saying it would come home seven. Whereat the writer chafed so she fears she will be never the better for it. Servants never use her well. Sent [Margaret] wardens and apples by Meredith; and by her own man a hundred of wardens and a hundred of apples to Mrs. Pughe, and two old turkey hens to herself—God grant they came alive. Gave the man that brought the letter the beginning of Christmas sixpence, yet heard he demanded money of her. Gave him as brought A. Paulmer 2s., and a groat to feed his turkeys by the way.

[early January].

Perceives [Margaret's] own man is more honest than others. "I have sent hearpes". 307.

The sister is Martha Wateis of Burway, near Ludlow; Harley is probably Thomas Harley of Brampton Bryan; while Mrs. Pugh is probably of Mathafarn (close to Dolguog). The last word in the postscript is difficult to interpret; it may be the personal name Earp.

1610/11

93. [Sir] Tho. Roper to Sir Edward Harberd.

Has given him advertisement of the claims that divers of this country make to the best land and almost the greater part of what the writer holds from him. Has from time to time put them off, to his great charge. Now he has got the survey, they have with one consent put up petitions to the Lord Deputy. For aught he can perceive thirty ploughlands are like to be evicted from the seigniory. Has sent this bearer, who can amply describe this business, to persuade him to send some man of understanding speedily, to maintain his title. It would be a great wrong to the writer to lose these lands after he has made estates out of them to divers that have been at charge in building and planting. Would rather buy the lands, whatsoever they cost, than engage himself to those he is bound to "defend", and if Sir Edward will direct him he sends out to buy those lands [certain to] be evicted, he will take it as a right done to him. The survey cost him £200; but thinks it not ill-bestowed, seeing he has brought it from £280 a year to £40. Although he undertook to defray the charge, nevertheless, seeing it amounts to so much, he hopes Sir Edward will not refuse to bear half, £100, which he entreats him to deliver to his man.

Afaune,
16 February. 361.

The reduction from £280 to £40 which Roper referred to was in the crown rent due out of the seigniory of Castle Island.

1611/12

94. [SIR] THO. ROPER TO SIR EDWARD HARBERD AT HIS HOUSE AT CHARINGE CROSS OR ELSEWHERE. AT THE GOLDEN HORSESHOE IN THE STRANDE "YOU SHALL SERTAYNELY HEARE OF HIM".

Has, to his great charge and trouble, brought down the survey of Sir Edward's land in Ierland from £280 to £40, but all that labour will be lost if he does not send over the "pattin" that a new one may be passed. Unless it arrives in Dublin within two months the Deputy and Council say he shall receive no benefit of the survey, the patent not being surrendered according to His Majesty's letter, and that they will ease the writer for the time he holds the lands, it being no fault of his. If Sir Edward takes not this opportunity his lands in K[erry] will never be worth anything. Perceives he is willing to contribute to his charge, which shall encourage him to spend money in defending Sir Edward's land when any part comes in question.

Dublin.
19 January.

Sealed with a merchant's mark 32.

[1611/12]

95. THOMAS ABRAHALL TO RICHARD PRISE.

Memorandum for him to move Sir Edward and Lady Herbert to grant him a lease of the lands in co. Lymbarike that Sir William Herbert had of one Edmond Hubert or Herbert, paying £4 a year for sixty years, but some small rent the first three years to see whether he can get it by law, which will cost great charges. Hopes to have Sir Edward's furtherance to obtain his right. Also to move him for a lease of a place called the Nochvale, which Sir William bought of the Knight of Kerre, paying 20s. a year, as Prise paid when he had it, for the like term. If he recovers it by law he will be no ungrateful tenant. God send him a merry journey. "Your lovinge gossip".

Newport,
19 January. 396.

1611/12

96. WILLM. JOHN ROSSER TO SIR EDWARD HERBERT AT MOUNTGOM[ERY] CASTELL.

Thinks it good for him and beneficial to his heirs to accept Thomas Abrall's offer for his unexpected lands in Irland that Sir Willm. Herbert bought in his lifetime, as appears by evidence he has from St. Julianse. If he accepts, he must send the evidence—will take security for re-delivery of them, with a draft lease—with his directions and furtherance in the suit at Abrall's cost. Leaves the rest to the relation of this bearer, who means to go over with Abrall next spring. Thomas Abrell is an honest man and sufficient to answer for anything he undertakes.

Llyssavyry,
20 January.

Endorsed: Letters concerning the concealed and purchased lands in Ireland. 313.

1611/12

97. Mary Forster to Mr. Roberd Bery at his house in Ludloe.

The first ten lines badly torn. . . . . bold to entreat his help. . . . creditors . . . and has found them all very rea[sonable and willing?] to release her husband and content [? to receive their m]oney at such times as her poor [? husband can a]fford, but she has forborne to give them . . . till she cau agree with all, for it work[s to] no purpose to agree with some and leave but one at liberty—her husband would live a banished man notwithstanding, and she not able to help him. Therefore prays him to go with this bearer unto Sir Charles Foxe to procure him to a composition; hears he has paid £100 principal debt for Mr. Forster. Will strain herself to pay £50 at Michaelmas or Ladyday twelvemonth if he will accept of it and release Mr. Forster. Will put him in good security. Sir Thomas Whorwod once spoke with Sir Charles Foxe concerning this. Prays him get it under his hand that if he has security before the end of Easter term he will be content, for so she has of others. Means to secure them all by that time and send for Mr. Forster, who is in Ireland.

24 January.

Her husband lost almost £80 by Sir Charls Foxe's sister, Lady Wodruf.

314B.

According to Shaw's *Knights of England* Sir Thomas Whorwood was not knighted till 1624, although an Edward Whorwood is listed as having been knighted in November 1611 (pp. 151 and 185); this Edward is not described as a knight in Armytage and Rylands' *Staffordshire Pedigrees*, 1664-1700 (p. 243).

[? 1612]

98. [Sir] Tho. Roper to [Sir Edward Herbert].

Received a letter by Mr. Cuttur that he should send over the late survey of the seigniory and the Order of the Council table for abatement of rent, upon receipt of which [Sir Edward] would send over his patent and make the writer allowance for part of his charge in the business, and his wife would acknowledge a fine confirming the writer's estate. All which he takes very kindly. Received his letter while coming towards the Isle of Man, and the papers are in Kery. But assures him that not one acre is left out. Will bear his servant's charges that brings over the patent if he finds it not so. Prays him send some "sofetientte" to be in Dublin the beginning of Michaelmas term, where his agent shall meet him and they shall get the new patent, which by the Lord Deputy's favour may be passed. It will much strengthen [Sir Edward's] title to some lands which had been long since recovered from him but for the writer. Might much have advantaged himself had he forborne prosecuting them that brought those lands in question. But [Sir Edward] has not lost an acre since the writer's coming over, which no seigniory in Ireland can say, although the last survey and this business have cost £500. The order for payment of £40 yearly is but till a better survey for His Majesty, which can never be after the patent is altered, for they will have those words left out. Asks for a new estate for the three lives in his former lease; and permission to alter one of those lives at pleasure (the party being in perfect health) will much bind him.

Thought his lease good, but finds it is but during [Sir Edward's] own life; is altogether ignorant in businesses of this nature, therefore entreats him to ask counsel how his estate may be made perfect. Could not send a "hake" this year, but if he will send a man over he will not fail next spring, or will deliver it to Cuttur; and [will send] one of his best colts, bred upon [Sir Edward's] land. Will never write more of altering his patent if he does not send it by Michaelmas.

The Isle of Man,
20 July. 393.

By a "hake" Sir Thomas no doubt means a hawk.

1614/15

99. RIC. PRYTHERGH TO SIR EDWARD HERBERT AT FLORENS.

Received his of 12 December and that from Augsburgh about the same time. Sir Fraunces Newport has sent order to pay Mr. Baker's mortgage money, and that Sir Edward will have it hereafter sold; Mr. Baker has great occasion to use money. Hears nothing of his bailiff of Munmouth shire; has received no money. If he means to stay abroad he must take some other order to supply himself, for his bailiffs will not keep touch. He has locked up some of his business; will take the best care he can for the rest. He writes to him to pay "presently" money taken up. Prays him write to some friends to be bound with the writer for money to his use, and it shall be paid. Looks to receive from Mr. Charles Herbert Sir Edward's fine for his livery this [? term]. But Burch will not acknowledge any certain [? agreement] but to have all the livery out and 40s. for his pains. Here is no news but [that] Sir Edward shall have a pardon for his money and his faults when he comes over. His friends wish him quick and safe return.

26 January

Hopes he has received two or three other letters. Goes to Anglesey about Shrovetide. *HM*2.23/1.

1615

100. JO. DA[N]VERS TO [SIR EDWARD HERBERT].

Heard by a letter [Sir Edward's] mother received from the Hague that he desired his letters directed to Sir Henry Wooton's. Sent a packet and letters of credit for him to Amsterdam upon receipt of his by Mr. Calvert; gave account of his business and told him he might find other packets at the Abbey of St. Martin in Paris, where [Sir Edward's] brother is. Knows not whether his cousin Newport's knighting is news to him – in which "you have your part of the obligation". His mother and the writer hold their journey into Shropshiere. Mr. Dekam has the reversion of Sir Thos. Parrye's place. The Lord Treasurer is "on the mending hand" and was led between two yesterday to take the air. The Bishop of Winchester, they say, shall be Councillor and Lord Privy Seal. Received a letter from Sir Edw. Cecill that [Sir Edward] was hasting homeward. Hopes he received some of his letters.

Charingcross,

24 June, *st. Angl.* 314A.

Danvers was Sir Edward's step-father. "Cousin Newport" is Richard Newport, later 1st Baron Newport. John Dackombe was knighted and had Sir Thomas Parry's place of Chancellor of the Duchy of Lancaster when the latter died a year later.

[c. 1619]

101. ——————TO [SIR EDWARD HERBERT]. *Part only.*

". . . Moins au Palatinat, que sa Ma'te est obligee a eux. Ce qui est bon au Roy en ce sujet leur sert aussy et a plus forte raison qu'il les touche moins. Bien confessent Ilz avoir declaré a sa Ma'te Imp'le et a la ligue Catholique qu'ilz entreprendront la Protection du Palatinat. Ce a esté sur la ferme confiance qu'ilz avoient qu'en vertu de l'alliance sa Ma'te seroit de la partye, et que par consequent non seulement les Unis et plusieurs correspondantz seroient fermes sue le pied qu'ilz ont fiché avec eux, mais aussy plusieurs autres Princes de l'Europe qui ont loeüil fiché sur sa Ma'te se declareroient a son regard favorables.

"Tout cela venant a manquer si sa Ma'tie tarde plus et les Unis prennent party ailleurs ou se refroidissans, les autres faillantz de courage, et aucuns de force et de moyens. Les differentz de la religion recommencans a renaistre par l'artifice des communs ennemys des nouveaux et dangereux partys si glissantz avec pretendue apparence de plus de repos et de moindre peyne, ne voyans aussy de ceste facon aucune fin ny esperence de sortir de la grande despence en laquelle Ilz sont desia.

"Lon espere que sa Ma'tie ne trouvera mauvais si on leur fault du costé dequel lon avoit faict et debuoit faire plus de fondement. Les unis previennent de bonne de ne demeurer courtz aussi de l'autre. Ilz quitteront a la verité a leur tres grand regret un des premiers membres de leur union, les Enfans et Nepueux de sa Ma'te et les pauvres subjectz et Etatz d'un si bon voisin et allié. Mais la necessité n'ayant de Loy et nulle charité reglee tribuant plus a autruy qu'a soy mesme, Ilz seront excusez et deschargez envers Dieu et le Monde, envers leur Ma'te de Boheme mesme et envers toute la posterité du changement de leur resolution. Si non seulement elle n'est approuvee mais aussy declaree injuste ou pour le moins precipitee et telle qui soit cause de se priver des effectz de lalliance par sa Ma'te mesme, qui y estant plus proche et plus interessee et tant sage et provoyange, ce qu'ilz feront a son occasion et a son example ne leur pourra aucunement estre reproché.

"Ce sera a la verité un pitoyable et mal assuré remede et un relief pareil a celuy des Compaignons d'Ulisse (qui estoit d'estre mangé le dernier). Car nous scavons bien que l'affaire de Boheme et des provinces unies perdue et le Palatinat redigé en servitude, que ny foy ny promesse, ny paction aucune nous garentira. Mais Il n'y a pas autre moyen, et tous ne peuvent comprendre cela qui croyent, le temps y peut apporter du changement ou pour le moins des traverses, si non a jamais au moins leurs vyes durant. Qu'il . . ." 324A.

This is clearly part of a letter (there is no clue to the identity of the writer) addressed to Herbert, while ambassador to the French king, during the opening stages of the Thirty Years' War. In dealing with it I have been greatly helped by Mr. Owen Taylor (formerly of the University College of Wales, Aberystwyth) and Mrs. Denise Taylor.

[1619]

102. [SIR EDWARD HERBERT] TO————. *Draft or copy; French.*

Received letters from the P. of the Rh[ine] asking the writer to thank him for his offers, and begging him to understand that he, the princes, and united states have given orders for a number of soldiers, foot and horse, for their defence if need be in the midst of so much trouble brought upon the Empire. Affairs, however, are not yet at such extremes that there remains no hope of peace, and they have not so far taken resolution to raise foreign troops without first seeing what course affairs will take. He should not put himself to trouble or expense for that purpose. Nevertheless, if occasion presents itself, His Highness will have remembrance of his offers and merits.

Endorsed in the hand of William Boswell, Herbert's secretary : "A Mr. . . . (*blank*) . . . de la pt. du Roy de Boheme". 325.

1619/20

103. JOSIAS DEANS TO EDMOND DEANES, KEEPER OF THE FORT OF ST. AULBAN'S IN THE ISLE OF JARZYE AND CUSTOMER OF THE SAID ISLE.

"Lovinge Brother Edward Deanes". Received his letter by Mr. Foinnes of Plymouth, merchant [? dated] 12 July 1619, and thanks him that he has not forgotten his love towards him. Mr. Foinnes has employed himself for the writers' liberty ; could want no money of him, for in this galley few are bought out for money. Seeing he could not be released, he has taken of Mr. Foinnes twelve French crowns, which he prays his brother pay willingly, as Foinnes lent it, to supply his wants in this miserable place. If "our" governor has acquaintance with the ambassador, he prays he would write to him—he can do more with a word to the General of the Galleys than money can do here. Thanks him for his instructions, which he will peruse until such time as God sends him his liberty. Prays to be remembered to his brother's father and wife.

Marseall,
14 March.

Brief endorsement in the hand of Sir Edward Herbert's secretary. 316.

The use of both "Edmond" and "Edward" is inexplicable. "Mr. Foinnes" may well be Thomas Fownes, who was then mayor of Plymouth. The governor of Jersey was Sir John Peyton. Edmund Deane is recorded as one of the soldiers in the garrison of Castle Elizabeth in Jersey in 1617—"age 35, of Somersetshire, married"—while the father is probably the Francis Deane of St. Aubin's—"age 60, of Somersetshire"—who was cannoneer at the same fortress (E. T. Nicolle, "The Report of the Royal Commissioners sent to Jersey in 1617", *Bulletins de la Société Jersiaise*, Vol. V, 1905, pp. 389-90).

1619/20

104. [SIR EDWARD] H[ERBERT] TO MR. BELL. *Contemporary copy.*

Long expected further advertisement from him and the company of English merchants at Bourdeaux concerning Fucher's business, as promised. Made diligent enquiry in this city to have him apprehended, and obtained promise from the chief counsellors of state that he should have neither interdiction to stop proceedings nor evocation to remove the cause from the court-parliament of Bourdeaux. If there be any demur, he prays them let him know, and he will give all assistance. Would be glad to know from someone of their company of any occurrences of note in their quarter.

Paris,
23 March, *st. vet.*

Endorsed: "A Mons. Boltor &c., Merchants Anglois, 5 April 1620, a Bourdeaux, touchant Fuchier". 33.

1620

105. T. HARLEY TO SIR CHARLES FOXE.

Understands by his son that Sir Charles expected Steven Godwyne, who came to the writer on Thursday from Beawdley, and to whom he made known the conclusion of the business concerning Godwyne's land —according to Sir Charles's offer of £600 to him and Mr. [? Brace], £200 at the sealing and the other £400 at such day as they should agree upon. Sent Godwyne presently to Lundon to Mr. Samuell Cranmer with a letter for the conveyance, the fine which Godwyne and his wife passed to the writer, and the writer's conveyance to Mr. Roe to the use of the said Cranmer, [etc.], that cousin Watyes might make Sir Charles assurance of the lands. Thanks for his kind entertainment.

Brompt[on] Castell,
21 May. 330.

This is Thomas Harley of Brampton Bryan, the son he mentions being Sir Robert Harley.

[1620]

106. [SIR] RICH. PRISE TO SIR EDWARD HERBERT, LORD AMBASSADOR FOR INILAND AT PARIS.

Wishes occasion for showing his thankfulness for the manifold favours he conferred upon him in Paris. Delivered his letter to "my lord", who lately told him there was order taken for the money due to Sir Edward from the Exchequer. Goes into Walles this vacation; will do him any service, and will tell him how things are carried there. Makes no question but he daily hears the news from Ingland.

York House,
23 June. *Armorial seal* 317.

The seal makes it clear that the writer is Sir Richard Pryse of Gogerddan. "My lord" is no doubt the Lord Chancellor, Lord Verulam, who lived at York House. The date is supplied by an endorsement.

1620

107. [THE EAST INDIA COMPANY] TO SIR EDWARDE HERBERT, AMBASSADOR TO THE KING OF FRAUNCE.

Have intelligence from their servant Paull Triggs, now resident in Paris, that after many years' suit and expense of almost £10,000, His Majesty of France has granted a commission for a taxation in satisfaction for the great damages sustained by the depredation of those of the port of Odierne upon their ship and goods from East India belonging to the fourth voyage; and the same is now upon the point of execution. For assistance whereof they have sent this bearer, Mr. FRauncis Tayler of London, merchant, interested in the said voyage, for whom they pray his furtherance.

London,
19 October.

Tho. Smythe — Robt. Jhonson
Henrie Robinson — Wm. Ferrers
Robert Bell — Richard Burrell
Reynoulde Greene

315.

"1621" [1620/21]

108. J. HAMILTONN TO [SIR EDWARD HERBERT].

"My Lord". Could have wished a better subject had broken his silence. All the ways he has come in[to] France he [n]ever heard of the intolerable extortions exercised against His Majesty's subjects on passage from and to Germanie by the ministers of the bureau.... Since the taking of Freidburg no other passage is open. Left a horse with his caparison in their hands that cost £30 in Antwerp in July last. Could have redeemed it for half a crown, but wanted occasion to "reprime thair debordit Licensis". Encloses copies of "past acts"; the pass mentioned [includes] his son, who quit him at Mets. Took another afterwards who promised to caution his fidelity in Amiens but stole his pistols and ran away at Moncormet, with "signall indices of Intelligence betwixt hem and le doux arrester". His lordship's word will be taken that the writer is no horse-merchant, nor will the horse arrested be for the market yet, for he has been hard travelled this six months. Would to God he could "participat" agreeable concurrences from whence he comes. Lack of counsel and deliberation are the causes. If he can do him service, the Marquess of Hamiltonn will find him out.

[? Stabin],
24 January.

Bears an endorsement in the hand of Sir Edward's secretary. 54.

There are a number of letters from this writer, addressed to William Trumbull, King James's agent in Brussels, in the *Trumbull MSS.*, Alphabetical Series, Vol. XXVI in the Berkshire Record Office. It seems from them that Hamilton had been, until recently at least, agent in Antwerp, but for some months before the date of this letter he had been writing from a number of different places on the Continent. Trumbull's endorsements usually describe him as Captain John Hamilton, but occasionally the forename is given as Jehan.

1621

109. [Sir Edward Herbert] to Lord Brook. *Draft or copy*; *Latin.*

No dignity is conferred upon him without some part coming to the writer. . . . Therefore congratulates not only him upon his increase in honour, but himself also. . . .

Paris,
28 March, *st. Ango'*.

Endorsed: "My Lord Ambassador" to Lord Brook. 324B.

Fulk Greville had just been created Baron Brooke.

1621

110. Tho. Murray to Sir Eduard Herbert, Lord Ambassador Resident for His Majesty by the French King, at Paris.

Received his of 25 April yesterday, with the discourse of the Spanish king's death and will, which the French and Venetian ambassadors divulged here fourteen days ago. His Majesty believes the particular anent the Infanta's marriage was coined by the French ambassador in Spaine, who gave it out that the marriage of our Prince with the daughter of France was concluded. But the letters from Spaine, France, Italie, etc., most agree that she should be bestowed upon the Emperor's son. Within six months the truth will appear. His Majesty is not satisfied with the answers to his demands proposed by the Marshal de Cadenet, but is much pleased with Sir Edward's care in enquiring [as to] the authors and printers of these infamous libels dispersed in Paris against His Majesty. Lord Digbie is to go towards the Emperor within ten days, but many wise men doubt the success of his negotiations both in Vienne and Madrid. In case the French king besiege the Rochellers His Majesty is resolved to assist them. Thanks God His Majesty and his parliament agree. The Lord Chancellor's sentence was given yesterday . . .(*details*). . . . He is also deeply fined, which he can never pay by reason of his weak state. Sir Jhone Bennet is shortly to be sentenced. Sir Henrie Yalverton brought before the Lords for drawing of divers patents, having given satisfaction in divers points, rashly, or madly rather, fell in[to] most bitter speeches against Lord Buckinghame, charging him with assuming regal power, and admonishing him to read the articles of Hugh Spencer's conviction in the time of Edward II, thus wonderfully offending His Majesty as pointing at him as another Eduard II; the Lords are to call him in question.

London,
4 May. *Armorial seal* 318.

Murray was Secretary to Prince Charles.

1621

111. Rich. More to Sir Charles Fox at Bromfield.

Prays him let his keepers kill the writer's fee doe with as much speed as may be. Sent before by his servant Abley but has heard nothing.

Linley,
31 October. *Armorial seal* 326.

[1623]

112. WALTER ACTON TO HENRIE FOXE OF THE HURSTE, ESQ. *Contemporary copy.*

Had such an old commission of the peace as Fox writes of from cousin Charles Foxe, which Mr. Clifford borrowed of the writer's father and sent to Fox's father. Thinks his brother has it. He shall have the loan of it.

Endorsed: Written a little before the said Walter Acton of Audenham sent the said commission to Henrie Fox to be transcribed. 8 October 1623.

There follows a historical note on the Staffords, Dukes of Buckingham, and on the royal title as rulers of Ireland, designed to prove that the date of the commission was 36 *Henry VI.* 310.

In the *Visitation of Shropshire*, 1623 (ed. Grazebrook and Rylands), in the Acton of Aldenham pedigree (pp. 9 and 10) where appears "Thomas Acton of Longnor . . . Esq., 36 H. 6", while "Hen. Foxe" is one of the three signatories to the Fox pedigree (p. 194). It seems very likely, therefore, that this letter is connected with preparations for the heralds' visit. No. 21 in the Appendix is almost certainly a copy of this commission of the peace.

[? early 17th C.]

113. RYCHARD BEVAN TO——————.

Humbly desires him to "tolerate" with him this half year's rent, 20s., for two months. Is constrained by the cruelty of Sheparde to place his sons in service, which has weakened him. Finds Shepard a very conscienceless man, for he has had the value of £3 a year in the past more than his bargain of £20. "God . . . deliver me frome him". 387.

[? early 17th C.]

114. RYCHARD BEVAN TO——————.

"Righte worshipfull my verye good Landlord". Beseeches him not to take this motion distastefull[y]; had rather lose the land than his love. He having granted the writer some timber, he desires likewise the continuance of his accustomed goodness in sparing him the loan of £10 for half a year upon consideration as formerly. Is in hand to match his eldest son, with his worship's consent, but his housing is so ruinous that any stranger will fear to lie in it. Will not break time for repayment, for his whole estate is his worship's tenement. Security shall be his three "doles", containing ten ridges, in his worship's meadow called Vartnall, now in the hands of Mr. Thomas Byrry from year to year, which are well worth 30s. by year. 388.

1628

115. T., [Lord] Baltinglas, to Lord Herbert.

Promised him a hawk or a horse every year in lieu of the woods, which perhaps were not so well looked to in the writer's absence. Assures him his woods of the Island of Kerry will never be decayed. Never did himself, nor suffer any other, to make a pipe or hogshead stave there, nor would he give 2d. a tree to Sir Valentine Browne for 10,000 oaks that [ad]join Lord Herbert's. They are not so well looked to now as when in the writer's custody. Mr. Herbert, who has much informed against the writer, detains half a plough-land of the Island that was never in his father's possession; intends to put him in suit for it. Knows of no other lands detained from Lord Herbert. Will give good assistance if he will have a commission for "preambulating" the lands.

Acknowledges he had a good bargain from him. Desires they may have no suits. Will be ever willing to perform more than the law compels. Will do any reasonable matter in building up a convenient castle, although not tied to it. But to build upon the ruined walls is to no purpose. There is hope of his lordship's repair into this kingdom; the writer's house will afford him lodging, and he will attend him to see his lands in Keary. And although he takes himself to be freed from the promise of a hawk or a horse, yet has sent him a hawk which he hopes will prove a specially good one—Lord Steward and Sir William Herbert told him that a hawk he sent Lord Herbert formerly proved the best in England. Hopes he will prosecute no further suit.

Ropersrest,
10 July. *Armorial seal*

Note at the foot in another hand: Mr. Weavers dwells in Garston parish between Preston and Lancaster. 329.

"Lord Steward" is probably Andrew Stewart, 1st Baron Castle Stuart—at the burial of the 2nd Baron's wife in 1635 her husband was called "Lord Steward of Castle Steward" (*Complete Peerage*, Vol. III, p. 96); but it might be Lord Stewart of Traquair. Sir William Herbert is presumably he who was created Baron Powis the following year.

[? c. 1620–40]

116. Pacience Langford to [? Margaret Herbert].

Although it is long since she was sent to for a receipt to ease the pain of the stone—hopes the party is recovered—yet she makes bold to send these few receipts that she had from two good "vesisyons" long agone.

Endorsed in Margaret Herbert's hand: . . . Medicines for the stone and "a meddicin of llilloabls". 391.

[? c. 1620–40]

117. Margaret Herbert's household notes.

Detailed notes on the cutting up of two cows and an ox . . . Then is there yet two cheeks and the tongue of the bull and six pieces of cow to spend between this and Christmas; and the leg of the bull and the two neck chines. "Joice Sonde and I . . . appointed hir to barrell up" . . . (*details*) . . . which will make in the barrel, of cow beef 43 pieces and 28 of the best of the bull, the pieces left out to be in brine in a "mitt" by themselves.

St. Andrew's day.

On the dorse : Made of one half of the cow, besides the roasting ribs, etc., 24 boiling pieces ; but the next half will yield but 18.

23 December. 311.

[1632/3]

118. [? HENRY BAKER] TO [LORD BALTINGLASS]. *Contemporary copy.*

Received his and the £10 from Sir John Byngley. When the writer spoke of the danger that might ensue from [Lord Baltinglass's] parting with possession of the Island, Lord Herbert rightly apprehended it and is tender thereof, and willing to accept of the profits of the woods and all other profits and increase of rents that may be raised over and above £500 a year clearly paid [Lord Baltinglass] by his receiver. For concluding whereof they were to have Mr. Lowe's advice, who could not attend it before the holidays. . . . Touching the marriage between Mr. Tho. Roper and Lord Herbert's daughter. . . . *Breaks off unfinished.*

[? early March].

Endorsed : Copy of part of a letter from Lord Baltinglasse's servant . . .

333.

This projected marriage for Beatrice Herbert did not, of course, take place.

1632/3

119. T., [LORD] BALTINGLAS, TO HENRY BAKER.

Received his letter with Lord Herbert's propositions. Would be glad to continue the treaty concerning the match, but fears his lordship's daughter is too old for his son, and the writer's estate not answerable to Lord Herbert's expectation. But if his lordship comes into Ireland he shall fully understand his estate, and then they may draw the treaty to conclusion if he thinks £1,500 per annum of inheritance and £1,000 in mortgages a sufficient estate, which his son shall enter upon after the writer's decease, clear from all incumbrances. Does not tie himself to more, yet upon conference he will be drawn to do any reasonable thing. Would have him carry the writer's son to present his service to his lordship, and if he holds him worthy of his daughter the writer will recall him from the Low Countries.

Concerning the increases of rent to have twelve years added to the leases, if his lordship holds his resolution of coming into Ireland and [has] conference with the tenants, they will sooner be drawn to a good increase. And what rent soever is made, the writer will only expect £500 a year, according [to] their last agreement, during his interest. Is willing Lord Herbert should take a year's time more from 1 July to advise whether to take the lands into his possession or no. Is very thankful to his lordship for not being willing to put him out of possession of the Island, fearing it might prejudice him or his wife if his lordship deceases before them.

Holds no lands of the Island nor near it but from Lord Herbert. Has often advertised his lordship that the freeholders pretend to one half of the seigniory, and that he could get in their estates for little or nothing with his lordship's and his lady's consent ; their estates are good in law. Lord Herbert was contented to leave the repair of the castle till his own coming over. The tenants know the writer's interest is but for two lives, and their leases are made accordingly—if for years, they are to enjoy them only if the writer's estate continue so long.

Roper's Rest,
22 March.

Endorsed : True copy of so much as concerns Lord Herbert.

Phil. Scudamore   Henry Baker
Thomas Hallely
Edw. Lloyd

Endorsement by Lord Herbert : Copy of a letter from Lord Baltinglasse wherein he professes he holds no lands in the Island "but as under mee".

331.

1633

120. [SIR] WM. RYVES TO THE LORD OF CASTLE ISLAND AT LONDON.

Had speech with Lord Baltinglas concerning his letter, who promised Lord Herbert respite for a year longer to consider the former agreement, and that Lord Herbert's action of waste should be saved to him in case he should not then agree. Lord Baltinglas promised to send the former agreement made by Lord Herbert's agent to the writer, but sent only a packet close sealed directed to Lord Herbert with a message by word of mouth that he condescended to every point of Lord Herbert's request. Can testify it if he should deny it.

Dublin,
9 July. *Armorial seal* 332.

1633/4

121. T., [LORD] BALTINGLAS, TO LORD HERBERT.

Has divers times advertised him the dangers they both are in concerning the Island seigniory. The rent of [£]160 reserved upon Sir William Harbert's patent is reduced to £40 by the late King's letter, which is now void in regard it was not passed under the broad seal (which he would have done had he prevailed for Lord Herbert's consent). Now the Lord Deputy is so desirous to be a good husband for the King that [all] undertakers desire to compound by fine or, augmenting their rent, to pass their patents *de novo*, and so have their estates confirmed by Parliament. Desires he advise with counsel and advertise his pleasure. Is informed there are divers defects in the first patents to the undertakers of Monster, as well [as to] the survey as mistaking of names. If he can procure His Majesty's letter for passing his lands without fine or for a small fine at the lately reduced rent it would much facilitate passing the patent. If difficult there, better to labour it here [even] at some charge. Hears the Lord Deputy goes in person to see all Monster . . . . . . (*torn*) . . . . next spring or summer, and then it will be too late. Desires his absolute authorization to pass a new patent ; Sir William Rives may see all the lands are in it. If omitted or delayed they will certainly come to pay the whole rent and arrears, which will be more than the seigniory is worth.

Ropersrest,
5 February.
Armorial seal (*the arms of Herbert*) 334.

1633/4

122. T., [Lord] Baltinglas, to Lord Herbert.

He shall have a year, or two if he please, to advise whether he will take his seigniory of the Island into his hands at £500 per annum, according to their former agreement, to which this letter shall tie the writer. Earnestly desires his consent to the passing of the new patent, at the writer's charges, and no increase of rent till Lord Herbert's estate be confirmed by act of Parliament here. If he omits this opportunity the land will be certainly brought to the old rent, with all arrears, for there is no colour to continue the rent as it is unless a new patent be passed, with all the lands the writer now enjoys, many being omitted in the former patent. This will secure all the lands to Lord Herbert and his heirs for ever. Has received none of his letters, and it seems his have miscarried.

Ropersrest,
15 March. *Armorial seal* 336.

[1633-c.1635]

123. Memorandum of Lord Baltinglas's Proposals.

On 3 April 1633 Lord Baltinglas gave the writer a particular of twenty-eight plough-lands he was possessed of under pretence they were parcels of the seigniory of the Island of Kerry, but none of them found for the Queen nor in Sir William Herbert's patent. He said he could buy them in for £120 but Lord Herbert would not consent. Therefore he desired the writer's consent to passing them upon Lord Dillon's book of fee simple to the use of Lord Baltinglas and his heirs . . . . Or if the writer would purchase so much on Lord Dillon's book of fee simple as those plough-lands were rented at, be at the charge of the patent, and grant Lord Baltinglas and his lady such an estate as he had in the seigniory, he would pay 20s. a plough-land; and ever afterwards the writer should have them. Both which he rejected as not honourable, especially for Lord Baltinglas, tenant to Lord Herbert at so easy a rent. Cannot find the note of the names of those plough-lands . . . . . .

Endorsed. For Lord Herbert. *HM*2.22/1.

The author of this memorandum is probably Francis Lloyd, Lord Herbert's agent in Dublin. Lord Dillon was then a minor and his lands in wardship.

[1634]

124. Lord Herbert's Petition to the King.

The hundred of Cherbury was granted by patent by Edward 6th to William, Earl of Pembroke, his heirs and assigns . . . . with as full liberties and profits as any had [it] . . . . Queen Isabell, dowager of Edward 2nd, having had [it with] fines for licences of concord, issues of jurors, and other the profits of the green wax, together with return of writs. Now the [e]state of the Earl is come to the petitioner, who has not yet claimed the profits of the green wax [etc.]. But His Majesty having given him his title of barony of that place, he desires to hold it in as ample a manner [etc., etc.]. Beseeches all fines [etc., etc.] hereafter [arising] in the said hundred . . . . with return of writs [etc.] . . . more desiring it by His Majesty's favour than by any other title. The profit is small, and no benefit to be had of the green wax during certain grants . . . for years yet in being.

Endorsed: The Lord Treasurer and Lord Cottington [are to] certify their opinions whether he has any title to [these] fines, etc., and how they are leased . . . . Fran. Windebank

The Court at Whitehall,
10 April, 1634. *HM*2.12/8.

The profits of the green wax are those arising from estreats to be levied in the county and issued (ordinarily to the Sheriff) under the Exchequer seal in green wax.

1634

125. [Lord Herbert of] Cherberry to Lord Baletinglas. *Copy in the hand of Francis Lloyd.*

Received his of 6 July 1633, 19 October 1634, and 6 December 1634 all together; it seems there has been some negligence in his messengers. Received £10 from Mr. Peeter Richards's man but not the £10 Lord Baltinglass says he paid Hollies; prays him take order that he receive it, and the £10 for this year. Likes well that the patent be new[ly] passed at Lord Baltinglass's cost (as he offers) upon condition all the plough-lands of the seigniory and all others adjoining in Lord Baltinglass's possession be therein. Prays him again to send two copies of the patent he would pass—for more expedition one copy to his son at Birch Farm (not half a day's journey from Chester)—and they will presently return answer to his contentment if it be so much to their good as he pretends. As for the overplus of the £500 yearly which he offers to pay, he desires to know how much it may be brought to if the writer and his son join to make leases; prays to be satisfied "ingenioussly" without concealing the true value.

31 December.

On the dorse is a copy of No. 120. 337.

[1634/5]

126. T., [Lord] Baltinglas, to Lord Herbert.

Goes out of town tomorrow or the next day. Will not fail to pass a patent with all the lands if in his power, and at his own charge. If Lord Herbert comes into Irland, he will not fail to pay him £100 within ten days. Will do his best to get Lord Herbert the £10 from Hollis, though he paid it upon Lord Herbert's acquittance. Will take order with Mr. Ricards to pay £10 yearly . . .

[? January]. *Armorial seal* 335.

1634/5

127. FRANCS LLOYD TO RICHARD HERBERT, ESQ. *Contemporary copy.*

Delivered his letter to Sir Valentine Browne, who promises his best assistance, also the power of his friends, and says he and they are well acquainted with the title of the seigniory. At the end of the parliament "wee" have agreed to go towards Kerry. Knows not how Sir Valentine stands to Lord Kerry. Finds him forward to discommend Lord B., Herbert's tenant, who sometimes, he says, lived in the castle now grown to ruin (£4,000 will not repair it) and the woods wasted to the value of £3,000.

Has no help against the pretenders to the estate from Lord B.; he inclines to obscure everything than give light. Finds by tenants he here converses with [that] so long as Lord B. is their lord, they will give the writer little respect and less intelligence. First thing is to put Lord B. out. Hears he is poor; believes if any consideration to part with his estate be offered he will accept. If they cannot impeach [his estate] upon the point of the livery—[if] the tenancy by the courtesy is destroyed by the livery, being (as most say) demised for lives thirty-two years since—that lease being surrendered upon the taking of this lease Lord B. now claims by, he should be advised by Mr. Ellis if [Lord Herbert] by the surrender be entitled again to be tenant by the courtesy, at the time of the second demise having issue.

If the lease be good in creation, then to see if it may be avoided by the defeasance therein; the words being: To pay the King's rent within a month after it is due or keep [Lord Herbert] harmless. He may easily compute the arrear of the old rent, Lord B. paying but £40 English per annum since the order taken 9 June 1612. Cannot find the King's letter to reduce it; fears neither it nor the order will discharge the land [of] arrear of rent reserved by patent and incurred in this king's reign unless a new patent had passed with reservation of £40 yearly . . . It is dangerous to pass a new patent before Lord B. be brought to his apposal, and the arrear satisfied, if thought fit. If he be not able to pay, then may his estate be avoided upon the condition of defeasance.

[Believes] the King's letter was grounded upon a false surmise—pretending most of the seigniory to be evicted, where in truth he is still in possession of all. A suit is depending for [some]. Had a sufficient survey been made, according to Lord B's covenant, the extent of the seigniory [had] been known, and as free from pretended titles as other patentees'. There is no land detained from him but what his grandfather bought, and no part of the seigniory plantation.

Finds Lord B. fallen in the opinion of the gentry of co. Kerry, "and willinge they be to tread him downe". The election of knights of the shire has made the county factious; Sir Edmund Denny made a partial return of Sir Thomas Haines; upon a committee the return was reported unjust [and] Lord Kerry upon a new election righted. Hopes to use both factions.

It is said there is an act to pass this parliament to confirm the estates of heirs and assigns of patentees who renew their patents with the Commissioners here for Defective Titles for Plantation Land; their estates shall be good against the King, notwithstanding any jeofail in the patent, and all pretenders. He should procure the King's letter for passing the rectories as appendant to the seigniory, [also] all the chief-rents. Touching the grant of the next avoidance, the Bishop of Audforte refuses to show the instrument (though Lord B. sent the writer) saying he would be advised by counsel, and that he deserved it as well as the best chaplain [Lord Herbert] has. Told him the rectories were not in charge in the First Fruits Office, nor ever presented unto, but donative by the lord of the seigniory. This instrument of Lord B's. might make it presentative for the benefit of the clergy, to the prejudice of the lord. Did Lord B. pass this in his own right by usurpation (upon his frequent presentation and resignations gained) or as lord pro tempore ? He says Lord B. made no challenge but as tenant of the seigniory, and that "your" clerk Cooke had not yet resigned. Cannot see Cooke before going to Kerry, and has no confidence in a needy man, so will prefer his petition for a caveat against the Bishop; will send a copy after the Lord Deputy answers it.

There are so many good laws made this parliament for securing men's estates, goods, and lives, that persons of all countries will come to live here, and land will be dear. There was no act against excessive interest, as £20 and £30 in the hundred yearly, which made [? the money men] forbear to deal for lands unless by mortgage. Now there is an act that above £10 in the hundred must not be taken. The seigniory will be improved to £900 per annum, if he lease in possession. As yet it is not well peopled. What they call bog with draining and good husbandry will make good meadow.

Is at 20s. a week charge for diet and chamber. Asks what suit counsel advise against the Bishop—"you canot begin in a better time". Mr. Walleyes must send him a warrant for more money; must else return. Received £20, and is in debt £10 14s. for a suit and cloak. His expense in travelling is here extrordinary. Yet Sir Edward Trevor amd other[s] he diets with can say he is no more expensive than is necessary and fitting. He should direct letters to the sign of the Seven Stars in St. Nicholas Street, near the High Cross.

Wrote of his purpose to fall to practice. Will (if recommended by the King's letter) buy all apparel and necessaries in England—they be here as dear again; will send for his books.

The Seven Stars, Dublin,
27 February.

Received £5 of Mr. Walleyes at Chester. Has sent for his books and man. Finds copies cost 6d. a sheet—can at less charge keep a man. Labours, by the petition, to keep all persons from presenting and Cooke from resigning. If Cooke do resign, or the church is in lapse, the writer's brother, that lives in this kingdom, is in England—if it please Herbert to give him the next avoidance, it is encouragement for the writer to abide in the seigniory and do Herbert service. He may make his own conditions with his brother, who, by himself and his wife's friends here, will requite his courtesy, and reside here with the writer—hopes they will increase Herbert's plantation and reduce the inhabitants to live in fear of God and His Majesty's laws. Doubts not, if the church is in lapse, the Lord Deputy will present whom Herbert nominates. It may draw on the writer's father "to setle his estate upon me" . . . if Herbert nominates his brother.

Advised this afternoon with the Attorney, Sir William Rieves, what course to take for discharge of the arrear of the old rent in this reign, the order qualifying it to £40 yearly binding King James only—he is clear of this opinion . . . . and says it is good to call Lord B. to discharge it in his lifetime and free the lands. Mr. Attorney will send out process of seizure . . . Must then call to Lord B. to clear the lands and "sure" [Lord Herbert] and his heirs for the arrear, according to the lease; and if he fails, to enter for a forfeiture in [Lord Herbert's] name—he must keep good correspondency with his father. It is the condition and covenants which defeat the estate and reduce it to "my Lords Grandfather" unless he can prove the first lease to Lord B. to be for lives and livery made before issue born, by which estate by the courtesy is destroyed; then the condition reduced the estate to Herbert as heir . . . Must next commence suit upon the covenant of waste. Must have a letter of attorney from [Lord Herbert], "ells my sollicitor may be penall unto me".

Finds by some words of Sir Edward Trevor's, speaking of deputy lieutenants in co. Denbighe, that if Sir Thomas Egerton, Lord Bridgwater's elder brother, had lived (that died here in Dublin) and come to be Lord Lieutenant, as Lord Bridgwater is, he had been a deputy lieutenant without striking for it. If he please to use means to Lord Bridgwater to make Sir Edward one, it will be gratefully accepted; he is in very good respect with the Lord Deputy here, and has many matters referred to him to order or certify his opinion, and is conceived one of the wisest privy councillors for this Kingdom.

1 March.

Sir Edward Trevor says it is Herbert's best course to come over, or at least procure the King's letter touching the defects in the patent also to have wrongs redressed. *HM2.22/2.*

"Sir Edmund Denny" should, of couse, be Sir *Edward*. The phrase "the money men" is conjectural—the actual words in the text are "your money wee", but this is clearly a mistranscription. The phrase "my Lords grandfather" also makes no sense; probably "grandfather" should be grandson, the meaning being that if the lease to Baltinglass was good its term was so long that it would fall in not to Richard Herbert himself but only to Lord Herbert's grandson. Richard Herbert's mother had died in the preceding October, hence this discussion of Lord Herbert's right to continue to hold her Irish estate by the tenure known as the courtesy of England.

1634/5

128. FRA. LLOYD TO RICHARD HERBERT, ESQ., AT BURCH OR ELSEWHERE.
Contemporary copy.

The persons presented to the rectories under Herbert's title Thomas Hwyins by his grandfather, later Burges, and now Cooke by Lord B. as tenant—all had the several rectories united by patent into one. Hears this by Mr. Leanord Harsett and the Bishop of Ardeferte. None lies in tax for first-fruits. The book of *admittia* and presentations remains with the bishop and is not returned into the First Fruits Office. The advowson of the rectory of Deesert, which township is part of Herbert's seigniory, now belongs to the dignitaries of the bishopric of Ardeferte—to the treasurer, he thinks. The three rectories are worth £1,400 per annum, and unless he stands to it it will be appropriated to the bishop. The enclosed (part of the inquisition after the attainder of Desmond) [shows] which rectories he was seized of. Some concern others, as Trelie, to which Sir Edward Denny has presented (but the patent being "firme and . . . two generall", the Lord Deputy lately presented). Does not find the rectory of Balley Castland in the inquisition; it is reputed Herbert's and appendant to the seigniory in Desmond's time. No doubt many things were omitted, the office being so sudden after the attainder.

A petition preferred last Michaelmas term by one Willam Oge Gwin is referred to the two next justices; the parcels are Ballamuckhadam, Kilcushne, and Kilvan vaine, containing eight plough-lands, the best of the seigniory; they are not particularly named in the inquisition, and therefore several pretenders claim them. Nothing done upon the petition yet. Mr. Llittles, Secretary of the provinces of Monester and Leinster, will give expedition, the more if Herbert or a friend writes to him. Hopes he has received a packet with a copy of his patent; if not he will find it in the rolls for England, *anno* 31.

Finds the Bishop of London Derry more calm since his conference with the Lord Deputy touching the petition; he is content nothing be done for a month upon the writer's promise then to show Herbert's title. The bishop thought it was intended for the writer's brother; answered that he thought it not fit to speak for his brother [so soon]. He says Mr. Cooke is *criminosus*; if [so] he must resign "in Love" or be deprived. Told him that when the church became void Herbert would commend a learned and reverend person. If Herbert please to commend the writer's brother he will much advantage the writer and spare expense. The church being free it is no simony to contract for the next presentation. He must procure Lord Bridgwatter's letter to the Lord Deputy or the bishop, and his father's or his own, with the King's letter (else it will be thought the inheritance of the crown). Sir Edward Trevor has procured a letter from the Lord Deputy to Lord Bridgewatter.

Touching the arrears of the King's rent, Sir William Reeves is minded to send forth his *distringas*, but would have the writer petition that the land is encumbered with King's rent £2,000 in arrears. There is no relief due by the tenants to Herbert, but by him to the King, *post mortem* of his father, one year's rent (whether that reserved by patent or £40, according to the order of abatement, that is the question). If arrears are due according to the old reservation, he should see if he can beg it of the King. Means to tell [Sir William Ryves] before going to Kerry that this Ladyday's rent belongs to Herbert, his mother being dead and "his" lease void or forfeited, and to wish that the tenants reserve their rents till the question be determined.

Offers £40 yearly for a chamber for himself [and] his man, washing, and summering of a nag; £46 is demanded. He should direct letters to the "Vyen Stairs" [*recte* Severn Stars], St. Niccolas Street, Dublin, near the High Cross.

8 March. 35.

"£1,400" per annum for the rectories is perhaps a mistake for £140; see the next letter for a much lower valuation.

1634/5

129. FRAN. LLOYD TO RICH. HERBERT, ESQ., AT BIRCH. *Contemporary copy.*

Has dealt with a very active bishop this morning. Refused to show him Lord B's. lease or to say if the patronage of the Island churches were in it. He then desired to see if they were in Herbert's patent or the Queen's letter to warrant the same. Perceiving he would not discover the evidence, he showed him a copy of Cook's patent, which is enclosed. He observed that the bishop, not being named by his Christian name, had no authority to institute, and so the church is lapsed to the King. There is time enough to procure a letter from the King to have the rectories added to Herbert's seigniory. Finds the Lord Deputy and his creature, the Bishop of Derrye, bent to increase the church revenue in having it appropriate to the bishopric. The Bishop of Aldefert [who] found a title to the King to present [to] the church of Preetie [? *recte* Treelie] of which Sir Edw. Denny, son-in-law to Lord B., conceived himself patron . . . has no childer, is very poor, and lives within seven miles of the Island. [The Bishop of Derry] says few inhabit there but the bishop's soldiers, and that if he be incumbent he means to build and dwell there and preach every Sunday. He offered to corrupt the writer in tendering a grant for his brother of any dignity in his diocese of which he is patron—archdeacon, chancellor, or treasurer, which first happens. If he means to commend the bishop to these churches, or assent to the Lord Deputy or the Bishop of Derry, the writer would be glad to know, that he may receive the proffer for his brother. The yearly profits of the Island churches, as the bishop affirms, are: The Island, £30; Ballecustlane, £25; Killinterry, £22. The profits this year Lord B. receives by grant of Cooke, allowing for salary to the curate £[?5], and 14s. 10d. [? "Proxe"] to the bishop. Herbert may find out in the rolls in England if the rectories and patronage were granted by the Queen to his grandfather.

There fell to the writer's view a lease from Herbert's grandfather to Sir Hen. Bagnall of lands in Anglesey. What use is to be made of it and who enjoys the lands, Herbert may learn. Desires to know what to do touching the rent arrears if they fall due to the crown and "the Lord" be not able to save Herbert harmless. Thinks "hee is not being to pay" Alderman Packhurst £3,000 redemption of a mortgage this month. Thinks it best, by consent, to sequester the rents until the land be cleared. Fears [rent day] is Ladyday and Michaelmas; their first stage is Easter week in this kingdom.

Upon better consideration he desires not to put Herbert to the trouble of procuring the King's letter for liberty for the writer to practise, but asks for a word or two from Lord Bridgwater that he was admitted to practise before the Council of the Marches, and what abilities in him the judges gave assurance of (they being required [to do so] upon the variance between Mr. Turner and him, he being then Mr. Eure's, the Attorney's, deputy)—unless His Majesty's letter be that he have the place of a serjeant-at-law, the Attorney-General or Solicitor, or the Attorney of the Wards. Hears Mr. Eure is made one of the judges at Council.

Mr. Aldersey's house near Copp[er]Alley,
14 March.

Has here agreed to lodge and diet by the year or quarter at a more reasonable rate. 36.

1635

130. [LORD HERBERT]TO THE KING. *Holograph copy or draft.*

Wise princes have ever received counsellors' advice on foreign affairs with jealousy. For, often corrupt, when most sincere they have appeared perplexed . . . . . Which might have deterred him from writing ; not that he imagines His Majesty has any sinister concept of his integrity, but that, being more remote than others from affairs, he will not be able to [form] a solid opinion. Yet, because His Majesty has [made] him of his Council of War, and the tenor of his commission therein extends to foreign affairs, he begs leave to offer a brief discourse on the state of His Majesty's kingdom in relation to other[s] ; being ready further to propose a cheap and important design for his service.

Princes ought to have most regard to those potentates next [to] them. And because that state is next which can soonest come and most offend, and no way is open to us but by sea, they will ever be nearest who have most shipping to transport and most soldiers to land. If both [be] in any European prince (though distant), he will be His Majesty's next and most considerable neighbour. [By] which rule France, Spaine, and the Low Countries seem most worthy examination.

France is strongest in men [and] most united, having "adjoyned" Lorraine, Alsatia, and the Palatinate countries, equal to a third of France. That king has now five armies on foot—in Lorraine, in Alsatia, this side the Rhine, on the other side, and in Picardy (in all above 130,000 foot and near 30,000 horse) ; besides which he is told of a sixth now raising in Languedoc and towards Navarre. As he is not so powerful in shipping as the Spaniard or Low Country man, so alone he is not much to be redoubted ; though when stronger by sea he would prove a dangerous neighbour.

Spaine has great sea forces but so diffused that he is not upon any occasion able to spare his shipping without hazarding the loss of his silver fleet to the watchful Low Countrymen ; and therefore not so considerable as France, and the rather that he wants men for the many occasions he has in the world.

The Low Countrymen have most shipping and the readiest for any purpose, and therefore may be accounted our next and most important neighbours ; though, being able to spare no men from their own occasions, are not to be feared [except] they associate themselves with some other.

It will be worth enquiring whether they may be induced thereto. With the Spaniard certainly they will not. But with the French it is questionable whether they may not (out of utility or necessity). Has heard great personages say "They durst not" ; considers their arguments : 1. They have so much use of our ports in foul weather that in short time our king might be master of the greatest part of their shipping; 2-3. They cannot subsist without our men and commodities; 4. They dare not put themselves into the hands of the French lest they renew their ancient claim to that country.

But to the first may be answered: If the French join them it may be doubted whether our castles and blockhouses (as they now stand) will be able to secure our havens, especially if they land with intention to take and fortify them against us; besides, as our shipping has many times use of their ports they may seize our ships in great number. To the second: Many other countries are able to supply men abundantly; besides, we should lose most, having there not only vent for our fiery spirits but a seminary for officers (two benefits that former times would have bought at a great rate). To the third: The profit from the intercourse of merchandise is mutual; we should lose as much as they. To the fourth: As long as the Spaniard is interposed the French will not pretend to any right in those parts.

Considers the advantages the Low Countrymen may make by entering into a league offensive and defensive with the French: 1. Strong assistance of men and money, more than from any other country. 2. The frequent diversions the French may give on the side of Picardy and Artois. 3. Enabling them to dispute the superiority of the narrow seas with us and consequently the drawing of all traffic into their hands; they would intercept many of our ships—recalls what a few Dunquerkers did. All which motives may be the stronger that the causes are common to both and therefore likely to be perpetual. [Moreover] necessity may constrain them thereto whenever we abandon them. Says nothing of their obstinacy, which is to sink or blow up rather than yield.

There is nothing therefore so much to be done as to keep the French and Low Countrymen divided. United they will hazard becoming masters of our seas and traffic, and have a bridge to pass over at their pleasure. For preventing which there is no so sure remedy as to enter into a strict league with the Low Countrymen, whereby: 1. We shall have the advantage of all they do, it being a maxim of state that where a stronger and a weaker join the stronger will have the benefit; also this will be the best way to curb them if they grow insolent. 2. We shall secure our own country. 3. We shall be masters of the narrow seas, ocean, and the whole element. 4. We shall give law to all maritime countries by taking their ships in passing or firing them in their havens. 6. We shall command all islands remote from the continent. 7. Joined together we cannot fail of intercepting the silver fleet; no history can produce a conjuncture of that importance so long neglected. 8. We may take that part of the West Indies which affords those treasures wherewith the Spaniard has corrupted the counsellors and invaded the dominions of the greatest princes of Christendom.

Conceives these puissant considerations fit to be embraced rather than any project of the French or Spaniard, who ever will sooner delude than assist us in the affair of the Palatinate. Neither are we to fear lest Spaine and France join against us, since no age can produce an instance that ever they jointly formed any war against any country; they can never agree who shall have the advantage. Besides, while we keep the superiority of the sea not all the world can offend us.

Hears the French and Low Countrymen have not only entered into a strict league, but desire His Majesty should come into it. Offers his opinion: As long as the French undertake the Low Countrymen's protection by land they ease His Majesty of a great burden, [for] if they did not, he, in reason of state, should, the Low countries being the outworks of his kingdom. And to induce them, the less His Majesty in appearance cherishes the Low Countrymen, so much more will the French do for them. Thinks it not amiss, therefore, to permit the French to do his business for him. But if by any contract, stratagem, or policy they make themselves masters of the Low Country shipping, or necessity forces them to have recourse to the Frenchmen's protection, it will redound to His Majesty's and kingdom's extreme prejudice; for preventing whereof he knows but two remedies—to join with Spaine, or to enter into such a league with the Low Countries for some sea enterprises as may take their shipping off from the French.

Conceives the first of these ways the worse. The Spaniard will shortly make himself so great as to admit no friendship with any (much less restore the Palatine) or will be so exhausted that he will not be able to assist his friends; besides, he would rather nourish a war betwixt us and France (with the Low Countries) than hinder it. This way is not to be thought on but as a last remedy. [The second way] remains; will offer a design both cheap and of importance.

Concludes with beseeching His Majesty to attribute imperfections [herein] to his not knowing divers particularities, [e.g.] the business of fishing. Presumes again to recommend that the way to reduce the Low Country men to know themselves and depend on us is to join with them in their sea enterprises, whereby they acquire that vast treasure wherewith in many places they make war against the Spaniard.

Neither is there any danger our nation should be drawn to approve their form of government; the wisest of them find that republics instead of one king have many, and we acknowledge His Majesty's government so temperate that we are happier than any nation living.

10 April. *HM*2.12/10.

The results to be obtained from entering into a league with the Low Countries do not include a number five. Either by error or because this was as much as Lord Herbert at first intended to write, there appears in the document after the sentence "while we keep the superiority of the sea not all the world can offend us", an appropriate concluding passage, but this has been deleted.

1635

131. Fra. Lloyd to Richard Herbert, esq., at Burch.

Contemporary copy.

Yesterday at the Council table was read Herbert's petition for stay of the suit at common law touching Ballamackhadaim and to have it read "at board", being plantation land. The Lord Deputy being absent, and Lord Corke saying to the Lord Chancellor "This is the Lord Baintingles", he was not granted an injuction but a rule to call them to show cause [etc.]; hopes Hollies will be here to serve it. Finds Lord B. labours on behalf of the "pretendans", seeing himself questioned for his estate. Like a poor-conditioned person, when he cannot help himself he helps Herbert's adversaries. Sir Edward Trevor said the lands concerned gentlemen living out of the kingdom, and ought to have "more deliberet and advantagious" course. The Master of the Rolls answered that the prosecutor was here. Herbert's friend Mr. Richard Blayney advises letters from Herbert's father and the Earl of Bridgewatter or other nobility to Sir George Ratlief, who is a lawer and an intelligent man—what he "wotes" the Lord Deputy most commonly orders. The land is not in the inquisition of attainder. The Earl of Corke lost £100 per annum to a "pretendan" out of this patent—God send it be no precedent. It's the vote of Sir George Ratclief that must help more than advice of the best counsel. Lord B. got his order of [? defalcation] of rent. There are suits at the provincial council of Monester by pretenders against Herbert. They say they will divide themselves, some there, some here. Cannot be in both places.

Asks him to procure the King's letter making the writer chief justice there, where the proceeding is like that at the Marches. The place is worth £100 per annum. Justice Gosnald that is in it stands outlawed; he is aged and has few friends, and has been judge there twenty years. Can practise here in terms and be there at sittings. The chief justice of another province, as young as the writer and no better lawyer, does so.

Mr. Alldersey['s], near Cooper Alley,
18 April. 37.

1635

132. FRANC. LLOYD TO RICHARD HERBERT, ESQ., AT BIRCH, NEAR ELLSMERE. *Contemporary copy.*

Has not received any money from Mr. Walleys. The Escheator, Mr. Persivall, intended to find an office after the death of Richard's mother this vacation; but understanding the writer would instruct him, they have agreed to go to the Island about St. James-tide. They expect Richard's coming; it will be costly—he should come well stored and instructed. The office must be found in the proper county by freeholders of the same. Although they will deal well with Lord B., yet will find opposition by the pretenders. Hopes they will find a "dyinge seised" in Richard's ancestor, and put Lord B. to prove his lease upon a traverse, and avoid it either in point of creation or by the defeasance therein. Mr. Persivall and everyone else wonders Lord B. is not called upon to clear the estate; he hopes no office was found by Lord B. *post mortem* Willm. Herbert, *milit.*, nor by "my Lady", nor any survey taken, and said Lord B. would not have any found.

Received 12 May his letter of 7 April. Has two or three suits against pretenders at Council table to stop them at common law. He should hasten over, or send recommendations to the Lord Deputy and Sir George Ratleafe, and money. There is no relying on Mr. Walleyes—"I am put to my credit and shifts . . ." He should be sure to bring from his father Lord B's counterpart lease if he means to sue upon breach of covenants at common law and take such damages as a jury gives. If Richard flies to equity, [Lord B.] will be ordered to repair part of the castle and make it tenantable. Touching the "most" [? *recte* waste], he pretends Hollyes was the overseer and disposer of the wood, and that he did "warre" [*recte* waive] his interest, and that Hollyes is liable in equity.

Mr. Cooke, the minister of the Island, is here. He says he will resign his rectories. It was in speech upon condition he might be parson of St. Owen's or dean of Lymirike . . . There is no danger of lapse if meantime Richard can procure the advowsons in his new patent.

The old rent is certified by the Auditor to all that have renewed and increased. Has found a commission in Queen Elizabeth's time to relieve the natives pretenders against the patentees, [also] the certificate of lands unjustly detained from the pretenders. Forbears till he receives money to apply therein. Has languished with the flux, the country disease, these three or four days. By the next Richard shall know if he mends . . . He should bring a note of his father's age and the time of the first lease, and if for lives. It is very material—some say his father was not of age. The Lord Deputy goes to progress the last of June. Capt. Price goes before him and meets him. There is no company here till September, or anything to be done. Mr. Cooke has given a particular of the seigniory except the Desart, which is out of his parishes. The bishop [says] he received a letter from Richard dated Mountgom[ery] Castle. Told him he believed it was from Richard's brother, and said he would be over shortly [and that] he may have proof from him [of] the age of Richard's sister and father . . .

Mr. Wolfe's,
20 May. *HM*2.23/2.

Part of the paragraph about Cooke the minister is garbled and unintelligible. This "Capt. Price" is perhaps Captain Charles Price of Pilleth, Radnorshire (for whose career see the article by Professor A. H. Dodd in *Y Bywgraffiadur Cymreig hyd* 1940, pp. 737-8).

1635

133. Fran. Loyd to Rich. Herbert, esq., at Burch. *Contemporary copy.*

Mr. James Fitz Gerrerd, steward of his seigniory, is dead, and his widow and one Piers (an attorney of the Court of Pleas) have wardship of his son. Cannot learn that he had above £40 a year of his own inheritance; he paid Lord B., as tenant of part of the Island seigniory, £300 per annum as men say (Lord B. says £200). They should be ready to oppose this office lest part of Herbert's inheritance be comprised in it. Wrote to Sir Valendine Browne (an opposer of Lord B. and a favourer of the natives in Herbert's behalf) to send some discreet person to see all court books, muniments, etc., sealed up and delivered to Herbert or the writer.

Mr. Wallys has as yet furnished him with no money. There is an inquisition found this vacation of a great barony called Idow in co. Kilkerry (*sic*); the Chief Justice of Common Pleas, the Master of the Rolls, and Sir Nathaniell Cattleme are appointed commissioners by the Lord Deputy and sent down to find an office to entitle the King. If Capt. Seryuer cannot procure a share in the great plantation [en]acted this summer in the Lord Deputy's progress through Connoht, there is hope he may speak in time for this ; is told it was the cause of his coming over. "Keepe it to your selfe".

He should be sure to bring over a letter of attorney from his father to enter upon the condition of defeasance and sue Lord B. for breach of covenant touching the waste, in which his father, though for Richard's benefit, is plaintiff. Else all is frustrate, and he may as well stay at home. If the writer, Herbert's agent, or any other should sue, [they] will demand his warrant of attorney ; if he cannot show it he is stopped by the court and ordered to give costs. Service to Sir Richard Newport, Herbert's lady, and Mr. Tho. Newport. God be praised upon recovery of the writer's health.

Mr. Walfe's, the attorney's, Castle Street,
20 May. 338.

1635

134. THE PRIVY COUNCIL TO [THE SHERIFF OF MONTGOMERYSHIRE].
Contemporary copy.

His Majesty has sent his writ to the sheriffs of North Wales and the mayors [etc.] of corporate towns [there] to provide one ship of 400 tons, furnished with men, tackle, munitions [etc.], to be set forth for the safeguard of the seas and defence of the realm. Are to let them know that he has upon weighty considerations concerning not only his honour and the renown of this nation, but the safety of all his subjects, sent [this] writ to all counties, that all might put their helping hands to secure this realm against those extremities which have distressed other nations and are the common effects of war where it takes a people unprovided. As His Majesty doubts not their readiness to contribute, so he requires their care in the ordering of it, that no inequality or miscarriage retard or disgrace it. For which cause they send the ensuing instructions : A ship of that burthen so manned and furnished will be £4,000, whereof co. Montgom[er]y may well bear £833 6s., [whereof] the borough of Mountgom[er]y £12. The charge upon the county is to be divided into hundreds . . . and those into parishes and towns, which must be rated by the houses and lands in them, as accustomed in other common payments ; saving that men of ability by reason of their "paynfull trades", stocks of money, or other personal estate, who occupy little lands and so in an ordinary "landscott" would pay little, be rated according to their worth, and the moneys applied to sparing and easing such as be of weak estate or charged with many children or great debts.

He is to send warrants to the constables of hundreds to call to them discreet and sufficient men of every parish, town or tithing to consider how the sums may be divided with equality, and return the same to him ; which done, he may order collection by constables, petty constables, and others usually employed for [such] collections. And when any refuse or neglect payment, he is without delay to execute the writ upon them.

Albeit His Majesty is resolved to maintain the clergy's privileges, yet because it has not been made sufficiently appear to him or this board what privileges have been allowed former[ly], he is to proceed to assess them as [others], bearing due respect to their persons and calling. Such assessments shall not be prejudicial in future to their privileges which upon further search shall be found.

White Hall, 12 August.

W. Cant.
Maynchester
Hambleton
Pembrooke and Montgom[er]y
Bridgwater
Kelly
E. Neuburghe
Cooke

Tho. Coventry, *Cust. Sigill.*
Lenoxe
Arndell and Surry
Dorcett
Hollandes
Fr. Cottington
Vane
Fr. Windibanke

*HM*2.12/11.

[1636/7]

135. Petition of Richarde Herbert, esq., to Viscount Wentworth, Lord Deputy General of Irelande.

Queen Elizabeth, upon the plantation of Monster, granted by letters patent dated March, 31st year, to Sir William Harbert and his heirs all the Castle of the Island with the lands belonging to it in co. Kerry and divers lands in a schedule annexed. Which lands descended to Mary Harbert as daughter and heir, who, being seized thereof, took to husband Sir Edward Harbert, now Baron of Cherberie [etc.], who were seized as of fee, Mary by her own right, Sir Edward in right of Mary. In 6 Jas. Sir Edward, without consent of Mary, did demise to Viscount Baltinglas, by the name of Sir Thomas Roper, for life, remainder to Dame Ann his wife for life, remainder to Sir William Harrington since deceased for life; by colour whereof Sir Thomas entered and was possessed. And the said Dame Mary died, whereby the premises descended to the suppliant as her son and heir, who, understanding of the act of the last parliament for securing the estates of the plantators in Monster that they [should] come within five years and desire the benefit of the act, is now come out of England and humbly prays benefit of the act and the Commission of Grace; and will put in good security to take no advantage of the letters patent now desired against Lord Baltinglas for avoiding the said lease.

Endorsed: Delivered Mr. Cusacke 22 Feb. 1636. 339.

James Cusack was Attorney to the Commission for Remedy of Defective Titles. Lord Baltinglass was actually dead when this petition was delivered to Cusack—he died on February 15th and was buried in Dublin on the 20th—but was apparently alive, or thought to be alive, when the petition was drafted. Lady Baltinglass was a daughter of Sir Henry Harington, brother of Lord Harington of Exton, which accounts for the third life in the lease.

1637/8

136. Benjamin Evans to [? Francis Herbert of Dolguog].

"Noble Sir". Has delivered to Mr. John Lloyd, d . . . . . .(*torn*) four cheeses to be sent to him, the weight whereof is underwritten. Hopes they will prove good ones. His servant Humffrey Davies came to the writer to enquire Mr. Edward Jones's age: Found it registered in St. Chad's in Shrewsbury—he was baptized 17 September 1570.

Salop,
1 February.

One weighs 25 lbs., the others 23 lbs., 20 lbs., and 16 lbs.

Armorial seal

Endorsed: For carriage and portage of these cheeses, received 7s. 6d. from Mr. Fra. Herbert. John Spencer.

Pencil jottings on the dorse: Star Chamber. Monday in Easter week at Cooper's house in Church Stretton. Morton Briggs, Rich. Ridley, Ar. Pr., Fra. Thornes.

Is at one of the clock on Monday to call on Mr. Churchman; at six in the morning on Mr. Willson to go to Mr. Turbervill. Should that day meet Dick . . . . . . (*illegible*). To call for "my" commission from Mr. Hillarye on Tuesday; for "my" subpoena for Som. Foxe from Holes . . . To bring "my" books to Juckes. Three breviates with [? Lanc], two with Juckes, one with "mee". The Star Chamber books are with Mr. Farrar to draw interr[ogatories]. To meet Sir Harrye Herbert under the elms at one of the clock. To go to Mr. Turbervill, by three of the clock on Tuesday. To be at the Star Chr. Office tomorrow by nine, at Churchman's by two . . . 340.

1637/8

137. M. Herbert to Francis Herbert, esq., at the Queen's Attorney's chamber, Inner Temple, London.

"Good Sonne". By a letter she sent him this morning by the carrier he will find she knew of some disaster; which is now come to pass, for this afternoon Sir John Bridgman is departed this life, and there is a most heavy house. The bearer desires his furtherance in some business that will be much to his preferment now Sir John is dead—maybe some pursuivant's place. Knows he will do what he can for him in an honest way—let it bind him unto Herbert to deal fairly towards him and his friends. " . . . Indeed I was in a terrible feare for you, but I trust now it was this which is come to pass, for indeed I have lost a true friend".

5 February. *Armorial seal* 303.

1638

138. The Lord Deputy [and Commissioners for Remedy of Defective Titles] to Mr. Richard Herbert. *Contemporary copy.*

Whereas he made suit to the Lord Deputy and Commissioners for Remedy of Defective Titles above a year since to be admitted to compound for and pass by letters patent upon the new Commission of Grace the manor and lordship of Castle Island and other lands in co. Kerry known as the seigniory of Mounteagle Loyal; and whereas the premises were at his request surveyed by one Richard Francis, an officer appointed to that service, whom Herbert undertook to satisfy for his reasonable charges; and forasmuch as he made return of the lands half a year since, and Herbert has failed to pay him, and has likewise neglected to compound with the Commissioners and proceed in passing letters patent; and for that there is a great arrear due to His Majesty out of the premises, and that Viscount Baltinglass, tenant, is lately dead, who, as Herbert alleges, should satisfy the arrear; and that His Majesty receives a prejudice by this delay, which wholly proceeds of Herbert's neglect: They have to this present borne with his remissness but now think fit to let him know that if he protracts longer than the last of next Trinity term his composition, etc., they will admit such others to compound for the same, and obtain new letters patent thereof, as shall sue for it, or otherwise to His Majesty's advantage.

Dublin Castle, Tho. Wentworth Adam Loftus
25 April. Gerard Lowther Rich. Balton
Cha. Coote James Ware
James Cusake 343.

1638

139. M. Herbert to Francis Herbert, esq.

"Good Sonne". Is grieved for his toil in these troublesome suits. The orders are so "slender" they make as much for their adversaries as for them; heard the effect from Ludlowe, and there are great brags how everyone is now at liberty to prove all their titles at this commission. Summerset Foxe's injunction restrained him [only] until the matter were determined in the Court of Wards, so now he makes account to trouble as much at this commission as at the last (last year at Shrewsbury). Prays God for good commissioners, otherwise the women may "finde" their lease. The brothers are all now at home unless it be those two that serve Mr. Attorney; they will now work what they can in the country amongst jurors, which old Corbett, an old juryman, has great acquaintance with. Mr. More of Linley said they could not have a more indifferent jury than the last, pointing to Hercules Kinnersley to be foreman; but he leans to Sommerset Foxe because his brother solicits his causes. Means to acquaint Mr. More with her fears and desire him to name some that will stand with the truth. Shrewsbury is not a fit place, the Corbetts having many friends thereabouts and in that town, who so worked with the jury last year that divers that went fully resolved for the co-heirs were clean turned. Between their smooth glosses and lordly promises they win many. Thinks it good to name Mr. More one of Herbert's commissioners—he is now able to travel, and is of great experience. Mr. Evan Phillips thought it best to name Sir Marmaduke and Mr. Adam Littleton at adventure—told beforehand they would be loth, but being told Herbert named them upon necessity or that the court thought them fittest they would not dislike; he said it was an ordinary thing to name commissioners and not acquaint them.

The Corbetts have many writings which her brother had of her against the finding of his office. They will do "us" little good, for they show her brother had more power to dispose of his estate than she wishes had been given him (unless he had more wit); that is in the deed upon his marriage. But if the opinion of his lawyer of the Court of Wards stands (that commissioners may reject proof of any conveyances or leases but what tend to finding an office for the King) it may do. But if the jury find the leases or Sommerset's deeds, how may the commissioners avoid what the jury find good? Follows the old adage: Ever fear the worst—the best will save itself.

Sent his sister the note concerning her Randell Owen. Wrote to Mr. Mathew Evans about his assistance to her daughter and concerning old Lady Price of Gogerthen. Told Herbert's wife she should not advise with Evan ap Owen unless he be there. Marvels the nag came so untowardly, for he was "slick" when he went hence; Cheese says he had ill fits in the night . . . There are few can be trusted, which makes her and him "live by the loss". Fears Evan did scarce meat him well by the way. If this do not "prouve", another must be enquired for for her nephew. Sir John Da[n]vers's mare is in the stable; will send for Broome about her taking horse.

Will get the Herefordshire lands drawn into a case. If agreeable to law he should get words in the commission to reject all evidences but what are for the King for finding of the office. Hopes he sees cousin Sommerset Fox has no advantage by reason her sister Marie's name was left out of the commission and she thereby not sworn. Hopes he has put in his second answer into the Court of Requests. Rawlins is dead; it was well they had his testimony.

He shall receive a note of the trespasses in Ellton and the names of the woods. None absolutely refuse to pay their rents but Marven and Richard Gough of the Signet. Keysell says he will bring in all he can get. Some of the poorer sort are unpaid; knows not what to do with them. Tedstill is behind £7, and Jennings Wigley and many of the beggarly people of this town, and some in Prior's Haghton. Mr. Lewes says Lady Paumer had attachments from all that refused to pay her rent—from what court he knows not, but she had possession ordered here at the Council, and her proceedings have been the President's. Prays God send good news of Sir Henry Herbert.

6 May.

Has not Mr. Usher's letter. The sum was £10 odd, and Mr. Trevor said he should have no more.

Thinks he has not delivered the state of the cause right to his lawyer about the copyhold lands. It cannot be forfeited because she and her sister made a letter of attorney to David John to repair to the court of the manor and lordship of Tytley, co. Hereford, to receive to their use at the hands of the then steward, Mr. James Dalley, seisin and admittance to the tenement and custom-lands whereof Francis Foxe, esq., died seized, unto whom they were sisters and next heirs. And they were admitted, and it cost for their copies 5s. 4d. apiece. And so they are become tenants to the lord of the soil, the Warden of Winchester, though Sjt. Hoskins has a lease. The copies may be amongst Bulkley's writings. It is thought Bulkley's lease cannot be good unless he had it confirmed at the next court. Doubts whether to acquaint Mr. William Littleton with it, for he was ever of Bulkley's counsel. Her brother should have sent two men that from his own mouth should have deposed that he had made such a lease.

Added below the address: Sent Mr. Spencer by this "Carry", Simmons, another cheese.

Armorial seal 304.

"Sir Marmaduke" is probably Sir Marmaduke Lloyd. "This town" is, of course, Ludlow.

1638

140. FRAN. LLOYDE TO [LORD HERBERT].

This day Mr. Attorney attended the Lord Deputy with the writer in the cause between him and Lady Baltinglas. The Attorney pressed it home [and] charged Sir Charels Coote that the articles were drawn according to his instructions and approved by Mr. Sjt. Sandbaich. They would not allow [Lord Herbert] a third part unless he discharged them of the covenant of building. It was objected as of old that the covenants of plantation were broken before the lease. It was answered that it was a real covenant entered into by Lord Baltinglas that runs with the land to tie the lady to build the houses, and is [Lord Herbert's] security to free him from the damage he must now sustain by stricter covenants upon the new articles of plantation in this Commission for Remedy of Defective Titles, upon the new passing of his patent, which he must do within the time limited by the statute.

Sir Charells Coote . . . alleged that in his instructions he had excepted the building of so many houses. Mr. Attorney assured the contrary. There was somewhat further given that by the late act here, enabling the heir to enter and avoid the estate made by the husband of the wife's lands, the lady's estate is to be avoided. It was argued she might remedy herself in a cause of equity, to which it was replied there was no relief in law or equity against an act of Parliament, to which the learned King's Serjeant could make no answer. Had he been so well read as he ought he might have remembered that the act is in the future tense—for any estate hereafter to be made. Moved that [Lord Herbert] had good cause of suit against her as executrix to her late lord; that sufficient assets will be found; and that [Lord Herbert] has his real covenant against her for not keeping the castle in repair. Sir Charells Coote answered that £500 would put it in repair, which they would disburse. Thus the debate in brief before the Lord Deputy.

After many days' attendance with Mr. Secretary, he understood the Lord Deputy's pleasure was to hold Monday last for the day. Received His Honour's commands on Monday to give the lady notice to attend by counsel, Sir Charrells Coote and Lord Dillon to have notice likewise. She hoped it might have been ended before [Lord Herbert's] departing. Lord Dillon said the lady and others troubled themselves more than needs, for if the conditions and covenants were inserted it might move [Lord Herbert's] son not to consent, and so turn to her prejudice. Sir Charrells Coote required the writer to send again lest he forgot the day. "So have you [his] humor . . . He must have duble notice". The Lord Deputy, who is most careful and certain in his word and commands, says he will write [Lord Herbert], and commanded the writer to call for it Monday next. Keeps his footman, who landed after [Lord Herbert] went on shipboard. Paid £5 10s. for copies of depositions. All things are dearer here than in London.

Cannot yet learn who has received from the Lord Deputy the petition to be read before the Commissioners for the Revenues to stay the arrear of pension, being assets to answer [Lord Herbert's] action. Moyses Lloyd has made no affidavit of service of the order on Lord Kerry and Mr. Roach to stay their passing and compounding upon the Commission of Grace for some of [Lord Herbert's] lands. He must send the original again—[cannot] serve them with a copy of a copy; if it comes by 1 October it's time enough. Prays his and his son's directions what suits to commence against the lady, with all the writings, especially his authority for entry.

Castle Street,
1 August.

Since the Lord Chancellor's troubles, "my gaines smaule, my expence greater". Unless by [Lord Herbert's] means to the Lord Deputy or greater power in England the writer has some competent promotion, he will not be able to subsist. 347.

The Lord Chancellor, Viscount Loftus of Ely, had recently been removed from office for irregularities—the "troubles" referred to in the postscript.

1638

141. [SIR] PH. MAINWARING TO LORD HARBERT OF CERBURY, OF HIS MAJESTY'S COUNCIL OF WAR.

Put the Lord Deputy this day in mind of Lord Herbert's business, who immediately gave it a new hearing at large, the event whereof he will understand from the Lord Deputy himself. There is a new hare on foot, scarce mentioned whilst Lord Herbert was here—they conceive he stands bound by his covenants to secure unto the lady her estate for life. His counsel must look into this. If Lord Herbert's passage hither had been as smooth and short as his return he would cross often. Will watch Irish occasions to do him service, if possible answerable to the obligations and lively memory he holds of Lord Herbert's mother, his thrice-noble patroness. Sees him enjoy himself in his park, breathing his perfect British air—it were a sin to interrupt his recreations since he leaves for London the middle of the month.

Dubline,
7 August.

His footman came the day he sailed for Ingland, and has been stayed for this. 344.

1638

142. [LORD HERBERT] TO [? THE EARL OF BRIDGWATER]. *A much altered draft.*

"M[y] . . . . h[onoured] L[ord]". Having with much labour and charge brought his business in Ireland to a point, he humbly offers an account thereof. If he releases his action of covenant and waste against Lady Baltinglas and joins with his son and her in a lease of thirty-one years to those who will give best value, the ninety decayed houses may be built up and a rent of £1,500 raised, whereof two-thirds to her and a third to him and his son. His son runs no great hazard confirming a sickly lady's life, and the lease will not be to his harm since lands are thought to be as high now as they will be hereafter. Only they must absolutely resolve her an answer by the end of Michaelmas term. Hopes his lordship, after speech with the writer's son, will vouchsafe his answer in the meantime to these particulars for the purchase of lands in Anglesea. Desires him to stay the sale of [certain] tenements which appertain to the writer only . . . . . being not sold above sixteen years' purchase . . . All which mistake arose because the commissioners were not sufficiently informed of the value. Since none will receive detriment but himself in his pursuit to right himself he cannot doubt but his lordship will give him a fair way therein. Is content the other lands be sold as agreed for, assuring himself his lordship will permit him the money according to the indentures.

15 August.

Endorsed: Copia vera. 394.

The Earl of Bridgwater is suggested as the recipient as being the person most likely to be asked to act as intermediary between Lord Herbert and his son.

1638

143. HUMP. WALCOT TO [? MARGARET HERBERT].

"Worthy Good freind". The goodness of her cause and the many promises he has made her and her son, Mr. Herbert, tie him to do her all the furtherance he can. Promised her son to be at Shrewsbury on Wednesday next, but his doubt is whether his absence may not avail them more than his presence. His ancient friend, old Mr. Corbett, his fellow justice, and his near kindred and dear friend, Mr. Actons of Aldenham, are earnest in her opposers' behalf, and they expect what favour and justice lie in his power. Will especially be pressed, as at the last meeting at Bridgnorth, for his opinion for the finding of their lease and their taking of the profits. . . Hopes her counsel will persuade the jury to forbear troubling the office with all leases, especially those against which there are so many colourable exceptions. Is not much perplexed with this, and the statute 2 Edw. VI, *cap.* 8, gives remedy. What troubles him is the point punctually put down in their commission, to enquire who occupied or took the issues, and by what title, at or after, etc. This will be hard pressed to be found according to the truth, and he knows not how to give opinion otherwise. But her son says this must not be suffered to be found by any means, which makes the writer loth to be in place for want of judgement to discern what his fellow commissioners may conceive forcible . . . Their friend Mr. More, his neighbour, and the other commissioners will do her all the good they can. [Will be] there if he can do them the least advantage, "though . . . I travaile sadly when I feare my jorney will be fruitlesse". Remembrance from his wife.

Walcot,

27 August. 341.

1638

144. [LORD HERBERT] TO [? LORD DEPUTY WENTWORTH]. *Contemporary copy.*

His son has recovered some strength, and has testified his assent to whatsoever the writer shall resolve concerning his lordship's order signified by letter in August, after the writer's departure from Ireland, about the differences betwixt Lady Baltinglas and him. Howbeit, as, for want of perfect health and of counsel learned where he now lives, his son has expressed himself only in general words, his further declaration will be sent by the next conveniency. Humbly desires him to require Lady Baltinglas's resolution concerning her submission to his order, as they purpose to do, and to detain the money due for her husband's pension, they knowing no way so valid and obligatory for bringing her to just reason.

23 November. 345A.

[1638]

145. [LORD HERBERT] TO [FRANCIS] LLOYD. *Contemporary copy.*

"Cosen Lloyd." His letter came this day, 26 November. Understands the money was too little, whereof he will advertise his son, who is to contribute to the charge. Hopes he will take order that they suffer no detriment if the trial for Ballom[a]cAdam proceeds. Lady Baltinglas's sickness, being but the gout, may prove not so dangerous, but if otherwise than well happen to her, legal entry should be made in the writer's name—or if something may be done to prevent the arrears falling on him. Wrote to the Lord Deputy and Sir George Ratcliffe of his son's recovery and intention to submit to the writer concerning an accommodation. Lloyd's Irish harper shall be welcome if he can play by the book after the English manner and speak good English. Service to Mr. Sjt. Eustace and respects to Lord Dillond. Hopes he can procure answer from the Lord Deputy by Mr. Secretary. 345B.

1638/9

146. HUGHE OWEN TO MARGARETT HERBERT, WIDOW, AT PROMFILT.

On Monday the 11th the Bishop of Bangor sent a note by the [ap]par itor to demand 10s. "annuall" from the rectory of Llanegrin—in default, sequestration next court, the Thursday following. Sent to acquaint the steward (the collector) that the rectory of Llanegrin was never charged before with any charge or task from Bangor, and that the curate who served the place this fifty-nine years never heard of any demand but £8 6s. 8d. yearly to the King. The steward said the Bishop would not bate a penny, for it is in the records that Llanegrin is charged therewith, but for the writer's sake he would stay sequestration [until] next court, the last day of this month. Desires word what he should do.

Tallaypont,

18 February. 346.

The curate is probably the John Griffith or Gruffith who—his "title" in each case being William Tuder of Egryn—was made deacon in 1580 and priest in 1582 (Pryce, *The Diocese of Bangor in the Sixteenth Century*, pp. 60 and 62).

1638/9

147. MATH. EVANS TO [? FRANCIS HERBERT AT] BROMFIELDE. *Torn.*

Is glad to understand of that just and advantageous order he obtained in the Court of Wards, whereby he hopes all rubs for the finding of the office for the coheirs are removed. Received his letters in Mr. Lewes Hughes's behalf, together with his proxy and letters of induction, and has effected all for him in legal way. Hears Hughes had a windfall of late by the death of a man near Windsor, of whose living he had an advowson. If he recommends farmers to Hughes for this rectory, he prays him let the writer's brother John be one. Will keep the instruments till [Herbert] comes up.

8 March.

342.

1638/9

148. THO. DRAYCOT TO MRS. HERBERT.

Acquainted "my Ld." of Bangor with her letter, and he will stay proceedings till Mr. Francis Harbert has time to advise and return answer. Is of opinion that in times past it has been paid to the Bishop, though of late omitted. Mr. Herbert may resolve himself next term in London by enquiring in the First Fruits and Tenths Office whether ten shillings yearly was of old due for Llanegryn, and if the Bishop pays the King first fruits for those annuals—he says they are mentioned in his composition. The rectories of Towin, Llanvachr[e]th, and others in that county pay; and so in Carnarvanshire, Anglesey, and elsewhere in the diocese they pay the annuals and procurations in his lordship's visitation, though they are impropriations as Llanegryn is. Service to Mr. Herbert and his bedfellow.

Bangor,
10 March.

350.

1639

149. [SIR] PH. MAINWARING TO [LORD HERBERT].

Heard by chance that he passed lately through Chester in his return from the camp to Montgomorry Castle. Congratulates his safe return. His lordship's agents, counsel, and friends here are labouring to settle his business. There has been a petition in his name and everything granted that can be on those occasions, with all favour and respect, both because the Lord Deputy inclines to it and because others through whose hands it passes are propitious. It will fall to [Lord Herbert] to pay the last survey; everybody thinks it reasonable, and the Commissioners remember that his son undertook to discharge it. It will be money well bestowed, for May next he will begin to receive a good rent there, and for some time it will be growing. Lady Baltinglasse pays all arrear of rent from the composition, which will go hard with her. There is a gentleman that by directions of the Commissioners for Defective Titles has long since given the surveyor £60 part payment, and would be glad to have his money. They are about to pass a grant, by advice of [Lord Herbert's] counsel, in the name of Sir Georg Radcliff and the writer to his lordship's use. Hopes he and his posterity will reap great profit by it.

Dubli[n]e,
24 July. 352.

Lord Herbert had been with the King in his expedition to Berwick.

1639

150. Cuthbert Hely to Lord [Herbert] of Chirbury in Tuttle Street, Westminster. *Badly torn.*

Received a letter from Mr. Edward Whittingham by Roger Reignolds, at Lord Herbert's going hence. Sent him answer with copy of a tri-partite affidavit of some of the defendants. By the neglect of some absent, who had exemplification of Reignold's judgement against Dunn . . . . . . [tres]passer . . . . . . [and had it] not been for Mr. Attorney Euers's great [? care] his lordship's tenant had paid costs and the matter been dismissed. The order is as favourable as could be in respect Mr. Gilbert Jones and all the writings were absent. There was great struggling by the defendants and counsel and [attorney] . . . . . . who appeared for all the defendants except Wm. Rees *alias* Dunn, the chief actor. Not knowing what inconvenience might accrue by this order, he has sent copies by advice of Mr. Rees Jones, one of his lordship's attorneys. He is chiefly to consider whether to go to a new trial; secondly, whether to move this court to stay this order and go to a hearing for the misdemeanour. For the better effecting thereof they [should leave] the original unsigned—until signed by some of the judges it is no order. The old order was rightly pursued if it can be made appear that Tho. . . . . . . [and Wm.] Rs *alias* Dunn had notice of the trial. The scruple they stand on is that they had no notice, thinking Reignolds would never pay their costs. Besides, there was a slip in the order for the interruption, *viz*, upon notice to the defendants or either of them—Griff. swears he had no notice.

Ludlowe,
30 September.

Was last night after supper invited by Mr. Rich. Herb[er]t to "my Lords" presence to hear the two ladies, Lord Herbert's two grand children, and Mr. Coate sing. His lordship goes hence next Wednesday towards Aseridge or London. Sent this day sennight a letter from Mr[s]. Beatris.

Further addition : Received . . . [th]ese copies from Mr. Edw. Whi[ttingham] . . . [? Ri]ch. [? Th]ompson . . . [Received] also last night a letter which Lord Herbert . . . . Tho. Turnor to the Chief Justice, Sir Tho. Millward . . . . . (*So defective as to be unintelligible*). 351.

The host at the after-supper entertainment is clearly the Earl of Bridgwater, and the "two ladies" are no doubt his unmarried daughter Alice and her sister Mary, Richard Herbert's wife.

1639

151. Jo. Edwardes to Mr. Richard Halle at Ludlowe.

Has not seen Mr. Corbett, but his wife tells him that on Friday there were some men to enquire for him, he being from home . . . Will join with him in anything he shall be commanded unto out of any of the King's Majesty's courts, as far as his age and weakness enables him. Heard Mr. Corbett was all night on Friday in town. Remembrance to Mrs. Halle.

Bridgnorth,
9 October.

Hears Mr. Corbett is gone to London.

Endorsed: Is willing to join with Mr. Edwards and go with him or Mr. Corbett and do what is required [by] orders of any court.
Richard Hall 349.

1639

152. Richard Hall to Mr. Richard Marston at his chamber in New Inn or in the Crown Office, London.

Wrote to Mr. John Edwards, his fellow-trustee, that if Mr. Corbett came he should come with him or his messenger to Ludlowe that they might join in sealing the lease of ejectment and travel together to the land to execute it. Encloses Mr. Edwards's answer. Prays him acquaint Mr. Frauncis Harberte therewith. Entreats him and Mr. Harberte to assist them against Mr. Corbett if he proceeds against them for their unreadiness to seal the lease, and undertake that they will seal at any time, or, if they enter their action, that appearance be given, and so stop all clamours.

Ludlowe,
12 October.

The order is dated May. Had no notice till this month. 348.

1639

153. Fran. Lloyde to [Lord Herbert].

Delivered his letter to Moyses Lloyd. Perceives he will advise as to the letter delivered to him by Parry, the Lord Chancellor's secretary. The fiat for [Lord Herbert's] patent being long since delivered into the Hanaper Office, upon petition by Garrett fitts Patrick Piers, the pretender to Bala mc Adham, the Council stayed it till further order. Being prepared to move the first sitting day for a *procedendo*, Mr. Plunkett, for Garrett fitts Patrick, moved [first] for trial in Easter term and costs because the order last term for trial was opposed by [Lord Herbert]. Had direction from his son to stay the trial till his coming over. Lord Herbert's counsel yielded to these: To have it tried at the Exchequer by a jury *de circumstantibus*, and to rely wholly upon the mere right and title and not give the new patent in evidence, so it might pass meantime (the statute expires next March). But the Board rejected that the patent pass before trial, though security was offered it should not be given in evidence. Consented that the depositions be read and delivered with the evidence, to which Sir George Ratcliffe said: Let it be so, but let Garrett's counsel make election for trial next term upon reading of the proofs, or in Easter term with witnesses viva voca. "Aliquod latet quod non putet".

If Lloyd will follow the writer's directions—finds him cross—he will prefer the like petition to stay Lord Kerrie's patent till trial with him for [Lord Herbert's] land that he holds called Drumlegach, to see if the Board will put them in the same predicament.

Has been a builder this vacation on a farm he has contracted for with Sir Thomas Merredith within a mile of Dublin. It's worth £70 per annum in possession and £50 more in reversion if the price and rate of land hold. The house and out-houses cost £400 the building. It is a lease from Lord Moore for thirty-seven years to come, with £23 reserved to his lordship. It will cost the writer near £600. Lent Moyses Lloyde money; has not received from him [Lord Herbert's] gift of 40s. last term and this. It he will give him leave to receive the lady's rent, he will take this farm in [Lord Herbert's] name for security. Is to pay those moneys within two years; pays meantime £67 a year rent. Has some moneys of his own. If he obtains a fortune by marriage he will be the better able to repay [Lord Herbert].

Mr. Cadowgan being invited to supper where the writer diets by one Burke, a clerk in one of the offices of the Lord Deputy's secretaries, he asked the writer (there being divers at supper) why [Lord Herbert] had not returned the £30 to Mr. Carre, the Lord Deputy's secretary (who paid £60 to the surveyor). Told him he had [Lord Herbert's] letter charging Mr. Charells Walles for the payment; said he was very unmannerly to use his lordship's name [so]. He replied he did not believe it, that Mr. Walleis returned more money in a year than [Lord Herbert] was worth, that for [Lord Herbert's] son he had disbursed £15 and sent ten times before he had £10 thereof. Told him that had he known [Lord Herbert's] credit and honour at Court his scandalous tongue had spurned to utter such words, and made an assault on him. Being parted, he threatened the writer with a candlestick, called him "mr. Necessity that had now law", and said he never knew Castle Street without a woodcock since the writer came. It's his duty to acquaint him with this passage, which the instant he returned to his chamber was put to writing and attested by himself and his man. Stayed this fortnight in hope Cadwgan, being his countryman, would recant; but [now] informs him how he, his son, and the writer have suffered by this goose-quill varlet.

Castle Street,
16 November. 353.

1639

154. FRAN. LLOYDE TO [LORD HERBERT AT HIS DWEL]LING [IN TUTTLE] STREET, WEST MEST[ER]. *Torn.*

How his agents have spent their time will appear when they return. Cannot commend their diligence. This term they have not disbursed a penny to counsel, but put a motion or two upon the writer. The trial for Bala mc Adham will go on next term at the Exchequer Bar. Moves this day for an order that the records in the Auditor's office be brought to the Exchequer; a *constat* without the Great Seal is no evidence, and to bring a copy of the whole record is too chargeable. Hopes they will be in better readiness than they were at the Council Boards. Is both counsel and solicitor. Cannot see them once in a week unless he hunts after them—and not till after nine at night. Sent him one letter by Mr. Churchman, two by his careless countryman Mr. Parry, the Lord Chancellor's secretary, and another by one Harrison, a Scot. Has not received a line from him. Knows not how he stands in his favour, but is sure he takes more care in his suits than his especial agents do.

A purchase he has made here has brought him into debt. His practice will not help, so he has resolved to help himself by acquiring a good wife. [Lord Herbert's] old friend, Sir William Rives, has interest in a gentlewoman here, one Mrs. Coope, a widow of good parentage and portion. Asks him to write to Sir William Rives, now one of "our Judes", to take the writer into his favour. Finds by Sir Richard Newport's letter that [Lord Herbert] and his son will give the writer lease of a good farm in the Island for his service here. This being intimated to Sir William Rieves may [assist] his demonstration of his possibilities to his father's estate in England.

Castle Street,
3 December.

This poor distressed gentleman, Capt. Steele, comes over wearied out with suits, to supplicate his grievances to the Lord Chancellor.

Armorial seal 354.

[1639]

155. Lord Herbert's Petition to the Lord Deputy of Ireland.

Being seized of the manor of Mounteagle Loyall and other lands in Ireland for life as tenant by the courtesy, reversion in fee to Richard Herbert his son and heir, articles were made between him, the said Richard, and Viscountess Baltinglas whereby she was to have the lands for life upon certain rents, etc. Being desirous the lands should continue in the suppliant's name and blood, an indenture was made 6 April, 12 *Car.*, between him and Richard Herbert on the first part, John, Earl of Bridgwater, and Edward Herbert esq., the Queen's Attorney, of the second part, and others of the third part, settling the lands upon the suppliant for life, remainder to the said Richard for life, and remainder to Edward Herbert, John Herbert, and Richard Herbert, sons of the said Richard, and the heirs male of their bodies, one after another in seniority. And provision was made that Edward Herbert, the suppliant's second son, should receive £2,000 portion, for the better performing of which Richard jointly with the suppliant authorized agents in Ireland to pass a new patent of the lands upon the Commission of Grace, which is drawn and allowed by the Lord Deputy and ready for the Great Seal. But some defect happening therein the said Richard takes advantage thereof and intends himself to pass a new patent, thereby (as the suppliant fears) to avoid the agreement with Lady Baltinglas and recede from his covenant to the disherison of his own children and the defrauding of the suppliant's second son of his portion. Therefore beseeches that if Richard Herbert be admitted to pass patent he be ordered to perform the agreement and indenture, and that if he refuse or delay, the suppliant be admitted to pass the said patent.

Endorsed: 6 January 1939/40. Conceives the request just and honourable. Will not give way for the passing of the estate by patent in any other way than is desired unless good cause be shown, [as to] which he apprehends not what can be offered. Has entered a caution with his secretary that no such grant pass the writer's hand till, [etc., etc.].

Wentworth 355.

1639/40

156. M. Herbert to Francis Herbert, esq., at London.

"Good Sonne". Has sent the white nag and his mare; caused Cheese to take her to Eale, the best horse-leech in these parts. The grey gelding will endure no travel—must sell him for a coach-horse. The "ball" gelding is very lusty.

Prays God he has come to some agreement in this troublesome business. He does well not to consent to Whitmore's motion for friends in the country to have a hand in it, for they will never yield to reason. Herbert's best friends are "above"; he has none in the country to equal "his" but Sir Robert Harley—knows none but him and Mr. Moore that they can trust. The Herefordshire lands were a fair portion for "them" to have, paying all the debts out of them, too. Elton, if it were out of lease, is well worth £160 a year, and Rushock £140. Lady Foxe holds £100 of Hereford shire lands per annum. So it comes to £400 in all—more if racked. [As] for Corbett's title, if Mr. Whitmore and Herbert agree, he might easily be put by, but if they agree for a sum of money they will yet have a suit with them for those lands. Whittmore's wife and her brothers could easily prove his claim "little woorth", for they know her brother's meaning was to revoke that as well as Summerset Foxe's deed. Had they not used deceit in it to please their brother, Ned Corbett would have stormed more at the other business. But thinking to have all that land and his share too in Lady Foxe's jointure, he was content with the assurance to his sisters, of whom no doubt he had promise of a share if he stuck to them with friends made by his alliance in Shropshire. So Mr. Whitmore may easily make Corbett's title to the Hereford shire lands void if his wife and her brothers will; and Millarte the priest knew well the deceit of it. Hopes if Herbert agrees for one he agrees for all—means his suit in the Arches, which is the worst of all. If there be no remedy as to the suit in the Court of Requests she must abide the smart of it; her conscience was tender in it, and they would have proved an agreement had she denied it, for Millarte the priest and others would have sworn anything. Hopes, if it go against her, they will not put charges upon her. . . Paid 40s. costs heretofore because it was pretended she had not answered fully. Lent her brother £30, and he had hay of her that year worth £110; and she gave him her father's signet, and the armour they detain still. But what he yields to she will be content with; prizes her ease and quietness and her peace of conscience above all.

His sister Owens writes that Pugh is gone up a very confident man to have his cause sentenced; he brought his wife and daughters great bravery against Christmas and new liveries for his men, and has laid £300 out upon lands in Lanbrinmaire parish. After all this to have a new bill put in will trouble his mind. Thinks the lease Pugh had of Sir Thomas Middleton may be ended before [the suit]; the country needs to look that they do not agree with him for longer than he has. Remembers Herbert's counsel told him he could not dispose of the commons because it was the King's.

8 February.

The rents of Elton, which she sent to London by Mr. John Lloyde, were £53 11s. 2d.; sent of David John's rent for part of Rhusock that he holds from year to year, 53s. 4d.: £56 4s. 6d. in all, which, if he can get it, will be a good help for next term. Gough of the Signet paid his rent into the Court of Wards, which should be £9 at £3 a year, for he paid none since her brother died. No arrearages come in. Has done all she can to "feare" them—seized Tedstill's yoke of oxen and sent them to Shrewsbury, where Keysell took them at £8, and she is to have a colt to make up the rent. It is great trouble and charges, but there's no remedy. Made Tedstill an example to terrify the others because he in open court made it so dangerous to pay rent to them without security. Cousin Whichcott must take up Keysell's bond.

Has sent 10s. by the boy to buy a couple of good, thick, large, old ling, which Boswell might get his brother, being a cook, to choose. The best ling looks very yellow. Last year Normcott chose what was not right old ling, being green. He should have a couple of the best for 7s. or 8s. The 5s. in gold enclosed is to pay cousin Mary Lawley for a commodity she is to send Herbert's wife.

There is great spoil in the "coppyes" by John Hardings. All the men at the ironworks fetch what pleases them. It were good to have a writ to trouble some to make the rest afraid. That "coppy" would yield a good sum if sold now. Phillip Marvin was buried on Friday; it was well they got somewhat of him. Prays Mr. Woodforde be well, for she has been wonderfully troubled with him in her sleep. Hopes Herbert received by Whittingham's man a little trunk with lozenges and a long, red box for cousin Lawlely. Bulkleys came yesterday from Leighton. The cause was [postponed] by reason Lord Cottington was sick, but was heard last Tuesday. Tedstill has cut down above sixty springs of young birches in Bromfields wood in such a way as destroyed sixty young trees; Green and Griffeths met him coming out, and Will Harding and his brother found him cutting them. Is persuaded this lewd villain did it of mere spite.

Armorial seal

Added below the address: Has given the boy 10s. for his charges.

Endorsed with notes (torn) concluding: . . . Perkes's oath in the Court of Wards. 305-6.

1640

157. [Lord Herbert] to Moses Lloyd. *Contemporary copy.*

Perceives he has been to the Island of Kerry and taken security of the tenants for payment of £500 on 8 May. If Sir George Radcliffe will appoint some citizen or merchant of Dublin who may receive it and give security for payment of half here and furnish the rest for the writer's occasions in Ireland, he desires that way. But if Sir George will not recommend any, then Lloyd is to detain the rents in the tenants' hands if safe, or appoint two or three able tenants (Bartstable to be one) to carry the money to Dublin and put it in the hands of Sir Philipp Persevall, an officer of the Court of Wards, to be disposed of as above, telling him the writer takes this boldness by recommendation of Sir Philipp Mainwaring.

Desires all diligence in the passing of the patent; money may be supplied out of [the £500], out of which the King's rent must [also] be paid. He must tell Humphry Githins and the tenants that the writer has made no agreement with his son, so until further order under his hand and seal before witnesses they are to continue payments to the writer. Encloses a letter to the tenants. Prays him enquire when the new Commission of Grace comes to the Hamper Office, and procure all the additions he can to the patent, putting in the names of the plough-lands with as much certainty as possible. Perceives one of his letters came opened; cannot call to mind by whom it was sent, but prays him enquire. Gave no order to Mr. Francis Lloyd for receiving any of his rents, but will give him full satisfaction for his pains. Hopes the £20 sent lately will only be used upon necessary occasions. He shall hear further concerning the lawsuits as soon as he speaks with the Lord Lieutenant and Sir Philipp Mainwaring.

Tuttle Street,
21 April. 360.

1640

158. [Sir] Geo. Radcliffe's Power of Attorney to Moyses Lloyd. *Contemporary copy.*

Whereas Edward, Lord Herbert, has authorized him to appoint attorney to set all his lands within this kingdom of Ireland lately in the tenure of Viscountess Baltinglass deceased for the term of one year beginning 1 May next, he appoints Moyses Lloyd, gent., as his attorney, [etc., etc.].

In the presence of:
Rob. Meredith
Thomas Littell

11 May.

358.

"1 May next" is not apparently a mistake—see Nos. 161 and 162.

1640

159. Moyses Lloyd to Lord Herbert at Mountgom[er]y Castle.

Received on 9 September his of 17 August commanding him to take Sjt. Eustace's opinion concerning the additions in the new *fiant*. Sjt.

Eustace was gone the circuit into Mounster and returned 9 September; he could not "disspach mee" at his country house at Harris Town, but on the 12th at his chamber in Dublin he perused the *fiants*, and is of opinion the additions are very material and profitable to be inserted. Sjt. Sambedge was of the same opinion. On 10 September Sir George Radcliff landed in Irland. On the 21st Lord Herbert's counsel and Mr. Cussack met at Sir George's chamber, and after long conference were all of opinion the additions will be granted when the Commissioners sit, which will not be before the term unless he can prevail with Sir George to have a private meeting of it.

Is also to inform him that Garrett mc Pattericke Peiers with divers others of his confederates encroach [upon] and disturb Lord Herbert's tenants, as appears in the petition preferred against them in Lord Herbert's name by advice of Sjt. Sambedge (that is now King's Solicitor). None has appeared yet; hopes to have an attachment against them all. Sent the like letter to Londen for fear he was gone from Mountgomry Castle.

Lord Herbert wrote that he would send a draft of the deed that Sir Phillipp Mannwaring and Sir George Radcliffe are to seal unto him and Mr. Richard Herbert with the uses in the tripartite deed of 6 April, 12 Charles (that the land may be reconveyed back to his lordship and Mr. Richard Herbert). It should be ready to seal immediately the patent is sealed. He should write to Sir George Radcliffe to assist in his business here and to thank him, and to Sir William Sambedge in regard he is one of Lord Herbert's counsel. Had nothing to write by Mr. Frances Lloyd's man; could not trust him, for he reported in town he came over about Lord Herbert's business—knows the contrary. Mr. Francis Lloyd is not like to "come out", being charged with above £400; endeavoured all he could, but cannot please him unless he wrongs Lord Herbert and himself.

Dublin,
25 September. *Armorial seal* 356.

1640

160. Moyses Lloyd to Lord Herbert, one of His Majesty's Council of War, at Mountgom[er]y Castle.

Received by the bearer, David Price, his letter concerning the additions in the *fiant*. Brought Mr. Cussack to Sir George, who wished the former to insert the additions in the order of composition, and he would appoint a time for Commissioners for Defective Titles to meet and grant a new order. Sends a copy of what Mr. Cussack did and what must be omitted out of the *fiant*—Balla mc Adams, Tullig Edmond, and Drom le Gowgh, in regard [the first two] are recovered from Lord Herbert "as yett", and Dromlegaygh is not in his possession. Sent an attachment against Garrett Mc Patterick Piers and his defendants which will cost every man of them £4 10s. [for] their contempts; the pursuivant is gone for them. Parliament began 1 October, sat for one hour, and is put off till 5 October. Is advised not to proffer the petition against Garrett Mc Patterick Piers and Morris Hussy until they have answered the suit begun. Had the petition drawn according to the tenants' directions under their hands; told them if they failed in their proof they should stand to the charge of the suit. Delivered Mr. Frances Lloyd 40s. Will enquire what the tenants will do concerning building, and upon what terms the merchants of Youghall will return moneys.

Dublin,
1 October, 357.

1640

161. MOYSES LLOYD TO LORD HERBERT AT HIS HOUSE IN TUTL STREET NEAR WESTMINSTER.

Received his three letters—the last, dated 15 December, on the 22nd. Delivered Sir Phillip Percivale £250 to be returned to Mr. Orias Churcman for Lord Herbert's use. Delivered him the rest of the rents; he promised it should be returned without charge. It is reported he is for Londen, and Mr. Thomas Litle and many more. Moneys for the King's rents are ready. Received but £440 of this gale's rent, and that with much ado, for corn and cattle yield [only] half last year's value. The arrears are secured by able men to be paid at Ladyday; makes no doubt of the loss of any part. If he confers with some of the noblemen that have estates in Irland, he will hear them complain moneys were not so hard to come by this twenty years.

If he cannot come over himself, asks authority before Ladyday [to make leases], for every man will be providing then to settle himself. There are three principal tenants that hinder the raising of his lands—Mr. John West, Mr. John fits Gerald, and Mr. Garrett fitts Gearald. They hold half the seigniory and more, and are so great that none dares offer for their lands. But if he comes over himself they will raise their rents much before they part with their land. Mr. West has bestowed much in building, and has gained so much in that seat that no reasonable sum shall make him remove. Mr. Garrett fits Geareld has a farm under the Earl of Corke of four or five plough-lands joining the land he holds under Lord Herbert, and has built there very good buildings with Lord Herbert's timber; the tenants under him on Lord Herbert's lands, above 350 persons, pay the Lord's rent and more in cattle and other customs—which is the impoverishment of the poor tenants. Mr. John fits Gearald has no lands but what he holds under Lord Herbert, and will improve what is fit before he removes. If he cannot come over before Ladyday, he should look over the applotment the writer sent, and charge forty or fifty shillings upon every ploughland—more upon some, especially upon these three. He may improve his lands, hard as the times are.

[Reminds] him of a letter Mr. Cooke, the parson of the seigniory, sent him; he said he would resign into Lord Herbert's hand two parish churches, Ballakaslane and Killinterna, both worth £100 a year. No service has been read in either this twenty years, and the parishioners are all willing Lord Herbert should have the profit [rather] than Mr. Cooke. The Islands church is too much for Cooke unless he repairs the church and took more pains; he is a better lawyer than divine, and has some of the demesne for glebe. £8 yearly was applotted out of the tithes of Killinterna to make the sum £1,000; Cooke claims that and hindered the tenants paying it. Had a distress and left it in the appraisor's hands, but the tenants said Cooke would replevy; hears nothing yet. Is informed that if Lord Herbert please, Mr. Cooke may be outed from all his "bennefitts".

Humfrey Gittins has condescended before Lord Herbert's counsel to have the [? additions] in the *fiant*; he "complaynes for mayntenance", and has received from the tenants and the writer £14 10s. of the old arrears, promising Mr. Griffithes of Sutton should pay it to Robert Browne, Lord Herbert's bailie—has his bond for it. Knows no reason Lord Herbert should maintain "us both" here—he confessed his master charged him not to come over before the patent passed. If Lord Herbert be pleased he have moneys upon his bond, he is very sufficient. Mr. Francis Lloyd is at liberty, and demands forty shillings for his fee last term; knows nothing he did for Lord Herbert. No act is passed for passing patents yet; it is expected next sitting, which is 26 January. Lord Dillon and Sir William P[a]rsonnes were sworn justices 29 December. Will do nothing about passing the patent before hearing from him. Humfrey Gittins promised to satisfy Lord Herbert as to Balla mc Adamis. Has Lord Herbert's petition in the Clerk of the Council's hands since Michaelmas—but could not be read yet—for Balla mc Adamis and Tullig Edmonds against Garrett fits Pattruck and Husey. No doubt of receiving the lands if Lord Herbert were here in person. Has not given Mr. Littl the £10 in regard he has his lordship's moneys in his hands. [Neither] Lord Kerry nor Dominik Roch have rejoined to Lord Herbert's replication. They would [have] commissions *ex parte* to examine witnesses, which is merely to delay and put him to more charges—because the place is far off there could be no further proceeding because of the parliament, and of late no Deputy nor Justice.

Dublin,

29 December. *HM*2.22/3.

A copy of Sir Philip Perceval's receipt for the £250 is attached. Humfrey Gittins's "master" is Lord Herbert's son Richard.

1640/41

162. [Lord Herbert] to Moses Lloyd. *Contemporary copy.*

Hopes to get a copy of the new Commission of Grace here. Would have him send the opinion of Sir William Sambedge and the rest of the writer's counsel under their hands, that he may pass the patent upon the last Commission of Grace by virtue of the new act, or otherwise. And he is to wish Sir Phillip Percivall to write his opinion, and how long he thinks the parliament will last. Wrote in his last about Mr. West's and Mr. Fitz Gerald's improving 50s. in every plough-land, which he may show them. Also wrote to Mr. Cooke concerning his surrendering the parsonages. Allows all moneys in Mr. Thomas Littell's hands above £10, which he gave him, towards payment of the surveyors by direction of Sir Phillip Percivall, providing it exceed not £30. Understands he has deposited all rents in Sir Phillip's hands. Sent him power to set the lands for this year, but would not have him absent when the writer comes or sends to renew the patent in Parliament.

22 February.

Has written twice to Sir Phillip Percivall without answer, so forbears this time.

Copia vera: Rich. Boswood 362.

1640/41

163. [LORD HERBERT] TO MOSES LLOYD. *Contemporary copy.*

He seems to have forgotten the writer's postscript concerning Mr. West. Because he says it is requisite that one Mr. John Hassett assist him about the lands, he has written a letter for that purpose. Hopes he received the letter to Master Cooke and has got the money from Mr. Thomas Littell. Perceives the business[es] of Ireland are not so settled that it is fit to proceed [with] Balemac Adam. He promises when he goes to the Island to bring May rents and arrears and improve 40s. or 50s. in every plough-land. Has written to Sir Phillip Percivall. He said he could make Dr. Cooke lose one of his livings "and never bee seene in it"; prays him do it. Will allow him £10 towards his clothes upon bringing home the rents in arrear. Will expect a reasonable note of disbursements, but he may assure himself that if he has proceeded faithfully he will reward him. Takes it unkindly that cousin Frauncis Lloyd does not give more assistance.

23 March. *Cop. ver.*: Rich. Boswood 363.

John Blennerhassett, of Ballyseedy, was High Sheriff of co. Kerry this year.

1641

164. MOYSES LLOYD TO LORD HERBERT . . . AT HIS HOUSE IN TUTTLE STREET, NEAR WESTMINSTER.

Received his dated 13 March the last day of April; delivered a letter enclosed to Mr. Hashett, who promised to assist the improving of Lord Herbert's lands. The certainty of the improvement he is not able yet to inform him; they and the chief tenants could not have a meeting in the Island (the subsidies and quarter sessions the cause). Mr. Cooke, the parson of the Island, died Easter Day; has obtained sequestration upon the tithes of the three parishes in his and Mr. John Hashett's names to Lord Herbert's use. The tithes are not yet settled; hopes they and glebe will amount to £140 at least. There were great means made for the place, but Dean Graye, who is in stead of the bishop, granted sequestration and said Lord Herbert is to present within six months after he receives notice under seal of the court, [failing which] it falls to the Archbishop of Causiall. Has got a promise from an able minister to perform the place for six months. He may mind there was in Dublin a Caunaurvon shire man, very able; [he said] Mr. Thelwell of Place Gough and Mr. Jon Loyd of Rueedocke would write to Lord Herbert in his behalf . . .

Has sent to Dublin to enter caveats against all grants or patents until he can go [there]. Has received some arrears and very little of this half year's rent. Cannot resolve him concerning Dean Coate before coming to Dublin. As for himself, here entrusted by Lord Herbert, if ever he cozens him or takes bribes or courtesies from any to hinder him sixpence, let him suffer what punishment he pleases. If he has spent somewhat extraordinary in expenses, he will give satisfaction.

Island Town,
3 May.

If he will direct his letters from the Letter Office to Mr. Henry Williams at Sir William Sambedge's house near the Wood Quay in Dublin, he will convey them to the Island. *HM*2.23/3.

"Dean Coate" is William Coote, D.D., Dean of Down.

1641

165. [LORD HERBERT] TO MOSES LLOYD. *Contemporary copy.*

The improvements he has made in the seigniory this year are far short of what he expected, many who know the lands affirming they are well worth £2,000 per annum, let from year to year. Master Anthony Tierens has accepted Lloyd's bill of exchange; but he has much forgot himself if he did anything in this without Sir Phillip Percivall's direction. Desires a particular of the tithes of the three parishes (except the glebe, which Lloyd says are the writer's), the names of the two parishes he thinks fit to go together, and the form of a presentation in Ireland. He must send the names of those thirty-five plough-lands out of his possession and the names of those ancient men living that will prove them to have been in Sir William Herbert's. He must pay Sir Phillip Percivall all money in his hands, who will furnish his necessary expenses and [those of] the lawsuits. He must give Sir Phillip a particular of the plough-lands in the seigniory, with the number of acres in the survey.

6 July. *Cop. vera*: Rich. Boswood 364.

1641

166. ORDER OF THE HOUSE OF LORDS.

Whereas Sir George Ratcliff and Sir Phill. Manwaring have been entrusted by Lord Harbert and Rich. Harbert, esq., his son, for passing an estate in Ireland, now in Lord Harbert's possession, it is ordered that the lands be passed over by Sir George Ratcliff to such persons as Lord Harbert nominates, under the trusts expressed, and to no other; and that no danger accrue to Lord Harbert or Richard Harbert, or any claiming under them.

Jo. Browne,
17 August. *Cleric. Parliamentor.*
*HM*2.22/4.

The next document in the bundle, at one time stitched to this, is an 'office copy' of the order.

1641

167. FRAN. LLOYD TO LORD HERBERT . . . AT HIS HOUSE IN TUTTLE STREET, NEAR WEST MESTER.

"In this millitary time, and of the event of this Rebellion . . . for the Rebellion it does grow in the Kingdome more and more". . . (*unfinished*). Scarce a secure place in the kingdom—the further part of

Monester the securest. For the service on "our" side six companies marched on Saturday from Dublin with half of Lord Ormond's troop, with powder and arms to relieve Drokeda; being appointed by the Lords Justices [and] the Lord General to march through on Sunday night, Sir Henry Tychborne with one troop of horse and five foot companies coming to meet them for a convoy. On Monday morning, being very misty, within three miles of Drokeda, near Lord Netterfild's house, a horse-scout, discovering the rebel, gave notice to the captain of this half troop, Capt. Wayes, and Sergt.-Maj. Roper, leader of "our" half regiment, of the rebels being half a mile off, their foot being near 3,000 and horse 300; the like caution being given by Lord Goromaston. [That] morning they [had] marched from Bal Rudrey, and were advertised by his lordship not to march on. However, they marched on in this great mist, and, being within a quarter of a mile of the rebel, the captain of the troop and Roper (a younger brother of the Lord's, a beardless boy) had a parley. The sergeant-major, being within musket shot of the rebel, drew his own and the next two companies into a body and marched on [with] the ammunition in the middle, and the other three companies in file and rank after him. They marched from the plain, over a ditch, a lane, and another ditch, to the field where the rebel was. The foot, being out of order in climbing over those ditches, were brought on by Roper breast and face to the rebel, his own company first. Where the poor soldiers expected the word of giving fire, he gave the word "to the Right Hand File counter march", which—he is informed by one Phillip Price, a Seropshere man in Capt. Alederidge's company—[put] their backs to the rebel. Thereupon the rebel gave the charge. Some of Roper's company said they have ordnance. Thereupon his company did fly and the rest followed. The enemy horse pursued them and all the English to slaughter. Where the battle was fought were killed but Capt. Allderidge and one Manwaring, his ensign-bearer; the rest killed in pursuit. They cast away their arms, and the ammunition was all taken. This man says further that Capt. Wayes charged the rebel with his troop, and, having brought them to rank again, charged the second time; he saw but three fellows of all the troop give fire with him, they being all Irish and Papists.

Capt. Patrick Waimes writes from Drokeda to the State, confessing that he promised Col. Tychborne to be with him Sunday with the foot, but the first day could make them march no further than Swordes. He says that when he was ready to charge, one of his troop rode up and said all the foot were fled; thereupon the trumpeter sounded a retreat, and only he gave fire. He discovered the rebel foot to be in three bodies; and three troops of horse, the first with pistols and "ceribins", the other two with demi-lances or half pikes. In short, the horse puts it on the foot, the foot on the horse—the loss, the poor English and ammunition. "Thus wee are like to perish," unless aid come suddenly out of England.

Dublin, Wood Quay,
2 December.

Of "our" six hundred there be five hundred killed and fled to the enemy. Col. O Reeley was the rebel commander, one that Sir Piers

Crosby knew in France, colonel of a regiment of foot, afterwards commanding the horse for three years. "We" need experienced commanders, and the soldiers to be English, Welsh, and Scots. "Els I must not live longer."

Armorial seal 365.

"Wayes" and "Waimes" are Sir Patrick Wemys, recently knighted. Sergeant-Major Christopher Roper was apparently a younger son of Lord Herbert's former tenant of the Castle Island estate. This account of the Battle of Julianstown, though in general agreement with others, differs in some details and adds some new ones.

1642

168. RICH. HERBERT AND JO. BLAYNEY TO THE CHIEF BAILIFFS OF THE TOWN OF MO. AND TO THE SERJEANTS-AT-MACE. *Contemporary copy.*

These are in His Majesty's name to require them to assess and levy £6 upon the freeholders and inhab[itan]ts of the said town and liberty for providing two soldiers to bear the arms of their town to serve the King at garrison at Bridgnorth. Hereof fail not [etc., etc.]. If any refuse they are to bring them before the signatories.

Montgomery,
16 November. 366.

1643

169. EDWARDE FOXE TO SIR CHARLES FOX.

Has not been well this five weeks. Spoke with him at the Crown about the £7 10s. rent long due for the coal-mines. Bore with him in respect he owed him money—for which he paid use, for Sir Charles had of Mr. Walter Langford for the Valetts Woods in Bouth Leasow sixteen nobles and the crops of hedges. Besides, the writer's wife should have had £50 for her good will for acknowledging the fine of the lordship of Sintton, to which consent was procured but by the writer's son and Charles Prince. Once again sends this poor bearer for the rent, hoping his conscience will better consider thereof. Was always willing to pleasure him, and joined with him in any cause. Means not to send any more, "but as you deale with me, so god reward you".

Has sent an obligation of Sir Charles'. . . . Sir Charles had some writing[s] of the writer's lands that Jhon Powell had for the warranty of the coal-mines; requests he sends them.

Endorsed: Received by Jevan Davis the last of Decmber 1643.

309.

The writer is probably Edward Fox of Ludlow.

1644

170. [LORD] MUSKERY TO LORD HARBERT.

The writer's cousin Butler has been very importunate in Lord Herbert's business of the county of Kerry, and has brought to the writer at Killkenny the Lord Lieutenant-General's letter, with a certificate of credit which tells that Lord Herbert's tenants have no way tasted the miseries of war, yet make that their pretence to deceive him. Answered the

Marquis's letter that so soon as cousin Butler returns (by which he hopes the peace will be settled here), bringing Lord Herbert's authority, he shall have both the writer's and his friends' assistance for settling his estate and recovering his arrears.

Dublin. 368.

The year was inserted by the writer, but no date.

1644

171. Lieut.-Col. James Till's Undertakings to Lord Herbert.

James Till, gent., Lieut-Col. of Horse, promises in the name of Sir Thomas Midleton that no violence shall be offered to the person or goods of Lord Herbert or any within his castle of Mountgom[er]y. They shall have liberty to go out and carry away their goods whensoever they will. A good convoy shall be granted as far as Coventry and recommendations given for their further conveying to London. Meanwhile an inventory shall be taken of all the household stuff, books, trunks, and writings in the castle. All horses and cattle in and about the castle and all victuals, wine, and beer shall be for the use of Lord Herbert. No money, silver, gold, or plate shall be taken from him or his family. The castle with all the goods, books, and arms shall be restored to Lord Herbert if God sends peace or Parliament orders it. Meanwhile Lord Herbert with his daughter and family shall continue in or return if they please to the castle, and carry into it all provision necessary.

James Till

Witness: Jo. Burton

It is further agreed that Sir Thomas Midleton shall sign and seal this if Lord Herbert require it, and shall assist Lord Herbert's bailiffs for levying his rents, and also preserve his woods and deer.

Half past 12 at night, James Till

Thursday, 5 "August". Jo. Burton

And it is further agreed that as long as Lord Herbert or his daughter continue in the castle there shall not exceed (*blank*) persons or soldiers unless imminent danger appears. And no trunks or doors under locks and keys shall be broke open. And if Lord Herbert [leaves] he shall have half a dozen men-servants within the castle to do his business and three or four maids to attend his daughter. And if anything be required for his further contentment it shall be lawful to add the same.

James Till

Witnesses: Hugh Pryce, Edw. Price, Oliv[er] Herbert, Rowland Evans, Daniel Edwards

*HM*2.9/1.

"August" is a mistake for September.

1644

172. Capitulations between Lord Herbert and Sir Tho. Myddleton

(*Consists of Lieut.-Col. Till's undertakings, as in the preceding document, with the following added.*) Whereas there is doubt what goods should be removed out of the castle by Lord Herbert, it is agreed there shall be left six beds for soldiers, one suite of hangings in the dining-room in the new castle, one suite of hangings and furniture for a chamber in the said castle wherein Sir Thomas Myddleton shall please to lodge, and one bed with furniture for a captain. And no person shall enter into Lord Herbert's library or study or the two rooms adjoining. And Lord Herbert shall remove all his [other] goods when he thinks fit.

"I am content to stand to all the abovespecified agreemente . . ."

6 September. Tho. Myddelton

Hugh Price Edw. Price
Sam. More Oliver Herbert
Rowland Evans Daniel Edwards

Copia vera: Rowland Evans
John Pulford Ja. Heath *HM*2.9/2.

The counterpart of the original of this document (i.e., that signed by Lord Herbert) is printed in full in *Royal Commission on Historical Manuscripts*, *6th Report*, Pt. 1, p. 28, and in *The Autobiography of Lord Herbert*, ed. Lee, p. 154, n. 1.

1644

173. LIEUT.-COL. JAMES TILL'S AND CAPT. SAMUEL MORE'S ACCOUNT OF THE TAKING OF MONTGOMERY CASTLE. *Contemporary copy.*

Sir Thomas Middleton, coming suddenly to Mountgomry upon Wednesday 4 September with about 800 foot and horse, and the King's soldiers lodged there and in adjoining parishes retiring there, sent Lord Herbert a summons to yield; who entered into a parley, and by Capt. Samuel More offered a large sum to free him and his tenants and neighbours from plunder and his castle from a siege, desiring answer the next Friday morning at nine; which was granted upon condition Lord Herbert would discharge some of his garrison, because they meant to place great store of powder, newly intercepted in Mountgomry shire, within the outworks for that night (pretending that if the garrison remained entirely there the powder might be seized), this condition being accepted by Lord Herbert. James Till, Lieut-Col. of Horse, accompanied with strong forces, and having a petard with him, came into the gates of the castle upon Thursday night about twelve, and causing a trumpet to be sounded, required that the castle be "presently" yielded. Whereupon Lord Herbert came to the gates, and finding Lieut-Col. Till with others between the gate and drawbridge, desired them to retreat, since the business was deferred until next morning. But [Till] requiring a present answer, and affirming he had a petard, gave that terror to Lord Herbert's servants and garrison that some leaped over the wall. Others cried quarter, which perceived by Lord Herbert he demanded again that Lieut.-Col. Till retire. Which though the lieutenant-colonel refused, yet he said he would give all reasonable conditions. Whereupon Lord Herbert entered into a treaty with them and obtained conditions subscribed by Lieut.-Col. Till and afterwards by Sir Thomas Middleton.

James Till
Mountgomry Castle, Sam. More
10 September. *Copia vera*: Rowland Evans *HM*2.9/3.

1644

174. [SIR] THO. MYDDELTON TO [THE COMMITTEE OF BOTH HOUSES]. *Contemporary copy.*

Finds that Lord Herbert did not appear at any time in the Commission of Array, though appointed a commissioner, and was not at any of the assemblies of the Lords at Yorke, Oxford, or anywhere else, but has been at home two years three months attending the recovery of his health; he furnished no money for dragooneers, as alleged in the House of Commons, and has done nothing to offend Parliament since his departure thence. Believes he has been ever careful to observe respect to both Houses, though many times pressed to things that might argue the contrary. Certifies the truth hereof to the intent Lord Herbert may be clear in their good opinion and restored to his former place and goods. And if Lord Herbert's health serve him not for public business, he desires leave to attend it by the advice of physicians. As for the manner the writer is in possession of his castle of Mountgomry, he refers it to the enclosed and Lord Herbert at his coming up (which shall be shortly, being desirous to be where remedies for his health may be had).

Mountgomry Castle, *Vera copia*: Rowland Evans
18 September. Dan. Edwards

*HM*2.9/4.

The enclosure is presumably Till's and More's account, No. 173.

1644

175. [SIR] WILL. BRERETON, [SIR] JO. MELDRUM, AND [SIR] THO. MYDDELTON TO THE GOVERNORS OF OSVESTRIE, VEM, STAFFORD, DERBIE, COVENTRIE, OR ANYWHERE ELSE IN [LORD HERBERT'S] JOURNEY TOWARDS LONDON.

Whereas Lord Herbert, engaged within his castle of Montgommerie by a siege, has been relieved by the King and Parliament through forces under "my" conduct, and desires to retire to London for his health, these are to entreat all governors and officers where his lordship and his train happen to pass for assistance by a convoy of a hundred horses if he requires the same. It is intended he be at no charge in this convoy but at his discretion.

Montgommerie Castle,
18 September. 367.

1644

176. [LORD HERBERT] TO SIR THOMAS MIDDLETON. *Contemporary copy.*

Has acquainted his daughter with some business in which he desires his favour and assistance, particularly concerning levying and returning his rents to London or where else he shall be; also that he would certify the Committee for Both Kingdoms what losses he sustained and is likely to sustain upon quitting his castle, that he may receive satisfaction, but above all that he be no loser of his goods in London. "I pray you at least love mee (as y'r father charged yow) and my Grandchildren"—hopes Myddelton will take care they may not want necessaries. Doubts not he will punctually perform the agreement [of] 5 September.

Stafford,
ult. September. *Copia vera*: Row. Evans.

Endorsed: Sent per Whateley. *HM*2.9/5

1644

177. CHA. GERARD TO COL. RICHARD HERBERT, GOVERNOR OF THE TOWN AND CASTLE OF NEWPORT.

Authorizes him by virtue of "the right you challenge by Patent" for the lordship of Llebeneth, co. Monmouth, to seize the estate of (*blank*) Vicaridg of Bristoll, now in London and in rebellion against His Majesty, and to demand and receive all rents, etc., due from his tenants. And if any refuse he is to take a party of horse or foot and seize their persons and estates as disaffected to His Majesty.

19 October.

Endorsement (*barely legible*): . . . of [? William] Jenkyns' land of Brad Street in the parish of Nashe . . . 1644. Marye Gylles tenant.

*HM*2.12/35.

Col. Gerard (the later Earl of Macclesfield) was Commander-in-Chief of South Wales. The person referred to here is doubtless the Richard Vickris, Bristol merchant, whose losses "to the enemy" had been mentioned six months earlier (*Cal. of State Papers, Domestic*, 1644, p. 120).

1644

178. [PRINCE] RUPERT TO——————.

Is informed that £100 by way of privy seal was imposed upon Sir Basill Brookes, which Sir Abraham Shipman pretends to be assigned to him and thereupon has imprisoned divers of his servants. Desires they be forthwith enlarged if there be no other just cause of their restraint, and what of that £100 remains unpaid be not collected by Sir Abraham. It is assigned to be paid at Oxford, and undertaken to be performed as soon as he certifies the arrear, which he is to do with speed, likewise what is in arrear from others for privy seal money, in particular from Sir Thomas Whitmore, who was assessed with his son at £200.

Oxford,
18 December. *HM*2.12/36.

1644

179. CERTIFICATE OF THE LOSSES OF LORD HERBERT AND THE INHABITANTS OF THE TOWN OF MOUNTGOMERY UPON THE SURRENDER OF MOUNTGOMERY CASTLE.

Losses of Lord Herbert in his castle, parks adjoining, farms, and non-payment of rents from his tenants, that have been heavily plundered by the armies assembled late at Mountgom[er]y:

	£	s.	d.
Plundered by the King's arms from his farm at Stallo, 40 kine, 12 oxen, other cattle, corn, etc.	520	0	0

	£	s.	d.
Lost by his tenant there.	600	0	0
Plundered from his farm at Llyssyn, 18 lean kine, 6 oxen, 200 sheep, horses and mares, butter, cheese, and household stuff by the King's army.	182	10	0
Plundered and lost in his farm at Walcott Lodge.	100	0	0
His two parks thrown open, woods cut, pales, rails, and posts burnt and taken away, deer, game, and fish-pools most part destroyed by the two armies coming into Mountgom[er]y shire, and the continual destroying of it.	1500	0	0
Loss of rents for this year in Mountgom[er]y by the armies' continual scoutings.	698	5	8
Loss of rents in Chirbury.	318	6	8
In Anglisey and Carnarvon shire, loss of rents.	228	0	0
Loss of rents this year by the coming of the armies in his lordship of Llanwothen, parish of Llannervile, Llangadvan, etc., in the collection of Wichan Jones, John Lloyde, and Evan Lloyde.	472	12	0
Loss of rents in the collection of Edwarde Richardes and Lodoick Lewis.	134	0	0
Loss of fees and rents from the audit of Northwales this year.	27	0	0
Plundered out of his two parks in cattle and horses.	120	0	0
Loss of the profits of the hundred of Chirbury.	40	0	0
R. Thompson	4940	14	0
Moyses Lloyd	[*sic*]		

Losses, plunderings, and burnings that the inhabitants in the town and liberties of Mountgom[er]y sustained, by particulars on record in the town, by the King's army under Col. Broughton and other damnifications by Parliament's army under Sir Thomas Midleton: Richarde Davies, bailiff, in cattles, household stuff, money, etc., £137 2s.; Philemon Mason, bailiff, in cattles, household stuff, his shop, etc., £98 14s.; Richarde Whittingham, in cattles, grain, household stuff, etc., £176 11s.; John Mason, mercer, in house and shop, etc., £140; William Coote, doctor in divinity and rector of Mountgom[er]y, in tithes, books, etc., £60; Richarde Thompson, in cattles, money, household stuff, etc., £223 15s.; Hugh Bennett, mercer, in his shop, two houses, etc., £150; Roberte Powell, in burning of house, goods, and loss of cattles, etc., £124 15s.; Reighnald Lloyde and John Lloyde, in goods, cattles, etc., £114 10s.; John Justice, £64 5s.; Mathew Lowe, £46 15s.; (*the list continues with sixty-four further names, the amounts ranging from £2 2s. 6d. to £140*). Total, £3,066 12s. 10d., besides some that have not brought in their particulars.

Richard Davies } Bailiffs of
Philemon Mason } Mountgom[er]y

Moyses Lloyd

Charles Broughton }
R. Thompson } Aldermen
Hugh Bennett }

*HM*2.9/42.

The second total, like the first, is incorrect, so also is a grand total of the two. In the continuation of the second list the £140 was the claim of Lord Herbert's servant Moyses Lloyd; one other amount exceeds £100, seven are between £50 and £100, nineteen are between £25 and £50, and the rest are under £25. Three houses, besides Robert Powell's, are mentioned as having been burnt.

1644/5

180. ESAY THOMAS TO FRAUNCIS HERBERT, ESQ., OR IN HIS ABSENCE TO HIS MOTHER, "MY DEARE AUNT", MRS. MARGARET HERBERT, AT BROMFIELD.

His man left £32 of Herbert's money to be disposed of in buying "w'tt Rags, yow know where". Doubts not he heard of the writer's intended surprisal, an unsavoury requittal for his constant love to the good of those parts. What could not be then performed, though Herbert's dear sister participated, is now this week acted, two horse-loads of tobacco, costing £26, being plundered. To conclude the tragedy he is informed that John Evans, the writer's agent and Herbert's servant, was surprised on Thursday in Machyntleth and carried away to Aberustwith Castle upon pretence he "hath already and knowes to some Money of myne". In addition, there are plundered and taken with John Evans six webs of those Sane Day paid for, by the practice of Sir Rich. Pryce, Thos. Prise of Ynnysgrigogge and his son, and Col. Whitney. Knows not where to desire relief "soe Remoate" otherwise than to Herbert. Requests his uttermost endeavours by his letters and friends, letting them know the writer has protections at large, both from the King and Prince Rupert, for his person and estate of every kind. Supposes John Boswell acquaints him how Mountgom[er]y garrison took on Tuesday night Jno. Pugh Rees, Jno. Galler, Rowland Thomas, Thomas Swayne, Jno. Evans, carrier, and Thomas Parry, all in their return from Shrewsbury, with their horses and carriages and above £20 worth of good hops of the writer's, which cannot be got off upon any terms, nor they enlarged. So he may discern his causeless oppressions on both sides. Lives in hope of some comfort from him in support of his drooping spirit.

B. C.,

15 February, very late.

Addition by Mrs. Thomas: Her husband gone to bed scarce well. Robert Evans, newly come, confirms all above written and desires some letter or warrant from Sir Michael Woodhous in case he cannot send to Prince Morrice in so short a time. Longs for the release of the poor man more than the loss of all her goods. Sarah Thomas

Armorial seal 369.

The letter is written from Bishop's Castle, for which borough Thomas was Member of Parliament.

1644/5

181. ORDER OF THE HOUSE OF COMMONS. *Contemporary copy.*

Upon a report this day from the Committee for Sequestration (to which Lord Herbert's petition was referred by order of the Lords and Commons) that it was of opinion, and so ordered 1 January last, that he should have £20 weekly: Ordered by the Commons that £20 per week be allowed him, £10 by the Committee of the Revenue and £10 by the Committee for Advance of Moneys at Haberdashers' Hall.

H. Elsynge, *Cler. Parl., Do. Com.*

25 February. *HM*2.9/9.

1645

182. CERTIFICATE BY ROWLAND EVANS.

These are to certify that he heard John Thomas of Dudston tell Lord Herbert that he (being with Sir Thomas Middleton a little before the coming of his forces to Mountgomry Castle about 5 September 1644) heard Sir Thomas say he would not meddle with Lord Herbert nor his said castle . . .

8 April. *HM*2.9/10.

1645/6

183. RIC. HERBERT TO FRANCIS HERBERT, ESQ., AT RHUSAISON.

"Honored Father." His brother and he have viewed [one another's] letters from him, according to his command, and trust to have grace to follow his instructions. Was in fault in not taking more care in writing his last letter; intends by no means to neglect either his book or pen, which if a man wants he is nothing esteemed. Preston said the writer's father would have him come up, but his grandmother would give him no credit. Service to his aunt Owenes and respects to his cousins and cousin Randall.

Oa. Park,
21 January. 370.

"Aunt Owenes" is Elizabeth Owen, widow of Athelstan Owen of Rhiwsaeson. "Oa. Park" is Oakly Park, near Ludlow.

1646

184. [Colonel] THO. MORGAN TO ALL OFFICERS, SOLDIERS, AND OTHERS.

Commands them to do no violence to the persons of the Hon. Richard Herbert, his lady, children, or family at Carlyon or St. Gillions, nor to plunder horses, cattle, household stuff [etc.] provided he be obedient to every order and ordinance of Parliament. . . . .

The leaguer before Raglan Castle,
9 June. *HM*2.12/40.

1646

185. [LORD] HERBERT TO MR. ROBT. GRIFFITH AT MONTGOMERY CASTLE OR SUTTON.

"Honest Ro. Griffith." Encloses a letter to his daughter, which he prays him deliver when he has perused it. He may see therein his intentions. 'Tis no longer answers but money he expects, which he is to seriously require from her. If she fails immediately to send as much as she can (and is due out of his rents, etc.), reserving to herself only

£70 for the half year, he will not trust her for the time to come, and she is not to meddle with the Michaelmas rents.

1 September.

His letter of attorney to her is not irrevocable as she pretends. But he will not take his trust from her if she satisfies him by next post-conveyance. Nothing will serve his turn but money; she must trifle with him no longer. He is to read the letter twice or thrice before delivering it and pursue the meaning thereof. Commendation to his father and family.

Armorial seal 371.

[1646]

186. Lord Herbert's Petition to the House [of Commons]. *Contemporary copy.*

Has since the beginning of these troubles been constant to Parliament, and in sequence thereof delivered himself and his castle of Montg. into Parliament's protection under a capitulation dated 6 September 1644, which is in the custody of the Committee for Both Kingdoms. After the surrender he was besieged by a great army of the King's forces, and on that occasion, as also by [Parliament's] keeping a garrison there (which still continues), he suffered losses of many thousand pounds, besides total loss of his lands in Ireland (a third of his estate). All which he will be ready to prove.

Desires, in regard these losses are fallen on him since putting himself into Parliament's protection, the House would take them into consideration. And meanwhile that the allowance of £20 weekly granted for his subsistence may be continued two years longer to begin 1 January next, and arrears satisfied out of some receipt where they may be truly had, his payments in Haberdashers' Hall being very bad for want of money, as is alleged. And if it please God to restore him to sight and hearing he will (so far as his age, 65, will suffer) render all possible services.

[December].

The Earl of Mowgrave had his allowance of £50 weekly until his death. Neither does the order whereby pensions were taken "from those of the Howse of Comons" take away his, since it was granted by both Houses, and given in part reparation for his losses since he surrendered.

*HM*2.9/7.

Lord Herbert slightly exaggerates his age—he was sixty-three at this time. The next document in Volume IX is apparently a draft of a motion in the Commons, based upon this petition (see No. 41 in the Appendix).

[1646]

187. Lord Herbert's Case. *Contemporary copy.*

The "degrees" by which he desires his request to the Commons may be represented by Sir William Waller: 1. His castle was required from him by Sir Tho. Middleton in the way of putting himself under Parliament's protection, as appears by his letter to Lord Herbert dated 4 September 1644. 2. In sequence thereof and of a constant adhering to Parliament he surrendered his castle into Parliament's protection, as appears by [the] capitulation, which, with a certificate of his faithfulness, the Committee of Both Kingdoms has again offered to the consideration of the House. 3. If it be too long to be read he would please acquaint the House with its effect, particularly the clause that he should be assisted for gathering his rents; and that an article was inserted that he might add or explain anything for his advantage—desires the benefit of it for making good his rents.

4. Has not received the fifteenth part of his rents these two last years. And suffered the destruction of all his horses, cattle, deer, and two parks, even to pulling up of post and pale, besides the pulling up of quicksets (laying his grounds waste and common), burning and throwing down of houses (divers of his best farms being deserted for want of tenants), and cutting down of woods at and since the siege of his castle; as he can prove by many witnesses and Mr. Esai Thomas (a member and his next neighbour, who has been lately in the country and can testify) to the value of many thousand pounds. 5. Hopes they will give speedy reparation.

6. Both Houses gave him the £20 weekly, yet he is in arrears many weeks; desires it be "presently" made good and the allowance continued.

7. The Earl of Mulgrave had £50 weekly paid to the last day of his life. Hopes the Houses will not be less favourable to him since his castle and estate were so freely delivered into Parliament's protection, his case differing from those who lost only [in the] wars. His age (65) and defects of sight and hearing render him . . . . not able to be active in their service. And the Houses still keep a garrison in his castle.

[December]. *HM*2.9/12.

The document is endorsed, in a later hand, with the date 1645, but this is clearly wrong. Myddelton's letter referred to under the first head is no doubt the summons to yield mentioned in No. 175.

"1644" [*recte* 1646]

188. [LORD HERBERT] TO MR. FROST. *Contemporary or nearly contemporary copy.*

Having attended a great while the order of the Committee of Both Kingdoms, which was to be reported by Sir William Waller, the writer has prepared his friends for tomorrow to second him in some points which he will propose to the House by the means of Sir William. And because (next Saturday falling within Christmas) if he loses this occasion he will suffer much, he desires him before nine o'clock this night to have the order ready written. It would be convenient also that a copy of the capitulation and the certificate from Sir Thomas Middleton were delivered to Sir William.

Friday, 18 December. *HM*2.9/6.

Gualter Frost was Secretary to the Committee of Both Kingdoms. Sir Thomas Myddelton's "certificate" is No. 174.

[? 1646]

189. MEMBERS OF THE HOUSE OF COMMONS TO ASSIST LORD HERBERT'S REPORT FROM GOLDSMITHS' HALL.

X Sir Anth. Irby, reporter; Mr. Salway; X Sir Robert Harley; Mr. Hen. Herbert to present the petition and "make Mr. St. Johns etc."; X Mr. John Selden; X Sir Benjamyn Rudiard; X Mr. Knightley; X Sir Symonds D'Ewes; X Mr. Scawen; X Sir Willm. Lewes; Mr. John Herbert; Mr. Oldsworth; X Sir John Merrick; X Mr. Arthur Owen; X Col. Willm. Davies; Sir Edward Baynton; X Mr. Esay Thomas; X Mr. Ansloe; old Mr. Salway; Mr. Vaughan, "by my brother"; Mr. Hunt; Mr. Hen. Pelham; Mr. Peregr. Pelham; Sir Tho. Pelham; Mr. Asher [and] Mr. Darley, by Mr. Pulford; Arthur Trevor, "to make Freinds"; Mr. Kylvert, "to make frnds"; Mr. Gape, "to make frends"; Lord Carbery, "to make"; Col. Will. Herbert.

Endorsed in a much later hand: 18 Dec. "1744". *HM*2.21/10.

Not all these were members of the House. The crosses possibly indicate those most to be relied upon, or perhaps those who had already given a promise of support. The phrase "make Mr. St. Johns" apparently means to make friends with Oliver St. John, the Solicitor-General. "Ansloe" must be Arthur Onslowe, member for Bramber. Vaughan and Hunt are probably Henry Vaughan, member for Carmarthenshire, and Thos. Hunte, member for Shrewsbury. There were two Darleys in the House, Henry, representing Northallerton, and Richard, representing New Malton. From Kilvert onwards is in a different hand.

1646

190. ORDER OF A COMMITTEE OF LORDS AND COMMONS THAT ARE OF THE COMMITTEE OF BOTH KINGDOMS. *Contemporary copy.*

That it be reported to the Commons that it is the opinion of this Committee that the outworks of earth of Montgomery Castle should be slighted; and that without further slighting the castle with all goods, ammunition, and arms belonging to Lord Harbert be delivered to him according to the capitulation. And that the capitulation and Sir Thomas Myddelton's letter of 18 September 1644, also a paper given into this Committee by Lord Harbert 24 July last, be also reported to the House. And that Sir Willm. Waller be desired to report the same.

Gualter Frost

22 December. Secr. to the Committee

*HM*2.9/17.

Whether this slighting of the earthen outworks was carried out at this time is uncertain, for the outworks are mentioned again, two and a half years later, when a much more drastic slighting was decided upon (see Nos. 208 ff). This decision to slight the castle had actually been made some months earlier, for the essential part of this order is printed in *Montgomeryshire Collections*, Vol. XX, p. 24, under the date 3 July 1646.

1646

191. HENRY SEILE TO [FRANCIS] HERBERT, ESQ., AT OAKE[LY PARK]. *Much decayed.*

Was glad to see the old handwriting—more glad when he can write some good news. On Saturday the £200,000 was conveyed hence towards the north for payment of the Scots and setting them out of this kingdom. Maj.-Gen. Skippon, who is to be governor of Newcastle, has the guarding of it; his son, as his deputy, is made governor of Bristoll. One moiety is to be paid at Northallert[on], the other five or six miles beyond Newcastle on their march homewards. On Tuesday last the House of Peers voted His Majesty to return to Newmarket with honour and safety. Yesterday the Commons voted his return, but to the Queen's house of Holmby (in the midst of Sir Tho. Fairfax's winter quarters), but have added this morning honour and safety too. On Monday last the Earl of . . . . . disclosed a plot for conveying the [Duke of] Yorke into France . . . . . . [a]gents in the business one Villiers . . . . . . Grandison, Hill, "my Lords owne Bar . . . . and . . . . son". The first two are in custody, bu[t] . . . . . . [f]led.

London,
Christmas Day. *Armorial seal* 372.

Seile was a bookseller, whose shop was at the sign of the Tiger's Head, in Fleet Street. The final passage refers to the disclosure by the Earl of Northumberland of the plot involving Col. Villiers, Richard Johnson or Johnston (one of the King's servants) and others (see *Journals of the House of Lords*, Vol. VIII, pp. 622 and 624-5).

1646/7

192. EDWARD SPENC[ER] TO FRANCIS HERBERT, ESQ., AT OAKLEY PARK.

Understands by his letter that he has received the things sent, but would be glad to know how they fit his body or mind. He and his wife thank him for the good, large cheese, and his charge of carriage. Showed Herbert's postscript to his brother, who will give an account as soon as he can speak with Mr. Okeley or Mr. Moore. His brother has notice from Mr. Jo. Lloyd to pay the writer; thanks Herbert for his care therein. His brother paid what was appointed at Goldsmiths' Hall and delivered the rest to Mr. Okeley.

Lond.,
16 January. 373.

Herbert had the previous August been fined £318 for delinquency, and the fine was passed by the House in November (*Cal. of Proc. of Com. for Compounding*, p. 1240).

[1646/7]

193. [LORD HERBERT'S] ANSWER TO THE HOUSE OF COMMONS. *Contemporary copy.*

Defended his castle above two years against all attempts by the adverse party to put a garrison in. In August 1644, finding he had lost one eye through a defluxion and was in danger of losing the other, and being very infirm, he settled his estates (as appears by an indenture of the 7th of that month, which he has showed to Mr. Speaker) and resolved to come to London, the country being destitute of remedies.

The Parliament forces coming shortly after and desiring him to put himself into Parliament's protection (in those terms he was required), he surrendered his castle to . . . . . Sir Thomas Middleton upon conditions in a capitulation dated 5 September, observance whereof he desires according to the true meaning, which by an article he has liberty to explain. Desires they appoint some committee to consider the capitulation, and he or counsel shall represent what conduces to the right understanding thereof.

Hopes that since he surrendered his castle freely the House will as freely deliver it again without more assurance than is required from others "Members of both Howses", and that he will not be subject to any condition not in his capitulation. And that, according to the true meaning thereof, reasonable compensation be made for his losses before and since the siege, for which he will offer a just particular, and yet will take less than his due. For the rest, he asks that the House will believe that he will no way depart from that fidelity which he has, since the beginning of these troubles, manifested "in a perpetuall sequence", as appears by a certificate of 18 September 1644; and that these testimonies may clear him from scruple. Nothing could grieve him so much as that any assurance should be demanded which reflects upon his reputation and honour.

Nevertheless, if more be required, desires that he with his counsel be permitted to speak before a committee to represent how dangerous it will be for him to depart from the capitulation, since it might make him responsible in life and estate if ill accident happen.

If it please the House freely to restore possession of his castle and give reasonable recompense for his losses, he will thankfully acknowledge their favour and give all testimonies of fidelity and respect.

[? March]. *HM*2.9/15.

The two preceding documents in Volume IX, Nos. 13 and 14, are shorter drafts of this; one is dated 5th March 1646/7.

1647

194. ORDER OF THE COMMITTEE OF CO. MONMOUTH.

Col. Richard Herbert of St. Julian's, a delinquent, appeared this day before them and desired to be tenant for all his real estate in this county according to the return of sequestrators. Ordered that he shall have the premises for one year from 2 February last, paying £100 and all chief-rents, taxes, and payments (contributions excepted).

Will Herbert   Will Morgan
Uske,   Willm. Jones   Chr. Catchmay
14 April.
Ror. Williams   *HM*2.12/42.

[1647]

195. [LORD HERBERT'S] PROMISE UPON FREE DELIVERY OF HIS CASTLE OF MONTG[OMERY]. *Much-altered draft.*

Clauses 1 *and* 2 *are substantially the same as in No.* 196. 3. In all businesses wherein he may show duty and affection to Parliament he will stand to the [promise he made in the House of Lords 21 May 1642, which he has kept inviolable (*deleted*)], which will be easier than heretofore, when many attempts were made to surprise him and put a garrison in . . . Hopes the House will without further difficulty . . . (*breaks off*).

Added: Mr. Speaker is desired to certify the House that his eldest son's petition to compound is admitted at Golds[miths'] Hall, and composition shall be purposed with all speed. *HM*2.9/26.

1647

196. LORD HERBERT'S PROMISE TO THE HOUSE OF COMMONS UPON RE-DELIVERY OF HIS CASTLE.

1. Will put no man in authority in his castle, or admit a servant, whom he knows or can discover to be ill-affected to Parliament. 2. If danger appear of any attempt against the castle, such as he principally entrusts with it shall advertise the next Parliament garrison, also Parliament itself, as soon as may be.

Desires the House to accept this promise and grant reasonable compensation for his losses, and meanwhile give order that the arrears of [his] £20 weekly be paid, and the allowance continued until compensation be paid, and no longer—though the Earl of Mulgrave had his £50, notwithstanding the order of 21 August, to the last day of his life.

H. Elsynge
Cler. Parl., Dom. Com.

Lord Cherbury's desires in this paper are referred to the membership of both Houses that are of the Committee of Both Kingdoms, as appears by order of 25 March 1647.

Copia vera

Endorsed: Presented 1 May 1647. *HM*2.9/16.

1647

197. CERTIFICATE BY THE COMMITTEE OF MONTG[OMERY] SHIRE.

Being of the Committee of Sequestrations for Northwales, they certify at the instance of Lord Herberte that from the time he put his castle of Mountgom[er]y into the possession of Sir Thomas Midleton for the use of King and Parliament he has sustained great damage by the violence of the war and disorder of soldiers entertained in his castle and others, the castle having been much defaced and suffered to decay, his woods exceedingly wasted, his two parks destroyed (the pale above six mile compass totally carried away and burnt), great number of his horses and other cattle driven away, his rents in great measure withheld by reason his tenants were plundered, and his demesnes and other of his farmhouses utterly ruinated; all which amount to many thousands, besides £1,200 per annum of his estate in Irelande wholly possessed by the rebels these five or six years (as they are informed).

Rich. Griffith
Evan Lloyd
Lodowicke Middleton

Mountgom[er]y,
27 April.

*HM*2.9/18.

1647

198. THE COMMITTEE FOR COMPOUNDING WITH DELINQUENTS TO [THE COMMITTEE FOR MONTGOMERYSHIRE].

Lately sent letters to sequester the estate of Francis Herbert of Doligeog, esq., for not sueing out his pardon according to order. Have received certain information, and are satisfied he has since taken out his pardon: hereby order [them] to make void the sequestration upon sight hereof....

Antho. Irby

Goldsmiths' Hall, London, 27 May.

D. Watkins, Ed. Ashe, Lawr. Brinley

Robert Jenner, Geo. Thomason, John Oldfeild

Jo. Leech

*HM*2.12/43.

The document is unaddressed, though obviously intact. "Geo. Thomason" is presumably Colonel George Thompson, not the well-known bookseller and collector.

[1647]

199. LORD HERBERT'S PROPOSITIONS "TO BE OFFERED".

That he be permitted to keep a garrison in his castle at Mountgomery of a number as may defend the same, he to appoint the officers. That he have leave to provide ordnance (of the smaller sort only) and ammunition for defence. That the pikes, muskets, "pouther", match, lead, and two small brass pieces, etc., which were in his castle be made good out of the arms now there, or otherwise supplied. That for better enabling him hereunto the £20 weekly allowed him by order of both Houses, and still in force, be paid henceforth out of the sequestration of co. Mountgomery. *HM*2.9/37.

[? 1647]

200. NOTE OF LORD HERBERT'S LOSSES.

Through decay of rents since putting his castle and estate into Parliament's protection, near £6,000. Losses in personal estate since putting himself into Parliament's protection, through cutting down of woods, destroying two parks to pulling up of post and pale, with loss of deer, horses, cattle, corn, besides pulling up of quicksets (thereby laying his grounds common), about £5,000. Losses since the beginning of these troubles till the surrender of his castle, about £4,700. Future losses in his lands in Ireland (not utterly taken away till he put himself into Parliament's protection)—being a third of his estate, and his rents better paid there than in England—are not to be estimated [not knowing] when they will be recovered; will give account when occasion is.

*HM*2.9/41.

1647

201. [LORD HERBERT] TO THE COMMITTEE OF BOTH KINGDOMS. *Contemporary copy.*

Whereas on 25 March last the House of Commons referred his desires, contained in a paper of the same date, to the Committee of Both Kingdoms, he has for their more ease extracted the substance:

1. Presents his losses since the beginning of these troubles until the surrender of his castle, occasioned by the quartering of soldiers of the adverse party upon his lands and the taking up of his rents for two years and three months, because he would not admit a garrison, in all [Northwales and the Marches *deleted*] no man appearing so openly

for Parliament in refusing to be of the commission of array, etc. Values it at £3,000.

2. Desires them to consider his losses since the surrender. It stands with equity (Parliament having had valuable consideration) to recompense them, as also according to the true sense of his capitulation of 5 September, 1644, where it is declared assistance should be given him for gathering his rents, so that whether in arrear since the beginning of these troubles or due since the surrender, he conceives these words comprehend them, even to the point of his losses in Ireland (where he formerly had £1,200 yearly).

3. Desires arrears of his allowance of £20 weekly because granted by order of both Houses and as yet unrevoked, and that he has little other means [while] enforced to keep guards in his castle.

4. Desires them to consider the means of defending his castle, both by enabling him to govern the guards and contain them in their duty, as also to call for assistance from the abler inhabitants of parts adjoining (especially the town of Montg.) when danger appears. And if the Committee will add some allowance to be levied out of the two next hundreds (Kerry and Kedewey) for maintaining only twelve foot and six horse, it would much ease his charges until God grant a happy peace or return him to his former means—has not received these two last years above a fifteenth part, and hardly hopes to receive this year above a fifth, which will but serve to provide for a guard to defend his castle.

Copia vera: M.C.

Endorsed: 1st paper . . . *HM*2.9/19.

1647

202. [Lord Herbert] to the Committee of Both Kingdoms. *Contemporary copy.*

Asks that the arrears of £20 weekly be paid forthwith, the Earl of Mulgrave having had his £50, notwithstanding the order of 21 August 1646, to the last day of his life, as by Alderman Averye's certificate (which he is ready to produce) will appear; the rather that he has little other means, and his occasions for reparations of his castles (much ruined since the surrender into Parliament's protection), also providing it with arms, ammunition, and victuals, and paying of guards there, are great, and himself disabled through decay of his rents . . . to furnish the charge his castle being frontier between England and Wales and more considerable than others.

Desires his losses, sustained for two years three months during which he defended his castle against all attempts of the adverse party to put a garrison in, be satisfied. Though £3,000 is the least it could cost, yet will accept £2,000, or have it deducted upon his eldest son's composition, who is £6,000 in debt (having sold half the £600 yearly the writer gave him on his marriage), with little more than £300 a year to maintain himself, his lady, and seven or eight children. Will make no advantage thereof towards his own losses.

Conceives his losses in Ireland are within the words of his capitulation. Asks for £600 yearly out of the Earl of Glamorgan's estate, he holding the writer's lands in Ireland and receiving £600 yearly from them, though worth £1,200 (the rent duly paid before these troubles). Demands but a moiety of his losses, and only till his lands in Ireland be recovered.

Does not yet know his losses since the surrender of his castle, being likely to continue. Might crave present reparation, but is unwilling to be burdensome, especially if the Committee will grant these desires, the most moderate he could devise for the ease of the state. Only exhibits a general view of those losses, according to certificates by the Committee of the shire and bailiffs of the town of Montg. . . . Will take a third less than is due, that payment be "presently" made.

Desires allowance out of parts adjoining his castle for its defence. Is not able to pay his guards and reserve competent means to subsist, much less provide for his younger children and innocent grandchildren. Cannot, besides, repair his castle and furnish it with arms, etc. As there is an express article in his capitulation that his arms, etc., should be restored, he hopes they will approve Governor Moore's leaving some at his departure, and give order that what is defective be made good.

Copia vera: M.C.

Endorsed: Second paper . . . *HM*2.9/20.

By his "castles" Lord Herbert means the old and the new castles at Montgomery.

1648

203. [Lord] Herbert to Mr. Richard Griffith at Sutton, near Mountgomery.

If he would set down particulars of his old infirmities, the writer would endeavour to get Dr. Mayerne's advice; but he should let the physician relate the disease. As for his castle, Griffith knows he is in no estate to bestow charges upon a garrison. Hopes those gentlemen who, out of kindness, would have soldiers to keep the castle, will pay them and be contented they lodge in the outworks, the reparation of which, with the towers in them, he has charged Moses Lloyd to procure (prays word if he performs it not). Is careful of Griffith's preservation, and doubts not he will preserve the writer's honour, state, and his propriety in his castle—must not suffer it to be alienated, especially now he must be absent in London. Prays him recommend the effect of this letter to Rich. Thompson. "Your ancient frend".

London,
16 May.

He should remember Mountgomery is unprovided of a preacher who may constantly reside there. 374.

[1648]

204. Lord Herbert's Instructions to Lord North to be presented to the House of Peers. *Contemporary copy.*

He is desired to acquaint the Houses that his request is in behalf of his eldest son, Col. Richard Herbert. Upon capitulation at the surrender of his castle of Mountgomery, Sir Thomas Middleton undertook that his rents should be made good, also that he might add or explicate [as] might be for his advantage; as by the capitulation kept by Mr. Walter

Frost at Derby House may appear. The capitulation was approved by both Houses. His losses amount to above £2,000. Furthermore, whereas by ordinance of Parliament the arrears of £20 a week [were] to be paid him in consideration of his estate lost and damnified in cos. Salopp and Mountgomery, arrears amount to £2,000. Desires in consideration [hereof] that his son's composition, with much rigour rated at £2,500 odd, be remitted. And if anything in his arrears be then remaining, he freely acquits the Houses. His last desire is that if his grandchild has anything to do before the Houses he may be favourably used.

Richard Herbert of St. Julian's, esq.: His estate in fee in possession, p.a., £50; for life in possession, p.a., £363 9s. 2d.; in reversion for life after his father's decease, p.a., £600; more in reversion as before, £400 and £120; tenement in Mountgomery lately purchased by his wife, p.a., £6 13s. 4d.; debts he owes, £7,000; his fine set at Goldsmiths' Hall, 30 June 1648, at a third, he having been a member of the House of Commons, £2,574.

[July or August]. *HM*2.12/53.

1648

205. Order of the Committee for Sequestrations for co. Mountgom[er]y.

It appears by an order from the Commissioners for Compounding of the 19th instant, and a particular of the estate of Richard, Lord Herbert, in co. Mountgomerie therewith sent, that he has submitted to a fine imposed for his delinquency and paid and secured the same . . . Therefore ordered that sequestration be taken off . . .

29 September.

Hugh Price
Rich. Price
Lodowicke Middleton
Evan Lloyd

Intrat. per
E. Mercey

Endorsed: Orders of the Committees of M. and Salop.

*HM*2.12/44.

The Salop order is wanting.

[1648-9]

206. Report on Lord Herbert's Delinquency. *Contemporary copy.*

Being a member of the House of Commons he deserted Parliament and was in arms against them. His estate: In fee per annum £50, for life per annum £370 2s. 6d., in reversion for life after a life £1,150; for which his fine at a third is £2,611 10s. Ordered that it be reported together with the fine that he is indebted £7,000. And that there was owing to Edward, Lord Herbert, his father, above £4,000 by Parliament, which he in his will (produced to this Committee) thus disposes of, viz: Due to him £2,000 arrear of £20 to be paid him weekly, and by his capitulation with Sir Thomas Middleton his losses and damage amounting to £1,200 were to be made good; remits it, desiring the Houses, for his sake, to remit to his son, Col. Richard Herbert, the £2,500 fine for his delinquency. *HM*.29/39.

"This Committee" is presumably the Committee for Compounding.

[1648-9]

207. Lord Herbert's Petition to the Commons. *Contemporary copy.*

£2,500 is imposed upon him for delinquency. Offers to their consideration: Is really indebted, as appeared to the Committee at Goldsmiths' Hall, above £7,000. Parliament was indebted to his father, lately deceased, £4,000. Besides, his father, during the late troubles, was damnified in his estate by adhering to Parliament £12,000; which by capitulation with Sir Tho. Middleton . . . was to be made good. He remitted the debt and damages to Parliament in his will and made it his dying request that in lieu they would remit the petitioner's fine. Addressed himself to the Committee at Goldsmiths' Hall, but they affirmed their rules would not admit them to extend favour to him, and ordered that, he paying in £1,000, his case should be specially reported to the Houses; which with great difficulty he effected. Now prays them to discharge him of the remainder of his fine. *HM*2.9/35.

1649

208. R., [Lord] Herbert, to the Committee for co. Montgomery. *Draft.*

They showed him this day an express from Col. Jones of the 16th, sent by order of Parliament, desiring to know whether he will maintain soldiers in Montgomery Castle, as his father undertook, or have it demolished, Parliament not being willing to lay such a charge upon the country. Takes it as an honour that where he has no power to conclude "I am not Concluded without myselfe". Is neither willing nor able, in relation to his debts and losses, to maintain a garrison. Enlarging the terms of the second [proposition] he readily consents that the castle be dismantled and made indefensible. Proposes that the outworks be totally slighted, the grafts before the new building filled up, and the drawbridge taken down; the graft between the new building and the old castle filled up, the drawbridge taken down, and the old castle demolished.

The propositions following he desires they return to Col. Jones to present to the House of Commons and Council of State: 1. That all the materials be preserved for his use. 2. They would be pleased to certify how weak the new building is, being after the modern fashion of brick, and not long able (in that place) to resist the weather; and that as it is only part of a house and his only dwelling in those parts, it may be continued as it is. 3. That some persons be entrusted to see all particulars performed . . .

Poole,
27 April. *HM*2.9/21.

The decision of Parliament was that the whole castle, both the old and the new parts, should be totally destroyed. The order, dated 11 June, 1649, is printed in *Montgomeryshire Collections*, Vol. XX, p. 27.

[1649]

209. Lord Herbert's Petition to the Commons. *Contemporary copy.*

Whereas the House may think fit to order that his castle [of] Montgomery be demolished (it being his chief seat, for which he has compounded), he readily concurs for the good of the republic, not doubting they will, for the great losses he shall thereby sustain, give just reparation, as granted to others in like case. Prays allowance for it out of the remainder of his fine.

[? May or June]. *HM*2.9/36.

1649

210. Jo. Jones to Evan Lloyd, esq., High Sheriff of co. Mountgomerie, Col. Hugh Price, [and] Rich. Griffithes and Richard Price, esqrs., at Redcastle. *Contemporary copy.*

Is commanded by the Council of State to convey the enclosed, that the contents may be put in present execution. The damage which accrues to "my Lord" by demolishing the castle, they should certify with speed and exactness in point of value, that neither his lordship nor the State be prejudiced.

White-hall,
18 June. *Cop. ver.*: R. Hamer.

Endorsed: Col. Jones's to the Committee of Mountgomery-shire for demolishing Mountgomery Castle. *HM*2.9/22.

1649

211. [Lord] Fairfax to all Officers and Soldiers under his Command.

Requires them not to prejudice the house of Richard, Lord Herbert, at Llyssyn, or offer violence to his person or family, or meddle with or take his horses, household stuff [etc.]; [and] not to quarter officers or soldiers at his house, he providing his just proportion "abroad" . . . [and] doing nothing prejudicial to the Parliament or Army.

23 June. *Heraldic seal at top left* *HM*2.12/45.

1649

212. [The Committee for Montgomeryshire] to Col. John Jones. *Draft or copy.*

In pursuance of his order of the 15th instant for demolishing Mountgomry Castle, which came the 22nd, they met at Mountgomry this day, and after examination of the workmen and those that paid them in the late Lord of Churbury's time, find the new building comes to £4,731, and the old castle valued at £2,000—[but] conceive it was not built at double [that]. Made an estimate of the materials of both, as now impaired by the siege and a garrison these five years; cannot make above £500 of them, or indeed procure a chapman for them. By the opinion of able workmen the total demolishing of the castle cannot be less than £1,000. Therefore proposed the demolishing to Lord Churbury, who [will] undergo the charge [in exchange] for the materials, [having] three months for [it]; the outworks [to] be continued for the soldiers to lodge in until at least the old castle be totally demolished.

Leave to his justice and wisdom what he will allow Lord Churbury for his great damage by demolishing the castle, above that of abating his second payment, which he [says] comes to somewhat less than £2,000.

Mountgomry, Evan Lloyd, *Vic.*
23 June. Hugh Price Rich. Griffith

*HM*2.9/24.

A detailed estimate of the cost of building the new castle (bearing the same date as this letter) is No. 23 in Volume IX. Lord Herbert's "second payment", the balance of his fine, was actually £1,611 10s., he having paid £1,000 of a fine of £2,611 10s. (see Nos. 206 and 207).

1649

213. [THE COMMITTEE FOR MONTGOMERYSHIRE] TO RICHARD, LORD HERBERT.

Have received a commision from the Council of State dated 15 June for the total demolishing of Mountgomery Castle, and to appoint some fit person to undertake [it] and make the best improvement of the materials and keep account thereof for defraying the charges of demolishing and towards Lord Herbert's damages. Upon debate of the charges [which] would accrue upon the State by the demolition above the valuation of the materials, they hereby authorize Lord Cherbury to pursue it with all expedition, and appoint Mr. Edward Allen and Mr. Richard Thompson to keep a just account. Likewise authorize Lord Cherbury to dispose of the materials for his charges in the demolishing, and account for the surplusage; and in case [they] will not defray the charge, then he is to be considered for his charges over and above.

29 June. Evan Lloyd, *Vic.*
Hugh Price
Rich. Griffith

*HM*2.9/27.

1649

214. ORDER OF THE COMMITTEE [FOR MONTGOMERYSHIRE]. *Contemporary copy.*

Ordered that Mr. Edward Allen and Mr. Richard Thompson supervise the demolishing of Montgomery Castle; to be careful to preserve the materials, and give directions for the drawing of the old castle before demolishing the walls, unless "such parte as shalbe needefull for the throweing downe of the buildinge without wast"; and proceed according to orders of Parliament and directions from the writers . . . Conceive it fitting Mr. Allen and Mr. Thompson be satisfied for their pains out of the moneys from the materials.

Evan Lloyd, *Vic.*
Copia vera Hugh Price

*HM*2.9/28.

[1649]

215. ARMS AND AMMUNITION LEFT AT MOUNTGOMRY CASTLE BY THE LATE LORD HERBERT.

62 muskets fixed in good order; 2 dozen of bandolieros; 2 dozen of

rests; 4 halberds; 6 barrels of corn powder; 2lb. weight of mail; 1 drum; some quantity of bullets; some body-arms of little worth.

Edward Allen.

Endorsed: Arms taken out of Montgom[er]y Castle at the demolishing hereof, the right of "my Lords" son as executor. Col. Hugh Price took them away . . . . . *HM*2.9/25.

1649

216. THE COMMITTEE OF MONTGOMERYSHIRE TO RICHARD, LORD HARBERT.

Received order from the Council of State of 19 September for giving satisfaction to Capt. Allen of £135 disbursed for discharging the soldiers of Mountgomery Castle out of the materials; and to put it upon the account of disgarrisoning and demolishing the same . . . . . . Have given him his address to Lord Herbert, being certified the Council intends not his lordship's prejudice, but that the allowance the Council are to make his lordship will be some other way.

Evan Lloyd, *Vic.*
10 October. Hugh Price
Rich. Price

Armorial seal *HM*2.9/29.

1649

217. ED. ALLEN AND RICHARD THOMPSON TO THE COMMISSIONERS FOR DEMOLISHING MOUNTGOMERY CASTLE. *Contemporary copy.*

In pursuance of their order of 9 June [as to] demolishing Mountgomery Castle, they accordingly have seen the total demolishing thereof and kept account, by which it apppears the materials amount to £500 and the disgarrisoning and demolishing to £505 5s.

Mountgomery,
16 November. *Vera copia*: T. Herbert *HM*2.9/30.

"9 June" is a mistake, probably for the 29th—see No. 213. The certificate at the foot provides the first appearance in these letters of the Thomas Herbert (son of Mathew Herbert, vicar of Crickhowell) who went to Ireland a few years later as agent to Lord Herbert, and founded the family of Herbert of Muckross.

1649

218. LORD HERBERT'S PETITION TO THE COUNCIL OF STATE. *Draft.*

Upon Col. Jones's report from them to Parliament concerning Montgomery Castle, it was on 11 June 1649 resolved that it be demolished, the care of it referred to them [with] power to make allowance to him for his damages. On the 15th they appointed Evan Lloyd, then sheriff, and others to give order for it . . . There being no other that would undertake to demolish it, they authorized the petitioner, who effectually performed it; the damages being by demolishing the old castle at least £3,000, and the new building erected by his father above £4,000. Prays allowance of £1,611 10s., the remainder of his fine, and allowance of his twentieth part, with further reparation as shall seem fit.

18 December. *HM*2.9/38.

1649/50

219. Order of the Council of State. *Contemporary copy.*

That a letter be written to the Committee at Goldsmiths' Hall that by Parliament's order of 11 June 1649 this Council ordered the castle of Montgomery to be demolished, and Lord Herbert's damage is about £4,000; and the House ordered that what the Council allow him may be paid out of the second payment of his fine, of which there remains £1,611 10s.: That the Council is of opinion that the Committee give him allowance of the said £1,611 10s.

Whitehall, Ex. Gualter Frost, secr.
19 January. *HM*2.9/31.

A copy of a letter to the Committee to this effect, dated 22 January, is the next document in Volume IX.

1649/50

220. The Commissioners for Compounding to the Committee and Sequestrators of cos. Monmouth, Carnarvon, Mountgom[er]y, and Salloppe. *Contemporary copy.*

Whereas Richard Herbert of St. Julians, esq., now Lord Herbert, has satisfied the whole fine imposed upon him, it is ordered that his estate be discharged from sequestration except his right to advowsons . . . and that he be not further proceeded against for any delinquency in relation to the first war . . . unless he has been engaged in the latter war and has incurred re-sequestration, [etc., etc.].

Westminster, Tho. Lyster John Ashe
24 January. John Bourchyer John Fieldley
Peeter Temple Nicholas Love
John Leech Ri. Salloway Rich. Darley

True copy per Dav. Edwards

Endorsed: Examined . . . Tho. Herbert. 38.

"Fieldley" is perhaps Col. John Fielder.

1650

221. Richard Morgan to Mr. Daniel Edwards.

The bearer, William Owen Humffreys, gave up his tenement last year and would not hold it unless as formerly, for £4, although the book was for £5. So the lands were not occupied until the writer returned from Mont Gomery shire and wished him to make the best of it and hold it for the £4.

Llan Beder,
16 August. 376.

This Llanbedr is most probably the one in Langstone parish, a few miles from St. Julian's.

1650/51

222. THO. HERBERT TO LADY MARY HERBERT AT LLYSSEN.

Since his return to Ireland he has not forgot to serve her in relation to her estate in Kery, but being constant to the headquarters, which has been these six weeks at Kilkenny, he could but appear by proxy. By Dr. Harding's invitation from Corke by Lt.-Col. Staughton, a commissioner there for the Parliament (as she may perceive by his letter delivered by the bearer, Capt. Pearce, quartermaster-general of their horse), the writer was in a fair way to have deserved her thanks. But Castlehaven (since the surprise of Kilmurry Castle, near the Isle) being come into those parts and as far spread as Beer and Bantry, all is frustrated till it please God to reinvest them with possession, which he doubts not will be effected ere this kisses her hand, for Sir Hares Waller is advanced with such a force as will fright or force them out. God has appeared marvellously for them, and requires thankful acknowledgement from all who abhor their barbarities or wish the welfare of "pure" England.

Made suit formerly to Lord Herbert that he would let such evidences as concern Tynterne be delivered cousin Fr. Herb[er]t to be sent to the writer's wife in Petty France. Does not expect them otherwise than [as] consists with respect to him and continuing occasion of serving him, which his unkindness will inevitably alter.

Waterford.

5 January, *Armorial seal* 377.

The writer is Colonel Thomas Herbert, the traveller, later knighted by Henry Cromwell and then created a baronet by Charles II; for an account of him see "Sir Thomas Herbert of Tintern: A Parliamentary Royalist" by N. Mackenzie, in *Bulletin of the Institute of Historical Research*, Vol. XXIX, No. 79, May 1956. He had purchased Tintern from Lord Herbert some years earlier. Herbert was very soon to become Clerk of the Council in Ireland. "Dr. Harding" is almost certainly John Harding, D.D., formerly Chancellor of Christ Church Cathedral, Dublin, and later actively associated with the Parliamentary régime in Ireland.

1651

223. CERTIFICATE BY COMMISSIONERS OF THE MILITIA FOR NORTHWALES.

Richard, Lord Herbert, has furnished the State with two horses and furniture, arms and armour complete.

5 May.

Rich Price
Hugh Price
Evan Lloyd *HM2.9/33.*

1651

224. R., [LORD] HERBERT, TO ROBT. GRIFFITHS.

Mr. Sheriff being in town, and the writer's wife having writ both to the Sheriff and cousin Pulferd about the fee-farm rents of Llandinham, the writer desires Griffiths to interpose in his behalf, consulting all parties' interest; and that the estate be conveyed upon cousin William Browne; and that the writer may pay the moneys to his cousin the Sheriff's lady at Aberboughan (for in her brother the estate now lies, if he mistakes not) or to her husband upon his return.

Prays him consult about his Irish estate—upon reduction of Lymricke he conceives it clearly in the possession of "our" forces—whether he may be admitted to it without composition, having never acted in that kingdom. Prays him advise what course to steer; and about sending an agent forthwith, and how instructed for so considerable an employment. The soldiery will be busy about debenters or making estates for themselves, which unprevented may swallow things in expectation or gift. Wrote to this purpose to cousin Job Charleton; a little conference will make the work easier and the obligation greater—the benefit the writer receives will be for "you and yours". Mr. Pulferd may be very instrumental in this; believes him very "reall" in it. And Sir Jhon Davers has ever appeared most ready; whose endeavours he has warned again by letter. Major Sallaway has been the writer's great patron; an address to him will conduce much to despatch—will write to him on Monday by Watt Waringe. Must endeavour to make good these several troubles to "you or yours".

Mong[omery],
22 [November].

Love to Griffiths' bedfellow. Prays him deliver the enclosed letters, about Landinham and the Irish business. Believes Sir Rich. Saltingstall may, by the late sheriff, one day be very useful. *HM*2.23/6.

The letter is dated "22.9." The newly-appointed Sheriff of Montgomeryshire was Sir Edward Corbett of Leighton; his wife was Lord Herbert's cousin to the extent that her aunt had married Mathew Herbert of Dolguog. The "late sheriff" was Richard Pryce of Gunley, near Forden, Montgomeryshire. Some account of Sir Richard Saltonstall (who was son of the Lord Mayor of London of the same name and uncle to the Roundhead general Sir Thomas Myddelton) will be found in an article "New England Influences in Early Welsh Puritanism", by Professor A. H. Dodd, in *The Bulletin of the Board of Celtic Studies*, Vol. XVI, Part I, November 1954, pp. 30 ff.

[16]53

225. [Colonel] Tho. Herbert to Lady Herbert at Mountgomery Castle.

The distance he is from Kerry makes him less able to help their agent. The exclusion of most or all of the Isle of Kerry out of the protected line has rendered that seigniory of very little profit, save some corn sown before the order, which probably will be reaped by their tenants, who are but withdrawn to the border of the estate and ready to return when leave is granted. Yet such has been the destruction of man and beast by sword and pestilence that famine has ensued there (especially towards Beer and Bantry) and elsewhere. Lord Herbert will need to send a new colony. Is her debtor—cousin Harry Herbert came lately from Cork and said he saw a Welsh cheese with Hollys directed to the writer.

Dublyn,
9 July. *Armorial seal* 378.

1653

226. Order by the Commissioners for the Affairs of Ireland.
Contemporary copy.

The Commissioners of Revenue are authorized to grant licences to the proprietors of corn growing without the line to reap it, provided the persons employed be such as the Commissioners approve of, and that they bring in such corn to the garrisons of the Commonwealth. And where the proprietors neglect to reap the same, the commanders-in-chief of precincts are to cause it to be brought into their garrisons or destroyed.

Dublin, 22 July. — Cha. Fleetwood, Myles Corbett, Edm. Ludlowe, Jo. Jones

True copy: Jo. Hughes 379.

[16]53

227. THOM. LLOYD TO MR. ROBERT WYNNE OF CARNARVON.

Congratulates the recovery of his health. Saw an entry by John Gryffyth of Llanio, gent., on the parcels bought by Wynne's aunt in her widowhood of Wm. Jenkins of Carrog—Ffôs yr ynys, Tîr Batchwilog (two quillets), and Erw'r Llowdwr, all in the occupation of Watkyn David. Another, Tythyn garn vawr, is in the occupation of Jenkyn Reignald. They hold them with their tenements, which were part of his aunt's jointure while she lived, but then reverted to Evan Gwyn, younger son of Evan Gwyn Vychan, as bequeathed by his father, who purchased them of Rowland Gwyn, heir-at-law to Thomas Gwyn of Morva mawr. That young man (or, rather, his eldest brother, Daniell Gwyn, lately dead) compelled the tenants by threats to pay him the whole rent, although they lay no colour of claim to the parcels. Finds it vain to charge the tenants not to pay the brothers, or to demand [the rent] in Wynne's name. Advises him to sue them all, gentlemen and tenants, "aboveforth". One process will do it, especially a *quominus*. Cannot learn Wynne's title to the other concealed parcels held by Llewelyn, and doubts its validity. He that is to be sued for them is Francis Lloyd, son of Dd. Lloyd ap Reignald, who received them of "my Lord" according to Mr. Burton's notes. Delivered a twelvemonth ago to Wynne's sister, Mrs. Dorothy Wynne, the papers he received from Mr. Robt. Owen. Service to his lady and family.

Ber.,
23 September. 1.

Ten or twelve years earlier this Thomas Lloyd was, apparently, a member of the household of Sir Thomas Salusbury of Lleweni (see *Calendar of Salusbury Correspondence*, ed. W. J. Smith, pp. 179, 189 195-6 *et al.*). He writes from Berriew. The lands which are the subject of this letter are almost certainly close to the Cardiganshire coast, a few miles south of Aberystwyth. This and later letters dealing with the same matter (Nos. 257-8, 261, 271, and 288) clearly came to Powis Castle through the Herberts of Dolguog. "My Lord" is no doubt Lord Herbert.

1654

228. OLIVER P. TO THE COMMISSIONERS FOR THE COMMONWEALTH IN IRELAND. *Contemporary copy.*

Having seen the petition of Richard, Lord Herbert, and taking into consideration the losses he has already sustained in Ireland, his debts, and his many younger children unprovided for other than out of his estate in Ireland: Recommends him into them, that he may receive favour and encouragement for carrying on his plantation there . . .

White Hall,
18 May. *Copia vera*: Will Malyn

Endorsed: Attested by Mr. Maylyn, His Highness's privy secretary.
*HM*2.12/46.

1654

229. [LORD] BROGHILL, R. VENABLES, AND JOHN CLERKE TO [? LIEUT.-GEN. FLEETWOOD]. *Contemporary copy.*

"My Lord". In obedience to His Highness's pleasure concerning Lord Herbert's proposals, they are of opinion: That he be allowed to have one hundred firearms and one hundred pikes for such English or Welsh Protestants as he transports to plant his estate in Kerry and Desmond when they come thither, giving security they shall not be used against the Commonwealth. That a man-of-war be appointed to convey them provided they be shipped at some port of England or Wales where the State's ships use to come. That he be allowed to make a line of defence about his house of Castle Islands or any other place of his estate, so it be not upon navigable river, etc., the same to be garrisoned by the State if the public interest require.

27 July. 380.

Broghill was at this time Master of the Ordnance.

1654/5

230. CHARLES FLEETWOOD, DEPUTY OF IRELAND, TO ALL UNDER HIS COMMAND.

These are to require them to supply the bearer, Thomas Herbert, esq., with convoys of horse from garrison to garrison in his travel into Kerry and return, sufficient to secure him from tories.

Dublyn Castle,
31 January. 40.

Herbert—not Colonel Herbert—was making his preparations for going to Ireland as Lord Herbert's agent.

1654/5

231. ORDER BY JOHN NELSONN, COMMANDER-IN-CHIEF OF ALL THE LORD PROTECTOR'S FORCES IN THE PRECINCT OF KERRY.

Upon address of Thomas Herbert, gent., agent for Richard, Lord Herbert, to the Lord Deputy and Council of Ireland, he obtained instructions for inhabiting Lord Herbert's estate within this precinct and to advise with the writer what part may be planted and brought within the line without public prejudice. Upon view of the estate, etc., the lands named are declared to be within the line of protection, *viz*, to the top of the next hill eastward of Ardenegraph and Cnocheteemore, thence southward on the east side of Gortglass and to Adergavule, and to the east of Killsarkon, and thence westward to the top of Glanlea and Glanda ragh, and thence to Cnockboy in the barony of Magonihie.

All officers, soldiers, etc., are to take notice. Assures the inhabitants of protection from all public enemies to the uttermost endeavours of himself and his forces.

23 February. 39.

[1655]

232. LORD HERBERT'S PETITION TO THE LORD DEPUTY AND COUNCIL. *Copy in the hand of Thos. Herbert, Lord Herbert's agent.*

Has a considerable estate of inheritance in cos. Kerry and Desmond, which for fourteen years past, by reason of the horrid rebellion, has yielded no profit; and being for three years past secluded [beyond] the line of protection, lies now waste, no house or inhabitant thereupon, the most perfectly ruinated estate in those parts, to the petitioner's insupportable loss and to public prejudice. All or most will continue so unless he be permitted to receive such of the Irish as desire to continue his tenants. Therefore asks to be allowed to inhabit so much of his estate with Irish who have been inoffensive during this rebellion, and with such inconsiderable proprietors who, relinquishing their interests, upon account of their good demeanour during the rebellion are thought fit by the commander-in-chief for the precincts to stay exonerated from transplantation.

T. H., Agent for Lord Herbert *HM*2.22/6a.

1655

233. ORDER BY THE LORD DEPUTY AND COUNCIL. *Copy in the hand of Thos. Herbert, Lord Herbert's agent.*

Lord Herbert's petition is referred to Col. Nelson, Governor of Kerry, who is to consider granting licences to Irish tenants to reside on the petitioner's estate; and he is authorized (if it may be done without prejudice to the Commonwealth) to plant there with Irish tenants, provided they be not such as have been engaged with the rebels [since *deleted*] in the first year of the rebellion against the Commonwealth, nor have been officers or soldiers of the Irish party, or otherwise notorious[ly] against the English interest. And the Governor is to return the names of such as are permitted to stay.

Dublin,
3 April

Tho. Herbert,
Clerk of the Council

Int. and ex'd per J. D. *HM*2.22/6b.

1655

234. THO. HERBERT TO COL. HERBERT.

Waited upon his Excellency this afternoon, who commanded him to send this abstract of "my Lords" desires, promising he would move them to the Council this afternoon. 1. His lordship desires a pass to transport 150 persons (now in readiness) with their stock, goods, and cattle into his estate in Kerry. 2. That a man-of-war be ordered to convey them into Corke, Kinsale, or other harbour in Munster;

they will be at Milford Haven the latter end of this month or the beginning of next. 3. That in respect one Andrew Ellis has 200 beasts, 1,000 sheep, 20 breeding mares, and other considerable goods to be transported, it is desired he may have a pass "in perticular", for his encouragement. 4. That they be allowed to transport what fowling and birding pieces they have for their security and recreation. 5. His lordship requests a pass to come in person with his attendants, horses, arms, etc., into Dublin, that he may tender his services to his Excellency and the Council (before he goes for Kerry) and settle his affairs.

Dublin,
2 May.

6. It is desired Lord Herbert and his planters have benefit of the acts and ordinances in reference to goods, stock, etc., they import into Ireland (that they be) excise and custom free, as promised by the Lord Deputy and Council in their order of 24 January last.

Tho. Herbert
Agent for Lord Herbert

Endorsed: Orders to be drawn agreeable to the desires.

*HM*2.22/7.

1655

235. ORDER BY THE LORD DEPUTY AND COUNCIL.

Ordered that Richard, Lord Herbert, is permitted to transport out of England and Wales one hundred and fifty persons to plant his estate in Kerry, with their stocks and chattels, and to land them at any port in Munster without custom or excise, [as] provided by the Ordinance of 23 June last; and that for their better security and encouragement they be permitted to bring sixty fowling pieces; providing always they act nothing to the prejudice of the present government. Whereof all governors, officers, soldiers, etc., are to take notice

Tho. Herbert, Cl. of the Council

Dublin,
7 May. True Copy: Tho. Herbert 381.

The signatures are the same, and the whole document is in Herbert's hand.

1655

236. ORDER BY THE LORD DEPUTY AND COUNCIL.

Have read the petition of the nobility and gentry of the despoiled Protestants of Ireland, which took notice of this Board's order of 2 April 1655 requiring payment of all rents belonging to the late King grown due since 20 March 1653/4 and arrears since 21 October 1641, and also of the order of 14 November 1654 requiring payment of rents due from 2 May 1654 out of lands formerly belonging to archbishops, bishops, deans, etc., and arrears since 21 October 1641; and which [referred to] the waste of their estates by the war and by "Lines", their engagements contracted for their subsistence during the war, their present burthen of taxes, their inability to plant and improve their estates in a short time through scarcity of inhabitants occasioned by the war and transplantation, etc.; and which therefore prayed that the rents be remitted while the contribution is continued in such a manner as rents are or shall be remitted to adventurers and soldiers, the rather that by the ordinance of 23 June 1654 there should be no public tax or burthen whatsoever for the use of the State taken from owners of lands in Ireland but according to the said ordinance, which remits rents payable by adventurers and soldiers for five years and until the assessments of Ireland are [equalized] with those for England. The Lord Deputy and Council, taking the distressed condition of the said Protestants into consideration, have remitted all arrears of rents; rents growing due from 28 September next are respited until 10 November next, from which date all rents are to be levied according to law unless His Highness orders the contrary.

Dublyn, Tho. Herbert, Clerk of the Council
21 May. Entered: E.A.

True copy: Tho. Herbert

Endorsed in the hand of Thomas Herbert, Lord Herbert's agent: Copy attested by Col. Herbert. 42.

1655/6

237. THO. HERBERT TO [LORD HERBERT].

Encloses once more a positive discharge from the Commissioners of the Treasury, procured after long attendance. Hopes hereafter he will be never troubled. John Mason and he will state the account betwixt [Lord Herbert] and "my Lady" for last half year's rent . . . If his trial goes on next Monmouth assizes he should send to London to retain the ablest counsel . . . Gave Mr. Jones the names of the best that come the circuit; the three first must have 20s. apiece retaining fee, the rest 10s. Care must be taken for an honest jury, which cannot be from the hundreds of Gwenlloog or Caldicott. If he could have most out of the hundred of Sken-frayth and Monmouth he might find a civil undepraved generation. The other side of the county is so infected with the new disease that he may fail of a verdict be his title ever so clear.

Mountgomery,
26 January. *HM*2.23/47.

The writer is Lord Herbert's Irish agent. The discharge from the Treasury is dated 2 January—see No. 47 in the Appendix. "My Lady" is probably the Dowager Lady Herbert, Edward, the new Lord Herbert, having succeded to the title in the preceding May.

1656

238. RT. OUSLEY TO LORD HERBERT. TO BE OPENED BY THOMAS HERBERT, ESQ., IF HE BE COME FROM ENGLAND TO DUBLIN, OR ANY OTHER EMPLOYED FROM LORD HERBERT.

Desires to become his tenant for a longer time and more land than he took of Twyss for three years as introduction to a more competent lease. The lands contiguous are the plough-lands of West Meanus and Bally Marrascall and two half plough-lands of Lackeny kill and

Lishenbane, which, with what he has, make five plough-lands. Begs the tenancy, giving as much as any Protestant will give. Would soon build if encouraged.

Trallee,
18 May.

John Hollis presents his service, and hints how serviceable he has been in encouraging people (by building the first house in the seigniory) to come upon the estate; most that are here came upon account of his building and living here. The bearer, Ri. Twys, is a careful servant to his lordship.

Has in his custody a claim of certain lands entered by Lord Herbert's father, in which are some that at courts of survey the jury found to be in possession of Irish rebels in 1641—Bally mc Addame, Cloudane, etc. Tried to prevent the setting of them this year to the State's use. He should take speedy course to get them out of the public's hands, for possession is eleven points of the law. 382.

1656

239. George Davis to Lord Herbert.

Has taken a farm from his steward, "Weast Meanus" and Balley Masse, containing two plough-lands (but 120 small Irish acres), for three years; which is an inconsiderable time for a man that intends to bestow most of his sustenance in building houses and manuring, and would spend the residue of his time as Lord Herbert's tenant, if he will grant him a lease of thirty-one years at the [present] rent, £23 (more than he would give, but he has a great desire to live on Lord Herbert's estate—hears he is favourable to tenants). Would [also] take the plough-land of Dulage, giving at most £8 per annum, and to have the like time.

Balley Marsiell,
20 May.

Endorsed: . . . Answered in Tom Herbert's by Twisse, August 1656.
*HM*2.23/5.

In an endorsement the name of the farm is interpreted as "East Meanus".

1656

240. Ri. Ousley to Lord Herbert.

Sent him two letters desiring to hold land of his seigniory. Took a small farm as a beginning and built the walls of a small house, not doubting he would have a longer time and other lands. But understands that Mr. Twys's contracts signify nothing; to which he gives little credit. However, the noise of it, occasioned by Mr. Lloyd and others lately come over, has much dissatisfied those that were beginning to settle. Is all at a stand. Begs him to confirm what Mr. Twys has done. His estate had been fully settled had any been empowered to treat with those that will come provided they have 21 or 31 years—for three years none worth caring for will meddle.

Trallee,
15 June.

Endorsed: Answered by Twise . . . 383.

The identity of this Lloyd (or Floyd) does not emerge.

1656

241. [THE CASTLE ISLAND TENANTS] TO LORD HERBERT.

Have taken several plough-lands of his seigniory for three years beginning May last from Richard Twise, who derives his power from Mr. Herbertt, and he from Lord Herbert's father (so expressed in their leases). Many left former holdings and came above three score mile, many having had several invitations by letters from his father, to whom many were ancient tenants. Therefore think they should have been encouraged to build and improve. Assure him, had it not been of a desire to remain tenants during their lives they would not have removed for so short a time as three years.

Have now of late been wholly discouraged by one Mr. Floyd publicly reporting that these leases by Mr. Herb[er]t or Richard Twise are of no effect, which has much hindered building, [caused] great loss to the tenants, and hindered the setting of lands unset at Floyde's coming. If Lord Herbert does not speedily send them good encouragement to proceed according to Mr. Herbertt's and Twise's conditions, most of the estate will be waste as formerly, for they can have as good land at a far easier rate—only the desire to be his tenant is their tie. Believe that had he been here he would have afforded them that land at easier rates—the rent will appear by the rent-roll brought by Richard Twise. Could give some relation of Twise his servant—of his care and how he has managed Lord Herbert's affairs here; but that they will appear in another manner more proper than from them, they having desired him to make this journey to give Lord Herbert account of their conditions and his own. Ask him to send his agent "to setle us" for the future. Daily expected Mr. Thomas Herbertt; had they not expected him, with full power for term of years or lives, there had not been so many in the seigniory.

Island of Kerry,
16 June.

Roger Hollis

Cha. Bastable	John Hol[is?]
Richard Sellers	Nicholas Bagtor
Frauncis Rossington	George Hollis
John fitz Gerrald	Tristram Marshall
Donogh mc Fynen	Bryan Preston
Cnoghor mc Fynen	Connor o Daly
Godfery Dally	George Davis
William ô Dally	Richard Trant
John fz Gerrald	Wm. [? Trantt]
George Donn	William Collman
Richard Tayler	Derby mc Thomas

Endorsed: "A letter from most of my Tenants . . ." Answered by Twise in a letter to Tom Herbert, August 1656. *HM*2.22/8.

"Answered by Twise" means that Twiss was the bearer; for the sense of the reply, see No. 246.

1656

242. CHARLES BASTABLE TO LORD HERBERTT.

Has sustained great hindrance by one Mr. Floyd, lately come out of England with a lease from him of five plough-lands which the writer and Mr. Frauncis Rossinton (a sufficient Englishman, well stocked) had taken of Richard Twiss. Was dispossessed until Richard Twiss settled them for the present until they hear from his lordship. Has asked his brother in England to wait upon him. Desires a lease of all the lands his father held, with the mill. Will "build" them at his own charge. His father was at great charge two or three years before the wars new-building the mills, and never gained his charges. If Mr. Herbertt be come over he requests Lord Herbert's letter [to him]. Desires the land for three lives. Has brought many of his friends to be Lord Herbert's tenants.

Island of Kiery,
17 June. *Armorial seal* 43.

1656

243. THO. HERBERT TO [LORD HERBERT]. *Contemporary abstract.*

Promises account of the estate in Anglesea and hopes he will undertake the management thereof to the best advantage of his near relations and that only. Has represented to [Lord Herbert's] mother such reasons as may induce her to make him an offer of that estate.

Complains of Lloyd's carriage towards the tenants in Ireland; many are so terrified of his noise they are like to leave. Lloyd reports that the writer has no power to set the lands. [*Marginal note*: See the appeals from the tenants.] Lloyd has no stock for his lands, but would gather Irish tenants and such as he can get. Desires him to write to Lloyd to tell him of his errors and his incivilities to his agent; and to all the tenants to vindicate the latter.

Maj. Ousley desires the plough-lands granted to the writer; he is a civil person and Justice of the Peace, and may expect better conditions than others. He should write him a courteous letter that if he have a mind to other land he may have it, and refer him upon the main to the writer. Mr. Charles Barstable desires to be tenant of some of the demesne and the mill. But the demesne, being near the town, is fit to be set in parcels from year to year to the townsmen. It is fit the mill be built and held by [Lord Herbert]. [*Marginal note*: £50 will build it up.] Desires that the millwright that repaired his mills be sent over with Twisse, and two masons from Bp.'s Castle. Barstable is an affectionate servant, and will be pleased by a letter of thanks.

Desires that Mr. Mitchell, the minister that lives near Ludlow, be solicited to go over, or Mr. Whitle of Bromfield. Col. Herbert promises to get him a quarterly stipend out of the Exchequer till the seigniory be planted. Col. Jones's letter would augment the stipend and make his approbation unquestionable. Promises to retrieve the concealed lands lost by the negligence of Lord Baltinglasse, of which one Fitch Gerald got a patent and afterwards turned rebel. Advises him to buy out these lands—they will be [cheap] and will make his seigniory the completest and best in Munster. Prays direction how to dispose of Twisse and what to allow him; he has been a faithful servant. [Speaks also] of the mines in Carnarvonshire and of Mr. Edward Herbert.

The whole document (comprising Nos. 243-6) *endorsed*: Breviate drawn by Meredeth Lloyd. 384a.

[16]56

244. [THOMAS HERBERT] TO [LORD HERBERT]. *Contemporary abstract.*

Has put in a protest as to the concealed and detained lands, according to the advice of Col. Herbert and some of the commissioners his friends. The fee-farm rents are under the consideration of the Council. Will go for Kerry before the soldiery get thither. Col. Herbert's respects. Desires a place appointed in London where to direct letters. Letters may be directed to Mr. John Hogshawe's, next to the Star on Merchants' Quay, Dublin.

23 July. 384b.

[16]56

245. [COL. THOMAS HERBERT] TO [LORD HERBERT]. *Contemporary abstract.*

Account of the Council's order touching the fee-farm rents. In pursuance of the claim a bill is to be filed in the Exchequer, to be managed by Sir Maurice Eustace, a true servant of [Lord Herbert's] family. The Protestants intend to petition the Lord Protector touching the fee-farms, the petition to be carried over by Sir Paul Davies upon the general charge. Desires [Lord Herbert's] mother may have an abstract of his last letter.

5 August. 384c.

[1656]

246. [LORD HERBERT] TO MR. THO. HERBERT. *Notes by Meredeth Lloyd for a draft.*

He should write: Is sensible of the prejudice Lloyd has done—he is to be strictly tied to his articles and discarded upon breach or failure. Major Ousley and Mr. Barstable should have all the civil usage his authority permits. Answer touching the carpenter, masons, and minister. His sense as to the demesne lands and mill. If any lands are intended for near relations [Lord Herbert] should "hint" him that they be not let to Ousley or Barstable. His intentions touching Twisse. Does and shall approve what Th. H. does in the management of the estate, without gainsaying of Lloyd or any other. [*Marginal note*: This letter of vindication by itself, that the tenants may read it.] Thos. Herbert should be very careful after the claim, and go on warily with

Col. Herbert's advice. When the Protestants' petition comes over he and Col. Herbert should send their best directions how [Lord Herbert] may assist the petitioners that employ Sir Paul Davies, with the names of such as may befriend them in respect of power, interest, or intelligence. He should enquire whether this grievance be redressed in Parliament, and, if any parliament men are sent from Irland, some friends should be made amongst them and their names sent him. Whether [Lord Herbert] will purchase Fitch Gerard's lands.

[August].

At foot: One checking letter to Lloyd; one to Ousley; one to Barstable; one (if he please) to Col. Herbert. The letter of vindication may be also an answer to all the tenants. 384d.

1656

247. [Col.] Tho. Herbert to Lord Herbert at Mountgomery.

Must [report] the good effect of cousin Tho. Herbert's endeavours in Lord Herbert's affairs. He prudently discoursed his claim of lands concealed and got [them] withdrawn out of the Army's security. So also with the Council's answer to the despoiled Protestants' petition, craving remittal of rent or suspension of Exchequer process; the Board have respited writs, and though process is to be prepared, they [will] represent their condition to His Highness. Composition rents are put out of charge while the monthly assessments continue.

Rejoices in the agreement between Lord Herbert and his mother, hoping his estate in this nation will thereby improve for the preferment of the young ladies and their brethren, to whom he appears tender and zealous to complete what his father intended. He desires the writer's assistance to his servant, cousin Herbert; the salary Lord Herbert allows him and the perpetuated settlement made him in Kerry hold forth the opinion he has of him. Tho. Herbert's attendance here expose him to great expense, Dublyn being more expensive than London; he will receive satisfaction by his accounts as to his seasonably being here in this critical time when (through inadvertancy) lands not forfeited may be set out for satisfaction of arrears.

Dublin,
3 September. *Armorial seal.* 44.

1656

248. John Mall to Lord Harbert at Clussen.

Met Mr. Rowland Burton last week; enquired whether Lord Herbert had received an account from Sir Thomas Middleton concerning the business of Ireland that the writer went to him about. He said Lord Herbert had received a letter, and let him look it over; he conceived Sir Thomas and the writer did not understand one another. [Promised to] put down his proposals to clear any scruple. Sir Thomas wrote that he denied to give security. Confesses he denied security for the £600—conceives the building is, with "the stock uppon the work", good security. Proffered Sir Thomas to give security to pay £300 per annum in England for twenty-one years, if God send peace (or for so many years as God shall send peace). Conceived Sir Thomas was satisfied. [Sees] no reason why he should pay £300 per annum and give bond for £600 besides. Acquainted Mr. Walker and other gentlemen that are iron masters with his proposals, and all agree that a fairer motion cannot be made. Desires him to [decide] within a fortnight, that he may make a bargain in another place. Is proffered a far greater bargain in Ireland. Does not find by Mr. Burton any [other] difference but about security; which he hopes will make no difference, Lord Herbert having building on his land also £300 per annum.

Longnor Forge,
19 December.

Endorsed: . . . Delivered 29 December; about the iron works near Kerry. *HM*2.22/10.

1656

249. [LORD] H[ERBERT] TO MR. MALL. *Draft.*

His of the 19th came on Xmas Day. Will not recite all that passed between them as to a bargain in Ireland, but only as to the security for the money to be laid out in building. Conceives, when they come to securing the rent, he will propose nobody but sufficient and responsible persons. But as to the [£600 *deleted*] money, etc., he expects only security from him, added as an article obliging to those that secure the rent for the twenty-one years next ensuing. And when it has been laid out, in making a complete forge, then the clause shall be void. If he does not think this reasonable, the writer will not deal, and is sure he does not follow the advice of Mr. Walker, his old master.

26 December. *HM*2.22/11.

1657

250. ED., [LORD] HERBERT, TO [THOMAS HERBERT, CLERK OF THE COUNCIL]. *Contemporary copy.*

Has the unhappiness to have committed his whole Irish estate to a person not trusty or honest. "This Prologue spells Tom. Herbert". Has resolved to be in Irelande a fortnight after Christmas; until then will suspend accusations. [Must] take possession of his lands and secure his writings, which are (more is his shame) in Tom Herbert's "dispose", who took commission as his servant, yet received letters from others commanding the rents and gave him no notice of it—by that concluding the writer was not master of it. [Tom Herbert's] extravagances are such that the estate is too little to serve his riot; he has denied many planters leases unless they pay £10, £12, or £16 agency money (the new name of a steward's reward for engrossing the lease), so that the estate is not above £350 per annum, whereas it might have been £800. He came into Englande to clear his accounts, but has never so much as offered them. In a drunken fit (too frequent with him) he said he was to gather the writer's rents in co. Monmouth, etc.—this is "a straunger" to the writer.

Desires him to secure his writings in Dublin, or at least [Tom Herbert's] person, till he comes over (or somebody else in case of death). The writings in Castle Island will be secured by cousin Wm. Browne. Desires he be very private—would not wound his reputation so much but that he may gain other employment. Believes him a great instrument of the writer's unhappiness in relation to his father's debts.

Llyssin,
17 December.

His estate in Ireland yielded in '55 £100 (Michaelmas rent); in '56 £350. Tom Herbert had advance of wages £50 and by bill of exchange £10. Yet he has spent all that and the rents and is in debt £150. 385.

[? 1657]

251. [LORD HERBERT] TO SECRETARY HERBERT AT DUBLIN. *Draft.*

Gave in his last part of the grounds of his suspicions. It will be impossible to clear accounts such as Tom Herbert's [except] where the occasion was contracted. When Tom Herbert came down from London, to avoid any passion betwixt them—considering the warning he had out of Ireland—and not well understanding the charge of the lawsuit, he sent for two lawers (one a friend of Tom Herbert's) to take up the accounts. That of the law[suit] was allowed; but as to the other of the rent, disbursements, etc., Tom Herbert did not well clear himself. Thinks he can lay other things to his charge. But will suspend censure. Is more tender of doing a servant an injury than of receiving one—the one may blast employment for ever, but the ways are (or were) more obvious for a gentleman to clear himself of any imputation laid by his equal. Will hasten into Irland and bring Tom Herbert with him, and will continue tender of his reputation however his carriage shall prove. Sees it appears to him that the writer is not able to keep a servant at such wages. But his family is in a sad and weak condition; and though it might be expected (considering what an estate his grandfather had) that he should live according to it, yet he finds himself not able (if he should bargain to last even a very few years) without ruining his family. Is resolved to lay out his own endeavours for raising it again, and will not leave one way untried that he and others his friends and kindred shall advise.

[? late December]. 271.

1657/8

252. RICE VAUGHAN AND THO. JONES TO LORD HERBERT AT MOUNTGOM[ER]Y OR LLISSIN. LEAVE AT MR. STEPHEN DAVIES' AT THE HARP IN MARDALL, SALOP, TO BE SENT.

After perusing the letter of attorney, they addressed themselves to Sir Phillip Manwaring, who desired a day or two to advise with his counsel, Sir Orlando Bridgman, with what safety he might deliver the writings. He says he finds but one deed concerning him; it bears date 1639, and is between Lord Herbert his grandfather and his father of the one part and Sir George Ratcliffe and Mainwaring of the other, whereby they conveyed the lordship of Mounteagle Royal (*sic*) and many other lands in Ireland to him and Sir George for ever. No trust is mentioned. It was acknowledged before the Lord Deputy the Earl of Strafford, and enrolled. Will attend Mainwaring two days hence and give him reasonable discharge. Is not so happy as to be known to him, but had many obligations to his noble father.

Graies Inn,
7 January. 18.

This is Rice Vaughan of Machynlleth, author of *Plea for the Common Laws*, *Discourse of Coin*, etc.

165[7/8]

253. [LORD] HERBERT TO THE LORD DEPUTY, LORD HENRY CROMWELL, IN IRLAND. *Draft.*

["May it please your Exelency" *deleted*]. "My lord". Persons eminent in command and virtues have, as the sun, their influence upon all under their protection, for the disposition of persons commanding will show itself . . . And that there may be added to his advantage one thing (how many years thought below that quality)—a humility and particular care of the least dependant— suits with the ornament . . . The care His Excellency has laid out upon the writer, the meanest of his servants, in his late orders to two captains of frigates for transport, leaves him without words to express his thankfulness. But his greatest unhappiness is that, because of urgent occasions, he cannot use that high favour, nor give the personal acknowledgement that is his duty. Is called home, ending his thoughts for Irland till after next January, when, God willing, he will with all submission present himself to him. The enclosed is of a long date, yet he makes bold to convey it, having intended to make his first addresses to him by its recommendations.

Bewmaris,
March. 392.

1658

254. ORDER BY THE LORD DEPUTY AND COUNCIL.

Ordered that the officers of the Customs of this port permit Lord Herbert's servants to return into England or Wales with one bay stone horse, two grey mares, and one sorrel mare belonging to him, and lately brought over in expectation of Lord Herbert's following, but his journey deferred.

Tho. Herbert
Cl. of the Council

The Council Chamber in Dublin,
19 April. Ent'd and exam'd: P.O. *HM*2.12/49.

[16]58

255. [COLONEL] THO. HERBERT TO LORD HERBERT.

Although his lordship's extraordinary affairs at home deprive them of enjoying him this summer, they hope his good opinion continues . . . Is glad he has returned cousin Tom Herbert hither, who well understands his concernments in this nation; presumes he tells Lord Herbert of some late sinister endeavours to invalidate what the law awarded his lordship the year past.

Dublin,
22 April. *Armorial seal* 26.

1658

256. THO. HERBERT TO [LORD HERBERT].

Is sorry his troubles increase. Wishes he could countermine those that cause them. Would cheerfully obey his commands to repair to England, but [Lord Herbert] is unacquainted with the condition of his affairs in these parts.

1. Although Col. Sancky promised to waive his claim to Bally mc Adam, yet, encouraged by malevolent persons in this county, he directed one Bateman in May last to take possession (but he was kept out). Since, Charles Barstable (tenant to those and other lands of the seigniory) agreed to pay Col. Sancky £12 per annum rent if he recovers the lands from his lordship. Is troubled at this egregious knavery. But doubts not to defend his right with less charge than was laid out in the recovery of [the lands]. Barstable promised last year's rent at the Island fair, the 23rd of next month (till when there is no money in these parts); will tender him articles to oblige him not to act to his lordship's prejudice. About 4 May 1657 Barstable and other neighbours went with the writer three or four miles in his journey for Dublin, and he then treated for those lands, which were that year set by the Commonwealth commissioners, being not then recovered. Set them to him then, in the presence of Maj. Love, for 1658 and 1659, if recovered; he was to have them for 1657 from him that took them from the Commonwealth, paying the rent to his lordship. He was to pay £25 for this year and £27 for next. By his contract with Sanckye's agent he is to pay but £12 for ten years. Col. Sancky is expected every day; will replevy if he distrains for the rent. The best title he can pretend to is a paper order from the commissioners, whose office is not of record; their order can signify no more as yet than a scarecrow.

2. Has set twelve plough-lands for seven to thirty-one years. Doubts not to set most of the seigniory upon very good terms. Several that are removing out of co. Corke would become his tenants; would rather deal with them than with many here, for most are either English or accustomed to the ways of English plantation. They will be freer to build and quick-set. Besides, it is for his honour and safety to have Protestants. In a short time the smallness of the contribution in this seigniory will encourage others to come and plant here. A protection and indulgence to those that come is continually necessary. Met with many complaints of injury at his return. Came just in the critical moment to ease them in the last tax; hopes his lordship will not have to pay any except for the small parcel held for his own use. One or two assessments more and this seigniory will bear but a very slender part of the burthen.

3. Some of the justices of this county are very forward to transplant. If not stinted they'll make a great rout here, which will terrify other tenants from coming if these be removed. There are those that, to save their own concernments and relations, will not stick to sacrifice another. Although the power of the J.P.'s under the Act of Attainder of Ireland commenced but this month, they are severe already—some within the bowels of the seigniory, as Barstable, etc., have already presented some of his lordship's tenants as transplantable, and prosecute

them on the new Act of Recusancy. Doubts not to nullify their projects and let them know they have endeavoured to injure a noble landlord. Was ever unwilling to receive Irish tenants, but English are scant, and these Irish are received elsewhere. Knows not why his lordship's estate should lie waste to please a few knaves that under pretence of religion prosecute these poor people while their main ends are but to have the lands at their own terms.

4. Sent by post to Col. Herbert and the attorney to enquire after the exemplification of the inquistion; hopes it will come before the trial. Must [prove] his grandmother was *infra aetatem* when she made the original deed to Virgin, and also avoid the pretence of several descents cast. Has studied the point here in Lord Cooke's works. Good lawyers are scant in the circuit. Few have come of late to this county, there being usually but one judge, for criminals only—this is the first *nisi prius* since the wars. Some of the jury are no enemies to his lordship's concerns. His attorney is to give him notice as soon as the circuits and "Jesses" [? *recte* judges] are resolved upon.

5. No money to be had from the tenants till the Island fair, the 24th of next month, unless he distrains or forces them to sell their cattle.

6. This year or not at all the arrears of 1641 and 1642 must be recovered, for the rule against the Statute of Limitations granted for six years in favour of the English commenced Trinity term 1653. Suits may bring in a considerable sum, though many former tenants are dead or transplanted to Connaught and Clare, etc.

7. Richard Twisse says he cannot take less than a third of the grain he sows for his lordship's use—[Lord Herbert] finding ground, oxen, seed, ploughs, etc., he only finding labourers. In England husbandry is commonly divided into four—1. the ground, 2. the seed, 3. the compost, 4. the labour—and the farmer has but the fourth. But here compost is seldom used and the ground—limestone—rather better than commonly allowed for tillage there. Twisse says that in England the farmer has usually the fourth part of the profits of the dairy. Cannot offer the customs of this country because such bargains are not usual. Twisse will have thirty to forty acres of fallow this year. Corn in these parts is "but a very Drugg", for a barrel of wheat, nine Winchester measures, yielded not 25s. till these three weeks (now 30s.). Because of that they are victualling ships at Kinsale. Nine measures of oats are worth 7s., and the same of small barley malt 15s. (until now 10s. or 12s.). Stock is the most profitable. The lands next the castle he should either employ so or set from year to year or from three years to three [years], till he needs corn for his house should he live here. There are three and a half plough-lands reserved for him near the castle, one of Caherninard and two and a half of Claskaniffe. Another plough-land of Caherninard was set to Barstable for £8. The residue of Caherninard and most of the Craggs (part of the land whereon the town stands) Richd. Twisse has had the use of.

8. Richd. Twisse has not yet pitched upon any lands, but speaks of the best part of Kilbanevane and a plough-land called Ballimolyr.

9. Mr. Browne is troubled at his lordship's disallowing his mill; hears he intends to repair to England. Browne has received £30 and has stopped £10 more for corn had here in 1656, which the accounts

[contradict]. He says [Lord Herbert] promised to remit £12, the first year's rent of "the desert". Desires to know his pleasure in that and concerning the fee-farm. The survey will evidence how many acres Termgoose and Insy mc Markus contain. His lordship is to pay 4d. an English acre, according to the patent, and though it is not required at present it is requisite to reserve a rent accordingly.

10. Is sorry there is the likelihood of a difference between him and his mother. Doubts not to put this seigniory in so good a condition that within a few years he shall not only discharge the annuities he agreed to for his brothers and sisters, but also receive clear £300 or £400 per annum. But cannot hope this unless his lordship be here in person or gives the writer leave to continue here.

Has sent all needful for carrying on the suit with the creditors. Dare not go to London to intend it because of the debts he contracted there for his lordship's father and the writer himself, which Mr. Medlicott, Vanley, etc., would clap him up for. Hopes to set the greatest part of the seigniory by 1 November. Had Mr. Charlton known the condition of affairs here—an opportunity of receiving tenants now may not come again these twenty years—he would not have advised commanding the writer over. The fine and recovery shall be left till further orders. Service to Madam Frances and Mr. Jones. Is glad he and Mr. Vaughan have agreed about the lands in Llyssyn Park.

"At your Lordships Castle Island",
29 June. 45.

It will be noticed that Herbert names two consecutive dates for the Island fair. "The desert" is probably Dysert.

1658

257. Robt. Wynne to Mrs. Dorothy Wynne at Dollgeog.

"Deare sister". Is glad she is in a way of recovery. Hoped to have heard from her whether Mr. Lloyd had taken the Cardiganshire business on him; will submit to anything he does. Otherwise will desire that it be prosecuted. Understands the sessions are at hand; hopes the enclosed will "doe the doe". The sessions at Hereford are the 3rd of next month; brother Foxwist is to be there. Her sister thanks her for the yarn. Their mother is not so well. His and his wife's recommendations to both cousins Herbert.

15 July. *Armorial seal*

Endorsed: The lands in Llanurchaian parish are in the occupation of Llewelin Parry. 4.

[16]58

258. Thom. Lloyd to his cousin Richard Herbert of Dolgiog, esq.

Is glad Mr. Robt. Wynne has obtained the desired deed; is satisfied as to his title and the "noe colourable clayme" of Evan Gwyn. Sent to treat with that gentleman when lately in Cardiganshire, but could not stay his leisure; on conference he might soon be convinced. If he can engage any to undertake it Herbert shall know soon. Meantime would have Mr. Wynne prepare to go with his trial at law. Pains must be taken to find out witnesses in those parts; one Richard Tydyr an old servant of Mrs. Owen's, that lives (if alive) in the parish of Llansanfriad, is a principal one. When Herbert is ready for the bars or other iron it shall be provided. Service to his lady and Madame Wynne.

Beryw,
20 July. *Armorial seal* 2.

1658

259. MARTIN NOELL AND GEORGE CLERKE TO SIR THOMAS HERBERT, SECRETARY OF STATE IN IRELAND, AT DUBLIN.

Received his of the 25th. Mr. Lane delivered the box to one that takes in letters near Temple Bar, but did not pay the port. There is a rule that all such things (except the State's) pay here. Not finding any hand on the outside to show it belonged to the State or a member thereof, the person waited until Mr. Lane came and paid the postage.

Lno.,
31 August. *Armorial seal*

Endorsed: Concerning Lord Herbert's box. 46.

1658

260. THO. HERBERT TO LORD HERBERT AT LLYSSYN. HASTE . . . WITH SPECIAL CARE.

Encloses a bill of exchange for £100 payable at ten days' sight to Mr. John Myddleton in London, returned by Mr. Benjamyn Crofts, who had £3 for the exchange. It is his first bill—has another in case it does not come safely. The money is payable by Mr. Tho. Corbett and his compartners, near the Tower. God willing, will return £150 more by the term, and before that a perfect rental of the Michaelmas rent . . . Would have sent a bill for more if he could—was forced to come from Kerry hither before he could [get] this. Has not received one line from him these seven weeks.

Corke,
14 September.

Service to Lady Frances, respects to Mr. Jones. Will be unwilling to adventure more [until] he knows of the receipt of this bill. *HM* 2.22/12.

[16]58

261. THOM. LLOYD TO RICHARD HERBERT OF DOLGIOG, ESQ.

Is glad his lady bore her journey so well; believes frequent moderate journeys would confirm her health. May not meddle in the sale of Madam Wynne's brother's lands without instructions; his deeds will tell what it cost his aunt . . . (*directions as to selling follow*). Prescribed not quicksilver (crude mercury) for Herbert's horse for the bots, but precipitate, of which he now sends a dozen by Gabr.; it is to be mixed with the quantity of a hazel-nut of butter and made into a ball, closely lapped in a bigger ball of clear butter, and thrust on the end of a rod into the horse's throat. Davyd Prees has undertaken that the iron bars shall be ready Friday next. Will he send to the forge or have them brought hither? The way thither by Bwlch y fedwen and Llyssyn is only some three miles nearer than to this place. Has bespoken ninety foot of bars. Service and thanks from his sister.

Ber.,
11 October. *Armorial seal* 3.

1658/9

262. Tho. Herbert to Lord Herbert at Dublin. Leave at Mr. Ballard the apothecary's in Castle Street.

Is glad to hear of his safe arrival and prays for his good journey to Kerry. His concernments are in good posture except the castle, which last winter worsted very much; will hasten thither next week to endeavour to have one good room fitted for him. Is glad the fines and recoveries are finished; had been at Dublin to attend that.

Cullen,
12 February. 47.

1658/9

263. Tho. Herbert to Lord Herbert at Dublin. At Mr. Ballard the apothecary's in Castle Street.

Received on the 20th his of the 15th, with the unwelcome news of his being displeased with him. Offers to his consideration: 1. His lady was named in the concord because it was conceived she was capable of having her thirds out of this as well as any other part of the estate; at Bewmarris it was his content she should be named. Sir Maurice Eustace does not rightly apprehend his title in Ireland if he thinks it is upon account of the last wars and the new rules; his lordship claims it as an ancient propriety, and not as adventurer or soldier. Sir Maurice said a fine was requisite and would debar all pretences if claims be not prosecuted according to the statue 10 *Carol.* in Ireland. 2. He charges him with receiving David Lloyd, a servant to his mother (who, more's the pity, he conceives to be an enemy). Saw nothing in the letters he brought concerning Lord Herbert besides his own desiring the writer to pay certain moneys for her use. Was to be married the beginning of January, but business in the unhappy office the writer is in [delayed him]. Has not meddled in the recovery of the arrears. Mr. Denny, to whom it was recommended by Mr. Justice Santhy, can testify when the writer received the letter of attorney. David Lloyd came over merely to bring these letters and to know whether the writer was alive, none of his letters having come for several months. 3. Would have stirred about the arrears, but not receiving intelligence of the arrival of the commission he had no business at Dublin. Has writs ready, and he shall have an account to a penny when he comes of whatever the writer has received of arrears due in his grandfather's or his father's time. 4. Had he come to Dublin he would have delivered the writings to Sir M. Left some nailed in a box at Mr. Hockshowe's in Dublin, where he lay formerly; has written to Mr. Watkin Sands to deliver them to Lord Herbert. 5. Does not imagine his present office privileges him from paying him that respect or yielding the right due to him. Neither cares nor fears who his accusers are and does not dread the narrowest scrutiny.

Encloses a copy of the bill Col. Sancky put in. Ballimc Adam mentioned in it is part of what the writer recovered for Lord Herbert, and is in both the decree and the patent. Submits to Sir M. E. whether his lordship derives his title from the patent or the decree. Col. Sancky's order from the Lord Deputy and Council is but a paper order, so cannot take away his right. The Commissioners for Laying Out of Lands may have power to dispose of forfeited or concealed lands, but these are not.

Will wait on him where and when he commands the other side of Slevelogher and bring the best guides these parts afford. Is sorry the castle will not be in fitting condition to receive him; finds it much worse than when he left it. Cruel winds this winter not only uncovered it but destroyed most of the glass; has sent for glass to Corke and hopes they will find a glazier here. Suggests he defers his journey eight or ten days. Some beer might by that time be brewed. Found no French wine at Corke fit for him; there's some daily expected. The weekly markets provide little provision this time of the year, and since he forbids him to provide any other he will obey. Will bespeak a beef and some muttons. Hopes they will have enough "caddowes" and bedding to keep his lordship's company as warm, though not so cleanly, as in England. Clonmell, Mitchells town, Maiallo, and Glanturke will be a better way this season than through co. Lymerick, which is a deep heavy soil.

Castle Islands,
22 February.

Desires him to wish Mr. Gouldinge to get from Mr. Pheelip Harryes, the writer's attorney in the upper bench, the exemplification of the inquisition after Sir Wm. Herbert's death—Sir Tho. Herbert delivered it to him—and four blank writs. He lives over against the Sun tavern in Nicholas Street, Dublin.

Armorial seal 48.

Herbert's "unhappy office" was that of High Sheriff of co. Kerry.

1658/9

264. THO. FARRON TO THOMAS HERBERTT, HIGH SHERIFF OF CO. KERRY.

Has sent the "particullars" hereafter mentioned with the cost of them. There is no sherry-sack worth drinking in the town. Will send the price of some white wine lately come into harbour. Wheat is 3s. a bushel. Mr. Maior has cloth a-making for Herbert, and will use him as well as any in Corke, or better. Mr. Croffts says that about the beginning of April he intends for Kerrye. Will secure a crib of glass for Herbert with some drawn lead if any be come over. Has put the linen-ware in the cask with the other things, but the two dripping-pans are loose. Service to Mr. Browne.

Corke,
10 March.

6 lbs.	rice . .	3s.	2 ozs. mace	3s.
3 ,,	currants . .	2s. 6d.	4 lbs. starch	2s. 8d.
4 ,,	raisins . .	2s. 8d.	1 oz. blue	2d.
1 ,,	pepper . .	1s. 10d.	1 pottle of oil . .	3s. 4d.
4 ,,	brown sugar .	3s.	2 bottles . . .	1s.
4 ,,	white sugar .	4s.	200 of red herrings .	4s. 6d.
4 ozs.	nutmegs . .	2s. 8d.	200 ,, white ,, . .	4s.
2 ,,	cloves . .	1s. 8d.	1 firkin . . .	1s. 3d.

25.

A "crib" is a hundred or a hundred and fifty square feet.

1659

265. Job Charlton to Mrs. Florentia Herbert.

Is glad of her commendable care for her younger brothers and sisters. Could wish the deed were executed by his lordship, to prevent mortality. Would have no occasion of delay by tendering another, for if his lordship should die their condition might be sad. Yet the annuities ought to have been settled more particularly (as to days of payment, etc.). Also, if his lady does not join in a fine she may recover her dower, and the two parts left may not be sufficient for the portions and annuities. Cannot but think his lordship (being sufficiently obliged during his life) will take care [his successors] shall not have his brothers and sisters at their mercy. Sent her letter to Barbican, but the Earl is not in town.

Lincoln's Inns,
25 June. *Armorial seal* 386.

The Earl of Bridgwater, Lord Herbert's cousin german, had his London house in Barbican.

1659

266. [Lord] Herbert to Robert Griffiths, esq., at Sutton.

His advice and carriage towards the writer are so friendly that he will follow the one and acknowledge the other when he may be of use. Will send a letter to Lord Lambert, whom he thought at London, but hears this day is at Chirke Castle. Knows no fitting person of interest with him that can do more than present his letter, which he will send by his own servant. Would have given the trouble to him had his occasions allowed him to undertake it.

Llyssyn,
6 September. 49.

A few weeks earlier Major-General Lambert had crushed Booth's rising, in which Lord Herbert had been actively engaged.

[16]59

267. MEREDITH LLOYD TO MR. JOHN MIDLETON, GROCER, AT THE STAR ON FISH STREET HILL.

Finding him not at home, is forced to leave this to acquaint him that he must use £15 this day about "my lords" concerns; which he desires him to give order to his servant to pay to such as the writer shall send . . .

"At your Shop",
26 November.

Below, in another hand: Lady Herbert's receipts. *Lloyd's receipt for the £15 is on the dorse.* *HM2.26/3.*

1660

268. ROGER JONES TO LORD HERBERT. LEAVE WITH MR. THO. GERVASE IN POOLE TO BE SENT TO LLYSSIN.

No news worth the sending. The King adjourns Parliament tomorrow and passes the bills. Hears none is of public concernment but that relating to ministers, which is sufficiently favourable to the clergy of the Church of Englande—"thanks to your honourable house". The Spanish ambassador is hourly expected, but the Adelantado observes his national gravity. The peace with that nation was published yesterday. The D. of Glocester is well, and, he hopes, absolutely recovered. Will be moving homewards on Monday—stays for Mr. Lloyde of Berrywe's company. Service to his lady.

11 September. *Armorial seal* 50.

The Duke of Gloucester died two days later.

1660

269. CR. BROWNE TO LORD HERBERT AT LLYSSYN. LEAVE AT MR. THO. JERVISS'S AT WELSHPOOLE TO BE DELIVERED.

Encloses the letter which came out of Monmouth on the 12th. Has had the *distringas* and record sent down ready for trial. Sent notice to Mr. Ratliffe (to Mr. Rowland Myddleton to convey); hopes it will arrive Saturday, which will give Mr. Ratliffe time to go to Monmouth if he sets forward Sunday afternoon—little will be done as to trial between parties on Monday. Supposes Mr. Williams will prepare breviates and fee counsel.

Mr. Gillinghan has waited on the Queen's counsel in relation to Chertsey; they will not grant Lord Herbert the whole manor, there being farms of £500 a year within it, several already in the hands of person[s] of quality. But they say that if he pitch upon any one or two of those farms he shall not fail of them, paying as others do, which he hears is seven years' purchase at least, some say eight. The petition for Snowdon is delivered to Sec. Nicholas; money must be returned out of hand for passing the seals if there be a grant of it. Supposes he has news from Mr. Jones or another, but gives the good news of the Duke of Glocester's recovery, of the arrival of the Spanish ambassador this day in a great deal of pomp, and of the peace proclaimed with Spaine. Hopes he and Lady Herbert are safe at Llyssyn after their journey.

London,
14 September. *Armorial seal* 397.

A Rowland Myddelton was mayor of Shrewsbury in 1673. The following February Lord Herbert was made Chief Forester of Snowdon, Chief Constable of Conway Castle, and Steward of the manors belonging to Bardsey Abbey (*Cal. of State Papers, Domestic*, 1660-61, p. 522).

[1660]

270. [LORD HERBERT] TO——————. *A much-altered draft.*

The unwelcome news in his of the 14th might have hindered him from pitching upon "those lands" and making particulars ready against their assizes. But having done it he he is free to condole the loss of so excellent a prince, so great a pillar of their Protestant religion. Takes it it is the Duke of Gloster he means . . . God preserve the remaining stock of this royal family, and put it in the King's and the Duke of Yorke's minds to marry, that England, etc., may not be provinces to other princes. Has lost a good master [and might have bettered his fortune by His Highness's favour *deleted*] for [when he kissed his hands last *deleted*] he said, "What ever requests you make to mee you shall find my best endeavours . . .", and more to this purpose. But he sins against the public and his own thoughts . . .

[September]. 617.

The Duke of York was, of course, already secretly married.

1660

271. ROBT. WYNNE TO RICHARD HERBERT, ESQ., AT DOLLGEOG.

Received his from Dollgelly. Encloses a blank letter of attorney. If Mr. Lloyd will undergo the business no man is fitter. His sister can say how many years there are since his aunt's death; supposes it to be past nine. Asks that they make as much as may be in the valuation, for he has promised to part with the lands to Mr. Vaughan for sixteen years' purchase. His and his wife's love to him and his bedfellow.

Llanidan,
8 October.

His comrade and he will next summer give Herbert the meeting in any neighbouring county save Cardiganshire (unless at Mr. Vaughan's house there).

Armorial seal 6.

This Mr. Vaughan is probably John Vaughan of Crosswood (later Chief Justice of the Common Pleas). If these lands are the Cardiganshire ones referred to earlier see No. 227) they are very close to his house.

1660

272. [FRANCIS FITZHERBERT'S] NOTE OF THINGS RECEIVED WITH MR. BROWNE FROM MR. RICHARD THOMSON'S HOUSE IN MOUNTGOM[ER]Y.

A box of writings concerning Cherbury, delivered to Mr. Ireland; 2 great presses of ancient records; 1 great brass picture; 1 alabaster picture; 9 glass bottles for stilling; 1 harp; 1 weatherglass in a deal box; 1 large picture of Edward, Lord Herbert; writings concerning Monmouth and Mountgom[er]y Castle, etc.; 1 bag of coiner's tools; [furniture *listed*] left at request of Anne Thomson; *other writings and articles are mentioned also.*

22 October. 398.

The large picture was presumably of the 1st Lord Herbert, or we would expect it to be described as 'of my Lord' or by some such form of words.

1660

273. THE PRIVY COUNCIL TO THE EARL OF CARBERY, LORD LIEUTENANT OF SOUTHWALES AND NORTHWALES. *Copy in Richd. Herbert's letter-book.*

Whereas divers of His Majesty's subjects exempt themselves from the trained bands in most counties, or refuse to appear or send their horses and arms to the musters, he is to put the statute of 4 and 5 Mary in execution against them, and every year return a perfect muster roll of "that County" to this board.

Whithall,	Edw. Hide	Albermarle
14 December.	Linsley	Dorchester
	Ormunde	Valentia
	Will. Morice	G. Sarterett (*sic*)
	H. Howard	Mountgom[er]y
	John Nicholas	

Ex. Will Cowley *HM*2.14/3/4.

This and the following documents similarly described are copies made for Richard Herbert of Dolguog in a thin paper-bound foolscap volume; they are all official letters communicated to him in connexion with his duties as either Justice of the Peace or Deputy Lieutenant for Montgomeryshire, and range in date from December 1660 to February 1660/61, with two of November 1666 added at the end. "County" is possibly an error for country; or perhaps a particular reference in the original to Montgomeryshire has been omitted.

1660

274. HIS MAJESTY TO THE EARL OF CARBERY. *Copy in Richard Herbert's letter-book.*

Charles R.

Whereas several persons of loose principles and known disaffection have furnished themselves with such quantities of arms and munitions as gives suspicion of design to disturb the kingdom, he is required to make search, and where arms and munitions be discovered in the house of any disaffected person above what may be reasonable for his safeguard, they are to be seized and employed for the use of the public. And he is to use all diligence to prevent tumults, insurrections, and numerous and unlawful meetings.

Whithall, Edw. Nicholas
19 December. *HM*2.14/3/1.

1660

275. [LORD] CARBERY TO MR. SHERIFF AND [THE JUSTICES OF MONTGOMERYSHIRE]. *Copy in Richd. Herbert's letter-book.*

Encloses a transcript of His Majesty's of the 19th, which he received the 24th. Commends to them the speedy and effectual performance thereof, the Deputy Lieutenants not having their commissions, the writer's commission for the Lieutenancy of Northwales being but lately passed the Seal. They are with all diligence to hinder tumults [etc.]. All arms and ammunition seized are to be preserved, particulars to be inventoried between them, that they may give account to him and the Deputy Lieutenants who shall be "suddenly" commissioned. Desires frequent knowledge of their proceedings.

London,
24 December. *HM*2.14/3/2.

[1660]

276. R. L. TO HIS UNCLE MR. LEWIS PRICE AT HIS CHAMBER IN WELCH POOLE. *Copy in Richd. Herbert's letter-book.*

Has not neglected any opportunity to write. His last was to Mr. Moris this day sevennight. Sent before some books of Va. Pwell's to be distributed. "There is noe other yet which you Looke for". Many are committed to prison daily—most of the officers of the old army, some upon suspicion of the————plot, some for not leaving London, and some for refusing the oath; and divers others this day for opening their shops. The Princess of Orange died yesterday about twelve o'clock, some say of the smallpox, others by bleeding that could not be stopped. Had it from two preachers that came from Oxford that nine or ten are dead of N. Col., which was the first college that read the Common Prayer book, and that others of other colleges die; they are full of blue spots, which is doubtless the plague. A wind lately blew down part of the cathedral of Yorke and all the pinnacles. And it is reported the Hollander lost many ships and men with mighty store of wealth. Surely God is drawing near, loudly calling upon everyone, good as well as bad. ". . . How are wee as those people Daniell mencens chap. 9:13 . . . . . The Lord is willing to treate with us upon those . . . Condicons . . . in Lev. 26 . . ." Prays him when he has read this, send it with the enclosed to D. P. "together with one of my V. P. B. to J. Ts. of K. with his name upon it, and you shall receive one or twoe for it by the first trustie Messinger". Wrote to S. B. concerning himself and expected answer this day, but fears [they are] miscarried; it was to tell him that if upon any terms he could obtain his liberty, the writer has a good master, easy service, and £6 yearly for him; must hear speedily. Are well, though the writer had some sore fits of the stone. They keep a jolly Christmas.

[Christmas Day].

Hear little of Capt. P. and wife. Rem. to all from both and to all about and within town. *HM*2.14/3/12.

This is headed "A Letter from Vavasor Powell", but the initials at the end are R. L. Vavasor Powell was at this time a prisoner in the Fleet. The Common Prayer Book had just been brought back into use by the Restoration. "V.P.B." presumably means "Vavasor Powell books". The person to whom this letter was addressed is apparently not the Capt. Lewis Price to whom Vavasor Powell wrote in July, for he had left the neighbourhood by the beginning of August (*Cal. of State Papers, Domestic*, 1660-61, pp. 136 and 176); Lewis Price may, of course, be the "Capt. P." of the postscript.

1660/61

277. [THE EARL OF] CARBERY TO [THE DEPUTY LIEUTENANTS FOR THE COUNTIES OF NORTH WALES]. *Copy in Richd. Herbert's letter-book.*

"My Lord and Gentlemen." Having sent commissions into Northwales for Deputy Lieutenants unto them whom His Majesty has approved of, they shall receive a transcript of his instructions and of a warrant useful for despatch of those affairs. They should meet frequently that they may be upon his coming (which will be with all speed) in a good forwardness. They should make inquiry after all arms at any time charged in the country that they may be demanded for His Majesty's service; and if those who have embezzled arms refuse account, they are to inform the Lords of the Council, or if necessary take speedy course with them. They are likewise to inform themselves what arms are wanting, that the country may be with expedition and at the easiest rates supplied. They should impartially rate men's estates, that every one being justly assessed His Majesty's and the country's service may be more readily expedited. All arms and the persons of those disaffected to His Majesty they are without partiality to seize.

Before they were commissioned he sent to the High Sheriff and justices of their several counties a transcript of His Majesty's letter of 19 December; wishes them to call for account of their proceedings therein. Sends herewith transcript of a letter of the Privy Council the contents whereof they should punctually observe.

2 January. *HM*2.14/3/6

"My Lord" is no doubt Lord Herbert. The King's instructions to Lord Carbery as Lord President, dated 1 October, are also transcribed into Richard Herbert's letter-book. So also is the form of the warrant mentioned above; it is designed to issue from the Deputy Lieutenants of a county in Lord Carbery's lieutenancy to a high constable, requiring him to obtain and produce returns from petty constables as to persons having lands worth £5 per annum or personal estate worth £100, and also as to the number of the common arms formerly charged upon every district.

1660/61

278. THE PRIVY COUNCIL TO THE EARL OF CARBERY. *Copy in Richd. Herbert's letter-book.*

Notwithstanding His Majesty's gracious concessions, many factions retain their rebellious principles, and some have lately entered into plots which, had they not been discovered, would have endangered His Majesty's person, the settlement of the government, and peace of the kingdom. And it is evident by their frequent meetings and other actions that this wicked spirit continues in the minds of many others (yet undiscovered) in several parts of this kingdom, who have furnished themselves with arms and hold correspondency together to execute some desperate attempt. Therefore they pray and authorize him to disarm all such as are notoriously known to be of ill principles, or have since the Act of Indemnity shown disaffection or disturbed the peace; to administer to them the Oaths of Supremacy and Allegiance, and to take security for their good behaviour if cause appear. If any refuse he is to proceed against them according to law.

Whitehall, 8 January.	Dorchester	Edw. Hide
	Berkshire	Albermarle
	Norwich	Northumberland
	Valentia	Denzill Hollis
	Edw. Nicholas	Will. Morice

Ex. Will Cowley *HM*2.14/3/7.

1660/61

279. [The Earl of] Carbery to the Lord of Chirbury and the rest of the Deputy Lieutenants of Mountgom[er]y shire. *Copy in Richd. Herbert's letter-book.*

Sends herewith transcript of a letter from the Privy Council, directed the 8th and received the 9th, which they are with all diligence to put in execution. Prays particular, frequent, and speedy account; likewise with all expedition an exact account what forces, horse and foot, may be raised in their county, that arms may be provided.

London,
11 January. *HM*2.14/3/8.

1660/61

280. The Earl of Carbery to the High Sheriff and Justices of co. Mountgom[er]y. *Copy in Richd. Herbert's letter-book.*

Has received theirs of the 2nd and 14th, expressing their readiness to secure His Majesty and their country. Commends their diligence in raising those horse mentioned in their letter, as being of very good use until settlement be made in the militia, which has met with many obstructions, though he has done all in his power, having disposed of most of the commissions to the counties entrusted to him. Has acquainted His Majesty's secretary with what they wrote, and in due time they shall have direction for the management.

London,
18 January. *HM*2.14/3/3.

1660/61

281. The Lords of the Council to the Earl of Carbery, Lord Lieutenant of Wales. *Copy in Richd. Herbert's letter-book.*

By theirs of the 8th they authorized him to disarm all notoriously of evil principles or that have since the Act of Indemnity shown disaffection or disturbed the peace; yet considering the late bloody attempts in the City of London and many advices from several parts of the kingdom of some horrid design against His Majesty, they require him to give strict order to his Deputy Lieutenants, etc., to observe the motions of dangerous persons, and not only disarm but imprison such leading persons as they have good ground to suspect opposed to the government and may influence multitudes to disturb the peace and refuse to take the oath of allegiance, and all others as shall design to raise discontents or draw parties together to engage the kingdom in unnatural war; and speedily advertise this Board of his proceedings, that order may be taken with persons by him secured.

Whithall,	Edw. Hide	T. Southampton
22 January.	C. Howard	Berkshire
	Albermarle	Dorchester
	Valentia	Denzill Hollis
	Lauderdale	F. Seymour
	F. Cornwallis	E. Manchester
	Ch. Berkley	Ed. Nicholas
	Will. Morice	Edw. Walker

Ex. Will Cowley *HM*2.14/3/13.

The "late bloody attempts" in the City are those of the Fifth Monarchy men.

1660/61

282. Lord Herbert and the rest of the Deputy Lieutenants of the Militia of co. Mountgom[er]y to the Earl of Carbery, Lord Lieutenant of Walles, at his house in Newport Street. *Copy in Richd. Herbert's letter-book.*

Have this day issued warrants to the constables to make return this day fortnight of all that fall under the qualification of maintainers and contributors for militia, horse and foot. Will then proceed to the settling of this county, and meanwhile endeavour to secure the peace. But must desire him to speed down the commissions for the other Deputies, that they may act effectually, for the largeness of the county [and] ill-ness of the weather and ways do incommode much. Will likewise present him with the names of persons fitting to command the horse and foot, and submit to his determination. Fear the number of horse and foot will fall much short of expectation. But they will advance as much as they can without oppressing the country, which is much impoverished by the late troubles.

F. Herbert
Roger Moston, *Vic.*
Math. Price

Newtowne,
23 January.

*HM*2.14/3/11.

1660/61

283. The Earl of Carbery to the Deputy Lieutenants of co. Mountgomry. *Copy in Richd. Herbert's letter-book.*

Sends transcript of a letter dated the 22nd from the Council, which came yesterday the 24th. Desires their particular care [in it and] frequent returns of their transactions, that he may give His Majesty and his Council satisfactory account. Hitherto has not received such quick returns as these affairs required.

Expects account what numbers of horse and foot their county is able to raise, according to the abilities of each person chargeable with whole arms or part of arms, that arms may be provided and officers commissioned by him. Has bespoke a quantity of arms here at the best rates . . . They are to make speedy provision for returns of money hither for paying for them.

[25 January]. *HM*2.14/3/14.

1660/61

284. RESOLUTIONS OF A GENERAL MEETING OF THE DEPUTY LIEUTENANTS AND JUSTICES FOR CO. MOUNTGOM[ER]Y. *Copy in Richd. Herbert's letter-book.*

Whereas the Earl of Carbery, Lord Lieutenant, upon occasion of the insurrection at London, before the Deputy Lieutenants were commissioned, recommended the Sheriff and Justices to [see to] the security of the country, and whereas they caused divers persons to be secured, many of which remain under custody, since which time all tumults are appeased: It is therefore resolved (*nem. con.*) that all remaining in custody, upon taking the Oath of Allegiance, be discharged, finding security of good behaviour and to appear at next general sessions for the county.

6 February. *HM*2.14/3/15

1660/61

285. ORDERS AND RESOLUTIONS BY THE DEPUTY LIEUTENANTS OF MONTGOMERYSHIRE. *Copy in Richd. Herbert's letter-book.*

That there be 50 horse raised. That there be four companies of foot, according to the instructions, of 80 a company. That there be a volunteer troop of horse under Lord Herbert. That £60 per annum be raised "to find the foote and Armes" till further consideration. That £250 per annum find a horse and arms till further consideration. That Mr. Richard Owen of Rhusison, Mr. John Pugh of Mathravall, and Sir Mathew Pryce be captains for the foot. That Roger Mostyn, esq., High Sheriff, be captain of a company. The proportion of each hundred for raising the foot:

Llanidloes 48	Mountgomry 32	Machynlleth 32
New Towne 48	Poole 32	Mathravall 32
Llanvillyn 48	Caurse 32	Deythwr 16

The charge for horse:

Llanidloes 6	Newtowne 7	Mountgomry 5
Machynlleth 6	Poole 5	Mathravall 5
Lanvillyn 7	Caurse 5	Deythwr 4

Mr. Owen, capt.	The foot to be raised in Llanidloes and Machunlleth, designed for one company.
Sir Mathew Pryce, capt.	Foot to be raised in Newetowne and Mountgom[er]y, one company.
Mr. Mostyn, capt.	Foot to be raised in Llanvillin and Mathravall, one company.
Mr. Pugh, capt.	Foot to be raised in Poole, Caurse, and Deythwr, the fourth company.

Poole,
6 February.

Resolved 8 February that the next general meeting be 26 February at Mountgom[er]y at John Mason's. That meantime the Deputies within their precincts prepare list[s] of whole maintainers and contributors for horse and foot. For Lanvylling and Mathravall: Lord Herbert, Roger Mostyn, John Blaney; to meet at Llyssin 20 February, and the country be summoned to appear before them at Llanervill the same day and *a die in diem* till [it] be settled.

Resolved that John Mason of Mountgom[er]y, gent., be marshal to the Deputy Lieutenants, all prisoners from this day taken upon account of the King and Deputy Lieutenants to be delivered to his custody.

Poole, 8 February.	E. Herbert	John Blayney
	Roger Mostyn	Rich. Owen
	Mathew Pryce	Rich. Herbert
	Edw. Lloyd	John Pryce

*HM*2.14/3/17.

The reference to the £60 per annum seems to be garbled; it presumably means that every £60 per annum of land must provide pay and arms for one foot-soldier.

1660/61

286. LORD HERBERT AND THE REST OF THE DEPUTY LIEUTENANTS OF CO. MOUNTGOM[ER]Y TO [LORD CARBERY]. *Copy in Richd. Herbert's letter-book.*

Received his of 23 (*sic*) January, with the other commissions. Have had a general meeting at Poole for settlement of the militia and the high constables' returns of the ancient charge, and find it [three *deleted*] [two *deleted*] hundred foot and 35 horse; which they have increased to 320 foot (to make four full companies) and 50 horse, besides a volunteer troop of horse under Lord Herbert and a volunteer company of 50 foot which in April last were raised by Thomas Corbett, esq., Recorder of Poole, and will be by him continued for the town and liberties. Have nominated captains of the foot, which they leave to his confirmation by commissionating them, viz: Roger Mostin, esq., Sir Mathew Pryce, Richard Owens, esq., and John Pugh, esq., and for the volunteer company Thomas Corbett of Poole, esq. Unanimously comply with his nomination of Mr. William Browne for muster-master, and desire his commission for him. Conceive he will leave the under-officers to each captain; desire blank commissions for them.

The persons formerly secured, he referring the dispose of them to their discretion, they have now, after a general calm, discharged upon taking the Oath of Allegiance and [finding] two sufficient sureties of their own neighbourhood to appear at next sessions.

Desire his like care and direction for the trophy money of Northwales as he has taken for Southwales, that the country may be eased of some charge.

And whereas he sent down direction to the High Sheriff and Justices for securing the peace, they raised a volunteer troop of 36 horse and employed Mr. Henry Purcell to command them for securing dangerous persons (who was also upon the King's coming into England employed upon like account); recommend gratifying Mr. Purcell and his troop by £200 out of some public money.

Last they desire him to cause to be provided in London for the militia foot 200 firelocks and 120 pikes; will return money as soon as they are ready.

8 February.	E. Herbert	John Blayney
	Roger Mostin	Richard Owen
	Math. Pryce	Rich. Herbert
	Edw. Lloyd	John Pryce

Since writing they have made bold to pitch upon Mr. John Mason of Mountgom[er]y to be marshal. Their next general meeting will be at Mountgom[er]y the 26th of this instant; meantime have divided themselves to . . . (*torn*) . . . things. *HM*2.14/3/16.

1660/61

287. [Lord Herbert] to ————. *Draft.*

He will find by the enclosed what success his letter had with Lord Powis, and that his orders committing it to the fire will be executed. Was at a great "contest" how to carry himself, and gave no answer to his lordship till this day; sends a copy. Remembered his advice, that where there is a weaker it is a point of discretion to make compliance a civility. Labouring to reconcile a difference [between] Sir Mathew Price and Jack Purcell, he had the success to make them as one. Having united them "wee" may bid defiance to the lords of the soil—the old quarrel of this county with the tenants, now revived. For this time, as for the future, he hopes he has laid grounds of amity, that the gentry will stick to one another and be able to choose the knight. Choosing a burgess will not lie in their power unless Mountgom[er]y, being county town, may choose their own, which they did till of late—it being their misfortune to choose a burgess that could not maintain himself, to save charges they accepted of the rest to bear a share, from which time all other corporations have had voices in choice of burgesses. If which precedent be not "obliging", he may be sure of the place. Gave him no encouragement, yet has acted so that, without naming him or anybody else, he strives by friends interested in the several corporations to divide their interest. If upon computation they find they can deal with them, the other corporations shall not be "destated". But if he gives encouragement to Will Browne and Dicke Herbert of Kerry, "the way" will be followed. "Your affectionate Nephew . . ."

1 March.

Desires to have his presence at the coronation excused. The address of the Duke and Duchess comes so near his conjecture that it surprises less than a report that the King should declare he was married in France and has two sons by a great duchess (whose name he forgets) by whom he will have right to part of France again. Whom the King thinks fit to be Queen shall be honoured by him and his sons, "as farre as I have life", and defended. Hopes this is the sense of all true subjects.

*HM*2.23/7

This was probably intended for Sir Henry Herbert, Master of the Revels. The "other corporations" referred to are the other boroughs in Montgomeryshire, who claimed a voice in electing the burgess for Montgomery; the burgess actually elected for the borough in 1661 was John Purcell of Nantcribau. The rumour that the King was married to, and had two boys by, a French princess is referred to by Pepys in the *Diary* under the date of 18 February. Lord Herbert's undertaking on behalf of his sons need not be taken as evidence that he actually had any—he certainly had infant daughters at this time, but the sons were probably prospective only.

1661

288. ROBT. WYNNE TO RICHARD HERBERT, ESQ., AT DOLLGEOG.

Is ashamed that his unhappy business in Cardiganshire has proved so troublesome. Is glad they will deliver possession. Will be content if the tenants pay as much as they paid Mr. Gwine, or what they agreed with Mr. Tho. Lloyd, 28s. or 30s. A brother-in-law of Mr. Tho. Lloyd took possession in the writer's name. Wonders that Mr. Evans questions payment of arrears and charges of suit, seeing they yield possession. But he desires, "being about time", to rid Herbert from so constant a burden. Sorry to know of his lady's weakness.

Llanidan,
25 May. *Armorial seal* 7.

[? 1661]

289. NATHANIELL NANSCAWEN TO LORD HERBERT AT CLUSHING. LEAVE AT CONWAY TO BE SENT TO SIR RICH[A]RD WINNE AT GWIDDER TO BE DELIVERED.

Finds his orders punctually performed by Mr. Tho. Herbert. Showed the letter at Dublin to Sir Arth[u]r Denny, who imparted it to the Right Revd. Edw[a]rd Sing, Bishop of Limbrick and Keirry; had great favours from both. Was at sea three times before landing at Dublin, where he spent three weeks removing a cold. Lay at Mr. Hollis', Lord Herbert's tenant's, on 17 June. On the 18th, Edw[a]rd, son to Tho. Herbert, was baptized, Lord Herbert being god-father by a representative; there was a great feast. The plough-land and a half called East Mennis and Killaly More in Castle Island parish, which Peter Brian holds for £16 per annum, is most convenient for the writer. Brian's time is but from year to year. Humbly desires it for thirty-one years; will be very thankful for any abatement of rent. Is still such a stranger [here], but in his next will try to write satisfactorily to his commands.

Castle Island, "Your . . . servant and Beadsman".
19 June. 30.

L

1661

290. THO. HERBERT TO LORD HERBERT AT LLYSSYN OR LONDON.

Confesses it is some months since he wrote, because he could not perceive that his letters were acceptable. In one he sent the whole state of Lord Herbert's case concerning his seigniory, and told him how necessary it was to renew his patent and have his rent reduced. Had he not come his lordship would have lost Ballymc Adam, for which Col. Sanckey, "your honest tenant" Charles Barstable, and Samuel Morris of Ballybeggan had conspired together. His Majesty's declaration for the settlement of Ireld. [protects] those in possession on 7 May 1659, and though his lordship was in Ireld. that very day and took distresses for the rent of Ballymc Adam, yet Barstable swore that Col. Sanckey was in possession. They would have gained possession had the writer not casually asked Mr. Nest, their old friend, to watch for mention of his lordship's concerns. Barstable swore the writer got possession from him by violence. He and Morris swore so desperately that the court was inclinable to restore Sancky, but the writer insisted on his lordship's privilege of Parliament as peer of this realm. Has been advised to petition the House of Lords against Sancky and the rest of the gang for infringing the privileges of that House. Does not doubt the nobility will second it. Indeed, Lord Corke came purposely to Court to serve his lordship. Goes this morning to Lord Kildare, Lord Westmeath, the Lord of Ards, etc., to desire their furtherance. C. Barstable said plainly Lord Herbert should be outed of Ballymc Adam and the rest of the recovered lands. He has presented articles against the writer to the Lords Justices. In 1659 at Castlemane Barstable abused his lordship when he was in Sir Geo. Booth's rising in Cheshyre, saying he was a traitor. His lordship was not pleased to take notice of it. Is advised by counsel it is actionable upon the statute of *Scandalum magnatum*; yet by the Statute of Limitations in Ireld. the action would be lost if an original writ were not filed before the end of next month. Desired Mr. Moleneux, his lordship's attorney, to file a writ in the Common Pleas. If he please to prosecute it he doubts not Mr. Barstable will be sufficiently cooled and he have good damages—the action may be laid at £10,000 or £20,000.

Barstable bragged he did not doubt to see Killmurrey, etc., evicted from his lordship. Therefore it much concerns him to have them secured in a new patent from His sacred Majesty. There are many seekers after the recovered lands. Col. Sanckey aims at Bally mc Adam; the soldiers that are to have reprisals for lands taken from them would have Killmurrey and Carker; and Dominick Roch's grandchild would have Cnockanienagh and Tullileagh. But he may preserve them all if he can get a new patent or a positive fiat to have them passed here. He should take care it leaves nothing to the judgement of those in power here, for they are on oath not to lessen His Majesty's revenue, and that will be their excuse if anything be referred to them. It will not be amiss for him to step into Ireld. himself and to have leave from His Majesty to that purpose. When he has done that he may say he has one of the completest seigniories in Ireld.

Received his commands by Mr. Nanscawen when his child was christened. Made bold to call him Edward, and to entreat him to be godfather, he being born his servant and in his castle. Did not hear Mr. Nanscawen preach, but perceives him to be a worthy person, learned, orthodox, etc. The bishop likes him well and resolved to accept his lordship's presentation, yet insists to know (as all bishops do) his right to present. Assured him his lordship's grandfather had presented heretofore, and Lord Baltinglasse before that. But he expects a sight of the patent; advises him to send over the new fiat made in 1640 or thereabouts, that includes the right of presentation though the old patent does not. Beseeches him to write a kind letter to the Bishop of Lymerick and Ardfert, Dr. Edward Sing; he was born in Shropshyre. Mr. Nanscawen has set the tithes this year for £60 besides christenings and burials; he desires him to recommend the repair of the Island church to the tenants and allow timber for it.

Mr. Nanscawen desires to be his tenant for East Meanus, but Peeter Bryan will not part with it. The bargain with Bryan was for a year's warning, and the sooner he sends him that notice the better, for he intends to deal with his lordship as Barstable did for Bally mc Adam and attorn tenant to Drue. Bryan says he will not surrender the lands unless his lordship comes and uses it himself and lives at the Island. But the writer made no such bargain—it is like that for Claskaniffe. He should out Barstable and Bryan, for it is not right that those that do not love his interest or design to destroy his inheritance should enjoy his lands.

Since writing the former part he has attended on the Earls of Kildare, Corke, Barrymore, Mount Alex[and]er (alias the Lord of Ards], and divers of the nobility, and they were all willing to serve him. The Earl of Corke appeared his friend at the Court of Claims. The Earl of Kildare presented Lord Herbert's petition to the House this forenoon, and order is granted that he shall not be dispossessed of any lands he possessed forty days before the parliament, and that Sancky and Barstable appear at the Committee of Privilege. He should omit no time in getting positive order for the new patent, and get Bally mc Adam and the rest of the newly recovered lands inserted. Was also this forenoon with the Bishop of Lymerick, who asks for a letter of attorney to enable the writer to present Mr. Nanscawen. The Bishop assured him he would not take advantage by the lapse of time.

Wrote before about Caherninard. Hopes he will prefer the writer to the tenancy rather than his absolute enemies. Intends to remove out of the Castle this winter. Hopes that if he intends to set it and Caherninard for a longer term than yearly he will have other tenants than Barstable, their bitter enemy. The bearer, John Dillis, desires to remove to the Island; hopes he will give him tenancy of lands adjacent to the town. Though many would have been unwilling and fearful to displease their former alliances and relations, Dillis made it his choice to do so that he might more clearly serve his lordship. Kept Dillis these ten days to see the issue of the business of Ballymc Adam. [Being successful] the writer must do what he can to secure himself from the assaults of Barstable and Sancky, who are resolved to ruin him. Hopes his lordship will defend him if suits are commenced against him over

Bally mc Adam. His and his wife's service to him, his lady, his sisters, and Mr. Henry and Mr. Tho. Herbert.

Dublin,
10 July. *Armorial seal* 31.

This reference to Lord Montgomery as the Earl of Mount-Alexander is eighteen days before the date of his patent (*Complete Peerage*, Vol. IX, p. 306). Henry and Thomas Herbert are Lord Herbert's brothers.

1661

291. The Lords of the Council to the Earl of Carbery, Lord Lieutenant of Wales. *Contemporary copy.*

By advertisements from several parts of meetings and complottings of persons of dangerous principles, of seditious pamphlets daily published and dispersed, and of the [un]usual confidence in many that were active instruments in the late times of usurpation, it is evident there is still a mutinous spirit in some . . . Therefore by His Majesty's command they require him to use vigour in settling and exercising the militia, that he may prevent or suppress seditious practices; and to have a watchful eye upon particular persons notoriously disaffected, and upon any just ground of suspicion disarm and secure them.

Whitehall,
19 August.

Ormond
T. Southampton
Roberts
Ashley
Edw. Nicholas
Wm. Morice

Manchester
Tho. Wentworth
Cha. Berkley
Anglesey
Denzell Hollis
G. Carterett

John Nicholas

*HM*2.14/4/2.

1661

292. [Lord] Herbert to Thomas Herbert, esq. *Holograph copy.*

Finds from his letters, one by John Gerald, the other by London way, what care he has taken to stop Barstable's intentions, and his advice concerning a new grant from the King. Has sent him a letter of attorney to deal with Barstable. The words of scandal shall be interpreted to Barstable's detriment and the writer's advantage, for in the strict pursuit of his reputation he may reach his ends of disabling Barstable in reputation and purse. Has given order to warn Barstable out of his holdings in Castle Island town, etc. As to renewing his patent, counsel here in England advise [not *omitted*] to meddle in it now, when there is only £40 per annum chief-rent taken notice of, and the King's revenue is to be advanced and way wanting. Never to have the names of the ploughlands, etc., expressed in a new patent is the opinion of Arthur Trevor, who, to prevent future danger, advises an exact survey by inquisition, naming each parcel that is namable. Will get an inquisition drawn. Encloses Trevor's directions.

If he, Barstable, and Hollis agree that the writer may be chancellor betwixt them concerning the Cayarninards this year, he confesses he is more willing Herbert should have them, but must not "baffle" his agent so much as to cross his setting, unless with consent of Hollis and Barstable. Is loath to believe all he hears out of Irland; thinks better of Herbert than Herbert thinks of him. Hopes to see the seigniory next year, and then can make distinctions not possible at this distance. Supposes he expects no compliments; plain words are fittest betwixt them. Love to him and his wife.

Llyssyn,
23 August.

Prays him be punctual in paying the rents this time. His order is to have them brought or sent by the end of November—in which he thinks not fit at present to employ him. As to the parson of Castle Island, he has sent a presentation and a letter to the Bishop. Desires Killenterna kept in his hands, as in his ancestors'. 556.

1661

293. [THE EARL OF] CARBERY TO [LORD HERBERT AND THE REST OF THE DEPUTY LIEUTENANTS OF MONTGOMERYSHIRE]. *Contemporary copy.*

Encloses transcript of the Council's letter, which he desires they will put in execution with all expedition, that the militia of horse and foot may "suddenly" be in a posture to suppress the designs of dangerous persons. Conceives they are enabled by the Act and His Majesty's instructions (that the trained forces be completely armed according to the modern fashion) to proceed against such as shall not conform as contemners of His Majesty's authority—the law [referring] to former and future instructions. Therefore desires they will speedily (according to several directions sent) return moneys for the arms many months since provided. Intends by [his] next to return answers to letters from them. Asks to receive their proceedings therein, whereby he may before going out of town (within three weeks or a month) give His Majesty and the Council account.

London,
27 August. Ex. per Will Cowley *HM*2.14/4/1.

[1660-66]

294. ANNE, [LADY] HERBERT, TO LORD HERBERT, MEMBER OF THE HOUSE OF PEERS, AT WESTM[INSTE]R.

Received no letter from him, and fears lest some indisposition hinders her of her only comfort in his absence. Desires to hear from him [by] Friday's and Tuesday's post. Encloses certificate of Col. Joones's estate in this county; cousin Browne has sent Lord Herbert notice of his lands by Hoult, which Humberston says are worth above £100 per annum. Has procured £50 upon Higgens's bond from Mr. Kiffim, and has sent it to Salope to be returned. As soon as Andrew Ellis returns from Mounmothshire she will return what money he brings.

Found Jonson so faulty about the corn and shirking amongst the workmen that she has warned him to provide for himself; hopes he approves.

"Thy . . . wife".

Sent a particular of things wanting for the children. Forgot a pair of bodices for each. Nancy's must be packthread instead of whalebone. And a pair for Mall also. Hains knows their measure. Love to her friends, and duty to her father and mother if in town.

Armorial seal 480.

The date of this letter must be prior to the death in 1666 of Lady Herbert's father, Sir Thomas Myddelton; if the Col. Jones referred to is John Jones the regicide, the date is probably very soon after his execution in October 1660.

1662/3

295. JOHN GERRALD TO LORD HERBERT AT LONDON. TO MR. JOHN MYDDLETON, GROCER, AT THE ROSE IN GRATIOUS STREET.

Received his of 28 January. Has sent the acquittances for the King's rents out of his seigniory of Castle Islands: The first, 29 November 1660, for £20 14s. 6d., is enclosed; the second, 15 July 1661, for £20 15s., is in his second letter; the third, 10 June 1662, for £41 10s. 6d., is in his third. Would not presume to violate his orders in forbearing the rents of Mr. Thomas Herbert's lands. Mr. Frances Llyn exchanged £250 at Trally for Lord Kingston; the other £50 shall be endeavoured when Mr. Llyn thinks fit. Would have written more but that Mr. Edward Morgan wrote lately.

Castle Islands,
27 February. 22.

Gerald was probably deputizing for Thomas Herbert, who writes from London a month later. The "third" letter is attached; it is identical, *mutatis mutandis*, with this.

[? 1662/3]

296. [LORD HERBERT] TO MR. OWEN JONES. *Draft.*

Perceives that some of the Irish exhibit claims to part of his seigniory. Counsel are of opinion his case is not within the Commissioners' power, he holding the lands by patents and acts of Parliament in Queen Elizabeth's time, not as adventurer or soldier, or for anything relating to the last rebellion, or within any clause of this Act of Settlement. However, he has written the enclosed, which he should let Mr. Burton peruse, and deliver it to the Commissioners when they see cause. Is sitting in the Parliament of England; hopes that upon that consideration and the arguments Mr. [Gunter *deleted*] Burton and he may use, the Commissioners will suspend proceedings till this session be over or till July, when, if need be, he will come over. Desires speedy notice if they will not.

Has an ancient title passed to him by the Crown upon the attainder of Garrett, Earl of Desmond, etc., though he is in possession by a decree lately obtained. The lands were in possession of the claimants' parents at the breaking out of the last rebellion, though really the writer's. In the Civil Survey in the time of the late usurper, there being no agent or other to assert his right, they were returned the property of the said Irish (who were arrant rebels), and were like to be disposed of to the soldiers in satisfaction of arrears. To prevent this, he preferred a bill in the Chancery Exchequer in that kingdom, and Mr. Basill, then Attorney-General, and the pretended Protector's counsel, etc., opposed his right with all violence. However, upon full hearing it plainly appeared that all the lands [some of which are claimed also by Col. Sancky *deleted*] . . . . (*breaks off*). 620B.

1663

297. Tho. Herbert to Lord Herbert at Llyssyn.

Since the addresses to His Majesty have no quicker despatch, it is held advisable by friends and counsel that course be taken to prevent the proceedings of the Irish claimants. Encloses letters, drawn by the advice of Mr. Edisbury and Sir Tho. Myddleton, to be transcribed by Mr. Bowen and subscribed and dated by Lord Herbert as if in London. By the Act of Settlement made in Ireld. all privilege of parliament is waived, but, he sitting as a peer of this realm, it is possible they will not proceed against him till this session be over [or] at least till July, before which he hopes his patent will be perfected in Ireld. at least . . . Parliament in Ireld. have passed an Act of Periods, that all claims be determined by 1 August or be for ever secluded. Hopes those against his lordship may be in the number, for unless the commissioners incline more candidly towards the English interest, the Parliament are not likely to enlarge that time. If the letter to the commissioners does not prevail, they intend, when he is here, to move the King for a positive order to forbear proceedings against him, being employed in Parliament here. Has drawn a letter for him to send to Capt. Hassett, whose interest is not a little concerned. Wrote to Mr. Burton also. Prays him, if he approves of the letters, to send duplicates [the following week] lest any fail. Dorothy came hither with the writings last Thursday. Delivered the particular; Llanwothyn lands will not be taken because so far in Wales. He should bring the counterparts of the leases. Will try to get them to accept their whole security within the parish of Mountgomery and waive Cherbury, otherwise the Shropshyre lands must be granted them.

London,
28 March.

Would not trust his boy with knowledge of Lord Herbert's transactions concerning his countryman. Sends the licence for Richd. Herbert's nuptials. Hopes it will be for both their comforts. Is afeared he is angry, not having honoured him with one letter since his coming to this country. 27.

"Capt. Hassett" is Captain John Blennerhassett of Ballyseedy, whose son, Cornet John Blennerhassett, became Lord Herbert's agent in 1676. If the Richd. Herbert mentioned is Richard Herbert of Dolguog then he was married twice, for his lady has already been mentioned (in No. 258). His only recorded wife was Lord Herbert's sister, Florence. See No. 301 for more of this.

1663

298. RICH. BOWEN TO LORD HERBERT AT THE TWO COCKS OVER AGAINST ST. DUNSTON'S CHURCH IN FLEETSTREET, LONDON.

Received his of the 18th with joy at the news of his safe journey. Intended to be at Shrewsbury on Tuesday for return of moneys. The most he could get from Lateward and Tho. Owen was £40. The tenants have no moneys; cattle gave none these last fairs. To impound their cattle would be their utter ruin and no advantage to Lord Herbert, for the cattle are scarce able to rise, especially in Llanwothin. Will be in Salop on Monday with what he can get, which he fears will not exceed £100. The work goes on well. Are now providing for the cutting of turf; should he "remove" the barn in Nyath Wen lands for putting them in? Turnstill's colt is a horse . . . And Turk has foaled a horse colt, coal-black, a great blaze in the face, but a lovely brave colt. Lest they injure the colts bringing them up, Will Groome has gone with the horse down to the mares. Should he "discharge" Mumplum, who expects moneys from Lord Herbert?

24 April. 399.

1663

299. EDW. MORGAN TO LORD HERBERT AT LLYSSEN.

Fears lest often writing should offend . . . Will be faithful whilst he has breath. Has written several letters; rehearses only the last, mentioning Capt. Hasset's son's desire to pay Lord Herbert £300 or £400 in England and receive it again out of the next rents here. Which saving the hazard and charge of a return, he presents this way to Lord Herbert; desires to know, if he accepts, when and where [etc.]. And if Lord Herbert pleases to employ "any of us here" to receive and pay, he humbly begs it, not for any advantage, only that he may testify thankfulness. [Begs] he may once more be employed; now better knows the state of things here. Prays for the prosperity of that honourable family to which he has been ever related.

"Your . . . poor Chaplain".

Castle Island,
28 April.

All things here in good plight, only George Davis's clamour for possession of Ardnigraph, which against Lord Herbert's mind they durst not give. Have not received one line from him these two months.

*HM*2. 22/13.

1663

300. RICH. BOWEN TO [LORD HERBERT].

Came to Salop yesterday and he and Mr. Middleton were with all the factors, but could not get a return under six weeks. Left £80 with Mr. Middleton to be sent by what carrier he thinks fit on Thursday, and Middleton will write by Saturday's post where to receive them. Could not make it £100—had only £10 from Tom Owen. It is not Owen's fault; Dick Ranger and the writer were amongst the tenants, and they all said they could not pay but offered their cattle.

Salop,
29 April.

Proffered 40s. for a return upon sight and could not have it. 93.

[16]63

301. [LORD HERBERT] TO [? FLORENCE HERBERT]. *Draft, much altered and torn.*

Hoped since leaving Llyssyn that she would have given her afflicted servant some hopes upon his submission and repentance, whose errors, mostly "on the right hand", are impatience of delay . . . . Conditions and covenants referred to brother Harry, [Si]r Job, and the writer . . . It is the wish of all her friends here—in particular the Countess of Exeter —that she give the gentleman leave to proceed in his suit. The estate is not great but is unburdened with debt or a giddy manager. Her inclination must not receive the least of seeming force, which is not in the writer's nature, but it would be a great happiness to see this match perfected, for many reasons, besides the redeeming her reputation, now a little at stake about the licence. If ever she gave Dick Herbert leave to hope to enjoy her, which "you have not but by my brothers and my [mouthes *deleted*] selfe . . . soe my brother affirmes a tacite leave to send for the Licence". Her last to brother Harry implies that if the writer was not contented with the breaking off the treaty she should have heard from him, which raises hope that this letter may revive it.

2 May. 51.

See the note to No. 297 for a comment on this matter.

1663

302. [LORD] HERBERT TO [? CORNET JOHN BLENNERHASSETT]. *Draft.*

Received his of the 15th from Minieard and Parson Ed. Morgan's of 28 April enclosed, both offering an accommodation, they paying his Irish Ladyday rent this side the water for repayment in Kerry. Will with thanks accept £250 by bill of exchange on some able person in London at a week's or fortnight's sight. Is forced to use some money in Dublin; if he could from Bristoll draw £100 on some merchant in Dublin it would be useful. [Would] order Mr. Morgan in Kerry to gather the whole £350 for him or only £250. Expects, for one or both, "sudenly" bills of exchange, he keeping duplicates for himself and the writer. Prays letters, successively two or three posts, to Mr. John Middelton, grocer, at the Rose in Gratious Street, London; if bills be enclosed, to desire him to open them. Will not see him at Llyssyn unless he is stayed in England till July.

Next to the Golden Ball in Drury Lane.

28 May. *HM*2.23/8.

1663

303. MORGAN HERBERT TO [? RICHARD HERBERT].

Told his uncle all Mrs. Owen commissioned him to. Is at his father-in-law's in his way to Cardigan. Delivered the exemplification and Mr. Hunt's lease to Mrs. Owen's new attorney. His father's service to him; he has given the writer 40s. towards the old tables at Morva . . . and he thinks last year's lambs his, receiving none when he came in. The Trayare of Morva was set by his father for £8 4s., and by the present tenant for near £9. But Morgan Jenkin David's land, which the widow puts to Mrs. Owen's account, is in another grange and never belonged to Mr. Francis Owen's lease. His next shall give account of what was disbursed towards the chancel. [Keeps] the 40s. because the messenger's looks scarce speak him trusty. Sends one ferret; could not get another.

Kilkennin,
6 September. 400.

Morgan Herbert of Hafod Uchtryd (Hafod, the seat of the Johnes family in the next century) had married one of the daughters and co-heirs of Henry Vaughan of Cilcennin.

1664

304. J. BLENERHASSETT TO LORD HERBERT IN ENGLAND.

It is a year and [a] half since he advised Lord Herbert's agents in Kerry to pay the King's rent yearly; wherein they failed for two years ending Easter last. Last spring a pursuivant was sent with a warrant to attach the agents or tenants for a year and half's rent ending Michaelmas; which Mr. Morgan sent by the writer in Easter term—which would not be accepted until the other half year's, due Easter, was likewise paid. [Had] brought no more than would bear his charges here and carry him back; desired Mr. Owen Jones to try to borrow in Dublin—would be bound for it—but he could not. The pursuivant put his warrant in execution only upon Mr. Morgan, from whom he received his fee. No further process will issue until after Trinity term, before which he hopes the remainder will be sent. The year and a half's rent is left meantime with Mr. Owen Jones.

One Dominick Roch put in a claim to some of the lands Lord Herbert recovered, but durst not prosecute it in the Court of Claims. He now has some hopes (knows not by what means) to get his name into the new Bill of Settlement, and so be restored to his estate; the lands Lord Herbert got from him are Tulleleige and Cnocknenenagh. And young Thomas fitz Gerrald, from whom Lord Herbert had Killmurry, Carker, etc., likewise hopes to get into that Bill and so be restored. Gives him notice that he may endeavour to stop their proceedings. Desires his favour in hindering putting into that Bill likewise the name of one Capt. John mc Elligott alias mc Elligott of Bally mc Elligott, in whose estate the writer is concerned.

Dublin,
28 May.

Since writing, with much ado he and his son got £24, which is put into Mr. Owen Jones's hands to make up the two years' rent. Must leave the paying, etc., to Mr. Jones—this day they [start] homewards.

*HM*2.22/14.

1664

305. OWEN JONES TO LORD HERBERT AT LLYSSIN. TO THE POSTMASTER OF CHESTER TO BE SENT TO MR. THOMAS PRICHARD AT KEVEN-Y-WERNE, TO BE SENT.

Received his of 7 July. Continued in the country till last week. Searched the Auditor's office, Surveyor-General's office, and the Secretaries' offices, and cannot find any fiat, instructions, or patent to him of any concealed lands in this country. Conjectures the rumour false. Conceives it needless to send to Mr. Herbert's father unless he found something material. Had there been any[thing] he must have found it in one of those offices. By the enclosed he may perceive how much rent is payable out of the seigniory to His Majesty, and what fees were paid, saving the pursuivant's—4d. a mile and 3s. a day after Mr. Morgan's arrest till [payment]. There was a great stir to get it together. Has reduced the 3s. per diem to 30s. in the whole, and Mr. Morgan paid 45s. for the miles. In all £86 16s. 6d. Hopes his agents will prevent unnecessary charges for the future.

Dubl.,
31 August. *Armorial seal* *HM*2.22/16.

"Mr. Herbert's father" must be Edward Kenney of Cullen, father-in-law to Thomas Herbert, Lord Herbert's agent. The enclosure (the previous document in the bundle) is a copy of the receipt showing rent £41 per annum (£82 for two years), with 21s. 6d. fees.

1664

306. W. BROWNE TO LORD HERBERT AT LLYSSYN.

Is partly confident but £40 chief rent was paid in '41. The composition by Lord Balltinglas was before the war and before the estate came to Lord Herbert's grandfather. Since then there has not been more in charge or paid.

Weston,
12 November. *Armorial seal*

Endorsed: From Will Browne. 52.

This is the William Browne who married Lord Herbert's sister Frances.

1664

307. [LORD HERBERT] TO MR. BURTON. *Draft.*

His last gave the sense of the Duke of Ormond's answer, which was worded as if his final answer would be as now, and Kingston but his grace's echo. The latter offers a convenient way for accomplishing his design, provided Kingston undertakes there should be no stop this or the other side of the water. But they should consider his grace's and Lord Kingston's words, *viz*, that the writer needs not a particular proviso, for the act sufficiently provides for the English Protestant concern. Burton knows his case by Tom Herbert's long letter. It should be considered whether this or any act confirms judicial proceedings as well as settling lands in English possession at the rebellion's breaking out. (His case is only doubtful in that the lands he recovered in the time of Cromwell were in rebel hands for a long time before by the neglect of Baltinglasse.) If they are in danger of a new court of claims to try those not tried for want of time . . . . . (*the rest too much altered to be intelligible*).

Llyssyn,
12 November. 53.

The addressee is Thomas Burton of Longnor, Shropshire, who became Chief Justice of North Wales in 1689.

1664

308. [LORD HERBERT] TO MR. THOMAS BURTON. *Holograph copy.*

If sufficient care is taken for the English interest by the bill in hand, all [recent acts] of judicature are confirmed. Thinks his one of the nicest cases. The lands he recovered were certainly purchased by Sir Wm. Herbert. These and his whole estate were set by his grandfather to Baltinglasse, who made himself a viscount thereby, and a very negligent or knavish person, by suffering these lands to be alienated by the heirs of those very rebels by whose conviction Sir [Wm.] Herbert came to the estate. Lord Baltinglasse would hardly be guilty of negligence in the infancy of his fortunes. Fears these rebels will take a lease of such lands as they find forfeit to the King by the late wars and make their pretence by discovering the lands in their ancestors' possession during Baltinglasse's lease, which lasted till the wars broke out, for his grandfather was negligent. If so, Lord Kingston's proposition will be worth nothing. He should write to Tom Herbert. Believes the rent paid in 1641 was what he now pays. Posts are uncertain, and he will receive a quicker answer to London than the writer can here. If the chief-rent proves the same he will engage Lord Kingston in procuring a new patent particularizing the new-recovered lands, which for a certainty were not sold by Sir. Wm Herbert or his heirs. Deserves better of the King than to lose his lands to him, for if they are not the writer's they are the King's by a double forfeiture. This thoroughly discoursed to the Duke will incline him to justice. As to the chief-rent, if Lord Baltinglasse deserved a reducement, certainly (without citing his father's and his late sufferings for their loyalty) they who ventured their blood and estates to bring Irland under the subjection of the kings of England, and were at great charge to purchase and plant it over and over again, deserve as much favour. Will take his advice whether to write a second letter to his grace or a petition. His Irish estate has cost his family blood and such expense of money as could have purchased four times as much rents in England without hazard or charge for afterclaps.

14 November. 54.

[1664/5]

309. T. BURTON TO LORD HERBERT AT LLYSSEN.

When he last wrote he fully accounted to have got His Majesty's letter in a few days, but found when coming to Mr. Secretary's that the business was referred to the Duke of Ormond—the Duke and Secretary having, it seems, agreed that all Irish business should be communicated to him. Knew this reference would occasion much delay and perhaps prove hazardous, but resolved to make the best of it. Applied himself for several days to the Duke, and often missed him by his absence in Hartfordshire. Found the Duke very civil, but could not obtain the answer he desired, so resolved to engage Lord Ashley in a personal address to him. By reason of the great state affairs of both he found it difficult to bring them together. Several days these three weeks he has waited on Lord Ashley at his house and thence to the Court and House of Lords, but [only] yesterday morning could they debate his petition. The Duke could not deny it to be reasonable, and gave him directions to attend Sir George Lane for drawing up the report, which was promised for next week. It is his and Lord Ashley's advice that Sir George be gratified with £10 or £5 at least, for he may prove serviceable in Ireland. The fees of the reports, references, and the letter, and what must be given to the under-secretary, will shortly be to be disbursed, and his lordship must entrust some person here with a bill of about £30 who may see the laying out of it. Service to his lady.

21 January. *Armorial seal*

Endorsed: From Mr. Burton, the "contents" ordered to be paid him by Sir Henry Herbert. *Bears also a brief jotting about the next letter.*

144.

1664/5

310. J. Blen[n]erhassett to Lord Herbert at Llussen.

Wrote before, but mistook the county. Here are agents and solicitors from all counties of Ireland to promote the Irish interest, and four or five crafty companions out of Kerry to solicit for the Irish proprietors. Has an eye upon them. The way used by many is to give half or two parts to secure the rest. Here is one Col. Richard Talbott undertakes for many of them. Believes the Duke of Ormond's claim (upon account of chief-rent due to the Earl of Desmond) to Lord Herbert's new-recovered lands in Kerry will be passed by, his grace accepting other consideration by this Bill of Settlement, etc. Mr. Burton says that on his petition to His Majesty he had a reference to the Lord Deputy, and a very good report from his grace concerning the passing of all his lands in Kerry, new and old, in one patent, [as] one entire manor and seigniory, all under the same rent as in 1641. There needs to be great care in it—the King's letter needs to be very full.

The Golden Boy over against the King's Head in the Strand,
London,
28 January. *Armorial seal*

Postmarked 29 January and endorsed: Came to hand the last of January.

55.

The writer is John Blennerhassett the younger. Ormonde was Lord Lieutenant, not Lord Deputy, the latter post being held (during the Duke's absence in England) by his son the Earl of Ossory.

[1664/5]

311. T. Burton to Lord Herbert at Llyssen.

Is distracted with vexation at the strange carriage of his lordship's business. Acquainted him in his last how, in the presence of Lord Ashley, he had assurance from the Duke of a quick despatch. Could receive no account of the report before yesterday sennight, when Sir George Lane produced the petition and reference with the Duke's sense upon the back, which was that Lord Herbert was to pass patent of such lands as he or his father held in 1641. Told Sir George that was neither their petition nor reasonable. Drew up notes setting forth that Sir Will Herbert was seized of the lands in the Queen's time, that then an interest in them was granted to Baltinglasse, who by neglect or combination suffered some of the old attainted rebels to encroach, that Lord Herbert had even in the worst of times made his title evident, and by decree (confirmed by two acts of Parliament since the Restoration) had recovered them. Three days after, Sir George told him he had read the paper to the Duke, who yet continued in his resolution. Dissembled his passion for that time and entreated Sir George to bring him to the Duke. Attended Monday, Tuesday, and Wednesday, but was prevented either by the Duke's privacy or absence. If he fails he will obey his further commands in petitioning the King *de novo* and setting forth the case at large, however it may "distast" the Duke.

However, he will take Lord Ashley's advice and proceed with caution. His friends in Shropshire are very desirous to see him, and it was his intention to go down after the term. But will decline going the circuit rather than his lordship's business should remain imperfect. Received the £30 from Sir Henry Herbert, and is resolved to take no promises or anything less than performances from courtiers before he parts with it. These lines cannot give half the vent to his present disgusts.

[*postmarked* 9 February]. 143.

[1664/5]

312. [Lord] Herbert to Mr. Burton. *Draft.*

"My exelent frend". Was more joyed to find how friendly and cordial he is in the writer's business than daunted at the Duke's unreasonable proceedings. Would not have him expose himself to the danger of a frown from his grace, yet to urge what is fitting in the writer's behalf. If after failure with the Duke he renews the petition to the King, it would be referred to the same person, and then they would get an enemy and still fail. Would have him get Lord Ashley, well instructed, face to face with the Duke. And if this fails, then to take the Duke's report in order to a new patent, for the fixing of the chief-rent to £40 is more advantage than the loss of the new-recovered lands. If he could get words to this purpose—all the lands possessed by Sir Wm. Herbert in right of his patent or purchase not alienated by him or his heirs—it would comprehend these plough-lands. Would be much troubled that his business should hinder Burton's circuit affairs; sends the enclosed as a reserve. He should procure his grace's reason why the writer is not worthy of so just a favour—whether he stops it on a public or private account. It shall cost anybody the fee simple of the recovered lands before he parts with possession.

[February]. 142.

1664/5

313. [LORD HERBERT] TO SIR ARTHUR DENNY BY BOWEN. *Holograph copy.*

To whom shall he complain of the trouble he [has over] his rents in Kerry? Tom Herbert ever failed him, and will anybody in money matters—rather extravagance than dishonesty . . . Sent one Jones over afterwards; against him were laid plots to cheat and slight him, and there Tom Herbert finds a fit subject. Employed then John Gerald Dillis and Parson Morgan: "faith, they act by halfes", and run him into inconveniences in the Exchequer. Though the latter may want cunning in the law and management of an estate, Dillis did not. Then comes over Will Browne, now his brother-in-law. He "slates" all accounts and comes to an agreement with four that want not cunning to propose gains to themselves and ability to content the writer—Richard Trant, Charles Barstable, Parson Morgan, and John Gerald Dillis—these to pay the years' rent on Xmas Day in London, clearing arrears remaining [with] Dillis and Morgan. On Will Browne's return, not disliking the proposition, he [gave] them letters of attorney, and they send a letter that they will not fail; has not heard a word since. Which occasions his sending the bearer, his servant Richard Bowen. Begs Sir Arthur's countenance and favour for him, and his advice. Fears he'll find a "sturdy" paymaster of Tom Herbert. Said, when he was at Tralee, that the quarrel was that in all leases Tom Herbert made (by virtue of a power from the writer) to friends in trust for his own use, he put large provisoes: a longer day for payment; and, if no distresses on the land the writer may enter, but when Tom Herbert pays arrears he may re-enter. Had no time then to rectify it; Sir Arthur knows what happened suddenly after . . . Must desire relief from Parliament against him, unless he quit those covenants; for other tenants, to enter and set again if there be fault of payment and no distress is a ready way. Therefore prays his endeavours to persuade Tom Herbert to clear accounts, that there be less jealousy betwixt them. If there be any advantage to be made by commissioners the writer employs to receive his rents [only] this arrear and those covenants hinder Tom Herbert from a share.

Knows he is an excellent friend; desires his advice "on both sides" . . . and that he will give Charles Mason leave to be assistant to Bowen—that he may be despatched and the writer attend in London, where occasions call. So relied on his Irish money that he laid out his country rents to the dis-furnishing of present occasions.

Llyssyn,
13 March. *HM*2.23/9.

Charles Mason became Lord Herbert's agent in 1678.

[1664/5]

314. T. BURTON TO LORD HERBERT. LEAVE AT SHREWSBURY.

Could not give account before of the Duke's resolution. Great delays, week after week, chiefly by the great affairs lying upon Lord Ashley—though his lordship made several appointments to attend the Duke they were put off. But this week both the writer and Lord Ashley spoke with the Duke, who said he must not think to overreach him, and asked why he desired what was not in possession in 1641. Told him the neglect of another should not prejudice Lord Herbert. Could have come a little closer to his grace—Lord Herbert, had he known what the writer knows concerning some Irish patents, would have said what he durst not. The result is that his grace was, with some unwillingness, content he should have a letter for a patent with a saving to the rights of others. Does not intend this saving shall extend to any but the decreed lands; may find a way to make it ineffectual. Desires he will acquaint his lordship's brother of Lord Arrary being gone for Ireland; he desired he should not stir till perfectly recovered.

18 March. *Armorial seal* 56.

1664/5

315. [LORD] HERBERT TO THOMAS BURTON, ESQ., AT LONDON. LEAVE AT MR. PLACE'S, STATIONER, GRAISE INN GATE. *Holograph copy.*

Is glad the Duke of Ormond is forced to unmask and thereby declare that the occasion of delay is that it is his misfortune to have Ormond's interest contrary to his own. Since his grace is interested with a pretence to some of his new-recovered lands, he will produce his title, and his grace shall be chancellor—not that he is in dread of greatness in any person under that of his King. Will show how much his grace would wrong him if he endeavours to defeat him of those plough-lands. In equity the whole is his, and it must be a quirk in law that must defeat him. If his grace will stand on quirks, why may not he, on some small consideration, convey his title to the writer? Is from home, but has left word with the posthouse in Salop to have letters follow him.

21 March. 57.

1664/5

316. [LORD HERBERT] TO MR. BURTON. *Holograph copy.*

Knows "my Lord" is of a generous nature. Thinks it better things were submitted unless he finds the writer's strength able to balance his greatness. Better to bend with the willow than be broken . . . . A fine [? horse *illegible*] or some such thing may do it, for though his title be weak, yet the writer is in possession, and may be troublesome. Submits it to his judgement, and whether the letter be presented or not.

24 March.

While they are striving about these few plough-lands, the other of the rent may not be discovered. 58.

"The letter" is clearly the next document.

1664/5

317. [LORD] H[ERBERT] TO THE DUKE OF ORMOND. *Holograph copy.*

It is his unhappiness to find his grace concerned in his right. Thought his demerit only had been the occasion of it, though he always reckoned himself a great sufferer on the most ancient English account in Irland and the King's in England. Now he knows his grace's pretences, he has given Mr. Burton orders to show him the writer's whole right, and hopes the neglect of his ancestors, or rather the miscarriages of their tenant Roper, "now" Lord Baltinglas, shall not prejudice him. Begs the favour of the despatch of his patent. The chief-rent at £40 per annum is the sum paid by Baltinglasse and himself. Begs that he will suffer the patent to run clear for all the lands in his present possession, which clause, if he be not satisfied, shall not be pleaded in prejudice of his grace's title for three years to come. Derives much of his trouble from Zanky's information, against whom, when the latter had Cromwell's right and the sword in his hand, the writer had a verdict at law in Dublin—which his grace will not believe he could, in those days, in a country governed wholly by persons of fanatic principles, had he not made out his pretences very clearly.

24 March. 59.

Lord Baltinglass had, of course, been dead some twenty-seven years. "Zanky" is Col. Hierome Sankey.

1665

318. RICH. BOWEN TO LORD HERBERT AT LLYSSIN.

Hopes he received his from Holly Head. Arrived Wednesday night, though they went aboard Sunday morning. Were forced to land at Skerish, fourteen miles from Dublin. Mr. Owen Jones was not in town. Found the chief-rent unpaid and a pursuivant ordered down. Went with Major Broughton to Sir Daniell Bellingham the Treasurer, and the pursuivant was stopped with a small fee. Received £19 from Major Broughton to Mr. Harryes' use, and paid a half-year's rent due Michaelmas. As the last two years' rent was not paid until 24 August last, and that by a pursuivant, Sir Daniell had ordered the uttermost farthing should be taken. Shall not be wanting to tell Lord Herbert's [agents] of it, "and that home".

Enquired for returns for England; the merchants will not return under £5 per cent. But at last met one Mr. William Hall that lives at Jacob's Ladder on Corke Hill, and is "Corespond" to Alderman Backwell that lives in Lumbard Street, London, who, he said, would pay any sum in London without charge, being first paid to Hall in Corke or Limricke. Has written to Mr. Richard Middleton (in his absence to Sir Wm. Rider). Mr. Hall has written the Alderman that Lord Herbert has £500 ready in Corke, which the Alderman has occasion to pay next week in Limricke. Has taken a course with one Mr. Hughes who lives at the Pied Horse in Winetavern Street to receive and despatch letters etc. Mr. Middleton should treat with the Alderman for the future as well, for they have sometimes to give 40s. per cent to have moneys remitted here from England.

Has furnished himself with horses and intends to begin his journey for Corke on Monday; wrote to Mr. Morgans to meet him. The subsidies are paid in by collectors, so Lord Herbert cannot be prejudiced by non-payment.

25 March.

Endorsed in Lord Herbert's hand: Received 2 April. Sir Thomas and he have written to brother Middleton touching exchange. 60.

Richard Myddelton, citizen of London, was Lord Herbert's brother-in-law and Sir William Ryder's son-in-law.

1665

319. [LORD HERBERT] TO BOWEN. *Contemporary copy.*

Is sorry he found his affairs of the chief-rent so slighted by Jones in Dublin and Morgan, etc., in the country. Prays him tell them he suspects them rather knavish than foolish, and that some design is carried on by them for somebody. Would have him leave Sir Daniell Bellingham a better understanding of him. Is apt to believe they have not so much as £500 ready for exchange. It is his positive order to leave no arrears of public moneys due. If in in-gathering his just rights he disables some tenants, he is to get better in their places out of the country of Corke. Since Alderman Blackwell (*sic*) has "deareing" [? dealing] in Ireland, he hopes, by Sir Thomas Myddelton's means, to have constant returns gratis. But desires no credit from anybody. He is to take Jones's account and discharge him if he sees cause.

Keven y Werne,
2 April. 61.

1665

320. RICH. BOWEN TO LORD HERBERT.

Has not received one word from him, Sir Wm. Rider, or Mr. Rich. Middleton. The commissioners have not a penny but the £500 that lies in Corke. Yesterday all the tenants appeared before him at the Island. They had nothing to say for themselves, but pleaded poverty. His instructions are to re-enter in default of a distress. The poorest has a distress upon his lands, but no one in the seigniory will buy them. And [the distrained cattle] are so weak that they cannot be driven a mile. The tenants will not do anything unless severely dealt with. Will make them dread giving his lordship the trouble of sending an agent on purpose for the future. The commissioners' excuse in not paying the subsidies was that Mr. Tho. Herbert told them the revenue of the estate is settled by Lord Herbert for his brothers and sisters, and [by] the act no infant under twenty-one shall be charged. The Lord Chancellor of Ireland drew the settlement and will remember it. If they can be taken off it will save £190. He must send over the counterpart of the settlement, which his mother was to seal.

The commissioners deny they offered Mr. Browne £60 per annum to prevail with Lord Herbert to take both rents at Christmas. All that was said was by Charles Barstable, when he was drunk, as he says—that he would give Mr. Browne £60 per annum if they could have a year's rents in hand constantly, and pay in Corke or Limricke, the money to be remitted by Mr. Browne upon his own charge to London.

His letter was but what the commissioners deserved, excepting Mr. Morgans. Had they been careful they might have gathered all the rents ere this, for at Michaelmas the cattle were strong. Intends to wait upon Sir Arthur at Tralee tomorrow.

Kilcowe,
5 April.

Endorsed: Came to hand the 17th. The answer approved by Sir Tho. Mid. 62.

The Lord Chancellor of Ireland was Sir Maurice Eustace.

1665

321. RICH. BOWEN TO LORD HERBERT AT LLYSSIN.

Has not received one word from him, Sir Wm. Rider, or Mr. Middleton (from whom he will receive this) . . . . *Goes on to repeat the preceding letter.*

Kilcowe,
5 April. *Armorial seal*

Endorsed in Lord Herbert's hand: The counterpart of the deed of settlement sent 14 May to Major Broughton in Dublin to deliver to Bowen; Frost and Charles Herbert parties and Sir Mau. Eustace witness. 63.

1665

322. THO. HERBERT TO LORD HERBERT AT LLYSSYN.

Received his by Mr. Bowen and in it the sad intimation of his continuing under his displeasure. Wishes the hand that writes this may rot and all the plagues of Egipt happen to him if ever he intercepted letters between him and his agents here, or dissuaded them to hasten the rents. Wrote often to Mr. Richd. Myddleton to pay Lord Herbert the £120 he has of the writer's. Hoped so great and good a parcel of cattle and sheep as he sent over would have produced more money, that he might have paid some to Mr. Browne. Wrote formerly about the subsidies, which might have been avoided—but because it came from him his lordship would not think it worthy his notice. Knows not what he wrote concerning him to Sir Arthur Denny. If he knows wherein he had offended he would be willing enough to beg pardon without persuasions of a third person. His and his wife's duty to him, his lady, Mr. Henry etc.

Culcow,
6 April.

Will give Mr. Bowen his best advice about the subsidies, which come to £180. *Armorial seal* 64.

1665

323. [SIR] THOMAS MYDDELTON TO LORD HARBARD AT LLYSIN.

His kind invitation works much upon their affections, but their infirmities and pre-engagement for Vale Royall this Whitsuntide put a bar to their desires. If Lord Herbert hastens not too soon to London, they resolve this summer to give him a visit. Approves Lord Herbert's instructions to his servant. It is very necessary his commissioners collect his rents within six weeks after they become due, for then the tenants will have either money or cattle in good plight. The money should be returned to Alderman Blackwell (*sic*) . . . Times are unsettled, and to suffer his tenants to be in arrear may prove very prejudicial. Love to him, the writer's daughter, [their] daughters, etc.

21 April. 65.

Vale Royal was the seat of Thomas Cholmondeley, esq.

1665

324. RICH. BOWEN TO LORD HERBERT AT LLYSSIN. LEAVE WITH THE POSTMASTER OF CHESTER TO BE SENT.

Has written every week but has not received one line since his of 2 April from Keven y Werne. Mr. Middleton wrote that Alderman Backwell would not return under four per cent. The arrears cannot be raised before the Island fair, the cattle being so weak; has above a hundred in his custody. Then, by God's assistance, he will gather both arrears and Ladyday rent. The tenants have had great losses this winter. Lord Kerry's tenants ran away by droves leaving nothing but the cabins, so that he has above [£]400 per annum upon his hands unset. Sir Arthur Denny and Lady Ellen present their service. So does Franck Lyn—cannot get Mr. Henrye's money from him, though he swears by all the ale in Tralee he shall have it ere long. Waits here "at the sterne" in hopes to receive his commands which way to steer his course.

Castle Island,
1 May. 66.

[1665]

325. T. BURTON TO LORD HERBERT AT LLYSSEN.

Lord Ashley's business has so hindered him that till these few days Lord Herbert's petition came not to the Secretary's hands. Went to the Secretary (now Lord Arlington) who perused the petition and said it was fit to be granted, but desired to know why the Duke of Ormond refused to report upon the King's reference. Told him it was because Lord Herbert was not seized in 1641, though he had been before, and in 1654 had restitution. Lord Alrington (*sic*) was well satisfied, and sent Mr. Llee to Sir George Lane to know his answer, saying that if the Duke continued obstinate he would find another way. [Lord Arlington's] interest is too prevalent for the Duke to oppose. A letter to the Secretary would be seasonable; he is very obliging—whatever he promises he performs. Finds no clause in the Bill of Settlement to Lord Herbert's prejudice, though Mr. Hasset once persuaded him there was.

3 May. *Armorial seal* 67a.

[1665]

326. [LORD] HERBERT TO [LORD ARLINGTON]. *Holograph draft.*

Found the Duke of Ormond so tedious in a reference to the writer's petition now in [Lord Arlington's] hands that he was driven to condole himself for the demerits of his person, since a sufferer for his King and Country could not prevail upon occasion. A reducement from a florid and large possession of rents and castles, well-furnished, to less than a third; the demolishing of his chief castle and plundering of several of his houses; a persistence in his duty to serve His Majesty even in the last attempt in Chester; and brothers and sisters not provided for by reason of a debt contracted in the late wars—if these may evidence it, then he is a sufferer. And is a sufferer of the second descent, for (asks leave as a Welshman to revive his sufferings) [his father], best known as Col. Richard Herbert, [gave his services] in the writer's infancy, and he took up the cudgels with the first opportunity. Will no more reflect on Lord Ormond. Must take hold of his kind expressions [to Mr. Burton]—that if the Duke is obstinate he will find some other way. This revives a drooping sufferer and calls for many thanks.

[early May]. 67b.

[1665]

327. [LORD HERBERT] TO [LORD ARLINGTON]. *Another draft of the same letter.*

Found the Duke of Ormond so tedious [etc., etc.] . . . The demolishing and plundering of his castles and houses in England and Irland . . . Served His Majesty even to the last, Sir George Boothe's business . . . Being a Welchman he must give a pedigree of his sufferings . . . [His father] left him five sisters and two brothers to provide for . . . But will not more reflect on Lord Ormond, and will think the case well altered since his good friend Lord Ashley recommended him to [Lord Arlington]. Has not had so kind a regard as his kind expressions since the King returned home . . .

[early May]. 272.

1665

328. T. BURTON TO LORD HERBERT AT LLYSSEN.

Acquainted him of the Duke's promise to Lord Arlington to report upon the reference [awaiting] his resolution since 17 December. Sir George Lane said he should once more be brought to the Duke, which, after four days, was done, and the Duke plainly said he did not understand Lord Herbert's case. Desired his report, however. Could not obtain it before this day by reason of the Duke's going into the country. The substance is that the Duke refers the petition to His Majesty's counsel-at-law. The report being so insignificant, he did not give Sir George more [than] 40s. and 5s. to his clerk. Went forthwith to Lord Arlington's and delivered the petition, report, and Lord Herbert's letter to Mr. Lee. Could not speak with his lordship by reason of great affairs in agitation.

19 May. *Armorial seal*

Endorsed in Lord Herbert's hand: Answered the 23rd: Not to let the business sleep but finish it this side the water. 68.

[1665]

329. T. Burton to Lord Herbert.

On Monday last Lord Herbert's letter and the Duke of Ormond's report were read by Lord Arlington, who (Mr. Lee says) gave directions to one Mr. Williamson, another of his clerks, to draw up a new reference to the Attorney- or Solictor-General. Chose Mr. Solicitor and delivered him the petition, references, and reports, and a fee of £5, and likewise a copy of the decree in 1654, with Bellingham's acquittances. Did not think it wisdom to show the patent or the reducement—the one in regard of the reservation, the other for that it mentions the eviction of the lands they now desire to pass. The abatement of rent being made upon account of the eviction would evidence either no title or that the old reservation should stand; so concealed those writings.

[25] May. *Armorial seal* 95.

The rent reserved in the patent was £160—see Lord Baltinglass's letter of 5 February 1633/4 (No. 121). The letter was originally dated 5 May, but this has been altered in pencil (perhaps contemporaneously) to the 25th, and the postmark is the 25th. The Solicitor-General at this time was Heneage Finch.

[1665]

330. T. Burton to Lord Herbert. Leave at Ludlow.

His petition, etc., have been under Mr. Solicitor's consideration. Cannot yet obtain it by reason of the Solicitor's great business. Will endeavour to get the patent passed here, though it is to be weighed whether that be advisable, for it will be difficult to ascertain the rent in 1641, though in Ireland it will plainly appear that then and ten years before it was only £40. Here they may be forced to procure the old patent. Chiefly fears the Duke's interest with the Lord Chancellor—it is odds the Chancellor will acquaint him with it. On the other side he may, with the assistance of Lord Dungannon, etc., get it passed before the Duke comes over, which will not be these six months. If he resolves to pass it here he must write effectually to the Lord Chancellor and "make freinds to him" by Lord Carbery, the Lord Treasurer, etc.

1 June. *Armorial seal* 69.

1665

331. Rich. Bowen to Lord Herbert at Llyssin. Leave with the postmaster of Chester to be sent.

Has, after long engineering, met with a bill of exchange for £500, which is enclosed, likewise £50 inserted for Mr. Browne. Has sent the first and second bills to Sir Wm. Rider and Mr. Richard Middleton. Could not get it a penny cheaper than £5 per cent—Alderman Backwell's "Corespond" would not return under. To pay it in Limrick would very near have cost £5 besides the hazard of the removal from Corke—not long since fourteen persons well mounted robbed the Archdeacon's house and took above £300. Several other burglaries and robberies have been committed here of late by the Irish. Hopes he will not have occasion to use Major Hill's vessel, for he hopes to get all his lordship's demands here by the Island fair. When he comes to Dublin about

1 August he will take course for the King's rent due Easter and the subsidies—is assured it will be no prejudice in the interim. Has a barrel of Irish slate, but God knows when it will go—the merchants are so fearful they will not venture.

Corke,
6 June. *Armorial seal* 401.

The merchants were perhaps afraid of the Dutch fleet; in fact it had been defeated on the 3rd at the Battle of Lowestoft, but this news would hardly have reached Cork yet. Irish slate, powdered, was used for medicinal purposes.

[1665]

332. T. Burton to Lord Herbert at Llyssen.

Has been this night with Mr. Solicitor (having been three times before) to hasten the report; is still delayed, though in very obliging terms. Has been very pressing in regard of the great increase of the plague and the danger of staying here. Does not question but to procure a *fiant* before he comes down for passing a patent here, or the King's letter for Ireland. Is not sure whether he can pass a patent so suddenly. Lord Herbert hears from other hands of our great victory over the Dutch, wherein all their admirals but one are killed, and of 115 ships but 45 escaped. The Duke is safe; we lost only the Earls of Portland and Marlborough and the Viscounts Muskerry and Fitzharding, but no ships.

8 June.
Endorsed: 1665. 141.

1665

333. Rich. Bowen to [Lord Herbert].

Hopes he received the bill of exchange for £550. Sent also to Sir Wm. Rider and Mr. Richard Middleton. Received his letters of 29 May from Ludlow, etc. Understands the deed of settlement is safe in Major Broughton's hands. Mr. Herbert produced his lordship's acquittance for the £20 lent in London. (*Further details which are substantially repeated in the following letter.*) Herbert assures him he will pay the £23 11s. 3d. due, with arrears of the last year and a half's rent, at the Island fair. Encloses Mr. Herbert's letter.

When the miller and Barstable took the two half plough-lands they thought it was "nothinge but aske and have". Though it was concealed from his lordship this five or six years he could not evict them but by due course of law, because they had been so long in quiet possession. Believes Mr. Hassett will not withstand him; has commenced a suit against the other, but fears they cannot make it out a distinct half plough-land from Dromalton moor, which is part of Knor O Daley's farm. Sir Arthur and his lady present their service. He should direct letters to the postmaster of Corke, Mr. Vaughan, a good friend and countryman.

Culcowe,
21 June. 71.

1665

334. THO. HERBERT TO LORD HERBERT. *Torn.*

Finds himself charged £155 11s. 3d. and £20 lent in London, which is £20 more than he owes, as is evident by the account of Mr. Browne . . . Paid him at Llyssen £60 and returned by Mr. Richard Myddleton £120. Desires to be allowed the £6 he paid to Mr. Christopher Rye and £6 for the exchange of £120. Truly, that is all he had for 52 handsome steers and 260 sheep, freight, customs, etc., cleared. Knows the time when the very steers would have assured £160. Owes £23 11s. 3d. of old arrears, which, with the forementioned sums, makes £215 11s. 3d., which was all that was due from 26 November 1663. Will, God willing, pay [the £23 odd] to Mr. Bowen before he leaves.

Touching the alteration of some covenants . . . .—only desires that, in case of rebellion whereby the writer may be interrupted in possession, those years be not [counted] part of the term, and that no rent be demanded during such rebellion. Hopes he will not be offended; Ireland is subject to wars, and this is a usual [clause]. Has not made £10 out of those f[arms] . . . But thanks God he has discharged his burthen of arrears. Never obstructed the least letter from or payment to him, and hoped he would have examined it before he censured [him] in letters to Denny or himself.

Culcow,
21 June. 70.

1665

335. RICH. BOWEN TO LORD HERBERT AT LLYSSIN. LEAVE WITH THE POSTMASTER OF CHESTER.

Begins his journey for Corke on Monday, and so for Dublin. Sir Arthur and his lady prevailed with him to stay for Charles Mason, who is to come over for England with him. His stay has been long, but he has raised all Lord Herbert's dues here that were to be had "above Ground". Intends to return them to Bristoll, which is 20s. per cent cheaper than London, though the sickness continues. If he [fails] he intends to bring it to Dublin and get it returned to Chester. Has Mr. Browne's business in readiness. Will obey Mr. Harryes' commands in Dublin. Cannot get the moneys from F. Llyn.

Culcow,
29 August. 72.

[1666]

336. T. BURTON TO LORD HERBERT AT LLYSSEN.

Has been going for London this fortnight, but fear of the plague and [business] here in the country were the reason of his stay. Next to that great concern of his own family there is no business in which he is more busied. Is not a little troubled at the present suspension of Lord Herbert's business.

[? mid-May]. *Armorial seal* 97.

[1666]

337. T. Burton to Lord Herbert at Llyssen.

Came safe hither out of Shropshire. He must send £50 and upwards for passing the patent. Will try what can be done about the fairs, markets, and royalties, but fears ineffectually except by a new patent. Some he already enjoys. They are matters of no great necessity—but the shadow of other things which are of substance.

London,
26 May. 96.

[1666]

338. T. Burton to Lord Herbert at Llyssen.

After a fortnight's dancing attendance he has at last procured [this] reference:

Lord Arlington's reference: His Majesty refers this to the Lord Lieutenant of Ireland, and unless there appears upon the writs usually issued in these cases reason to the contrary, he is to give order for the granting of the fairs and markets desired, or certify his opinion. Then His Majesty will declare his further pleasure, with a gracious respect to the petitioner's loyalty and merits. Whitehall, 13 June.

Inserted the markets, though he did not mention them. However he may relish this reference, it is as much as can be procured. Was again about Lord Herbert's business with Madam Chiffinch, but she can give no more account than formerly. He must devise so to engage the Chancellor that his patent receives no stop before him. Forewarns him to be prepared against the worst.

19 June.

Endorsed: Answered the 25th, with a letter to the Earl of Clarendon.

73.

"Madam Chiffinch" is perhaps Dorothy, widow of Thomas Chiffinch, late Closet-Keeper to the King, she being Welsh, a Tanat of Merioneth.

1666

339. [Lord] Herbert to [the Earl of Clarendon, Lord Chancellor]. *Holograph draft.*

Has, after two years' waiting on the Duke of Ormond, Lord Arlington, and the Solicitor-General, ripened a request for the Great Seal in relation to his estate in Irland, which, from Queen Elezabeth's time, has cost the lives and estates of many thousands of his tenants and many of his name in the rebellions and massacres there. It had been presented last year but the plague disturbed all such proceedings. Asks him to let it pass the first seal, the rather because the gentleman he employs, Mr. Thomas Burton, is a lawyer and must attend the circuits. Many of his relations' and friends' being this summer-time in the country is the reason it is not presented by a person of greater quality. Presumes the justness of his request will speak better than the best of rhetoric.

Llyssyn,
23 June. 74.

1666

340. THE KING TO THE EARL OF CARBERY, LIEUTENANT OF NORTH-WALES AND SOUTHWALES. *Copy in Richd. Herbert's letter-book.*

Charles R.

Whereas the two Houses of Parliament, having received this session informations of the insolent carriage of Popish recusants, and apprehending . . . a public disturbance, have by their late address moved . . . that all Popish recusants that refuse the Oaths of Supremacy and Allegiance be disarmed: Forthwith all Popish recusants within his lieutenancy of Northwales and Southwales, or such as are suspected to be so, [that] refuse the oaths are to be disarmed. Expects account from time to time, particularly how armed he has found them. Arlington

Whitehall,
24 November.

He is to receive the arms into his own hands (or appoint them to be kept by some of his Deputy Lieutenants) giving account thereof.
Arlington

Copia vera: Ed. Agborowe *HM*2.14/3/18.

1666

341. LORD CARBERY TO SIR MATHEW PRICE AND OTHERS THE DEPUTY LIEUTENANTS FOR CO. MOUNTGOMERY, "TO BE SENT TO EACH OTHER". *Copy in Richd. Herbert's letter-book.*

Encloses a transcript of His Majesty's letter of the 24th, which came this day. They are to put the contents in execution and give account from time to time.

Ludlow Castle,
last of November.

Copia vera: R. Herbert, Dolgiog, 4 December

*HM*2.14/3/19.

1667

342. [THOMAS HERBERT] TO MR. BRISCOE, ATTORNEY IN CHANCERY. *Contemporary copy.*

He was retained for Lord Herbert in a difference of meres and bounds betwixt the lands of the Lord President of Munster and Lord Herbert in co. Kerry. Both desired a commission of perambulation. The Lord [President] ordered Mr. Hartstonge, his counsel, to exhibit a bill, and the writer desired Mr. Whittfield to draw an answer. A commission was issued 13 May, and Mr. Warburton (that waits on Mr. Whittfield) assured the writer that Sir Arthur Denny and Lt. Sands were commissioners for the Earl of Orrery, and Capt. John Blennerhassett and Mr. Richard Chute for Lord Herbert. But when he saw the commission, instead of Capt. Hassett he found Mr. Mellefont. If Capt. Hassett was altered without Briscoe's knowledge it is neither usual nor just. Also, the plaintiff's agents kept the commission from him till the 7th of last month. Lord Herbert's commissioners attended that day at Ballymac[Daniel ? *torn*], the Earl of Orrery's land. They would not consent to a jury then, and would only examine witnesses. Observing at least 140 on Lord Herbert's behalf, they were not well pleased, and would have stinted him to thirty or forty, their own not exceeding that, designing to bring *gens contra gentem*. Would not consent. Next day witnesses trod the bounds and they adjourned to Currens, (after [trying] to have the witnesses examined in the plaintiff's house) which was in difference. On Wednesday the 10th at Currens the plaintiff's commissioners would not proceed unless one John Creagh should be both clerk and interpreter and admitted to stay in the room as well when the defendant's witnesses were examined as the plaintiff's, whose clerk he was, while James Connor (clerk for Lord Herbert) should only stay whilst Lord Herbert's witnesses were examined. The whole day being spent in arguments, they would not proceed till further orders from the Lord President, to whom they sent John Creagh. On Saturday he returned with Lord Broghill, and it was resolved both clerks be admitted. They adjourned till the 14th to Ballygrillagh, four miles from the bounds in difference, when one Capt. Samuell Morris brought new orders from the Lord President, and they would not proceed unless he were admitted interpreter, which was consented to, John fz Gerrald being admitted interpreter for Lord Herbert. They then adjourned till Thursday and sent an express to the Lord President to Charleville (above thirty miles distant) [and obtained his consent] to a jury. The sheriff attended at Bally mc Daniell on the 22nd, but the weather being foul few appeared, and a jury could not be had till the plaintiff's commissioners ordered the sheriff to return some gentlemen present but not summoned—believes they came designedly, as a *tales*. Protested but was overruled, and a jury of thirteen were sworn, and the bounds [again] trod. From Wednesday to Saturday they examined witnesses, vilifying any produced on the defendant's behalf, though good and ancient, some eighty-five years of age and the youngest fifty. The commissioners on Saturday the 26th adjourned till Monday to Traly, which was burdensome for the writer, being seven miles from his house. [Their] witnesses being exhausted, forty a side being examined he produced as many more, but the plaintiff's commissioners refused, and put the commission in their po[ckets], without which Lord Herbert's commissioners thought it not safe to [proceed]. The jury were charged to go and "chant" on the evidence they had heard. On the 1st [and 2nd] of this instant the jury attended the commissioners and declared [three several times] that they could not agree, and last of all were adjourned till twelve at night (the last moment the commission was in force) and, being required, certified under their hands and seals that they could not agree. Whereupon there were no small threats that the jury and witnesses should be brought to Dublin. They say they will have the commission renewed; desires him not to consent till Lord Herbert's pleasure be known.

Culcooe,

5 November. 557.

[1655-78]

343. [LORD HERBERT] TO DICK THOMPSON. *Holograph copy.*

Received what writings he sent by his daughter and put them up in a box before her. Hopes God will restore Thompson to health again, and then he shall find them as he sent them, unless the writer be forced to send a rental to the trial betwixt Higgenson "and I"—the deed of the writer's mother's marriage is to be shown to prove the writer's father but tenant-for-life. If his strength will give him leave, he prays him cause to be amended any faults in a breviate Rice Morgan is to draw. Supposes Robert Browne with the rental will be sufficient to prove the writ. 273.

1668

344. MARKE ANTHONY TO LORD HERBERT. LEAVE AT THE DOOR OF THE HOUSE OF LORDS IN WESTMINSTER.

Would have sent before had he known where to direct a letter. Mr. Theodore Cocke shipped 28 March eighty tons of ore belonging to Lord Herbert and Mr. Bagnoll. The rest remains in the storehouse until the ship returns. Yesterday Robert Haywrd was here and paid for it to Mr. John Hill and the writer £420, which is now to be paid out to the workfolk and the country people for commodities for the workfolk's maintenance for eighteen months past. Except Mr. Hill pays some of the country debts and deducts it from the workfolk's share that he is to pay, it will "come too shorte". Asks patience till these scores be paid, when he will have as true an account as any man may make. Is not acquainted with making up accounts with men till their dues were satisfied; if some "fine" men constrain it or persuade Lord Herbert to require it he thinks it not convenient. Desires to have all scores cleared that they may have credit to proceed further, Lord Herbert to take whatsoever is over. Since October their best works were drowned out; now the workfolk would have the water drawn out for them to begin again. Such things must be borne out of the price of ore. Would that Mr. Hill for some time to come should provide for the proceeding in the works, with necessaries for the purpose, as iron, steel, candles, and corn, etc., for the people, and take what profit arises—he would not be so "fine", nor at leisure to visit France or Italy. Unless Hill assists the writer, all will be naught; when money is to be received he is ready enough. Concerning Edward Thomas and Lewis Harry, the former is a great favourite of Mr. Hill's who will be very unwilling to part with him.

It is hard to get in rents. Some of Lord Herbert's tenants of the highest degree are behind three years, some two. Of the poorer sort he is constrained to get corn, cheese, butter, or an ox or a cow to kill for the workfolk, and from some ploughing and harrowing instead of money. The several parcels of ore remain as they were; never shipped but twenty tons before this eighty. There is great store of "smeethen"; Major Hill has had forty-two tons and Mr. Griffith ten tons.

Pen Rhyn Du,
28 April. *Armorial seal* 402.

The reference to smitham makes it clear that the mines in question were lead mines. Penrhyn Du is in the parish of Llanengan, Caernarvonshire.

[1665-1686]

345. NAMES OF THE JUSTICES OF PEACE AND DEPUTY LIEUTENANTS OF SHROPSHIRE.

Sir Vincett Corbett of Morton Corbett; Sir John Corbett of Aherley; Mr. Newport of Eaton; Sir Edward Acton of Aldham; Sir William Whitmore; Mr. Child of Kinlett; Mr. Whitmore of Ludson; Mr. Weaver of Morvile; Mr. Weld of Willey; Mr. Lacon of West Coppice; Mr. Bentall of Bentall—deals in coals; Mr. Cressett of Cond—his wife was a Catholic; Mr. Fowles of the Grange; Capt. Ottley of Pitchford; Mr. Mackworth of Betton; Mr. Burton of Longnor; Mr. Baudewin of Shrewsbury; Mr. Prince of Shrewsbury; Sir Humphrey Briggs; Sir Francis Edwards; Capt. Robert Corbett of Albright Hussy; Mr. Langley of the Abbey; Mr. Adams of Longdon; Capt. Pope of Bridgnorth; Mr. Pope, jr.; Mr. Mitton of Shipton; Mr. Herbert of Bromfeild; Mr. Charlton of Witton—Sir Jobe Charlton's son; Col. Foxe of Conam; Mr. Bawldwin of Stocke; Mr. Walcott of Bitterton; Capt. Davenport of Hawne; Mr. Lutlowe of Bromcraft—Catholic; Mr. Walcott of Walcot, sr.; Major Oakley of Oakley; Mr. Waringe of Owlbury; Mr. More of Lindley; Mr. Newton of Heighley; Mr. Kery of Binweston; Mr. Powell of Worthin; Mr. Leighton of Watlesbourough; Mr. Leighton of Lawton, jr.; Mr. Kynnaston of Horley; Mr. Hunt of Boreatton; Mr. Corbett of Stanwardine; Mr. Kinaston of Ottley; Mr. Manwaringe of Eightfeild; Mr Powell of the Park; Mr. Mitton [of] Haultst[o]n; Mr. Lloyd of Aston; Col. Clive; . . . . (*torn*) of Longford—Cath.; . . . . Smith of Langley—Cath.; . . . . . . Carrington of Aston—Cath.; . . . . . Forester of Shefnall—Cath.; . . . . . Lacon of L . . . . .y—Cath.; Mr. Tho. Ireland of Albrighton—Cath.; Mr. Tho. Berrington of Morehall—Cath.; Mr. Hunt of Moreton—Cath.; Major Revell of Shefnall—Cath.; Major Loyd of Melverley—Cath.; Dr. Bostock, physician—Cath.; Mr. Henry Foxe of the Hurst—Cath.; Mr. Brookes of Madley—Cath.; Mr. Cleaton of the Lea, Mr. Hamage of Belzardine, Mr. Clough of Mindtowne—[all] *infra etatem*, all Cath.

*HM*2.9/50.

This list is of interest partly for the additional information it occasionally gives, and partly because there is a gap in the Shropshire Quarter Sessions Order Books between 1669 and 1684. It probably belongs to about the middle of the date-range assigned to it. Many of the names, of both persons and places, are in corrupt forms; the necessary corrections are provided by means of the Index. Miss Mary C. Hill, County Archivist of Shropshire, has given me valuable help in dealing with this document.

[? c.1670]

346. JAMES SCOTT'S PETITION TO LORD HERBERT.

Farmed a parcel of his land, by name Feyryes, near the Island, half a plough-land, from John Hollis for twenty-one years, paying yearly £11, whereon he builded a substantial "tacht" house, wherein he dwelled for a twelvemonth without interruption. Then one Laghlin Daly, a neighbour, encroached. Jo[h]n Hollis brought an order from the Presidency that he be not molested. Notwithstanding, Daly drove the petitioner's cattle out, which Jo[h]n Hollis replevied and took out of the pound. Afterwards a jury in the Island of Dalye's followers, friends, and relations awarded the petitioner to pay 44s. cost and lose a third part of his farm. Having lost what substance he had (considerable for one of his rank) by paying the aforesaid costs and the whole rent after losing the third of his farm and making improvements, he was forced to surrender his lease. Gave all he was worth for last gale's rent on going away, and ever since has lived on Sir Valintine Browne's estate in a distressed condition, praying for Lord Herbert's coming to "the Nation", not doubting to be then righted. His wife's father, Jo[h]n Ruane, was his lordship's father's and grandfather's servant, and she would not willingly live anywhere but under his lordship's wing, in expectation her child after her may be serviceable to him and live on some part of his estate. 612.

1671

347. [Thomas Herbert] to [Lord Herbert].

Acknowledges his of 29 March by post and two duplicates—per John Prichard's wife and by Ch. Mason. Had the first a few days before Easter. According to his commands he sold by Mr. Sanders' advice the twelve oxen to one Mr. George Crofts for £39 6s. Four were fat, four indifferent, and the others mere scrubs. Well looked to they had yielded near £4 apiece, but they were not housed or fed with hay till John Moyses went. Twisse in excuse says [Lord Herbert] sent directions only to keep them in good order, to be re-fed and stalled this year. Eight were turned to grass (for want of hay) the beginning of April, so but four were in when Mr. Crofts came to look over them, and not three nights' hay left. As [Lord Herbert] resolved to convert them into milch cows, the writer sent to Mr. Crofts, who was casually here, and he bid a fitting rate. Kept another year they would not have produced more profit, considering the charge. They now produce 25s. 6d. apiece for their keeping three-quarters of a year, which they reckon here a good return.

Pursuant to former orders, he had, before Mr. Mason came, delivered Mr. Sanders and Rd. Twisse £20 to buy cows at Listowell fair the 3rd of this instant; they bought twelve which cost (with the charge of buying and bringing home) £18 12s. 3d. Delivered the residue of the £39 6s. to Ch. Mason against Malahuffe fair, where he bought six more, dearer than at Lystowell. Milch cows are dear because of a great mortality of cattle last winter and spring, and many tenants much prejudiced thereby. Old and young Trant lost above sixty beasts, Mr. Sanders seventy (most great cattle), James Galloway above fifty, and so most plough-lands. But God be praised [Lord Herbert's] escaped with the loss of one cow and but five calves out of forty. Now hears there be three or four more drowned (by neglect in the cowboy). Mr. Mason has care of the rest of his stock and husbandry, by his lordship's directions, and promises exact account.

As to the buildings, the chimney shafts were finished by Easter, till when there was necessity to continue James Chatterton, John Seawell and the best masons of Munster being employed in rebuilding a great steeple to Corke cathedral. Was advised by Sir A. Denny and others that understand building to continue Chatterton to finish the shafts, that he might not excuse himself should they prove smoky. Then discharged him and the masons and labourers for the present, but the carpenters and shinglers go on. Most of the outside of the great house is shingled; will then with all speed shingle the stable. Chatterton grumbled much, and said he had it under [Lord Herbert's] hand to be continued his salary till the work were finished. He is still in the country, and would fain take the work, "by the Great", i.e., plastering the house and all partitions, the stone steps to the house, and the entry. He asked £55 for them, [Lord Herbert] to find materials and he labourers—much exceeding his former computations. Would have agreed for a sum certain had he been reasonable—it would be well done. Will try to have it well finished more reasonably. The horses are yet so weak, fuel cannot be brought for the lime kiln—one of the first things to be done. Hopes to get the lime burnt before the house be shingled; will cover it with faggots [against] rain, and put a little door with a lock to prevent its being stolen. Will finish the house with all speed. Will he have casements in the windows, in which, and how many? Some, Chatterton says, will be requisite to let in air to the rooms; they are not included in the computation. Shall the furnace be put up in the great house or in the intended brew-house? If in the great house, it will spoil it with the "stemme", and Chatterton says the "stock" of chimneys in the great house may be prejudiced by any breach or rupture. The chimneys are very shallow, the biggest not above a foot deep.

As for the money due to Mr. Robert Hassett, he had, before [Lord Herbert's] letter, picked out so many of the best tenants as his money amounted to (with interest £86 12s.), and is paid most of it. Will call to him for [Lord Herbert's] bond and papers when he has had it all. Sent [Lord Herbert's] letter to Capt. Hassett about the year's value. He and his son John came and said they are not liable, that the Act of Settlement imposes it on the landlord, and that they expected to be reimbursed out of the rent. However, they said they would tell Cnocher o Daley they were forced to pay. The old captain said, "What I give, I give"—but will not be compelled to pay unless liable. Told him [Lord Herbert] needed not his gifts, and he was obliged to pay by contract. He said the Act indemnified him in that very particular. Wrote to Mr. Whittfield, who is of opinion the tenants are not liable, but [Lord Herbert]. However, Cnogher o Daley and his brother will not contend for it being told Capt. Hassett is to pay it. So his lordship will save £9.

The Sheriff, Capt. Samuell Morris, has a *levari facias* for £14 year's value on Bally mc Adam. Prevailed with him to forbear a month. It must be discharged either by him or Madam Browne—presumes he will do as much in favour of her as Capt. Hassett expects for his farm. Wonders why the *levari facias* should come when it was not in charge to the last sheriff. Prayed Mr. Whittfield inspect the records, lest by any device of Col. Sanckye's this should be put on [Lord Herbert]—presumes it was once discharged by him because not mentioned in the former sheriff's writ.

Mr. Bateman came by order from the Grand Farmers of the King's Revenue in Ireland and distrained on Bally mc Adam for £12 arrears of quit-rent (as they pretend). Paid all the crown rent last Michaelmas for all the seigniory, and has Mr. Bateman's, their collector's, acquittance. Replevied the cattle by replevy from the Presidency, and desired Mr.

Whittfield to apply to the Farmers and their commissioners at Dublin, and let them know that Bally mc Adam is part of this seigniory, that [Lord Herbert] enjoys it as such by his ancient and modern patents (also by decree confirmed by two Acts of Parliament), that his ancestors were in possession before the war, that he has been in possession these fourteen years; that though Col. Sancky passed them in his certificate and patent (with a saving to his lordship's right) he never had possession; that though he had the confidence to pass them in his new patent, that did not make [Lord Herbert] liable to pay quit-rent for them as forfeited lands; that if they expect quit-rent because they are in Col. Sanckye's patent they ought to charge him, not [Lord Herbert]; that any other part of Sanckye's estate passed by patent is liable to the rent for these lands, since he passed them at his peril. Hopes Whittfield will prevail with them to do justice.

Had not his letter of 24 April, by Charles Mason, till the 10th instant, after the post was gone; yet hearing Mr. Robert Hassett was going to Dublin next morning, he writ all night to Mr. Whittfield instructing him how to discourse with Col. Sancky to perfect the agreement about Bally mc Adam. This is the first the writer heard of it. Desired Mr. Whittfield to assure Sancky that if he performed his part faithfully as his lordship's counsel advised, he should have his 100 guineas or their value on the day agreed; and that [Lord Herbert] expected a verdict (and a judgement, for without judgement a verdict signifies little) and such other deeds as counsel advised. Mr. Robert Hassett could not be at Dublin till the 15th.

Will observe his directions about the Eastmeanus; knows no better way to effect it than by Sir Arthur Denny, who has been these seven weeks ill of an ague, and like to die, but now on the mending hand. Charles Mason brought message from Sir Arthur that he will write as soon as he is able. Sir A. Denny spoke to him some years since for some accommodation in that business of Eastmeanus, by the procurement (he thinks) of Drew. Will do it warily and effectually.

[Lord Herbert] gave orders by his letter from Dublin to set Rackenderry for three years, which is done. Last year Mr. Sanders had it; he would not take it longer, being afraid of that desperate fellow Thomas mc James. Whoever told him mc James stayed by connivance of the writer's told a [lie]. Sent John mc David the sergeant to warn him off those lands and demand possession for Anthony Palmer, an Englishman to whom he had let it (and improved the rent 20s. for each year). Thomas mc James would not believe [Lord Herbert] would have him begone [until] he saw his orders; then he promised to leave. Will [otherwise] indict him of a forcible detainer this quarter sessions. Values one iota of his lordship's commands more than Mc James's soul and body. He vows the writer's ruin, whose misfortune it is that [Lord Herbert] thinks he countenances Mc James there, when *he* thinks him the only one that caused him to be removed. Mr. Prichard reported Mr. Mason was to be married to some rich widow about Mountgomery (thinks her name is Couchley). Thought it better to set the lands with advantage than hazard them "at 6 and 7". Is troubled his lordship is offended with him upon every information. Has good security for the rent. Thomas mc James shall not enjoy one foot of the seigniory—has already to some, and will signify his pleasure to that effect to the rest of the tenants. At the least opportunity of rebellion Mc James would cut the writer's throat as he would bread when hungry. Told him in former letters that Mc James and one Major Barry (that came one day to his lordship here with young Fitz Gerald) were hatching mischief about Killmarrey; but he is not pleased to take notice of it. Has been confirmed by some discourse with Sir Rd. Kyrle, who was here visiting his old friend and new brother-in-law Sir Ar. Denny; he said they were informing Lord Kingston that [Lord Herbert] had no right to those lands, and that [they were *omitted*] concealed lands within that commission formerly mentioned. Told him they were damned liars, and that he hoped Lord Kingston was so much a lover of [Lord Herbert] and of so much honour as not to credit such rascals, who designed to set the English noblemen in a flame to warm themselves thereby . . . Hears of no proceedings yet on that commission of enquiry.

Among the tenants that Mr. Robert Hassett pitched upon to pay his money was Richard Trant, but he came for allowance of that £12 he lent Will Lloyd on his lordship's account, for which [Lord Herbert] gave his bill. Told him he had no orders to pay it; prays his pleasure therein. Will not demand rent from Will. Lloyd, according to his command. Spoke with Mr. Sanders about some moneys for Will Lloyd by Michaelmas, but he has been at great expense in building and had great losses in cattle, so cannot accommodate him yet. Sanders supplied Will Lloyd with some this spring, and the writer did with £5 since Christmas—not yet repaid.

Set Fyeryes last year to John Wms. for £9 10s., but he had great loss of cattle, and has not paid; has secured what cattle he has left for the rent, but will not appraise or meddle with them till he hears [Lord Herbert's] pleasure.

He ordered him to supply the bearer, Mr. Thomas Corbett, with £10, which he did, and 40s. more; has his bonds for it, and upon his lordship's [? certificate] that it is paid, he is to cancel [the bonds] in Morgan's presence. Received the enclosed lately from Dr. James Vaughan, saying there's £50 left him by a sister, which he desires [Lord Herbert] to receive and charge the writer with a bill of exchange or receipt for it here.

Has been troubled with a spice of "the contrey disease" for three or four months, but escaped the gout. This is a very sickly spring—ague, smallpox, and fever raging in divers parts. Hopes he will pardon the badness of the paper. His poor wife and his lordship's godson present their duty.

Culcooc,
16 May.

Service to his lordship's brothers and sisters. Garrett Gerald that looks to the horses desires to know whether he shall come over to wait on [Lord Herbert] or be discharged here. If here, how much shall he give him; if sent over, how much shall he pay him? The horses are in pretty good order, being "scowrd at the Marsh". But they were misused in the winter, being frequently rid by Mr Hassett, as the boy complained to the writer with tears. *HM2.22/19.*

The Act of Settlement had specified one year's 'rent and profits' of all lands which had been set out to officers and soldiers for their arrears of pay in 1653 as one of the sources of a fund to be raised for paying the arrears of commissioned officers who served the King in Ireland before mid-1649. This explains the references here to "year's value". "Madam Browne" is Lord Herbert's sister Frances, the wife of William Browne. Thomas Herbert's apology for the badness of his paper is not superfluous—this long letter has not been easy to decipher.

[16]71

348. [SIR] HENRY HERBERT TO COL. WORTHEN AT COURT. *Holograph copy.*

If the Hon. Capt. Herbert consigns £110 on the writer for him, it shall be paid on Capt. Herbert's order the 28th of this month by eight in the morning.

"My House" near Millbridge, Westminster,
19 November. *HM*2.24/1.

The order to pay Robert Worden (or Werden) this sum of money is in the same bundle, with several other such orders of Capt. Herbert's.

[16]71

349. RO. WERDEN TO SIR HENRY HERBERT AT HIS HOUSE NEAR MILL BRIDGE, WESTMINSTER.

Indisposition permits him not to wait upon him. Sends the bearer (Francis Tompson) his servant with Sir Henry's note to pay £110 upon Capt. Harbert's consigning so much to the writer's use; which consignment the bearer brings, the writer's receipt upon the back, to be delivered to Sir Henry upon his paying the £110.

Whitehall,
27 November, at night.

Will, if he thinks this receipt not sufficient, send any other discharge. *HM*2.23/16a.

Werden was at this time a major in the Duke of York's Guards.

1671/2

350. JOHNE MURAY TO RITCHARD HARBERTT, ESQ., AT BRUMFEILLD, NEAR LUDLO.

Received his dated 3 February on the 5th. Glad to hear of his good health but sorry he thinks his bill unreasonable, which is contrary to the letter he sent, after receipt of his cloak, showing he was well pleased. As to the price of the buttons, he may please himself. A month before Christmas he wrote that the money was ready. Wanted it very much since—to follow his trade he must go now upon trust. If he had not liked the buttons when he received them they could have been changed as he changed the swordbelt [in] April 1670. Assures him that however Herbert mislikes his prices, this ten years "sinc I have wroght to your honor" he never had twelve pence a pound for laying out his ready money. So let it please him to return it as soon as he can. Entreats him in his next letter how he likes his last clothes and his son's; is not well satisfied that he never sent word.

Londone,
6 February. *HM*2.23/15.

[16]71/2

351. [SIR] HENRY HERBERT TO MONSR. HERBERT, CAPIT. AU RÉGIMENT DU COL. JONES, CHEVALIER, À PAGNE EN LORAINE PRÈS DE NANCY. DONNEZ À MME. PARIS À LA CROIX BLANCHE, RUE DE MAIRE AUX FAUBOURGS ST. GERMAIN, PARIS.

"A late Adresse was made to you" by Mme. Paris; hopes it is come to hand. He may be disappointed, for his colonel has ordered Frekleton to enclose no more letters in his packet. His colonel has given the King a sight of what Capt. Herbert wrote concerning his quarters, good usage, [etc.]. He shall receive a letter from his lieutenant and another from Mr. Edgcombe. His lieutenant's accounts were left with the writer by the colonel; finds upon perusal of them a charge but no discharge, which the colonel promised Izod should bring. Having a note of Mr. Edgcombe's payments, a balance shall be made. Has this day paid Frekleton £50, which with £13 added is returned by Frekleton to be paid Capt. Herbert by his colonel . . . Freckleton paid to Pearce [£]10, to Major Dutton [£]2, "and for his Horse" [£]25, [leaving] [£]13 returned.

Cobet is froward and will not budge a foot unless he have £20. Told him the £20 he had received might serve for both journeys, but nothing can prevail without money . . . Attested Capt. Herbert's handwriting to the warrant to Mr. Cooper for delivery of the goods to Cobet, and the person where Capt. Herbert lodged has done the like. The Lord Chief Baron's servant promised to assist delivery of the goods after trial; the Lord Chief Baron (sitting upon life and death at Stafford, where the prisoners are to be tried) is Sir Edward Turnor, and was "our" Speaker. All requisite shall be done to prosecute or cause Cobet's bond to be forfeited, and for recovery of the clothes in case he be refractory. Would willingly put the charge on her that paid the first £20 and retrieve his goods . . .

Has endeavoured to get the [£]30; the drawer owns the debt but pays not. He should chide H. Evry for not writing to his parents.

Near Millbridge, West[minster],
29 February.

Encloses a letter from Lord Brackley. *HM*2.23/17.

Henry Every, one of Captain Herbert's fellow-officers, was eldest son of Sir Henry Every of Egginton, Derbyshire, 2nd Bart., Sir Henry Herbert's son-in-law.

[1672]

352. [SIR] HENRY HERBERT TO [CAPT. HENRY HERBERT]. *Contemporary copy.*

His of the 25th, French style, was delivered by Mr. Frekleton on 29 March, English style, wherein it appears he has received the bill of exchange for £63, and that Frekleton has accounted for £73. To make up the £100 desired by him (whereof the writer furnished £50 for that Mr. Edgcombe cannot furnish moneys till [Capt. Herbert's] draper and Lieut. Izod are paid) he may expect performance from the writer rather than his occasions should suffer. Wishes he would draw less that he may have more here for extremities. The state of his condition: 25 August last, '71, Ed. Blackwell (*sic*) esq. paid to Capt.

Herbert's use . . .	£507	10s.	
Received of Mr. Edgcombe	50		
On Lord Herbert's bill of "imposte"	7	16s.	
	£565	6s.	
Paid to 12 January '71 for Capt. H. Herbert's use, as by particulars sent	333	11s.	9d.
Paid to Mr. Frekelton 29 Feb. '71	50		
	£383	11s.	9d.
	£181	14s.	3d.
Paid Vaughan, laid out for L.H.'s bill of impost.	1		
	£180	14s.	3d.

He shall receive £50 by bill of exchange on Thursday next. By whom is not yet known, for he purposes to be at the Exchange then to try how the exchange runs, and carry the money with him . . . [Capt. Herbert] had the good fortune to receive his money a few days before the check of payments out of the Exchequer.

The war was publicly proclaimed 29 March '72 against the States of the Low Countries. An encounter has been had with the Smerna fleet, commanded by Sir R. Holmes, who with seven ships undertook their twenty-four fighting ships, worsted them, and took eleven prizes. He deserves no news for he sends none. However, preserve his health and keep money in his purse is the best advice he can give in temporal matters.

[? early April].

Sir Henry Jones has ordered Frekleton to receive no letters for his packet, therefore the address given must be observed till [Capt. Herbert] alters it. The services of his wife and children. Harry longs to be with him—shall he be sent? Not a word from Capt. Everye. Desires a discharge for moneys paid him. *HM*2.23/12.

Sir Henry Jones was Colonel of Captain Herbert's regiment. "Harry" is Sir Henry Herbert's son, then not quite eighteen.

1672

353. John Read to Richard Herbert, esq., at Oakely Park.

Mr. Cheyne promises his lady's bodices shall be ready in time. Will bring with him Herbert's cornelian ring and his sword. His lordship sets out Wednesday and will be at Worcester Thursday night, where he hopes to find Herbert's coach. The directions for the tea are: A quart of spring water just boiled, to which put a spoonful of tea, and sweeten to the palate with "Candy Sudger". As soon as the tea and sugar are in, the steam must be kept in as much as may be, and let it lie half or quarter of an hour in the heat of the fire, but not boil; as soon as the ships are in he shall be furnished with "fresh and good". No news but that a Templar was clapped up in the Tower for telling news; how he'll be tried is not known. Some say there will be a peace. Capt. Herbert is very well—Lord Brackly had a letter from him this day.

Lo.,
29 June.

The little cups must be held over the steam before the liquid be put in.

404.

Read was Lord Herbert's servant.

[16]72

354. [SIR] HENRY HERBERT TO CAPT. [HENRY] H[ERBERT].

Informs him of his return from a short progress to Ribsford and Egington to see his daughter Every; as of [Lord Herbert's] purpose to visit the writer there—but was hindered by indisposition contracted at London, and made haste to Llussyn to take physic and to excuse his non-attendance on the Earl of Essex into Ireland (who is settled there, and Lord Bartlet returned). But [Lord Herbert's] thoughts are for Ireland, though he may be disappointed by a summons for Parliament in October, "when your personall aparance will bee Expected".

The enclosed letters were here yesterday at the writer's "landinge". Where the regiment is drawn into garrison, Capt. Herbert may have leave to do his duty here to the public and "intende" his concerns, which need him.

Near Millbridge, Westminster,
22 August.

Capt. Herbert's brother has sent by Montgomery carrier £50 in a bag sealed for him, which proves right "upon Tale" . . .

*HM*2.23/18.

"Lord Bartlet" is Lord Berkeley, the returned Lord Lieutenant. Why Capt. Herbert's attendance should be required in event of Parliament's being summoned is unclear, for he was not at this time a member.

1672

355. [LORD] HERBERT TO RICHARD HERBERT, ESQ., AT OAKELY PARK. BY WAY OF LONDON.

"Wee are all alive in Dublin . . . but misserably beetossed. Have escaped the Greatest Tempest that ever shipp lived in, and out of one place out of which never shipp scaped till this . . . Ile make noe discription—though I can make a very authenticke one, haveing discoursed with the Knowingest seafareing men about it—for feare of Trembling . . ."

Dublin,
19 October.

Prays him let Bowen and Parson Jones know he is alive. Twice they were nine days and nine nights at sea. Brother Tom desperately sick, but much better for it.

Armorial seal 75.

1672

356. [LORD] HERBERT TO RICHARD HERBERT, ESQ., AT OAKELY PARK.

Richard's letter of the 22nd of last month is the first dated since the writer's landing; perceives his being shipwrecked gained the general opinion. Perceives he has been staying at the Lymore; is well pleased if he had good sport. Finds sister Herbert's illness caused him to leave Rhusayson ere Bowen reached it. He says no word of the master of Rhusaysen. Thanks God he has had a little of the country looseness, which proved excellent physic; believes he will live longer than many wish. After Christmas he will march into Kerry after brother Tom, who now wholly enjoys "Peggy sweetelipps" the parson's wife and the writer's new house (which is so neat and fine that he wishes Richard such another at the same cost). For news they have alarms of the fanatics and the natives. [The latter] are most dangerous, because the fanatics can give the King's government no disturbance but at the same time they put themselves out of his protection, which is the common safety of the English planters. There is one, Walcott, before "us" now; but takes him to be maliciously accused, because he is no fool, and his accuser is lately turned papist. In Clare several rebels whose lands were distributed amongst the soldiers and [sold] since and settled by acts of Parliament [etc.] have entered upon their estates, saying the King has granted an act of oblivion and grace, and that they shall all be restored. This sounds like Irish insolence and Irish reason. Cannot blame a conquered people [for trying] to relieve themselves, but the conqueror never gave such relief. Fears not the worst the Irish can do as long as the English understand one another and preserve their faith to His Majesty. Yet the potent Irish are better heard in Whitehall than in any former ages. A few more insolencies will discredit them, and then all will be well. Fears he is tedious in an affair Richard is not concerned [in], "but here my shoe wrings mee"—he is concerned for his estate and throat. But they have an admirable Lord Lieutenant, newly recovered from death's door. They live at a jolly but sober rate, and play at "umbra" like mad after business is done. If he may brag, the method of proceeding as to the army is what he proposed first in London to his excellency the day after he was named. The army is kept in a moving posture, lying in a larger proportion about Dublin, where there is a body able to suppress any sudden rising. It is relieved every two months, so that the army of horse has its round of duty twice every year, which makes them able and willing.

Dublin,
8 December.

Hopes he orders Bowen to proceed in payment of the writer's debts.

On a separate slip : The surest way to send letters is through a friend in

London. Directs these to Mr. Henry Grice, haberdasher of hats, over against St. Clemen[t's] Church in the Strand.

Armorial seal 5.

Rhiwsaeson, Montgomeryshire, was the seat of Richard Owen, cousin to Richard Herbert.

1672/3

357. [LORD] HERBERT TO RICHARD HERBERT, ESQ., AT OAKELY PARK.

Despairs of seeing a letter from him when he moves to Kerry, which he intends within this fortnight. Will direct letters per Sir Henry Herbert. Letters directed to the postmaster of Dublin will find him in any part of Irland. Has to "eate and drinke" little ready money, so his abode here is doubly convenient. This country will keep him plentifully, and his estate in England will free him of all incumbrances, even in this time of lear. Could get no rents hence, so if he had stayed in England he [could have] paid no debts there. Prays him supervise Bowen and [see] how Andrew Ellis pursues his orders about stock. When the war ends and trade opens, he may expect to see the writer, for then it will be the same thing in what country he lives. Would have those parcels of land of poor Jacke Evans, deceased—betwixt the Lymore and Mountgom[er]y town, about £20 per annum—bought for him, though some debts be delayed; believes they are to be sold now his whole estate will be divided betwixt his sisters. Prays him contrive it; they will complete his demesnes. Purposes to build in the Lymore or by Black Hall, as he shall be advised, and to have 300,000 of bricks made the summer following next for the purpose.

Dublin,
14 January.

Is troubled that he hears not of brother Harry's return.

Armorial seal 76.

1672/3

358. [LORD] HERBERT TO RICHARD HERBERT, ESQ., AT OAKELY PARK. TO BE LEFT WITH MR. CRANKE, POSTMASTER OF BRIMIGHAM, FOR CONVEYANCE.

His of the 5th came [today]. Is obliged to him for paying the clamorous debts first. Would rather pay "use" for money than anybody should be at a loss. Questions not but as he is a good manager of his own affairs, so he will be to the writer's, which are wholly submitted to him. Is weaned from England for a longer time, "since my Misse is married, or to be soe ere long—but cheer up, wee must all live till wee dye. Bid my brother marry, and if I like his proceedings as a younger brother, 'tis two to one but hee may be an elder". His last letter says Lady Frances Brerton is dead . . . but . . . (*torn*) . . . confirms it not. He gives good news of cousin Owens of Rwsayson [being] in a way of recovery. Ned Humberston [would have] obliged him if he had pitched on the keepership of Llyssyn, being skilled in cattle and husbandry. If tenants are backward, Bowen and Whittingham ought to be diligent. Tom Browne is a happy, unhappy person in acquiring such an estate and losing such a benefactor. Rejoices that sister Florencia is mended, and their children in good condition. Will make sister Frances an honest return when her business is perfected. Richard's letters will be conveyed by the postmaster-general.

Dublin,
21 January. 77.

Lord Herbert's first wife, Anne Myddelton, had died in 1671 ; his second marriage—to Elizabeth, daughter of Lord Chandos—was seven months after this letter. Lady Brereton did not die until 1680.

1672/3

359. [LORD] HERBERT TO RICHARD HERBERT, ESQ., AT OAKLY PARK. LEAVE WITH MR. EDWARD CRANCKE, POSTMASTER IN BRIMIGHAM. . .

Received his of 28 January just as he took coach three weeks since at Dublin ; arrived here Friday last in much better health than he left Dublin. Kept his bed three days ; finding himself worse and worse of the cold, he "began to consider this body of mine was not for my use unlesse it would endure the wether", so got up, took leave of the Lieutenant, and proceeded next morn. Wishes Richard the like of the house he finds here at his price, and that if ever he builds he would take the model of it. Expected Mr. Pugh to act as he does, but is glad Richard and the rest of his friends stick to the writer's cousin and their own interest. Displacing the *Custos* without an offence is unpracticable ; supposes the Lord Lieutenant of Wales and Lord Powis too cunning to [try] any such thing, but Richard's advice will occasion a letter to the Lord Chancellor and Lord Bridgwatter.

The ill weather in England and Wales is well represented in Irland "and wee say noething of it". Prays him continue his care for his concerns ; he longs to be in a condition to serve his family, which cannot be if money be wanting. Longs to hear how Andrew Ellis disposed of the cows and what he buys in their stead. If Humberston had offered his service for Llyssyn he might have saved Andrew's wages ; but will not part with a worse man than Imgram to please him. Will need a hundred guineas about May ; Bowen is to send them, and at the same time may come four "parshall" saddles with holster tops and all other furniture, which Richard is desired to bespeak—two of red velvet with silk fringe and two of leather stitched with silver. The saddles should be fit for Som. Fox, to whom the writer's service. Love and services to "my sisters all".

"My Cabbin" at Castle Island,
18 February.

Brother Thomas never better in health. Is his bedfellow in a very large bed, "and yet . . . I smell his sweate, but I pay him of[f] at tother end".

405.

Lord Herbert was *Custos Rotulorum* of both Montgomeryshire and Denbighshire, but it is presumably his Montgomeryshire Custos-ship that is referred to here. "Fit for Som. Fox" apparently means that Somerset Fox was Lord Herbert's 'pattern for size'.

[16]72/3

360. [SIR] HENRY HERBERT TO LORD HERBERT AT CASTLE ISLAND. TO BE SENT BY MR. WARBERTON, POSTMASTER IN DUBLIN.

His letters gave the certainty of his safe arrival at Castle Islands, and of the great satisfaction he receives there. Presumes he has received the Captain's assurances of his safe return to Court and his duty in the Guards. He is come in time to assist public interest, much endangered by ill counsels. [The] Declaration of Indulgence has been examined by the Commons, and a vote passed that the penal laws could not be suspended but by Act of Parliament, which was presented to the King, who answered that he would consider of it. Some days passing, the Privy Councillors were ordered to move His Majesty, and answer was presented by Secretary Coventry, but not being satisfactory, the House made another address, to which the King answered that he would consider of it. The House expressed their discontent by putting off the bill of supplies. His Majesty on Saturday the 1st presented the papers to the Lords and desired their advice, assuring them he would be tender of their privileges. Yesterday the Lords voted that the King's answer to the Commons, referring the points to a parliamentary way by bill, was a proper and natural course.

The House of Commons has voted £1,260,000 at £70,000 a month, but it moves slowly for that the laws are not secured, and yesterday they made an address to the King (wherein the Lords' concurrence is desired) for removing papists from Court and banishing priests out of England, and putting them out of all military and civil employments, and that all retained shall take the Oaths of Allegiance and Supremacy and receive the sacrament. The bill for supply is adjourned to Saturday next, and is not likely to run post till better satisfaction be given. The bill for indulgence to Protestant dissenters is ready to be presented to the Commons, but must wait upon the bill for supply . . . (*The terms of the bill follow*). The King is almost constantly at the House of Lords, and was there this day till three in the afternoon. It is reported the Brandenburgians have defeated 4,000 French horse and foot in the Bishop of Munster's army, Munster taken and the Bishop besieged.

4 March.

The lady is not married, and Lord Herbert is fairer for her favour than Lord Mohun or any other. When the Captain entertains the journey, Hary may wait upon Lord Herbert with him.

Contemporary endorsement: Capn. Henry Herbert's letter. 403.

The Lords' vote described as occurring "yesterday" was actually on 4 March. The money voted by the Commons was £1,238,750 (25 Car. II, cap. l). "Hary" of the postscript is Sir Henry Herbert's son. The endorsement is a confusing blunder—there is no doubt at all that the letter is from Sir Henry Herbert, not Captain Henry Herbert.

1672/3

361. [LORD] HERBERT TO RICHARD HERBERT, ESQ., AT OAKELY PARK. TO BE LEFT AT MR. CRANKE'S, POSTMASTER IN BRIMIGHAM . . . .

Received his of 23 February two days ago. Is glad his rents are so well paid, but sorry his debts pay so slowly. Intended the corn at

Llyssyn should pay servants' wages, etc.; it will pay for some years a considerable sum, he hopes. Bowen should not neglect the buying of Jack Evans's lands below the church; can improve much by them. If Charleton "payes" there, they are to forbear a little if he endeavours to pay (with ready money) what he sets to others and increases his stock on the lands he occupies himself. If he fails in either it will be time to advise him to a remove hither, where, with a little stock, in time he may live extremely well. "I love the fellow and would not have him . . . impoverish himselfe." Will, he thinks, build at Stalloe, if he ever returns to be able to buy £200 or £300 to supply the rent of it. Will sow the whole Frith with nuts and acorns before he is two years older for a perpetual stock of fuel to his family's chief seat, which must be within a mile or two of Mountgomery.

Is Ingram married to Peggy Rantio? Believes she was more in love with the park than the man. Is loath to separate husband and wife, and will suffer them there. Humberston would take his woman again, and it is better to keep Ingram (that is careful of deer and horses) with an honest wife than the other (that loves neither) "with a——that will defile my lodge and pillage my goods". If Humberston "has a mind to me" he must come over with a sum in his pocket; can in a short time prefer him to a service in his own calling, if the writer makes no park himself. Is likely to live longer here than he purposed, all things pleasurable and convenient appearing more and more. Despairs ever to see Richard here; it is best he does not come lest he lose his love to his own country.

Is sorry his brother is not paid. Bowen must send over at May a hundred guineas, and the bed and stools, etc., of dimity wrought with green, which he intends to set up in his withdrawing room looking into the garden. Would willingly have his smith, Heylyn, old Kate, and Mault, drunken as the two former are, and arrant scolds as the two latter are. Both the gold (which they must carry concealed) and the bed may be sent by them. 'Tis less hazard though a little more charge to come by Dublin, where a couple of tits may be bought for 20s. to carry the maids and the things, and the good men may beat it on the hoof. Love to his sisters and to Richard and his little ones.

Castle Island,
18 March.

Is [sorry *omitted*] sickness has seized Sir Job as to displace him from his new honour and put Seymer into it.

Endorsed: About . . . Andrew Charleton . . . etc. 78.

Sir Job Charlton had become Speaker of the House of Commons early in February, but served only a fortnight before retiring on the grounds of ill-health.

1672/3

362. John Read to Mr. Richard Bowen at Coedtallog.

[Notes] that his trunk is sent, and that the six cheeses will be sent. Received 30s. of Mal. Wilson from Mrs. Arabella. Has already paid Mr. Robinson of Ludlow the 30s.; if he will be so knavish he deserves to be without his money this year. Will spend £20 rather than be abused for 20d. Desires to know the condition of Mr. Fitz Herbert's farm, and where the writer might find a purchase for the small sum he has to lay out. Would willingly plant himself in Mountgom[er]y shire or Carmarthen shire.

Asked him to advise with old Katherine, Malt the brewer, and Hylyn whether they come to Castle Island, and to send with them if they come her ladyship's wrought bed, [etc.]. His lordship has written to Mr. Herbert to send saddles, etc. He must send also two livery saddles over the stable. His lordship will not part with the cook, so Mr. Vaughan must provide himself with another. His lordship conceived on departing from Llyssyn that there was more money to be made out of the corn, etc., than would clear the servants' wages and workmen's bills. His lordship wanted him to pay them and himself and leave the rents. Desired him also to peruse the rentals and not trust his man. He is to enquire whether the smith will come over.

Castle Islands,
18 March. 79.

"Mrs. Arabella" is Lord Herbert's sister, Arabella Herbert.

1673

363. R. Herbert to Lord Herbert at Castle Islands.

Gave account in former letters of his discourse with Andrew Ellis and of Heylin's and the smith's being entertained at Lloydiarth, and that he had told Ned Hum[m]erston what Lord Herbert proposed for him. If Hum[m]erston undertakes not the journey the things cannot be despatched yet. Hopes he received the advices of Mr. Bowen's death; hopes "suddenly" to see his new agent or receive orders therein. Lord Herbert guessed "too right" at his brother's silence, who commanded the writer to give account of his employ this year, and at his return, God willing, will wait on him in Ireland. His brother says his business most at sea was to save charges, hoping to find the *St. George* frigate cheaper than London Town. [As to] the deer, the keeper Hickman rendered his loss at Llyssyn last winter at 150; the deer at Lymor stand well. Shortly expects Parson Jones; will tell him from Lord Herbert of the shortage of ink and paper at Beryw. Mrs. Devereux is dead; knows not how things will be now between father and son—the son is at sea. Has transcribed Mr. Bowen's accounts. Delivered the directions about the saddles to cousin Fox, who dined with him this day. Fox said he sat in the House of Commons by Sir Jon Trevor when Sir Jon opened a packet, one letter being Lord Herbert's mentioning the violin, etc. He said the best are Italian and would cost £60, but he supposes Lord Herbert means English make, and will take speedy course in it. Lord Herbert's sister's love, and their love to their brother Thomas. Has not heard from his brother Harry, but 'tis reported Sir Henry Herbert had [died].

Oakely Park,
22 April.

Annexed is a transcription of Bowen's accounts. 406.

The Revd. Roger Jones was Vicar of Berriew; the reference to the shortage of ink and paper is probably a sarcastic complaint that he had not written to Lord Herbert. Mary, the wife of George Devereux of Vaynor, died about this time; her death is recorded (without date) in British Museum Additional MS. 14,881 between entries of 1671 and 1674 (*Montgomeryshire Collections*, Vol. XIII, p. 419).

1673

364. [Lord] Herbert to [Richard Herbert].

Despatched Read upon the first notice of Bowen's death. Brother Thomas ill with a cold; his death, if it happen in Irland, will be laid to the writer's charge as "a great, Willfull sin". Till about three weeks ago no man so merry or healthy, but then he grew melancholy and peevish. Last night he slept and appears somewhat mended. Is glad they are all well. "God continue health to you and your whole fire side, and there's your Irish proverb for you."

Observes how Bowen managed Llyssyn; in parting not with all the servants as soon as the winter corn was in the ground (except Kate and her maid, Lewis, and one boy to look to the cattle) he followed not the writer's orders. To speak truth of the dead, he ever believed Bowen honest but to have much more compassion for anything than the writer's purse. Is sorry Mr. Andrew Ellis cannot do as he promised—doubts not but it is in prospect of making an advantage of the writer. Must at this distance submit. Leaves it to [Richard] to put the demesnes of Llyssyn in as profitable a way as he can. Milch cows are the dearest and most troublesome. Would have the other sort, if they be cheap, for summering in the hills and wintering in Llyssyn. Must the market continue so ill? Cannot suspect the failure of his interest in the country while [Richard] and the rest of his friends take care of him. Whether all things, as pensions, etc., run in the same stream is not material. But living or not living in Irland is the most important point of his life—which is carried for Irland. If he continues so for some years he will be able, by interest of money, to recover any interest shaken by his absence. The discovery of the £47 will help buy six black coach mares, which Read has orders to buy out of hand. When the keepers have accounted what male stock they have, [Richard] may dispose of them to himself and the rest of Lord Herbert's friends, preserving a strong male game according to the number of deer; and he should kill females young and old, that may be eaten baked, roast, or boiled. Sir Henry Herbert has orders for a brace of bucks out of the Lymore. Neighbour Vaughan of Lloydiarth may command a brace of bucks out of Llyssyn and a leash of does there next season.

Longs to see some of the Mountgomery shire or Shrop shire gentlemen here. When they returned they would have reason to say this is a pleasant and fruitful country. Hopes Heylyn's removing to Lloydiarth does not remove all the good things out of the garden with him. Could wish he had a "watter man" and six labourers (single men) to ditch and set quicks. Doubts not by draining and fencing to make his demesnes of [£]60 at least £200 per annum. Hopes Read is on his return. Prayers for all at Oakly Park.

"Deare Dick, Your obligd brother-in-law."

Castle Island,
6 May.

Since writing it has pleased God to take brother Tho. An impostume broke at five o'clock this morning, 7 May, which immediately suffocated him. He had a yellow and black countenance from the beginning to the end of this sickness. Letting a little blood yesterday eased him much and gave him an easy death. His impostume issued out of his nose and mouth in a torrent . . . . . . (*more details follow*). It is a miracle he lived so long, knowing how he came. He desired the doctors to ease him, and called to our Saviour to take him to his mercy. Doubts not he is now a glorified soul in Heaven. 80.

1673

365. [LORD] HERBERT TO RICHARD HERBERT, ESQ., AT OAKLEY PARK. TO BE LEFT WITH MR. CRANKE, POSTMASTER AT BRUMIGHAM.

Received a letter of 29 April from cousin Henry Herbert telling of his father's death. The writer's last gave news of brother Thomas's death . . . "But of that I say noe more". Has perused Christopher's accounts and Bowen's, and observes no compliance to his directions in either. Hopes Whittingham has set out all the lands about Mountgomry to give rent at Michaelmas, and has sold his fat cattle and made good money of hay this hard year—expects a considerable sum. Hopes debts will pay off quicker for the future and rents be more briskly called for. Doubts not Read has waited on him long since and is upon his return from London; longs to hear of him for important reasons. Hopes the violin and books of tunes came safely to him, and that the writer will receive them, the saddles, the guineas, and his mares ere long. "God blesse us from Violl Inns of 60*l*. price. I meant onely the best of English make." If he has not received it, prays him get Sum. Fox to write to "him"—knows not how to direct to him if not in London at his chamber in the Temple. Prayers for him and the writer's sister. Service to Som. Fox and Sir Job. Wishes the company of some good friend. Here is pleasure enough.

Castle Island,
13 May.

Endorsed: Fowles, Finch, Tempest, Courtney, Trevaynion, Woordon; *Cambridge*, *Resolution*, *Sweepstakes*. 28.

"Christopher" is Christopher Whittingham; he was steward of Lord Herbert's lands around Montgomery, Bowen having had charge of the Monmouthshire lands. The endorsement gives the names of captains and ships lost or reported lost in the first Battle of Schooneveld, 28 May 1673. Sir Henry Herbert, Master of the Revels, had died on 27 April.

1673

366. [SIR] VA. BROWN TO LORD HERBERT AT CASTLE ISLAND.

His lordship honoured him with his commands for some laths. The woodmen have not done yet with their barley sowing. If he please to employ the plasterer or another to cut what he will have, the writer's sergeant will show him the wood. His wife and little boy are his lordship's servants.

19 May.

Notes on the dorse in Lord Herbert's hand: To reset the two mills to "him" at £40 per annum for twenty or twenty-five years to encourage him to build two more mills at Killasoghty and another at Curranse, to pay for them £2 yearly for the first seven years, £4 for the next seven, and thereafter £8 . . . . (*further details*). 81.

[1673]

367. [LORD HERBERT] TO ————. *Holograph draft, much altered.*

Lives in a country wild and barbarous by reason of the ill ways to it and the dangerous inhabitants. There are many English and English interests that should have protection. But they have no army troop, company, file of men, nor garrison, nor so much as [a place] to keep a barrel of powder. They know none under whom to range themselves in their own country upon any alarum. Nor have they any place of strength with garrison nearer than Corke, Kingsale, or Limericke, the nearest at least forty miles. To some of these must they fly on all occasions, and leave wife, children, houses, and s[toc]ks to the mercy of a bloody enemy (as they are expected to be in another rebellion)—and 'tis possible they look upon themselves as now provoked. And he cannot question but the Romish clergy, that expect to be deprived of their livelihoods and incontrollable dominion over these blinded recusants, muster up their malice and consider their strength. This is their condition, and they hope a redress from their superior and his Council. Humbly proposes no place fitter for a magazine, and to be kept with less charge, than Rosse Castle, half a company of foot being sufficient to guard such a magazine as may well supply an army, or at least the hands of the country. 'Tis true it is a worthy gentleman's capital seat, but why may not the King gratify him in a good rent for it? It would be a visible strength under which they might kindle a force. If they can make good the field, this place of the writer's is the best from whence may be commanded all the passes in and out of the country in three hours' march—he knows the country better than the writer. Humbly requests he would discourse with Lord Orrery that he would use his interest that something be done. Begs not command, but to know, while in "your" country, whom he may apply [to] for authority to defend himself, it being as great a crime to arm men without commission as to neglect a trust [one] is commissioned for. Besides, he has, as a volunteer, been in sufficient hazard and expense, and he expects wages whenever he ventures upon service . . . (*Breaks off unfinished*). 614.

The words "Deare Madam", smudged almost into illegibility, head the sheet, but I assume that they have no connection with this letter.

[1673]

368. [LORD] HERBERT TO TOM HERBERT.

The rain prevents his waiting on Col. Macalecuddy to him to receive his advice. Understands the case thus: Sir Wm. Petty sent five armed men with an iron mark to mark the woods on the Colonel's lands (in his quiet possession by the King's orders this eleven or twelve years). Is desired as a Privy Councillor of Irland (or rather, Justice of the Peace) to grant a warrant for apprehending the persons, who made it a riot, offering to draw their swords and fighting with the Colonel's men. Asks word, after he has examined the Colonel's man (sent along with Mr. Gerald), how far he may proceed—is ignorant of proceedings in this country. 472a.

This is the Thomas Herbert who was formerly Lord Herbert's agent.

[1673]

369. THO. HERBERT TO [LORD HERBERT]. *Appended to the preceeding letter.*

Is so weak he can hardly speak. Both as Privy Councillor and Justice of Peace he may issue a warrant for the offenders and bind them over to assizes or sessions. Or, having examined witnesses, he may make a report to the Lord Lieutenant and Council, before whom Sir. Wm. Petty will be convened. Does not conceive Mc Gullicuddy lost possession because his [trees *omitted*] got the marking-axe. Hears Sir H. Ford's son was one of those there. "Your . . . servant till death." 472b.

[1673]

370. HEN. WHITFELD TO MR. PHILLIP HARRIS.

Lord Herbert has come to town and left with him this copy of an exemplification under the Great Seal proving Mary to be under age at the time of the feoffment. The patent and all other writings are left with Mr. Blennerhasset the younger. Lord Herbert is going for England and leaves the management of the whole to Harris, who is to retain counsel.

[? June-August].

Endorsed: For Traleey—*copia inquisicionis post mortem Will. Herbert, mil.* 473.

[16]73

371. THO. CORBETT TO RICHARD HERBERT, ESQ., AT OAKLEY PARK.

"Honrd. Cosin". Has sent his man purposely with the enclosed that Herbert may cause the writ for the sessions to be renewed and proclaimed at Poole, to be holden at Mountgom[er]y on 10 July. The writ must be tested by two justices (one of the quorum); it is not sufficient for the *Custos* alone to do it, as Mr. Lambard and reason itself say. He may put the writer's name to the test with his own. Lest he be not fully satisfied, he encloses copy of a letter he sent up to Sir William Weld, who lately came the Shropshire circuit, and is now a judge of the King's Bench. In case the Shropshire sessions be mistaken as to time he may do well to send that copy, and the Lord Chancellor's directions therein, to Sir Richard Corbett and join with him to have it new-appointed. Has been ill of a cold by going abroad too soon after taking physic. Service to his lady.

Dolley,

27 June.

Has directed the enclosed to the sheriff and justices. Desires word what he intends to do. 408.

The *Custos* of Montgomeryshire was Lord Herbert.

1673

372. [SIR] RICH. MASON TO LORD HERBERT AT MONTGOMERY.

Cousin Oakeley willingly accepts the honour Lord Herbert did him in choosing him for the arbitration of the controversy betwixt him and Mr. More. Upon arriving here the writer repaired to the Lord Chief Baron's house, but found he was gone into the country. Has been several times with Mr. Bertie and well disposed him for the matter. Their Majesties return for London from Windsor on Tuesday next; is going thither. The town is empty of company and news. Duty to his lady.

19 September. *Armorial seal* 82.

The Chief Baron was Sir Edward Turnor, and "Mr. Bertie" is no doubt Vere Bertie, his successor in that office.

[1673/4]

373. [LORD HERBERT] TO RICHARD HERBERT, ESQ., AT OAKLEY PARK, NEAR LUDLOW.

Jan. 28: Barnard Howard offered a petition to the House that those who were papists in conscience and not in faction might be favoured. It was rejected, but had many courtiers on its side. It set forth the suffering and loyalty of his ancestors and the sequestrations upon them in the usurper's time, that they could not provide for their younger sons; and now an act coming out against papists bearing office or pension, a papist must of necessity leave his country or suffer extreme wants; therefore desired that he and such as desired to live peaceably be allowed, taking the oath of allegiance, to bear office and pension. But the H[ouse] .... (*torn*).

Jan. 29: Sir R'bert Howard prefers a petition in behalf of Sir Samuell Morland's project for draining of water; it was referred to a committee. Mr. Right brought in a bill for ascertaining of measures, of coal, corn, billets, and faggots. Ordered that thanks be returned His Majesty for his last speech. Ordered that the Lords' concurrence be desired to the vote of the House concerning a peace with the Dutch; Lord Cornebery goes up with this. A message from the Lords that upon consideration of His Majesty's speech, they are of opinion .... (*torn*) .... to proceed in a treaty with the States General in order to a speedy peace; and so adjourned this day.

Jan. 30: The House went to St. Margaret Westminster, and heard sermons from Dr. Cradock and Dr. Loyd. *HM*2.23/88.

This letter, if it can be called such, is no doubt merely a copy of a news-letter received by Lord Herbert.

1674

374. [LORD] HERBERT TO THE DUKE OF MONMOUTH. *Holograph copy*.

His Majesty's answer to his request has infinitely perplexed him, the more considering how his family have for three generations wasted their estates and their time. What he desired of the Queen's jointures was in reversion, and no increase to present necessities. Now waives it. Would rather have something in Wales, where the rest of his estate lies.

And his grace may so order it that he has no benefit for a year or two, which will still respect present necessities. By which time he hopes the King will look upon the distresses the remaining number of his faithful subjects put themselves in by adhering to his interest while he was banished. Begs him to attempt this, and that when His Majesty has signified what he will give, and when he shall begin to reap the benefit, it shall be inserted on the back of his petition and directed to the Lord Keeper and Lord Treasurer to pitch on what in North Wales will answer His Majesty's intentions, to be settled on him for ninety-nine years. Begs him use all expedition, because waiting is chargeable. Would fain be at the wording of the grant ere he goes into the country or into Ireland. Desires to part with the burden of discontent this denial has caused, that he may not look upon himself laid by as a useless subject wasted in interest and estate.

31 March.

The lordships of Denbigh and Bromefeild "in" Yale lie very convenient, either of which for ninety-nine years would answer his desires. This lies in the King's power, although he cannot sell without act of Parliament.

409.

[1674]

375. [LORD HERBERT] TO [? THE DUKE OF MONMOUTH]. *Draft.*

"May it please your Grace". Is advised by all knowing persons that the likeliest design "to doo mee good" and within the King's power is a lease for ninety-nine years of some lordship in Wales at some small rents, with power to receive profits and lease copyhold tenements (the present rent to be reserved at expiration of the term), power to make benefit of encroachments by confirming titles to those in possession, and to enclose by agreement commons not yet enclosed (to redound to the benefit of the writer's heirs after expiration), and benefit of courts leet and baron "under 20*l*.", mines and quarries [etc.], and as large privileges as any the King's lordships, except mines royal. In fine, he begs the lordship of Denbigh or of Bromfeild and Yale . . . . . to be bound only at determination to leave the same rents to the Crown as the Auditors of the Exchequer make out are the King's present receipts . . . Begs the grant immediately, though the profit accrue not till Ladyday 1675, by which time he hopes the King's necessities will be in some measure over (if not, so small a thing will not be considerable to His Majesty). Would have meantime some employ to inspect the lordship.

*HM*2.23/73.

[? 1674]

376. [LORD HERBERT'S] PROPOSALS TO THE DUKE OF MONMOUTH. *Draft, torn in places.*

His grace has been pleased to consider his just pretences to His Majesty's favour. Has waived the proposal he made touching the Queen's jointure (which he observes fluxing out apace to several persons) understanding his grace [is] concerned in it. [Asks that] he attempt to get him a grant of one or more of the lordships in co. Denbigh at a small rent for ninety-nine years, with ample liberty for compounding for enclosed and for enclosing lands . . . only to be obliged at the end of the term to render the lordship chargeable with the rent he receives it under ; viz, the lordship of Denbigh or that of Bromfeild and Yale. If this fail, all the chiefries and rents due to the King out of Mountgomrysheire from the lordships . . . . . or a sum of money. If this fail, then [a parcel of money out of the King's . . . . . in case Parliament give him a new supply—if Parliament offer restrictions as to the using of it, then, being so supplied, his privy purse . . . . *unfinished and the whole passage deleted*] . . . to procure a parcel of money out of the hearth money or other present revenues, which will be at liberty if the King be supplied by Parliament. If this be denied, he will conclude that after three generations' service he is totally laid aside as a useless and unworthy person. This is the sum of his humble desires. *HM*2.14/21.

[? c. 1674]

377. Lord Herbert's Account of his Losses. *A fragment from his notebook.*

. . . . . horse at his own charge, with a[n] equipage for himself suitable to the design, which amounted to a great expense ; all lost again in his loyal attempts for His Majesty, and his estate sequestered and himself made prisoner till General Monk's declaring for a free parliament.

A great estate in Ireland better worth than £2,000 a year, lost for twenty-two years [in] the rebellion, and though now restored yields not a moiety of [that] ; besides the charge of replanting with tenants and cattle.

	£
1. Grandfather, E., Ld. Herb[er]t, sold lands of inheritance at 15 y[ears'] purchase, £4,000 per annum.	60,000
Remains unpaid of his salary as ambassador.	10,000
The Irish estate gave before the war £2,500 per annum; this lost for 22 years.	55,000
The Irish estate now yields £1,000 ; and the charge of new planting.	35,000
Demolishing Montgomery Castle and the plunder of other of their houses in the war.	30,000
2. Father, Rich., Ld. Herbert, sold £1,000 a year to maintain his regiment and troop in the King's service.	15,000
3. Ed., Ld. Herbert, his son, sold to pay debts transferred [to] him by Rd. Herbert.	3,000
Moneys and personal estate lost at Sir G. Booith's business.	5,000

*HM*2.26/1.

"The design" in the opening sentence is Sir George Booth's rebellion. These pages, detached from a small notebook, and written in the third person, contain what appears to be part of Lord Herbert's case in suppose of his claims upon the royal bounty.

1674

378. Statement on a Dispute between Lord Coventry and Lord Herbert.

About Thursday sennight three of Lord Coventry's men fell upon Lord Herbert's fowler and took from him his lordship's setting dog, betwixt Broadway Hill and "Stothoud" on the road, on Lord Coventry's liberty, as they say. He overtook them at "Shipton Norton" and desired the bailiff of the town to speak with them, and they said they had lost the dog. He enquired all about [for] a week for the dog. Being aware of Lord Coventry's coming down from London, he got one to write a letter, and had much ado to deliver it to his son, who said the dog should not be restored except he bring a letter from Lord Herbertt.

2 April. 410.

This is clearly Cotswold country—probably Stow-on-the-Wold and Chipping Norton are the places meant.

[16]74

379. MICHAEL CHEYNE TO RICHARD HERBERTT, ESQ., AT OAKELY PARK, NEAR LUDLOW.

Has sent the garments written for: A flowered gown laced, also an embroidered "body" of silver and gold of the best in London (which were made on purpose, there being none so large to be had); likewise a flowered petticoat unlaced with a "manto" coat and underbodice, the green petticoat with a silver lace between the other and one gold and one silver lace more than was on before—all sent Saturday, 9 May, by Edward Mills the carrier, that they might come in time. Hopes they will be to his liking.

12 May. *HM*2.23/19.

[? late 17th C.]

380. NOTE CONCERNING THE TENURE OF SIR WILLIAM HERBERT'S ESTATE IN MONMOUTHSHIRE.

Sir William Herbert died seized of: Three messuages in Caerlion; one capital messuage or mansion-house, St. Julian's, holden of Henry, Earl of Pembrooke, as of his manor of Caerlion in socage by fealty and the rent of 4s. 1d.; 163 Welsh acres of land within the manor of Caerlion; certain hereditaments within the manor of Llebenith, holden of Queen Elizabeth as of her Principality of Wales in socage by fealty and the rent of £3 7s. 3d.; 24 Welsh acres of land and pasture in Cawldrey, holden of the Provost and College of the Blessed Mary of Eaton as of their manor of Cawldrey in socage by fealty and the rent of 16s. 8d.; and divers messuages, etc., in Tyntarne (holden of Henry, Earl of Pembrooke, as of his manor of Tyntarne in socage by fealty and the rent of 9s. 4d.) and in Newport, Stowe, and Dyffrin (holden of [the same] as of his manors of Newport, Stowe, and Dyffrin in socage by fealty and the rent of 16s.). 479.

Llebenyth is "all that part of the Lordship of Caerleon which is in the level of Caldicot" (*Historical Traditions and Facts Relating to Newport and Caerleon*, Part III, p. 112).

[? c. 1675]

381. LIST OF POPISH PRIESTS AND JESUITS, THOSE THAT KEEP THEM, AND CHAPELS IN MONMOUTHSHIRE.

Mr. David Lewis, a Jesuit and Provincial of the Jesuits in that and adjacent counties, kept in the house Lantarnam, and protected by Sir

Ed. Morgan, bart., who is a Justice of the Peace and Deputy Lieutenant, and a popish recusant, and keeps a public chapel, and mass constantly said; and his brother, Mr. Ja. Morgan, suspected to be a Jesuit, was "bread and at" the Jesuit's college at Ghent. Capt. Syllyard, a Jesuit kept and protected by Mrs. Jones of Lunarth, widow to one Will. Jones, esq., who died a Justice of Peace and Deputy Lieutenant, and lived and died a popish recusant, and his son now bred in the College of Jesuits in France, mass constantly and publicly said by the said Syllard and others, the parish church wardens and constables papists convicted.

Hen. Milborne, esq., a Justice of Peace at this day in five counties, has ever been papist since he came into the commission (and greatest part of his family and household papists convict) in whose house one Mr. Dracot, a Jesuit, often lies, and two of his sisters, Mrs. Kath. and Mr[s]. Christ. Milborne do by reason of his power protect one Mr. Wal. Price, a popish priest, who constantly and publicly says mass for all comers at their house, who come in great abundance. A warrant has been demanded of the said Hen. Milborne to apprehend the said priest by Roger Seys, gent.; which was denied, and Seys threatened by Milborne.

Mr. G. Milborne protects one Fr. Dracott, a popish priest who constantly says mass publicly at Monmouth and Wenistone. Tho. Bodman, esq., keeps one Dr. Pugh, a popish priest who says mass publicly at his house at Black Brook. Wal. James, esq., keeps Jo. Lloyd, who says mass publicly and constantly at his house at Trevor. Col. Turbervill Morgan keeps one Thomas Lloyd as p. at his house at Lanvaire, who says mass publicly and buries, marries, and christens in the chapel. Mrs. Scudamore, widow, keeps a p. in her house at Penrose, where mass is constantly said.

Mr. Thos. Gunter keeps one Capt. Evans, a Jesuit, in his house, and has a chapel public to the street in a g[rea]t town, viz, Abergaveny, adorned with the marks of the Jesuits on the outside, mass publicly and constantly said, and hundreds of papists resort [to] it daily, and often at church time, and 100 go to mass there when not [? 40] go to church. Mr. Ricd. Crosse keeps a public chapel at Lanthonia, where one Capt. Pugh and Tho. Lloyd say mass publicly and constantly. At Lancothy [is] a house belonging to one Rowland Prichard, esq., now a Justice of the said county, though he lives at Bristowe, where mass is publicly said by one Mr. Thom. Elliot, a popish priest who was about four years since taken by Capt. Scudamore saying mass in his robes and sent to gaol and released by order of the said Justice; being informed it was a scandal to him, and dangerous to have mass said in his house, he answered he had £10 a year more for his house, which was more than the scandal could hurt him. Mr. Isaac Williams, who is Coroner . . . keeps public mass and has his children christened by a popish priest. John Jones, esq., has mass publicly said at his house at Dingston [and] Hen. Vaughan, esq., at his house at Courtfeild. Charles Progers, esq., now a Justice of Peace for the county, all his family papists convict and he vehemently suspected, mass said at his house at the Wearalthoe at the Combe, which house and £300 per annum belong to the church.

*HM*2.9/86.

This "Capt. Syllyard" is presumably a member of the Catholic family of Sulyard of Haughley, near Stowmarket, Suffolk. Walter James of Trevor may be identical with the Walter James who was steward to Lord Powis (see Nos 21-23). "The Combe" is The Cwm, in Llanrothal, on the Herefordshire side of the Monnow, four miles north of Monmouth; a House of Lords order of 1678 asserts (as this document does) that this house and £300 per annum in lands belonged to the Church of Rome (Foley, *Records of the English Province of the Society of Jesus*, Vol. 4, pp. 462 and 463).

1675

382. [LORD HERBERT] TO BROWNE. *Holograph copy or draft.*

"Cosen Browne". Is content to set to him the house, gardens, etc., which were Bastable's, the half plough-land of Keulgoram, Mc Gwire's close, the great garden which the writer had of Parson Morgans, the two plough-lands and a half of Glase ganiff, and the two plough-lands of Caharninard and Killynane, at £90 this year and £100 per annum afterwards . . . . . . (*more details*). Does not include the slang of Black Gorstyland, left out for increase of cottages and gardens (hears three are already built and more offer), nor a parcel within the ditch belonging to Corbett's holdings, nor the half plough-land of the Disert. The long slang of Black land was always before in nature of a common to the mill. Hereby orders positively that Parson Morgan be put in possession of the rest of Bastable's holdings, called Boherme laffe, at [£]27 11s.; expects he will quitclaim for the garden bought of Twisse, because the town will improve now the highway is made good to it, which will improve rents, etc.

If Browne expects Bally Mc Adam at Peirce's bargain of £45 per annum, he must repay £155 charged in his accounts for money laid out, and also defray the charges of the verdict to be had at the next assizes. Otherwise he is to make good the last lease, i.e., £66; but in favour to him he may have it at Peirce's bargain adding £15—the laying-out of the £155 deserves about £20 per annum as money goes in Irland. He is to build a sufficient house on it. Would rather be immediately reimbursed the £155 and have £45 per annum, of which the writer's sister is to have £22 during her lease.

Although he set East Meanus at £24 per annum, he would, to end all bitterness, accept £12 in fee for ever, they that were in Charles Mason's hands quitclaiming their general right in commons, etc., and to Farne Bracke and Killaly. So if he likes the seat there is [to be] paid but £4 more than the old fee-farm of £8 odd, and Farnybrac[k] may return to Deely's hand. Observes that Bateman paid, that the writer owes Capt. Hasset but £80, and that Mr. Ken[n]y paid one of the £100 bonds. Expects [to receive] these bonds cancelled, the bond for the money paid Mr. Morgan for Bastable, and the writer's note to Trant for £12 (paid).

Understands his tenants are grown very litigious and that Browne makes a profit of them as fees to the steward, although no profit comes to the writer. Prays him encourage not strife among them—enough will come to him from refractory persons—but take a care to raise the writer's dues from fines to keep men in good order and respect to the court and one another. Must have the old rental in Dillis's hand, whereto each tenant has owned his holding. Expects it by the next that comes to this country with acquittances for chief-rent. Mr. Galloway so long neglected his building that the writer took the timber as forfeits. It was half rotten and not worth a farthing. Allows him no other in their place. Prays him tell young Capt. Hasset that the writer must enter upon Killmurry in his father's time for default of building, etc. Since Browne bought not the writer's cattle before Jones returned, he has sold them to Charles Mason towards satisfying the debt. Has sent brother Harry order to receive this half-year's annuity, [£]75, from Browne.

Since he wrote about Browne's estate in Radnorshire there are such judgements, etc., against him that Cole denied to pay the £20, and says he'll give up his trust immediately. The bill is returned with a schedule of debts due to the writer, which he expects to be punctually paid; also a particular of "what I give you freely", for which he might justly expect payment. Hears much of Browne's extravagant way of life; he would do well to look into himself. Apart from what the writer gave him, Browne has got into his debt £205 10s. 5½d., without reckoning the £155 for Bally Mc Adam, or how he will compound for East Meanus; and his debts in England are considerable. Thinks Browne must lay aside thoughts of Baly Mc Adam and set it out. He should see if he can get his father-in-law to compound for East Meanus. If he sends Mr. Kenny's other bond and Hasset's bond, which with use to Michaelmas come to £192—£7 10s. 5½d. less than what he owes the writer (*sic*), he will freely acquit him. And if he can spare £100 for England he should let Cole do what he will, and Read shall endeavour to settle his concerns. They may turn over "that Rent" to the writer, which, with his salary, will render Browne's holdings in Irland almost rent-free.

Prays him have a care of the tenants lest by too much severity in gathering rent they be frightened off the writer's land. Wishes he had suffered Jones to remove more of the writer's goods hither. Better to make the best of them by sale while their cost is fresh in the accounts, with the person that bought them to testify it. Charles Mason has orders to take an exemplification of the writer's last patent, to clear Bally mc Adam at the trial, and to lie [ready for] all occasions.

14 April. 83.

The recipient is Capt. Thomas Browne, Lord Herbert's newly-appointed agent. His father-in-law was Cornet John Blennerhassett (John Blennerhassett II). "Young Capt. Hassett" is presumably Cornet Blennerhassett's son (John Blennerhassett III), who died in 1709.

1675

383. J. BLEN[N]ERHASSETT TO LORD HERBERT.

Admires [that] Mr. John Reade denies the £80 due by bond from his lordship is his; he put the money into the writer's hands to lend his lordship as the writer's own, in order to receive interest. When Capt. Browne came into Ireland last July he brought a letter from Lord Herbert signifying that Browne had undertaken payment of that debt, but he has paid [nothing]. Sent his son Robert Blenerhassett the middle of this month to demand it, and he said he will pay—with interest but from that day Robert demanded it. Desires a letter ordering Capt. Browne to pay next Easter gale at furthest. Was never so troubled about any debt.

Bally Sheedy,
28 December.

Endorsed; Capt. Hassett's letter . . . 558.

This is John Blennerhassett I, the grandfather in the three successive John Blennerhassetts who were alive at the same time.

1675/6

384. J. BLEN[N]ERHASSETT TO LORD HERBERTT. TO BE LEFT WITH MR. GRICE, HABERDASHER, OVER AGAINST ST. CLEMENCE CHURCH IN THE STRAND, LONDON.

Received his this night about eight, and, it being post night, he replies. Will "suddainly" step over to Capt. Browne and discourse Lord Herbert's resolutions to him. Will discharge Jo[h]n Deely, knowing the crime is pardonable, and exonerate his recognizances. Will not fail to remember the tribe of F.G., though Rogere Downe sold his interest in the mill of Killmurry the other day, unknown to the writer, to Tho. Fitz Gerrald the uncle; will eradicate him if Lord Herbert pleases . . . The old man is yet living and hearty. Lord Herbert commands him to be with him about Candlemas. Asks time till 1 March; before that a parliament is expected here, and the writer's father will by that time "informe us som what, and both these I would willingly see". Will attend him sooner if required. "And soe concluds yett John Oge . . . your Lordships . . . servant."

4 January. *Armorial seal* 84.

The writer is John Blennerhassett the son—Cornet Blennerhassett; he identifies himself by the description "John Oge" (i.e., the younger).

[1675/6]

385. SAM. SCUDAMORE TO CAPT. HENRY HERBERT.

Is happy with news by his father of Capt. Herbert's recovery. Wishes him every day better assurance of the safety of his leg; hopes the good woman and his patience have overcome his misfortune. It is here reported that he is parting with his company to one Mr. Goare; which he does not believe—is sure he would let him have first refusal. It is not fit to say anything of "our concerns" at this time. Had a very hard time of it. He [may] give Mr. Edgcombe a receipt for the company's money from 1 Jan. '74 to 1 Jan. '75, having cleared with the writer. Honest Brewse is the same man as ever, "improufed in liying" if possible.

Yorke,
9 February.

Has been very ill but is recovered.

Endorsed: . . . 1675/6 . . . from Lieut. Scudamore . . .

*HM*2.23/21.

1676

386. [LORD] HERBERT TO MR. FOWLES. *Draft.*

His agent Thomas Browne is "stepped aside" [through] making use of the writer's money without leave in his stewardship of his estate in Irland. Browne intends he shall be satisfied out of his estate in Wales. There is above £700 due. Has no satisfaction in prospect but out of £120 per annum, of which £60 is a widow's for life and the rest clogged with extents. Has now placed the "manage" of his Irish estate in one

Cornet John Blen[n]er Hasset, a man of £800 or £900 per annum, rich and beforehand in the world.

Mr. George Mountagu, the writer's uncle by his wife, uses him and his sister Brownelow as ill as possible . . . in the sale of Havering and Purgoe. Bringing him to reason is left to sister Brownlowe with advice of Sir Richard Mason, she to be supplied with the writer's share of the charges. [Hopes] that after these troubles he will have more considerable sums in Fowles' hand. Asks whether he has applied himself to Sir Richard Mason about the writer's title to Havering and Purgoe. If he can make a good title he can come to a conclusion with Fowles and pay off his debts.

Llyssyn,
15 April. 85.

This is Thomas Fowles, goldsmith, of London, who was now acting as Lord Herbert's banker. George Montagu of Horton, Northamptonshire, was brother to Susan Montagu, wife of George, Lord Chandos, whose daughter Elizabeth was Lord Herbert's second wife. Margaret, Lord Chandos's elder daughter, was the wife of William Brownlow of Humby, Lincolnshire, who in 1697 succeeded to the Brownlow of Humby baronetcy; Brownlow had been previously married to Dorothy, daughter and coheir of Sir Richard Mason of Sutton, Surrey.

[16]76

387. SAM. SCUDAMORE TO CAPT. HENRY HERBERT.

Is troubled that he cannot from his own hand receive some account of his health. Lately received a letter from Mr. Beavour that the Colonel has ordered him in Mr. Edgcombe's place to receive the moneys of the regiment. Desires he will order Mr. Beavour to pay and be accountable to the writer for Capt. Herbert's company's money. His last account with Mr. Edgcombe was to Jan. '75/6; was debtor to him £12 18s., which he desires he will order Mr. Beavour to pay. Capt. Herbert's old friend George Moore is dead; fears the bitch his wife, who killed him with hard duty, may trouble Capt. Herbert for money upon the old account, to prevent which the writer paid him or her more, he is sure, than ever Capt. Herbert owed; she promised she would not come near him. Brewse, Murry, and Kenedy present their duty.

Yorke,
24 April. *HM*2.23/22.

The writer was a lieutenant in Capt. Herbert's company. "Mr. Beavour" is probably the Richd. Beavoir who became adjutant to the Duke of York's regiment in March 1675/6 (Dalton, *English Army Lists*, 1661-1714, Vol. I, p. 231).

1676

388. [LORD HERBERT] TO [CORNET JOHN BLENNERHASSETT]. *Contemporary copy.*

Received his with bills of exchange for £250, which he will transmit back to London to be paid to Mr. Thomas Foules. For the future he should direct bills to be paid to Mr. Foules to the use of Edward, Lord Herbert. Did he have any abatement of £10 per cent for exchange? Reckons it wonderful hard to leave his money in the merchants' hands for two months and yet pay £10 per cent. Is told Lord Corke, by leaving his money some time in the merchants' hands, has it paid in England without allowance; prays him enquire. Asks to have the rest of May and the whole of Michaelmas rent in London a fortnight before Christmas to supply his occasions at the next sitting of Parliament, which he would not miss, it being likely to be of great consequence. Relies upon supplies from Ireland to support him there, for what he has here is employed in building. And is now in a chargeable suit for a very rich lead mine discovered upon the waste of the lordship of Cherbury; and [is at charge] putting workmen on upon another lead mine discovered in his enclosure near Montgumrey.

He may tell Mr. Thomas Browne that not clearing Bally mc Adam out of the Exchequer after he had paid so much of the writer's money (to Col. Zankey, in journeys to Dublin, and at the assizes) was a knavish neglect. Zankey is obliged to assist taking it out. Prays him tell Mr. Browne he is barbarous and must be so used, and that not a place in the King's dominions shall protect his person from the law; will post his reputation and effigies in all trafficking ports if he flies. He is to be very strict in gathering the rents of Bally Mc Adam, etc.; and the demesne, where he has no distress, he should add to Browne's accounts. And he is to certify the writer whether he has come to any agreement touching a settlement of Browne's lands on [Blennerhassett's] daughter—he should not do it without a salvo for the writer. Notices he is a little shy in answering this query. Desires to be satisfied when [Blennerhassett's] father died, what day of the month Mr. Tho. Browne made the settlements if any, and their substance. Assures him if he takes no care for the writer in it, "I shall . . . be very angry with my frend John". But he will believe his only complaints are to Tom Browne, who is the basest fellow on the face of the earth—would tell him this in the bottom of a saw-pit—notwithstanding he is such a desperate bravo.

Prays him clear Bally Mc Adam and the Meanus, and send the whole year's rent without abatement other than chief-rent and exchange . . . The house and demesnes were waste this year; hopes he, his lady, and family will live in it, else he will have reason to say Cornet Hassett can no more endure a good house than Capt. John Hassett.

Llyssyn,
25 September. 559.

[16]76/7

389. THO. FOWLE TO LORD HERBERT AT LYSSEN.

Sir Thomas Grosvenewer sealed the writings. Paid him the money; also the bond, which he was very willing to dispose of, and conveyed his interest in it before Mr. Yeat [*or* Geat] to the writer.

London,
25 January. 86.

[16]76/7

390. ARTHUR VAUGHAN TO LORD HERBERTT AT MOUNTGOUMREY.

Would have waited upon him, but has to go towards Chester, and peradventure to Ireland about his concerns there. Delivered to his man 5 bushels, i.e., 10 Winchesters or "stricks", of wheat at 5s. 7d. a bushel, and 12 at 5s. 10d., amounting to £4 17s. 11d., which he desires him to deliver to the bearer.

Tretherwen,
1 February. *Armorial seal* 87.

1676/7

391. JAMES DOWNSE, MASTER OF THE COMPANY OF DRAPERS, TO MR. WHITTINGHAM, RECORDER OF MONTGOMRY.

Here sends him by Lord Herbert his order, which his lordship approved when here: An agreement of their Company for keeping a "flanen" market at Montgomrye the second market in every month in which there is no fair there, also the four fairs in the year. All subscribed except six or seven zealous men for Poole market—though they [say] they are content and will come to Montgomry at the said days. Next month they have a fair, so the second market in April will begin their agreement. He should take his lordship's advice to give the country notice; desires him to impart this to the bailiffs of his town, that course be taken to bring in the country with their "flanens".

Salop,
14 February.

Have done their utmost for his town; heartily wish it successful.

Armorial seal *HM*2.9/52a.

A copy of the order, of the Company of Drapers of Shrewsbury, dated 31 January, accompanies the letter.

[16]76/7

392. ED. WHITTINGHAM TO LORD HERBERT AT HIS LODGING IN LONDON.

Received the enclosed Thursday last from Mr. James Downes. It is requisite to have his advice speedily, that this agreement may be read in churches, whereby the country may repair with their flannels to "our" fair and market—15 March at Mountgom[er]y. Service to his lady.

20 February.

Endorsed: Returned effectual answer. *HM*2.23/23.

[16]76/7

393. RO. JONES TO LORD HERBERT. TO BE LEFT WITH MR. THOMAS FOWLE, GOLDSMITH, AT THE BLACK LION WITHIN TEMPLE BAR.

Received his of the 11th and 14th; will send the bacon by return of the carrier. Mr. Griffiths went on Friday to Ludlow; will go for Llyssyn as soon as he returns. The carpenters hasten the staircase. The masons continue cutting the earth; a day or two will being them to the cellar. Tomorrow the stairs to the upper gallery will be all laid, then they'll fall to the arches and partitions. A door is cut into Lord Herbert's dressing-room and the other shut up. If he were here he would make his lady's dressing-room into a closet, where the bed may be continued, and make the chamber where the "fellamote" bed is her dressing-room (to which there would be a convenient closet under the stairs) and a door into it by the window; which means the hangings will fit, and the same door [will serve] to come out of the gallery into Lord Herbert's whole apartment. The "paintado" room (the back stairs being taken away) would make a convenient lodging with a closet. This will save charges several ways. This way affords his lady the same prospect.

Has this day set £22 odd of Broughton's farm; hopes tomorrow to set the rest, and keep up the rent. Cannot persuade Jo. Bushop to continue the mountains; will hardly get a tenant for it. Has raised the rent of Great Pen Spitchell 20s., the greatest that ever will be had for it.

Has continued the collier to make a full trial, and he has taken two miners and a lusty workman to be his partners; now the work goes on furiously, his partners to have a share of the £20. They are all in great hopes, and the town of Mountgom[er]y for their better encouragement (if they find coal) will add £5 to the £20. As soon as Mr. Read comes from Monmouthshire notice shall be given him to send the account.

Lymore Lodge,
18 February.

Is informed Mr. Nichols purposes to make "it" a mine royal and lease it from the company that farms the mines royal.

Due to the fishmonger is about £4, £10 to Wm. Lloyd the grocer. Told the fishmonger to wait upon him.

Endorsed: £10 to be paid Mrs. Mary Lloyd.

Further endorsement: Mr. Walker at his chamber in Clifford's Inn or at the Exchequer Office in the Temple. *HM*2.9/53.

The mine that Nichols proposed to make a mine royal might be the coal mine, but the reference may be to some other mine, perhaps a lead mine, which could more properly be claimed as a mine royal. This "Mr. Nichols" is no doubt the Nicholls who seems to have been lord of one of the manors or petty manors within the hundred of Chirbury (see No. 401). The building works that were going on are almost certainly at Lymore House, which (to judge by this and subsequent letters) was undergoing a substantial reconstruction.

[16]76/7

394. RO. JONES TO LORD HERBERT. TO BE LEFT AT MR. THOMAS FOWLES . . . AT THE BLACK LION WITHIN TEMPLE BAR.

Encloses accounts from Mr. Read for the £470 10s. Sent two flitches of bacon to Sallop to be sent, but the Mountgomery carrier, who delivered it to Rees Pugh, forgot to bring the carrier's name and lodging in London, so cannot [yet] tell him where it may be found. Received his letter to engage the Mountgomery burgesses for Sir Richd. Corbett. There were but three in the town, and those engaged for Kinaston three months ago; could not persuade them to stay at home—all he could do was to engage three others in the neighbourhood to give their votes for him. There was the greatest labouring for voices that ever he heard of. The report is that £5 was given for a single vote on Kinaston's account. If so he'll be sure of the rabble party that wants money, and will probably prevail unless Sir Richd., who has the mayor and officers on his side, can outwit the drinking party and prevail with the mayor to make a return. At Llyssyn Mr. Bond said the enclosed account was due over and above his wages, which are £22, being two years and three quarters. No deer taken at Llyssyn since Lord Herbert left; but brought five from the Frith Hickman to Lymore.

Lymore Lodge,
25 February. 88.

Sir Richard Corbett was contesting (and won) one of the Shrewsbury seats against Edward Kynaston of Hordley.

[16]76/7

395. Ro. Jones to Lord Herbert. Leave with Mr. Fowle . . . at the Black Lion within Temple Bar.

Received the garden seeds. Sent his letter to Mr. Read; presumes he is at Dolgiog or [near] about Mr. Herbert's concerns. The bacon was left at Sallop—whether by the carrier's or Mr. Rice Pugh's neglect he cannot learn. The carrier is Tho. Forrester, and lodges at the Cross Keys in White Cross Street.

The masons are cutting the passage under the great staircase to the inner cellar. The tilers are at work. Jo. George and the carpenters are making the stairs to the upper rooms over the great hall, and then they'll finish the great staircase. A fortnight hence the house where Powell lived shall be removed to Lymore and carpenters erect it to Lord Herbert's order.

Sent Mr. Bond's account; he stays at Llyssyn till Lord Herbert's pleasure is received, and then will be gone. Great frost and snow the first four days of this month, and since great rain; fears it will much prejudice the deer and lambs, yet they stand pretty well. There's great striving for the election at Sallop; they have been seven days already. Received a letter last night that Sir Richd. Corbet will certainly be returned burgess.

Lymore Lodge,
9 March. *HM*2.9/54.

[16]77

396. Ro. Jones to Lord Herbert. Leave with Mr. Thomas Fowle . . . at the Black Lion within Temple Bar.

This day being at the coal-pit the colliers say they cannot continue unless Lord Herbert allows them £3 a yard for sinking, the rock being so hard that the last fifteen days they sunk but two feet three inches. Some ironstone they found, but no quantity. Offered 20s. a yard till they get five yards deeper—level with the "smutt" found on the riverside, and they refuse. Has for this week put them on day-wages, that he might receive his order whether to continue them. They have sunk in this pit but fifteen yard two and a half feet. The inhabitants of Mountgom[er]y desire he will speak to Sir Job Charlton ere he comes his circuit that the second assizes may be there.

What tile they had are laid, and more preparing at the quarry. The masons have finished the passage between the two cellars, and Jo. George is finishing the stairs over it; then the plasterers will fall to work—they have already lathed it. John George asks whether he will have "banisters" both sides the door in the partition [a]cross the gallery to give light in the passage. Lord Powis's agent demands £4 odd, a year's rent for the lands about Llyssyn; told him it should be paid.

2 April.

Endorsed: From Jones at Lymore Lodge. *HM*2.9/55.

"Smutt" is a black earth taken as an indication of the presence of coal.

1677

397. W. MORGAN TO LORD HERBERT AT HIS LODGINGS NEXT TO THE BULL HEAD TAVERN IN SOUTHAMPTON STREET, BLOOMESBURY.

In relation to his affair in this county with Capt. Browne, Col. Freeman and the trustee for the children are content Lord Herbert should have it continued in his hands upon payment of the use and securing the arrear, about £40, until the children are of age to be placed abroad. This performed, there will be no encumbrance upon the estate save Mr. Mathewes's judgement, which he will assign to Lord Herbert upon payment of debt and interest, about £76. Arrears of rent before his judgement in August last Lord Herbert cannot meddle with—only Michaelmas, this Ladyday, and Christmas rent he has a right to, about £58. One David Jones, that pays £10 15s., is become insolvent and goes off leaving only two ricks of hay (eight wain-loads or eighty drag-loads), and the building quite ruined; has set it for £8, but if he does not approve, upon payment for ploughing it will be surrendered. Had to rebate 40s. in Maud Prees's tenement, otherwise she had left; likewise to set Coome Meirick to its value in the inquisition (the building being quite fallen down); also Croes Gynan at £20, Morris ap Evan at the old rent of 40s., and Coome Batha at the old rent of £5—£53 in all. The increase would not quit the cost of repairing the houses, there being neither wood, building stone, nor thatch within miles. Being obliged to pay £9 per annum for use, his lordship's receipt will not be near the interest of his money, but there are hopes of th'other in reversion.

His commission against Niccolls is to be executed in Mountgom[er]y in Easter week, where the writer may understand his resolution. The land lies not much further from Mr. Read than from the writer; will give him meeting if he appoints Read to view it.

Boultibrooke,
7 April. *Armorial seal*

Endorsed: From Wm. Morgan touching Tom Browne's estate in Radnorshire. 560.

There is more about the commission against Nicholls in Nos. 400 and 401.

1677

398. SAMUEL THOMAS TO LORD HERBERT AT THE TWO PINE APPLES IN HOLDERN ROW, LINCKOLSINFEILDS.

Received his letter that he would, if moneys came in, [pay] what he could conveniently. £100 here or in London would be a great kindness, being the time of his greatest want. Proposes to be in London the beginning of May, and will wait upon him. In the interim two lines of comfort will oblige.

Salop,
11 April.

Since writing he has had notice of Lord Herbert's loss by a servant. Will do his utmost, for this town and what other places he comes in, that if such a person be seen there may be a discovery.

Endorsed: Mr. Samuell Thomas touching his shop debt. Answered.
*HM*2.23/24.

1677

399. WILL. GOMELDON TO LORD HARBERT AT HIS HOUSE IN LONDON.

His father has given account of their proceedings [thus far]. The first night he arrived here he sent his lordship's man to Deale with a good friend to search both houses and ships. Meantime he got Lord Herbert's paper translated into French, which is now printed at Callis and sent to all the seaport towns from Bullen to Newporte. Caused the pacquet-boat to be searched so that neither trunk, valise, nor person escaped before it went off. Likewise sent an attorney to the mayors of Folkston, Heath, and Rumney with description of the man and goods, with order to let no boat go to sea [unsearched], and to stop any boat hired for Fraunce till they have order from the writer's brother Gomeldon, a justice of peace living "in the Midd Way", there being more felons pass by those by-ways, where they go undiscovered, than by any of the great ports. Gives this account that he may see he was not negligent—hears from his father that Lord Herbert has taken his man and goods.

Dovor,
13 April.

Sends him the account enclosed. 411.

I am greatly indebted to Dr. Felix Hull, County Archivist of Kent, for help in dealing with this letter. He tells me that there was no Gomeldon in the county commission at this time. It seems probable, therefore, that Justice Gomeldon was a Baron of the Cinque Ports—this would account for the wide jurisdiction attributed to him here. Dr. Hull suggests that "the Midd Way" may be a road or street in Dover.

[16]77

400. RO. JONES TO LORD HERBERT. TO BE LEFT WITH MR. THOMAS FOWLE . . . AT THE BLACK LION . . . LONDON.

Received his of the 17th. Had discharged Mr. Bond by paying him £22 wages and telling him Lord Herbert's pleasure as to his other demands —done in the presence of Mrs. Judyth six weeks ago. Went to Llyssyn yesterday. In his return to Mountgom[er]y he met Bond going thither; told him he must take his things and be gone. Discoursed Nicholas and Humberston about the deer at Llyssyn; fifty died—four prickets, one sorrel, one buck, four old does, and forty fauns. At Lymore and Frith died about forty; cannot give [exact] account—the keeper was hunting in an outlier.

His commission about Ritton ended Thursday; in the judgement of his commissioners all appears very fair by proof of Mr. Niccolls' witnesses as well as his own. Mrs. Judith will have "suddenly" ready sixty yards of blanket two yards broad, forty yards more a yard and a half broad, 140 yards of web, cloth for furniture of one bed, and sixty yards of hempen cloth. The web she designed to sell to pay weavers and walkers; forbad it till she heard from him, for it gives little in the market, and it were better to have it coloured and hang two rooms. If he [keeps] the web Mrs. Judyth desires £4 to pay the weaver and walker, who are very poor.

At Llyssyn are twenty calves "for reare" and two for slaughter; already at Lymore three and one killed and one cow that has not calved. Purposes next week to send up all the young cattle, and turn out the store and feeding cattle. Must keep the great ox and working oxen in a fortnight yet. Will send the sheep to Fryth Park, but must keep the horses here. There is no grass at Llyssyn hardly to preserve sheep alive. He wrote him to take up the young mares bought of Mr. Herbert, but two are in foal. None of the horses are in order for sale till grass has fattened them—those that have been out this winter. Shall Nicholas turn out those at Llyssyn?

The carpenters have taken down Powell's house and "fallen" other timber for the stable. Four men are at work besides sawyers and squarers. The plasterers begin the great staircase today, glass being ready for it this fortnight. John George is making the dormant in the upper chamber over the great hall, having done the great staircase from the cellar up (which is sunk throughout to the depth ordered).

Is glad to hear he has retrieved the jewels and taken "my fellow Gamester (as your Lo'p is pleased to call him)"; he needs not fear the writer will betake himself to those courses . . .

23 April.

Endorsed: Delivered 28 April. *HM*2.23/25.

The nature of the dispute with Nicholls appears from the next letter. The dormant is the great central beam supporting the joists.

[16]77

401. W. Morgan to Lord Herbert at his lodgings next to the Bull Head tavern, Southampton Street, Bloomesbury.

Mr. Niccolls' endeavour at the first commission was to make distinction between the manor and the hundred of Chirbury by limiting the manor to the parish; and that Lord Herbert had no right to the soil of the waste, [it being] in the lords of the petty manors. But Lord Herbert's proofs having cleared these points, at this last commission he bent his evidence towards making out that the place has been time out of mind his freehold, and produced an aged witness who was so far from proving it that he remembered the place to be common for eighty years. The rest of his witnesses endeavoured to make Ritton in the lordship of Kinnerton—which the defendant admits to be in the hundred of Chirbury. On Lord Herbert's part were thirteen witnesses who prove the place to be always common before the enclosing, that the inhabitants did suit and service at his court, and (by processes issued thence) debts levied in the place by taking of cattle; also that the inhabitants of Mucklewick and adjacent townships always had common of pasture there. When the depositions are published Lord Herbert may proceed as counsel advise.

As for the concern with Capt. Browne, he will confer with Mr. Read speedily; meantime will file the inquisition at "our" sessions, which begin next Monday.

Boultibrooke,
24 April. *HM*2.23/26.

1677

402. KATHERIN ANWILL TO LORD HERBERT.

Has long waited his pleasure touching the debt due upon his father's bond to Mr. Anwill, her late husband, being unwilling to be over-troublesome by frequent messages. Did not doubt he would remember his promise that the debt should be one of the first. Now understanding that some of his father's debts have been paid, she desires to know by cousin Evan Vaughan [the bearer] when she may expect "them". The original debt was £300 and the forbearance long, and but £150 received. For what remains due, what he thinks reasonable will satisfy her.

Llwyn,
5 May. *Armorial seal* *HM*2.23/28.

The husband is probably Evan Anwyl, third son of William Anwyl of Park, near Penrhyndeudraeth, High Sheriff of Merioneth in 1611 and in 1624; Evan's wife was Catherine, daughter of Morus Williams of Hafodgaregog.

[16]77

403. RO. JONES TO LORD HERBERT. LEAVE WITH MR. THOMAS FOWLE . . . AT THE BLACK LION . . . LONDON.

Received his by Mr. Fowlks. Finds he would have some of the young horses taken up and "Man'd", which shall be done. The rent in Nicholas's collection about Llyssyn amounts to but £78 4s. 8d. in the whole year, besides what's allowed to Wm. Evans the tailor and where the rye is, so there remains £57 unpaid of the £135 13s. 4d. Thomas Oliver the husbandman is discharged. At Llyssyn the young horse is now at grass in the Calaes pasture below the stable.

Lymore,
5 May.

Mr. Rice Pugh's bill is £27 odd, Mr. Baker's £32 odd. 145.

1677

404. [LORD] HERBERT TO MR. THOMAS FOWLES . . . *Holograph copy.*

Has he sent to Mr. Daniel Arthur to know whether Mr. Ignatius Gould has received the contents of the £300 bill, that the writer may account with him? Prays him send by the bearer, Tho. Castle, £30 . . .

9 May. *HM*2.23/29.

[16]77

405. RO. JONES TO LORD HERBERT. LEAVE WITH MR. THOMAS FOWLE . . . AT THE BLACK LION WITHIN TEMPLE BAR.

Was at Llyssyn last week; the workmen's bills amount to a considerable sum. Has taken the accounts of several that Lord Herbert owes money to in Sallop, etc., but Charles Jones of Poole and Rice Pugh of Sallop were not at home. Presumes the [only] way of satisfying them is by taking up money at London, for it's not to be had in this country upon any condition, those that are to tender Lord Powis his dues from Mr. Howard having not left any that could be procured at double use—they would not let this opportunity pass lest Lord Powis become possessor of the lordship and use such tyranny among the inhabitants as he does in Mountgom[er]y shire. The coach mare, etc., are come safe to Lymore by Thomas Lloyd. The cloth which Mrs. Judith provides for a bed shall be coloured green as directed. The tradesmen will be continually dunning for their money; [wishes] Lord Herbert could be furnished with a sum rather than daily to vex at the importunity of such men. Mr. Page and partner were with him today and say they cannot forbear longer. When Lord Herbert comes to the country course may be taken to lessen his family at Llyssyn and elsewhere. If a bargainer cannot be had for Llyssyn dairy it were better to set out part of the land than continue several houses and families upon his hands.

Ludlowe,
12 May.

This day the under dairy maid at Oakley Park was buried; she died of the smallpox. This frightened Mrs. Herbert and the children out of the house. They have been at Ludford a fortnight, and will not return for a fortnight yet. 90.

At the time of writing this note the Powis Collection in the Shropshire Record Office has not been catalogued, but I am greatly indebted to Miss M. T. Hill, Assistant Archivist, for a good deal of information from the collection which makes it seem probable, at least, that the lordship referred to here is the lordship of Clun, and that the "Mr. Howard" is the Honourable Robert Howard of Hoar Cross, co. Stafford; the relation between him and Lord Powis with regard to this lordship does not appear, however.

1677

406. JO. READ TO LORD HERBERT AT HIS LODGINGS NEXT TO THE BULL TAVERN IN SOUTHAMPTON STREET, IN THE FIELDS, LONDON.

Mr. Jones showed him his letter dated the 9th, and they have [considered] what was most fit as to raising money in these parts. The usurers have made so many purchases of late that they have taken up money themselves, and pay double use for it, and without land security will not part with a farthing. To speak truth, in two or three places he used all the interest he could, but they answered plainly, if they had money to lay out they would not deal with a person of quality. So conceive he must be supplied in London or nowhere. The former judgements and daily encumbrances that fall upon Mr. Brown's estate will frighten a third person to lay out money. Will try what can be done.

Is glad the city agrees with him. Prays God it be not destructive to his purse. If he affects a city life, this summer he should convert most of his demesnes to rents. He wants the Statute at Large to this day; if he will send it to the Lodge they will carefully keep it.

Llyssyn.
21 May. *HM*2.23/30.

[16]77

407. THOMAS STRADLING TO LORD HERBERT.

If his occasions will not at present suit, prays him send a bill on Mr. Fowles payable in a month or two or three. Is sure nothing can be more reasonable.

2 June.

Endorsed: From Capt. Stradling . . . Sent him a bill for his whole, forty guineas, payable September. 89.

1677

408. CHAR. HESLERTON TO LORD HERBERT.

Has sent the goods. They were all of Lady Brownlowe's and Miss Bunty's choosing, but if he or his lady dislikes any they shall be changed. Lady Brownelowe has put [in] a pattern of scarlet velvet, which will be 30s. per yard. Likewise she has put some patterns within the coloured silk; the petticoat may be changed for any of them. The alderman requests he will be mindful of the bond of £133 which Lord Herbert gave at his departure hence, and that he make some return before Christmas, when they will have extraordinary occasion for money.

London,
27 September.

Endorsed: Mr. Hasleton's . . . *HM*2.23/31.

[? 1676-8]

409. DOWNE FALVEY'S PETITION TO LORD HERBERT, ONE OF HIS MAJESTY'S PRIVY COUNCIL FOR IRELAND, AT LLYSSIN. LEAVE AT MR. THOMAS FOWLES . . . AT THE BLACK LION . . . LONDON.

Farmed from him, when he was at Castle Island, the grist mill of Drom Iltanebeg and another which the petitioner made since at Ballinarde in Killmorry, at a great rent, to his loss by reason of that new mill. Of late there has been a way found to impose so many fines upon him for taking the usual toll which is the custom over all the county, that is, the sixteenth part; in lieu of which fines his goods to the value of £3 are upon the recorder's hands. Being not able to pay the rent if course be not taken for stopping those fines, he [begs] order to Robert Blener Hassett, esq., to deliver his goods until his lordship's coming; and then when he hears the custom in Lord Kerrye's, Sir Vallentine Browne's, and Esquire Dennye's estates, he may order as he thinks fit. 619.

1677

410. [R.] BLEN[N]ERHASSETT TO LORD HERBERT AT LLUSSIN. TO BE LEFT AT MR. THOMAS FOULDS, GOLDSMITH . . . LONDON.

His brother Jo[h]n Hassett has employed him to receive his lordship's rents and duties due Michaelmas and All Saints', which he is daily collecting and distraining for. Former letters gave account of his brother's disbursements for the three gales to May last. His brother is very ill and keeps his bed.

Killorglin,
4 December. *Armorial seal* 561.

1677

411. SAMUELL WILSON TO [LORD HERBERT].

Cornet Hassett died on Tuesday the 4th. In obedience to his lordship's commands he has called in great part of [Lord Herbert's] goods. Madam Hassett delivered up all she had, mostly pewter. The three dozen old plates are much worsted, which she promises to satisfy him for or, upon [Lord Herbert's] arrival, to change in Corke. But Mr. Rob. Hassett produced a letter as from his lordship—did not have the perusal of it—that the collection of 'em was to be his, they to be delivered to the writer. If he is remiss in a true or speedy collection, the writer will resume the power, otherwise the possessors of 'em will think "we" do but trifle—perceives by their denials some damage will be had.

Caused the windows to be mended; but before he could make fires he was forced to get a mason to raise the hearths, which were sunk from the boards. Concerning joining the writer in commission with the next agent, he begs it may be in full and equal commission, that nothing be done without his consent. Expects not the least gratification, holding himself sufficiently already rewarded. If he thinks fit to commissionate Mr. Mason with the writer, he dares promise better service than any before have done. "In the houre I am not . . . true . . . let me be noe more . . ."

Noghovall, "Your . . . Chaplain".
5 December. 562.

Wilson was rector of the Castle Island parishes. He had been ordained only this year. He became Chancellor of Ardfert in 1684.

1677

412. GEORGE CROFTS TO LORD HERBERTT AT LYSSYN. TO BE LEFT WITH MR. THOMAS FOULDS, GOLDSMITH . . . LONDON. *Franked*: JA. H.

Advised him 3 March last that Mr. John Hassett would order into his hands £200. Mr. Hassett sent it and within three days advised him that his lordship had drawn on him for £300, [so withdrew] it. Received 11 April Lord Herbert's bill of £200 payable to Mr. Daniel Arthur's order. Mr. Hassett [said] he had not a penny to answer it and begged the writer to stop it, so he desired Mr. Gould, Mr. Arthur's friend, who had the bill, not to return it. Did not receive a penny till the Island fair, and a good part not till a month after. Was forced to give Mr. Arthure a bill for £200 without exchange. Mr. Hassett promised many times he should have the exchange, £10, or at least the interest for four months. Begs to be allowed [something] out of the rent of Clasganneff.

There is no hope of Mr. John Hassett's recovery. Is willing to undertake all Lord Herbert's affairs in Irland. Will be just between him and his tenants, and will pay the rents [through] Mr. Daniel Arthur at the lowest exchange that goes. Will not give longer to the tenants than he orders—knows forbearance to some does good, to others harm. Every tenant, if he leaves his farm, shall be bound to get one that will give as much. Has great concerns in Kerry, and can take Castle Island in his way. Is sure that by his dealings with Lord Herbert's tenants he pays two parts of their rents, so the receipts will be easier to discount. Will leave it to him for one year to allow him what he pleases. Is "in the peace" in co. Corke and can be in co. Kerry on the least application to his friend and landlord the Lord Chancellor, so that none shall wrong his lordship's concerns there. Castle Islands house wants repair.

Corke,
7 December.

Mr. Hassett is dead. *Armorial seal* 565.

The frank is that of James Hickes of the Letter Office. The Lord Chancellor at this time was Archbishop Michael Boyle.

1677

413. [R.] BLEN[N]ERHASSETT TO LORD HERBERT AT LLUSSIN. TO BE LEFT AT MR. THOMAS FOULDS, GOLDSMITH ... LONDON. *Franked*: JA. H.

On Tuesday night it pleased God to take his brother John Blen[n]erhassett. As intimated heretofore, his brother ordered him to collect Lord Herbert's rents, which he did till his death, and will, if he thinks fit, collect the remainder and have them in readiness whenever he is pleased to charge him with a bill of exchange . . . Will go on collecting provided the tenants will pay.

Killorglin,
10 December. 563.

[16]77

414. FR. FITZHERBERT TO LORD HERBERT AT LLYSSYN.

[Heard] from Mr. Roger Jones that his lordship was informed by Charles Mason that the writer [spent] £100 when in Engelande for Lord Herbert's letter for payment of his money. Notwithstanding his several orders, he has not yet received one groat. In his three journeys for Engelande he spent £100 besides £20, a whole year's rent—had no other motive to go for Englande. Is indebted for it to this day. But will change the scorn of this ungrateful story into a humble petition. Mr. John Blenner Hassett is dead, or will be before this [arrives]. Mr. Reade said his lordship had thoughts of employing the writer when Mr. Browne left. His brother will give £2,000 bond that he will clear with him once a year. If he disposes that otherwise, he begs to be admitted seneschal, solicitor, and assistant to his agent; or that he be allowed any small salary, as a servant, that he may have a colour to retire into that country, where all his pittance is. Appeals only to the chancery of his lordship's own breast. Service to his lady, sisters, and Mrs. Littleton.

Dublyn,
10 December. 564.

1677

415. CHARLES MASON TO [LORD HERBERT].

Promises to give security to pay in London, free from exchange, the year's rent at two gales, May rent at All Saints' and All Saints' at Candlemas. Intends to transport before August yearly goods amounting to the year's rent and order payment as soon as they are sold. Capt. Bro[wne delivered *torn*] to Mr. Willson the writings he had in the great house, and will deliver the deeds concerning Meanus which Mr. Jones will carry to Wales (whereby Mr. Robert Browne may never see them but by his honour's consent—he intends to serve Capt. Browne and the writer to Chancery to discover them, and affirms he was not bound to relinquish his interest in Comin or West Meanus woods, but did deliver a general release of the profits under the hands and seals of Mr. Gorsteloe, Mr. Drew, and himself). He says Mr. Hassett promised him some mountain farm equivalent, and he intends [to wait] upon [Lord Herbert] in Wales next May if he does not arrive sooner. Mr. Fittz Herbert is content now to accept £40 due to him for two years past, and denies receiving any tonnage money but the £8 10s. he accounted for in England. Expects answer from Mr. Whittfeild about Bally mc Adam and the tonnage. Mr. Robert Hassett is very earnest with the tenants to pay their rents to him—he thinks he will be allowed the £20 for gathering it, which, if his lordship please to stop it, will defray Mr. Jones's expenses in the journey and part of the exchange. Admires at Hassett's confidence, for his power from his brother is extinct with his decease. Mr. Willson cannot return the money till mid-summer, for with discharging fees, buying horses, etc., he has not £5 spare; he owes no man anything here. Mrs. Herbert is at her father's, and will send £20 for her son with the rent. Is this week for Corke; will enquire for good bills and the cheapest exchange. Will acquaint Mr. Kenny what his lordship wrote concerning the former's grandchild.

Noghovalls,
25 December. 16.

Mrs. Mary Herbert was the widow of Thomas Herbert, the former agent to Lord Herbert at Castle Island, and was the daughter of Edward Kenney of Cullen, co. Cork—grandfather to her son, Edward Herbert.

1677

416. DANIELL ARTHUR TO LORD HERBERTT AT LYMORE LODGE.

Being informed out of Ireland that Mr. Hassett, who managed his lordship's concerns there, is lately dead, one of the writer's acquaintance in Corck, by name Richard Trant, tenders his service and a relation in this town (an honest, able man) security for his fidelity. Believes it is a good occasion for his lordship to lay hold on. Cannot say that Mr.

Hassett has paid the contents of Lord Herbert's bill as yet, but believes there is no great matter behind. Mr. Loftus—presumes he heard he was wounded—is out of danger.

London,
27 December. 412.

1677/8

417. Tho. Fz. Gerrald to Edward Herbertt, Baron of Chirbry and Castle Island, at Clussyn.

Being hitherto discountenanced by him, through the means of persons contriving for themselves lest "any of us" (who were his ancestors' servants since their first concernment in this kingdom) should be a hindrance to their great profits and further claims—which far exceeded what "wee" ever expected—he dares presume only that his honour will seriously consider all this. Lets him know further that "your owne servant", the writer's nephew, Thomas fitz Gerrald, still awaits his favours.

Cordell,
22 January.

Sealed with a West Frisian doit 24.

1677/8

418. Charles Mason to Lord Herbert at Llysin. At the Post Office in London to be sent. *Franked*: Ja. Hickes.

Mr. Kenny and Mrs. Herbert intend to send for their son over this spring and keep him at Killkenny School till fit for Dublin College, and dispose of him after to what they find him capable of. They design well for him. Hears she has refused several matches merely of maternal love to her children. She will pay £20 to Mr. Jones or return it with the rents. Mr. Kenny and the whole family express great honour for his lordship. Mr. Robert Hassett would willingly gather the rent, but not all think the money secure with him. The £20 is better spared for Mr. Jones's expenses or exchange. Mr. Browne delivered what writings he had in his lordship's house in the Island, and promises to deliver those he has at Bantree; he is much nettled by Capt. Herbert's letter accusing him of betraying his lordship in the suit over Bally mc Adam—he and the attorney accuse one another. Is expecting answer from Mr. Whittfield. Neither he nor Mr. Willson has received anything from his lordship since his of 29 November. Several English packets have come since Mr. Jones should have been here. Cannot find any willing to build at the Black water, and it will be difficult to find any to inhabit there before his lordship settles in the Island (if he intends it) next summer. Provision should be made for gardening, beer, hay, and turf, and notice given to the tenants of the demesnes, that they may provide for themselves if they consent to remove, as is necessary—else where can he feed his beef and mutton, graze his horses, etc? It will be chargeable to "buy all things with the penny". Hopes Mr. Hassett took care in setting the demesne to have it surrendered when his lordship needs it. Was desired by Mr. Thomas Fittz Garold the elder to convey the enclosed; he can create trouble by promoting the interest of the Duke of Ormond or their's that have a gift from His Majesty of all the concealed lands in Munster. His lordship is sufficiently armed by the decree of the Court of Claims and the new patents, but there may be great charge in the defence—which he may prevent by a favourable countenance and reasonable bargain of a farm to Mr. Thomas Fittz Garold the younger, his lordship's late servant, for years or lives. If bestowing a small annuity upon Mr. Garold could prevent further trouble it were a purchase well made. He and Mr. Willson will keep all quiet till he arrives.

Noghovall,
22 January.

Sealed with the same coin as the preceding

Endorsed (*as one of a bundle*): Irish letters from Mr. Willson, Charles Mason, Roger Jones, Mr. Saunders, etc. 41.

1677/8

419. RO. JONES TO LORD HERBERT AT LLYSSYN. *Franked*: JA. H.

Found Mrs. Hassett removed to Corke, having sold all her goods, and Mr. Robert Hassett at Sir Boyle Maynard's, near Waterford, at the wedding of his nephew, Arthur Hassett, to one of Maynard's daughters. Does not find that Hassett has received any moneys since his brother's death. Daily distrains, but has not yet got above £5, and knows not what to do with the distresses he has, the cattle being so poor. Understands Mr. Robt. Hassett in his brother's lifetime received about £200. Sent to Cork to enquire for the clerk of the *nisi prius* at the time of the trial about Bally mc Adam, who has the books of several assizes; is informed he lives about Lymericke. Mr. Mason proposes for security Mr. Wilson and another parson of Glanerogh, named Palmer, who married a daughter of Mr. Morgan's—Mr. Mason says his benefice is above £100 per annum. Urged him to give other security, alleging the uncertainty of parsons' lives—generally they leave a number of children rather than an estate. Showed Mr. Mason Lord Herbert's instructions about having moneys in London to carry on the trials but he said he cannot answer his expectations. Shall he accept the security proposed?

Castle Islands,
26 February. 9.

1677/8

420. RO. JONES TO LORD HERBERT AT LLYSSYN. *Franked*: JA. H.

Met with Mr. Robert Hassett and got the paper concerning Capt. Browne's accounts, and the releases from Barry Drewe, etc., relating to Eastmeanus. Waited on him at Traley and elsewhere but cannot get the moneys. Has sent to Dublin for writs against him in the tenants' names from whom he received moneys. This will hasten payment, "or else Ile have his body for itt". Got instruction from the clerk of the *nisi prius* where to find the record of Bally ma Adam; sent to Dublin to have the *postea* drawn up and signed by the judge. Mr. Robert Hassett says his brother left the lease of Killmurrey to his youngest son, and that a friend shall wait on his lordship in Engld. to renew it and pay the fine. Old Hasset settled the lease of Tullileague upon Thomas Hasset, so that at the death of Mr. John Blener Hassett there were but two heriots due, one for Killmurrey and one for Mulluch M[ar]ky and Curraneduffe. Sent the serjeant and one assistant to distrain upon Eastmeanus for the rent due from Robert Browne and he made a rescue, for which the writer will have him indicted. He pretends there is but 3s. 4d. due . . . He says he will turn cattle upon any common in the seigniory; told him that will cost him more than the rent of Meanus.

Lymericke,
15 March. 10.

[16]78

421. Ro. Jones to Lord Herbert at Llyssyn.

Met Mr. Robert Hassett at Traley Castle to receive the moneys he received from the tenants, but he would not pay a penny unless allowed £20 salary for the half year ending Michaelmas last and given such a discharge as he produced ready drawn, which the writer refused. Finds in his brother's account £60 salary for three gales, it being but one year and a half and six weeks from the letter of attorney to his death. Told him he had no commission to allow £20 for six weeks' work, and that his lordship had not desired him to meddle with it. His brother charges himself with only £16 odd for grazing of Classganiffe and Cahirnard, and returns Killgoram as waste . . . £38 is due for grazing, of which Jo. Ma'David affirms £22 was paid to Mr. Hasset, besides two hogsheads of cider (for which £6 was offered by Mr. Hasset's servant that now lives in Bastable's house). Has sent to Dublin for a subpoena against Robt. Hasset, Tho. Hasset, and Mrs. Hasset, executors of Jo. Blener Hasset. Mr. Robt. Hasset owns he received £199 8s. 7d., out of which he paid Mr. Fitz Herbert £40 and the crown rent due Michaelmas. Distrains upon Killmurrey for the rent and heriots; the distresses shall be sold as soon as he can get a chapman. Acquainted Mrs. Hassett that if she does not give satisfaction of what's due from her husband and brother the rigour of the law will be [applied]. Took distress from Menus; Mr. Robert Browne says he will replevy and go to trial, alleging but 3s. 4d. or 1s. 8d. to be due thinking to force his lordship to show the deed. Is informed by counsel that to prove payment of the rent is sufficient evidence against him. Takes many distresses but has not received in money £100, nor can he get a chapman to buy one beast, for there's hardly grass to preserve cattle alive. As soon as he can make up £150 he will return it. John Hasset let the demesne, so Charles Mason cannot have any till Ladyday next.

Castle Islands,
27 March. 11.

1678

422. Charles Mason to Lord Herbert at Llysin. At the Post Office in London to be sent. *Franked*: Ja. H.

Went with Mr. Jones to Limbrike assizes to confer with Mr. Harris, Lord Herbert's attorney, [but missed him]. However, met with one

Mr. Jerves, who had his lordship's verdict for Bally mc Adam; procured his letter to one in Dublin to procure the Chief Justice's hand to it. Mr. Robert Browne says publicly that the writer is his greatest enemy. Mr. Ro. Hassett refuses the money he received except he has £20 for gathering it—which had been avoided had Lord Herbert accepted the writer's opinion, to send [someone] a commission for gathering the rent with command to conceal it till Mr. Hassett were past recovery. Finds Mr. Jones is to receive his and his securities' bond. His security is Parson Pallmer and Parson Willson, who have at least £300 a year, besides what he has. Believes Mr. Jones designs to prefer himself. If Jones or any other will undertake it upon the same conditions, he will think himself recompensed in being an instrument of saving Lord Herbert so much. Otherwise will serve him faithfully. One part of the instructions—that he would allow £3 per cent to have the May rent in London [by] Trinity term—he cannot answer for this year.

Noghovalls,
2 April. 15.

1678

423. FR. FITZHERBERT TO LORD HERBERT AT MR. THOMAS FOWLES . . . AT THE BLACK LION . . . LONDON.

Is just arrived out of the north-east circuit, where he had to settle his affairs, that he might attend his lordship's affairs in Kerry. Intends on Friday to begin his journey to keep the court leet. Received a letter from Mr. Jones that Mr. Robert Blenner Hassett detains the rents and denies payment unless allowed half a year's salary more than is due, so that he is forced to sue the executors. This stop, and the distresses not being fit for sale, obstructs Jones's return, which he fears will incur displeasure; Jones will go as soon as the writer arrives. Hopes to retrieve the record and get judgement on the verdict against Sanckey before going down. Jones informs him that Mr. Mason undertakes the agency. Asks him to "doe mee right" to his lady and sisters.

Dublyn,
16 April. 19.

1678

424. RO. JONES TO LORD HERBERT AT LLYSSYN.

Got the moneys from Mr. Robt. Hassett save £20; told him his lordship would not allow it and that next week he should be served with a writ. Took £250 to Corke to get exchange but only three men in the town had effects in London, and they would not draw under £11 per cent and twenty days' sight. Could not get any at Youghall under the same rate, but got a bill at Kinsale for £200 at £9 per cent. The merchants have drawn all their moneys from London at any rate for fear of war. Above £20,000 came over in guineas between Allhollandtide and Christmas, and now trade lies dead. Has 87 cattle distrained for Bally ma Adam and above 40 from other tenants, also sheep, horses, and corn. Disposes of the distresses as fast as he can that he may get hence. Mr. James Conor will not pay. Distrained upon East Meanus; Robert Browne replevied and put in a declaration that he is possessed of a freehold—will demur. He gives out that he will have a great part of Killgoram as parcel of Farnibracke. Outed the tenant of Killgoram and set the distressed cattle there to try whether Mr. Brown will impound them. Mr. Jo. Hasset had leased Killgoram to his servant, Carty, as part of his own estate, never mentioning his lordship's name nor reserving him any rent. Threatened to bring two justices to out him, but Carty surrendered possession. Mr. Kenny allowed the £30 due from Mrs. Herbert for her son's diet and schooling, and they both thank his lordship. Paid Mr. Keny £10 more to make up the £40, four years' interest, due to him. Mr. Kenny will write how they will have Mr. Herbert disposed of. Sent Mr. Fowle the bill of exchange, and wrote to Capt. Herbert to call to Mr. Fowle for the £150.

Kinsale,
20 April.

Mr. Fitz Herbert daily expected at the Island, for the great leet is on Friday. Mr. Robt. Hasset, who has the keeping of his lordship's bond, promised it next week. 12.

1678

425. Jo. Woolfe to Lord Herbert at Llyssin.

Mr. Loftus was advised to decline the reference; the trial came on yesterday. The evidence on Lord Herbert's side, which concerned sealing and delivery of the deed of settlement by Lord Chandos, was proved by the Countess of Castlehaven. But execution, by livery and seisin and attornment of tenants, there was not effectual testimony of, the witnesses [being] dead; [but] their deaths and handwriting [were proved]. It was conceived the case stood against the serjeant; but three of the four judges inclined (by directions to the jury) to think his title good, and this morning the verdict was brought in for him. Mr. Loftus will not sit down with this foil if further evidence be discovered to clear scruples about the tenants' attornments, which he has good hopes of. The charges of this suit cannot but be considerable.

2 May. *HM*2.23/32.

The settlement in question is no doubt that made on Lord Herbert's marriage to Lord Chandos's daughter. Lady Castlehaven was Lord Chandos's sister.

1678

426. Richd. Salter to Lord Herbert at Lymer Lodge.

Received his by Mr. Herbert, with a particular of Lord Herbert's [debts] in this town. Showed it to Mr. Dan. Jencks, Mr. Richd. Gryfiths, and Mr. Tho. Baker—Mr. Pugh was not at home. They say the particulars are much less than is due to each. What is due to the writer is near £7 less than Lord Herbert charges himself with. As to furnishing money to pay off these debts and put them in one hand, none of these persons can do it, nor can the writer. But if he please they will all endeavour to find where he may be furnished with £250 or £500 upon a Bristoll bargain for seven years upon land or personal security.

Salop,
8 May. 91.

1678

427. Tho. Browne to Lord Herbert at Llyssyn.

Delivered to Mr. Jones East Meanus and co. Lymmerick deeds and Mr. Shawe's bond of £1,000, and the rest of his lordship's writings to Mr. Wilson. Never endeavoured—as Capt. Herbert writes—to keep the least scroll; hopes he may know who [so] informed him. Paid Mr. Jones the arrears. His matching into Hassett's family displeasing Lord Herbert has almost ruined him. Acquaints him that there are several that aim at [a] great deal of his lordship's estate here. Has desired Mr. Jones to get him a chapman for the reversion of his mother-in-law's lands in Presteigne. All he aims at now is to clear with Lord Herbert, and hopes for his favour and that he forgive miscarriages past. "Your . . . poore Kinsman".

Castle Island,
10 May. *Armorial seal* 566.

1678

428. Ro[b]t. Browne to Lord Herbert.

Has acquainted him of a hardship put upon him by Lord Herbert's late substitute here. Agreed with Cornet John Blenerhassett last March twelvemonth touching East Meanus, Farrenny brak, and Killally as follows: Was to get his brother Drew's, Mr. Gorsteloe's, and Mr. Newton's discharge for the mean profits (for which a suit was commenced against Lord Herbert in Chancery); Mr. Hassett was to deliver the writer possession of Killally and the deeds of Meanus, etc., belonging to Mr. Newton (the deed of fee-farm by Sir William Herbert to Virgin and his assignment to Newton). Cornet Hassett gave him Killally but said Capt. Browne would send the deeds. This agreement was before good witnesses; did not have it reduced to writing, knowing he was dealing with a gentleman that durst not do an ill thing, especially acting on behalf of his lordship. But Cornet Hassett dying, he is to this day without the deeds, and has lost the mean profits, above £400. And now Lord Herbert's new agents—Mr. Wilson, Mr. Jones, and Mr. Mason—refuse the deeds, though they have them. Entreats him to perform the agreement or give up the discharges, and he will give up Killally and recover it at law if he can. Will release the commons of mountain, given by Sir William Herbert for cattle without number, upon his granting the writer a lease of three lives of Gortnycople, Gorte Glynny, and Knocky olly, containing two plough-lands (mountain) lately in the tenancy of one Taylor, at £20 a year (the new improved rent being £24) paying a half-year's rent to renew a life, and so for ever, and giving up the deeds aforesaid. Refused Michaelmas and Ladyday rent, finding he has paid more than his due, being credibly informed the rent reserved in the deed is but £6 yearly. Must remove it into Chancery, and hopes thereby to have the deeds brought into court can prove by no worse persons than the Lord Chief Justice and the whole jury that they were in Lord Herbert's agents' hands at the assizes. But his hope is that Lord Herbert will make good the agreement. All proceedings are by consent stopped until his pleasure be known.

16 May. 567.

1678

429. SAMUELL WILSON TO LORD HERBERT.

Hopes he has not incurred displeasure in being surety for Mr. Mason. Is herein partly a means of saving him £60 or £80 per annum [exchange]. All the papers from Capt. Browne are in his custody and an inventory given to Mr. Jones. Others, relating to the Meanus, which they thought it not prudence to see (among them Rob. Browne's deeds, which he threatens to bring them upon oath to produce) are sent out of their custody to his lordship's own hands. His seigniory much wants one in commission of the peace; there is none within eight miles. Other justices are so addicted to their own creatures that his lordship's tenants expect little right from them. If he approves of Mr. Fitz Herbert's proposals 'twill be no loss, for he promises to solicit in Dublin and save many counsels' fees. Has moved into his lordship's house, and designs at his own cost to give it what external ornament he can. If he forbids it not, he intends to run two rows of Dutch willows, sycamore, or other spreading trees of quick growth from the front of the house towards the bridge, with a gate at the end, and an orchard below the bridge on the castle side. Has moved the building of a market house in obedience to his commands, but finds a great aversion to it, most [preferring] the building of a free school, which may prove as advantageous to the Island as that at Charlivile is to it. From those who almost daily offer he will not want English Protestant tenants. But covenants of building are ill performed; only Mr. Morgan, Saunders, Trant, and Cnoghore o'Dally have [built]—the rest live in mere cabins.

21 May. *Armorial seal* 568.

FitzHerbert's proposals are in the next letter.

1678

430. FR. FITZHERBERT TO [LORD HERBERT].

Left Dublyn about 19 April and arrived here the 24th and kept the court leet and next day a court baron. There was not upon record so much as the names of the resiants, "decimers", and inhabitants in the seigniory. Made a new [record] by Mr. Mc David's memory, but issued warrants to the constables to make a [full] return within five days upon pain of 40s. apiece. Finds estreats of the courts only of the two last years, which he delivered to Mr. Jones to have collected; they amount not to above £10. They have been so long uncollected the tenants [etc.] are persuaded his lordship will remit them; told them his order is to the contrary. Has ordered the recorder to engross on parchment the fines of the last courts. Cannot out Mc David at present, but has checked him and joined George Twyst with him; has given them his lordship's orders concerning forfeitures, fines, heriots, amerciaments, and other royalties, and what he will allow them above their accustomed fees. The tenants complain for want of some powerful person to protect and punish. Finds by conversing with merchants here that Mr. Mason's undertaking will save at least £60 or £70 per annum for returns, besides the advantage of receiving the money twice a year at London.

In answer to Mr. Reade's letter, he well remembers making entry upon part of Worthyns Moors within a year or two of his being steward, in old Thompson's time. Upon the lord of Worthyn's refusal to appear they made entry, but upon his submission did not proceed.

Begs leave to represent his own condition. The best of his practice lies in the north-east circuit, where he has been eight or nine years, and gets £40 to £50 per annum. Must quit it to attend here. If he will allow him £20 per annum with the fees of the court (not above £10 betwixt the recorder and himself) he will live amongst the tenants and encourage their virtues and punish their vices, and will solicit all his concerns at Dublyn and save counsels' fees except at common law and Chancery trials.

Finds papers in Mr. Willson's hands of former proceedings betwixt Drue and [Lord Herbert] about Meanus, etc.; will advise with counsel at Dublyn about them. Hopes he remembers how the writer was used here by Mr. Thomas Herbert in drawing the last leases (having no more than paid for parchment and engrossing), and that he will have the drawing of the next. Mr. Jones has put Mr. Willson, Mr. Mason, and the writer in possession of his lordship's house. Encloses a request from the recorder to become tenant in the country and in the town, having neither house nor land within the seigniory; his father is an ancient tenant. Mr. Jones has a petition from John Mc David.

Castle Islands,
21 May. 569.

McDavid is described in a later letter as the "serjeant".

1678

431. CHARLES MASON TO LORD HERBERT.

Delivered his bond and security to Mr. Jones. Mrs. Hassett lives in Corke, where Mr. Jones will receive her answer. Mr. Robert Hassett will answer his lordship only by post. Hopes Mr. Fittz Herbert will finish the concerns of Bally mc Adam this term, and free it from quit-rent. Gave the collector of His Majesty's revenues in this county two guineas to forbear distraining till after the term, which will save £10 or £12. Wishes he would grant Mr. Browne a lease of Taylor's farm conditionally that they quit-claim to all but what they have in possession. Mr. Jo. Hassett left Capt. Browne and his wife but a bare £20 by will. There is no entering on Killmurry till the expiry of the lease. If his lordship accepts of Mr. Fittz Herbert's service upon his conditions it will save money if there are law-suits, especially if he proceeds against those that possess the purchased lands in co. Limbricke.

Finds no effects of Mc Cragh's promise, and the father is ancient, so it is necessary to begin the suit. The rest of the money will be remitted this week. Finds the Goralds much inclining to his lordship's interest; they have sent their request by Mr. Jones. They have a great influence on the people of this country, and may [otherwise] occasion him some expense. [Offers] his opinion if he disposes of any lands here before he comes over. Mr. Robert Browne and Mr. Jones could not agree about a mortgage of Killally. Asks order to treat with Browne in his own name or another's; Browne desires but £60 for seven years at £8 a year.

Had he mentioned it to Browne from his lordship he would have been very "high". Browne has Virgin's and Newton's interest, but not Drewe's, who has a lease from Newton about forty years unexpired. The reversion of Meanus and Farnybrake and the present interest of Killally are in Browne.

22 May. 13.

1678

432. EDWARD KENNEY TO LORD HERBERT, ONE OF HIS MAJESTY'S PRIVY COUNCIL.

Thanks him in particular for his care of his grandchild. Has received £30 from his daughter on Lord Herbert's account, and £10 from Mr. Jones, which complete the interest due. He wrote that Ed. Herbert may be bound apprentice to his lordship for a term of years; his father left him to Lord Herbert by his will, and if he may be serviceable to him, he is bound enough, both by the will and by his many obligations from his lordship. Has been sick this long while.

Cullen,
27 May. *Armorial seal* 570.

1678

433. SAMUELL WILSON TO LORD HERBERT AT LLYSSIN.

Mr. Croffts pretends to more years in Glascanyff than the present one, by grant from Mr. Hassett, and [failing that] intends to rent those two plough-lands at the same rent of £30 per annum. His lordship can expect no improvements from him, by way of ditching and quick-setting, who scarce makes up his outward fences, letting his cattle run promiscuously through the in-land, breaking down fences formerly made. And the usual rent of £30 is too little, for the tenants of Disert came yesterday and said that if he would rent it of his lordship they would give (as under-tenants) £1 13s. 9d. a gneeve for the whole, and bind themselves to improve as strictly as others do. This will amount to £40 10s. per annum. Would have discovered some long-smothered plots against his lordship in relation to concealed lands, but perceives Robin Browne has done it by Mr. Fitz Herbert. His lordship has enemies, and such a seneschal is absolutely necessary.

Castle Island,
27 May.

Old Bastable paid £36 for the land.

Armorial seal 20.

1678

434. THO. MA CRAITH TO LORD HERBERT AT LYMER PARK. [TO BE LEFT AT MR. THOMAS FOULES AT THE BLACK LION . . . LONDON. *Deleted.*]

He commanded the writer, when he left Kissyn last August, to send exact account of his estate here and what it amounts to as set by Charles Mason. Has sent it by Mr. Jones. Will, if he wishes, send a list of the joint farms divided in parcels and an account of the work and other duties that accrue to every chief tenant out of every plough-land. If it were known here that he should send that account they would burn him in the house. Is faithful to serve him; will not see him abused by any of his servants. Has now four cows by the two Lord Herbert gave him. Grazing is very dear and the grass bad. If he will order for him ten acres of pasture and meadow, getting some abatement the first years, he will divide it and quickset it and pay yearly five shillings per acre. It is the only thing he wants, and the first vacancy of [the place of] John Mc David the serjeant or [that] of the recorder. If he writes he should enclose it in Mr. Wilson's or he will never have it. Beseeches him to keep this and all other letters from him from the sight of Mr. Jones or any other that has correspondency here.

Castle Island,
29 May. 301.

[16]78

435. Fr. Fitzherbert to Lord Herbert at Llyssyn or elsewhere.

Since Mr. Jones left Kerry several have been tampering with the writer to solicit Lord Herbert for new leases, with considerable increase of rent. Had £20 offered him by one person, but will never [take] a penny but what Lord Herbert's generosity affords. Has this day with difficulty and some charges obtained judgement against Sanckey although some of the records were lost (which was never done before). Mr. Trante has sealed a lease of ejectment against Mr. Hassett's tenant.

Dublyn,
8 June. 571.

1678

436. Charles Mason to Lord Herbert at Llysin.

Mr. Fittz Garold is concerned that his lordship will not answer his letter, and suspects the writer hinders their reconciliation. Mr. Patricke Pierce, Fitzgerald's relation, is agitating something to Lord Herbert's prejudice; he and Mr. Fittz Garold were lately in co. Corke, either with the Earl of Barry More or the Earl of Orrory. The latter has a commission from the Duke of Yorke to enquire after concealed lands. Pierce, assisted by Mr. Fittz Garold's writings, intends to prove all that was Mr. Garrett Fittz Gar[o]ld's to be concealed, and will bring all the new-recovered lands under the same notice. Pierce is troubled that Capt. Browne enjoys the lands Lord Herbert made him a grant of. Those his lordship has to deal with in it are potent. Mr. Thomas Mc James says that if Lord Herbert would be favourable to his nephew he would stop the mouths of all those clamorous people. Prays him promise to be kind to the nephew when he comes.

One year's stay will settle all his concerns, so that he need not come again except for pleasure. Offers to supply his house with all sorts of provisions "of the growth of this Contrey" (by which he excepts wines, fruits, and spicery), and also hay, oats, and straw, and firing for the house, in consideration of £300 a year and the benefit of the demesne. By this means Lord Herbert will ease himself and his family of a great deal of trouble. Suggests he commands Mr. Fittz Herbert to prepare the business of co. Limbricke for a trial next summer. Suggests the purchase of Mr. Bateman's interest in Knockenegore, as besides that there is not one foot but derives from him or his ancestors. When bought he may add to it so much of Curranes and Malaghmarcky as lies between it and the lane from the Island to Thraly, which will make a good farm. Proposes Carkir, etc., be divided, making six inland farms with sufficient mountain grazing. Suggests he defers disposing of any part of this seigniory till he arrives, for no man can inform him at this distance of the advantages of each farm. Lord Herbert granted better bargains at Llysin than he would had he been here. Besides, his presence will encourage English tenants to come.

Mr. Fittz Herbert will find by enquiry in Dublin whether there are any judgements against Mr. Robert Browne. If not, his interest in Killally will be sufficient to secure for £60. Hopes he will send Mr. Fittz Herbert hither with a commission of the peace; he will be serviceable not only to him but to the tenants, and what he will save by soliciting and in counsels' fees will be more than he asks. By reason of the rumours of war his correspondents advise him to forbear trading to sea till times are better, which has occasioned him to propose to the tenants that if they will pay along with each rent 12d. per pound he will forbear Ladyday rent till Michaelmas and Michaelmas rent till Christmas. Some accept with thanks. This will pay part of the exchange. These are troublesome times. Would rather lose by paying the money in Corke and so remit it hence to London than venture the seas as things stand.

Castle Island,
11 June.

Prays his favour in reading what he writes—cannot find anyone he can trust to transcribe his letters. 17.

1678

437. John Richardson to Lord Herbert.

On 16 June 1677, when he left the writer's house, he gave him a bill for £18 10s., to be paid with interest on 1 January. But his lordship not coming to town, and the writer not hearing from him, he desires him to pay the bearer, Mr. Weatherly. Hopes he will not fail him.

Southampton Street,
24 June.

There is also due 20s. for things lost and broke while he was at the writer's house.

Endorsed: John Richardson's £18 10s. *HM*2.23/33.

1678

438. Th. Corbett to Lord Herbertt at Lyssyn.

Makes bold by Mr. Jones to present a few rude lines in acknowledgement of his favours, and to certify him of the death of Mr. John Hollyes, to whose oath the difference over bounds between Mr. Sanders and the writer was referred. Hollyes being Mr. Sanders's friend, and the writer not having power to force him, he could get nothing done. Mr. Sanders, by his greatness and power, wrongfully keeps from the writer the land formerly in the possession of John Hollyes and others for fifty-six years (as was proved by Mr. Cnohor O Dalley) as part and parcel of Caragh, and of Mr. Twisse and John macke David ever since they were concerned in his lordship's seigniory. Could produce a hundred to prove it if he could but get them unto their oaths. The wrong he sustains in paying rent for land Mr. Sanders enjoys will be much to his prejudice unless relieved. Prayers for him, his lady, and family.

Castell Islands,
8 July. 29.

1678

439. SAMUELL WILSON TO LORD HERBERT.

Wrote by Mr. Fitzherbert, to be left at the post office at Dublin. Mistook the two plough-lands and a half at Glascaniff for two. In old Bastable's time near £50 was made of them. Mr. Crofts brags of a long lease from Mr. Hassett, whose power his lordship knows best. If Mr. Crofts can be disposs[ess]ed the writer will find a sufficient tenant or become tenant himself at the old rent. If Bastable set it at £1 13s. 9d. a gneeve the old rent of £35 is not unreasonable. Confesses £5 or £10 more will accrue to the writer yearly by tithes the way he now proposes. But assures him his greatest design is to advance his lordship's rent; the next is to see if he can bring a hedge near the town of Castle Island.

Intends to erect a gate and a handsome wall at the lower end of the walk leading over the bridge, which will be convenient in stopping up the road too frequently made through his lordship's yard. Presumes to do it at his own charges. Was the other day in company with the Earl of Orrery's steward, who spoke of Killmurry, saying it would infallibly fall under a trial, but thought it was by the means of some ill instruments and not out of his master's disaffection to Lord Herbert; he was confident Lord Herbert's letter to his master would stop proceedings, or that by his presence those incendiaries would be detected and nothing denied him by the Earl. In answer to his last commands, he believes few buildings are performed according to covenant. Mr. Mason has called in their leases. They design next week to ride throughout the seigniory and give him a particular account. Would have paid his lordship's money before this, but is not sure whether the bookseller had sent them. Is sure no such ship came to Corke. Mr. Jon. Goold never heard of any such. If Mr. Millington can show a receipt from the master of the ship, he will send the money by a bill of exchange (though they refused him one this week for so small a sum, and he was forced to send by Tho. Francis). It is his seigniory's prayer to see his lordship here next summer, but he will miss the noble recreation of hunting for want of dogs. If he will bestow a couple upon the writer he will breed out of them against his arrival.

Castle Island,
11 July. *Armorial seal* 21.

1678

440. Samuell Wilson to Lord Herbert.

Cannot imagine why the bearer is posting himself over for Wales. Has tried to pump it out of him. He [says] he's commencing a suit in Dublin, and "by his pretty Consequence" must infallibly be at Llyssyn a fortnight hence. Suits are not so easily determined. Concludes he's sent over by the joint consent of the seigniory. There has been a close cabal amongst "our Grandees" these three weeks to procure the old tenants new leases ; it grieves their hearts that Lord Herbert is proffered so many new English ones. Wishes he were present to encourage them, for the seigniory greatly wants such. When he last waited on him his lordship was laying out for beds among the tenants. Has already fitted up curtains, counterpane, etc., to the Grey Chamber bedstead. If he gives warning of his coming, he'll take the whole upon himself and borrow or buy such as become the largest bedsteads.

Castle Island,
13 August. 572.

1678

441. Charles Mason to Lord Herbert.

Has [already] acquainted him with the advantage in not disposing of this seigniory till his lordship is present. Begs, if he accepts his proposals, he will give him time to make provision. Knows not what occasion the bearer has to make this journey. Is informed the tenants intend to petition for a refusal of their own holdings. They have made little improvements, so he may reasonably set them to those that will advance the rent and make a proportion yearly of ditch and quickset it. Capt. Browne replevied the cattle Mr. Jones distrained for arrears, so did Mr. Robert Browne those taken for the rent of East Meanus, etc. Expected his further order before this. If there be no proceeding against Capt. Browne in the sheriff's court, it will be dismissed. Made an attorney the first court after Mr. Jones went, but knows not how to put in an avowry. The other action lies in Lord Herbert's own court. Mr. Robert Browne is about some bargain about East Meanus, Farnybracke, and Killally ; the latter is his in possession, and the fee simple of that and the rest is his. The opportunity is not like to present again. Mr. Browne is gone to his brother Drew (who intends to purchase his interest) and removes to some other place ; if Lord Herbert please to deal with him he should hasten his orders. Browne wants money, and must deal with somebody.

13 August. *Armorial seal* 573.

[16]78

442. [Sir] R. Mason to Lord Herbert at his house at Montgomery.

Prepared £100, but Lord Herbert directed not the receiver to take it, so it lies dead in his hands. He should never doubt his own credit nor the writer's finance to supply him. It will be infallibly satisfied if Lord Herbert's depositor be findable. And for security in "cases" of mortality,

Lord Herbert will please cause Mr. Reade to sign an obligation; which otherwise he would not ask.

Yesterday the Lord Chief Baron dined with him at Worcester with his lady, son, and daughter; he has wrote his sense fully to his niece. Is of the Chief Baron's opinion: "Wee should butcher your concerne to putt it on the Tappy in this conjuncture". Will gladly hear Sir Thomas Bridges, but cannot think his skill or interest exceeds the Chief Baron's; will rejoice if he has found something to Lord Herbert's service that they could not. "Compliment . . . for me your cosin Betty . . . God send her a sonne".

12 October. *Armorial seal* *HM*2.23/34.

Three years later we find Sir Richard Mason dunning Read for payment of what is perhaps the sum referred to here. By his niece the Chief Baron—Sir Wm. Montagu—no doubt means Lord Herbert's wife, her mother being his first cousin. To put something on the *tapis* is to lay it open to discussion.

1678

443. JO. WOOLFE TO LORD HERBERT AT LLYSSIN. TO BE LEFT AT THE POST-HOUSE IN SALOP.

Received the £100 from Sir Richard Mason. Applied half of it in satisfaction of the principal on the enclosed bond (not doubting he will return the interest, £4) . . . Is glad to hear of the new encouragements from Mr. Loftus for bringing the cause to a second trial; which may be more seasonable by the death of Mr. Serjeant Newdigate, though happening very lately. Supposes there is no suit yet commenced.

19 October.

His commands to Mr. Graunge shall be performed.

Endorsed: Bond of £50 cancelled, money lent by Wolfe "or his mouvement". His promise to pay £50 to Mr. Grainge.

Further endorsement: . . . Trial for lands in right of Lady Eliz. Bridges . . .
*HM*2.23/35.

This suit is mentioned in No. 425. "Lady Eliz. Bridges" is presumably Lord Herbert's wife, *née* Brydges.

1678

444. FRAN. BLAKEWAY TO LORD HARBERT AT CLISON.

Acquaints him with a small debt for a gown of flowered silk, £7. He bespoke it on 15 February 1676/7. Brought him a bill two days before he went out of town and he sent answer that he would send it from the country. Fears it is out of his mind. Desires an order to receive it here of Mr. Fowles, or that he will return it from Salop.

The Three Crowns, Cheapside, London,
26 October. 92.

1678

445. CHARLES MASON TO LORD HERBERT.

Procured, with much trouble and riding, bills of exchange for £345, which he sent the 22nd of last month. Remitting cost £6 per cent. A little before exchange was two or three per cent, and was falling till news of the popish plot arrived, which startles and amazes the English in this kingdom, and trade is worse than before, though then bad. Could not foresee the troubles that have happened in these kingdoms since his proposals were made. Encloses his account and a perfect rent-roll of last May's rent; the duties are paid at All Saints'.

In Corke Madam Hassett assured him she would pay every penny. Mr. Robert Hassett says rather than contest with his lordship he will refer the difference to two gentlemen or to a lawyer with Mr. Fittzherbert; his counsel says the renewing of the first life is lapsed and advises him to tender the £30 for renewing the last life. But if his lordship may re-enter for non-payment of the first £30 he will gain more by new-setting than double the £60. The tenants pay £35 per annum above the rent.

It is true that if Capt. Browne's bill to Mr. Kenny had been accepted, and his cattle sold, he paid near £50; but those failing, it wants something of £30. Mr. Sanders says he paid Browne in money for the wheat, and Mc Craigh says he weighed but eleven barrels of barley and agreed for it at 9s. per barrel. The suit is continued by Mr. Fittzherbert's advice. The captain has done well in disposing of his farms in the seigniory; he set Killcushney to Mr. Thomas Fittz Garold, Lord Herbert's "sereant", and Bally mc Adam to Counsellor Roach (who lives in the writer's sister's house), and intends to dispose of the lands Lord Herbert extended or the reversion of his mother-in-law's jointure to satisfy what he owes Lord Herbert. Mr. Robert Browne of Meanus submits at length to payment of £8 [a] year, only craves time. Has not had time to wait upon the Earls of Barrymore and Orrory since Tho. Francis came; intends it next journey to Corke.

It is reported the King sends hither ten thousand men out of England. If he uses his interest at Court he may have a company of foot or a troop of horse quartered in this town; possibly, upon acquainting the King and Council with the necessity of a garrison in this county, and that this is the most convenient place, His Majesty will grant it. Command of a regiment and the government of this county would produce great advantages to him or his brother. Begs pardon for this presumption.

Castle Island,
2 November.

Mr. Fittz Herbert stayed his journey for Dublin twelve days. Hopes the money is paid to Mr. Fowle, but sends second bills.

Attached under seal: A perfect rent-roll of the seigniory of Mount Eagle Loyal for half a year's rent due 25 March "1675" (*sixty-three items totalling* £469 9s. 6d.; *the account of disbursements and disposal of this sum follows*).

Armorial seal 575-6.

The figures of the year in the title of the rent-roll are quite clear, but it is apparently an error for 1678.

[1678-9]

446. Lord Herbert's Answer to the Duke of York's Commissioners.
Holograph copy.

Has no estate but what is of Queen Eliz.'s title. His grandfather let it to Lord Baltinglas for three lives, who suffered several parcels to be embezzled—having but a term, he suffered claimants to enter, then as at present great disturbers of the English proprietors, as far as impudence, perjury, and forgery avail them. Enjoyed the whole of his seigniory in Cromwell's time as his legal right. One Col. Sanky entered on part as forfeited; but had a decree against him, in the usurped times, for the whole. Has enjoyed it ever since, and set to tenants since the King's restoration. Had the benefit of the Act of Settlement, and has passed the view of the Commissioners for View and Review, and all other disturbances that malice could procure.

But finding himself under the danger of a great chief-rent he got a new grant from the present King to reduce it, which recites his old patent at large, and what passed in general words. Is settled as well as law and the King's grant can secure him. Yet has been alarmed frequently since, firstly by Lord Ormond's grant, then by Lord Kingston's, and next by the D. [of] York's. But the informers could make no advantage as to the two first, nor did the commissioners proceed as to the last, his title was so firm [despite] Patrick Peirce, the fitz Gerards, and their relations in Kerry who style themselves of Kilmurrey in his seigniory—one of the parcels usurped in Lord Baltinglas's time, or at least since Sir Wm. Herbert died (his [great-]grandfather, employed long in public affairs to the prejudice of his estate). Col. James fits Gerald in the rebellion seized all the rents of the seigniory and totally extirpated the English inhabitants, and had possession of all or most of the estate. But when the times settled he was restored in possession as true proprietor.

A son or grandchild rather (he supposes) of this fitz Gerald was taken into his brother's family, who there carried out his treacherous design against his brother, Ed., Lord Herbert—not suspected till, notice being given out of Irland, his letters were intercepted, in which were a rental of several plough-lands, the present rent, and improvements, by which to solicit good bargains for his kindred, also directions [how] to come to the writer's papers and then make hay while the sun shone. His brother [then] parted with him. They since lay out threats and sometimes fair words—that if he sets Tho. fitz Gerald a reasonable bargain of Killmurrey they will stifle those claims . . . But he not consenting, all this disturbance [is] contrived from time to time.

Endorsed: Answer by Ed., Lord Herbert, to the Duke [of] York's commissioners touching pretensions to some of the Irish estate.

*HM*2.22/18.

The whole paper is in the hand of Henry, 4th Lord Herbert, but it is clear that his brother must have composed the first two paragraphs, probably shortly before his death, Henry adding the last paragraph and copying out the whole.

1679

447. Pat Crosbie and S. Morris to Mr. Davyes.

There is a reference to them from the late-going Justices of assize in some controversy betwixt him and Mr. James Hariyn. Give notice that on Wednesday 8 October at Traly they will be between nine and ten in the forenoon . . . . . . to examine and determine the difference or state the form of it to the next justices of assize for this county of Kierry.

25 September.

Added at foot: To Teige o'Daly, Jo[h]n mc David Gerrald, Donnogh Quollety, Morrish Hinchy, Morrice Cahane, Jo[h]n mc Bryan,——— Connell, ——— Ruorcke . . . . . (*torn*). 577.

[1679-81]

448. ————TO EDWARD KENNY, ESQ., NEAR KING'S SALE. *Draft.*

[Spoke] to his honour about Kenny's being tenant to the house and demesnes at Castle Islands and taking the agency of his concerns in that kingdom, and finds him very sensible of Kenny's respect and faithfulness. He should forthwith apply himself by letter, proposing being his immediate tenant, and not do it by Mr. Browne (as formerly) or any other, which will not be satisfactory to his lordship. His honour will insist that he pay for the house and demesnes £50 per annum (being the rent proposed by Mr. Brown on Kenny's behalf), and that it be returned quarterly—which he may easily do [by] his great interest in merchants at Corke and Kingsale. He should not scruple to give Capt. Meade and his brother Ken[n]y as security. His lordship is as yet altogether a stranger to his concerns . . . *Breaks off unfinished.* 270.

Capt. Meade was the second husband of Mary Kenney, widow of Thomas Herbert, former agent at Castle Island.

1680

449. HENRY BLAYNEY TO LORD HERBERT. LEAVE AT MR. RUSSEL'S HOUSE OVER AGAINST THE DUCHESS OF YORK'S HEAD IN THE OLD PAL MALL, LONDON.

Capt. Edward Lloyd reports that the King and Council have discharged him for the words he sent the writer, which the latter put under his hand to Lord Herbert; which words he will make good upon oath, with other things he knows of Lloyd, if Lord Herbert please to order that he be sent for by Parliament.

Gregynog Hall,
14 October.

Desires a messenger be sent for him, otherwise [Lloyd] will think he comes voluntary.

Armorial seal *HM*2.23/36.

[16]80

450. ED. WHITTINGHAM TO LORD HERBERT AT MRS. RUSSELL'S HOUSE OVER AGAINST THE DUCHESS OF YORKE'S HEAD IN THE PALL MALL, NEAR WESTMINSTER.

Encloses account of the second election, and two libels which Mr. Browne and Mr. Davies have dispersed (the author is Mr. Browne) which reflect upon the magistrates of "our" town. The occasion is laying aside Edward Davies [as] bailiff. [They] obstructed the sealing of the writer's lease for the toll, drawn in pursuance of Lord Herbert's order (hopes he remembers it was referred by the writer, Mr. Bailiff Herbert, and Mr. Read to settle, being then in dispute). Had a right to it, and was forced to sue an injunction out of the Marches to quiet himself in possession. Lord Herbert heard it at the Lodge before he [left], and ordered him to pay 20s. yearly to the town and take a lease for twenty-one years, quitting his right. Never made clear four nobles a year. Was the only person that brought the drapers of Sherewsbury and drovers to the fairs—they have small sale of cattle or sheep, only swine. Cousin Math. Price perused the lease, and can say how he is unjustly dealt withal. Hopes he will confirm the order. Mr. Bailiff Morgans has not been at any court since these libels, "neither" the writer but twice. Discontented persons that "live by the spigotts" are the disturbers.

18 October.

Endorsed: Misdemeanours by grand jury in Montgomeryshire.

*HM*2.9/58.

The account of the election (of the second of the two bailiffs of Montgomery) is No. 57 in Volume IX, and the two libels are No. 59. They are listed in the Appendix as Nos. 79 and 77. The endorsement apparently means that this letter was used as the wrapper for a bundle dealing with the topic mentioned.

[1680/81]

451. T. Burton to Cousin Read.

There is now an opportunity for him to appear the writer's friend by engaging the votes of the underwritten burgesses of Salop. Intends to stand for a burgess of parliament next election for that place. Lord Herbert will also give him thanks.

Longn[o]r,
21 January.

Walter Haynes of Westbury.
Gittins of Aston Rogers.
Thomas Purcell of Wolstermine.
Edward Peers of Llancastell.
Will Foster of Marton.
George Peake of Worthin.
Corbetts of Newton.
George Peers of Montgomery.
Gittins of Brocton.

Endorsed: 1681. Mr. Burton's to Jo. Read. *HM*2.9/61.

The year endorsed would ordinarily mean 1681/2, but probably means here 1680/81, since there was an election in the February of that year. The likely explanation is that the endorsement was added later in the year 1681.

1680/81

452. [Lord] Herbert to Mr. Roger Jones, his agent in Ireland. *Contemporary copy*.

Requires him upon sight hereof to deliver to Mr. Charles Mason his bond, he having given security [for] his account.

7 March. 578.

1681

453. Petition [? to the House of Lords] regarding Fines in Wales. *Draft*.

In many parts of Wales pro- and post-fines are in farm to the person who sets fines upon alienation, or his trustee, so that he sets very high rates for his own advantage. In some counties of Wales as great a fine is set (by these farmers) for bare security of money upon mortgage as upon a sale of lands. 'Tis desired the Welsh may be at liberty to levy fines at the Common Pleas or their own Great Sessions, as they think best. Or that no man may set a fine where he is farmer of them . . .

*HM*2.9/62.

The next document in Volume IX is a draft bill limiting fines in Wales.

[16]81

454. RO. JONES TO LORD HERBERT AT HIS LODGINGS OVER AGAINST THE CROSS KEYS IN THE OLD PALLMALL, LONDON.

Never received his letters about employing Mr. Edw. Kenny to take the care of his concerns in Irland. Twiss said it was intended. Mr. Wm. Kenny, [the] brother, with his sister and Capt. Mead, [came] to Kerry to the farm Mr. Herbert holds from Lord Herbert. Waited on them to know whether Mr. Kenny had received such orders; they said there was no such thing . . . Neither did he hear of Mr. Griffith's going into Irland, until at Mountgom[er]y Will. Rondle said he was gone by Bristoll. Would have stayed till further orders had he [known]. Wishes he had been at Castle Island when Mr. Griffith came or in England when Twiss and Mason came over; would have discoursed them before his lordship. Did a person of repute accuse him it would trouble him; but he knows their reputation where they live, and that no credit will be given them there, whatever his lordship does. Lord Herbert will in time know these people.

As to his purchasing lands in Irland, he has had a mortgage on Twiss's interest above three years, and another upon the interest of Mr. Corbet. The money he lent Twiss was to redeem his mortgage to John Pooke for £34; he was so well known he could not [borrow] £5 to save his life. The writer having brought £100 out of England to lay out there, lent him the money and took the same bargain as Pooke. Twiss had £12 more of him for other debts; had the rent for three years in lieu. So he was to have from Twiss and Corbet £19 10s. yearly, and the mortgage money at Ladyday from both. But Twiss was returned in arrear by Mr. Mason £18 18s. 8d., and nothing to pay but the corn on the land, which the writer was forced to seize. Eight days after he had seized it (the usual time) he went with the appraisers to appraise it, then Twiss begged eleven days more; but not a penny could he get, nor any man to deal for his corn (the year before he received £14 from a merchant in Corke, which is this day unpaid and the corn undelivered). When all failed Twiss desired him to buy his interest in Kilbanavane, which he did for £40, and stopped out of it the arrears due. The lease is for ninety-nine years determinable upon three lives. Presumes his lordship has the counterpart, and that Twiss could dispose of it, otherwise the mortgagee, whose deed was drawn by counsel, would not have lent.

His money lent [to] Corbet and the yearly "comeing in" from him and Twiss were above £100, out of which he paid £40 to Twiss. Twiss endeavoured to put several tricks upon him, but failing, took his way to England to complain to his lordship—this by the advice of Sullivane, MaCragh, White, and others of [that] crew . . . If such people be credited he will receive little rent out of Irland and may find the trouble of providing a new agent yearly. As for the rent he collected at Mountgom[er]y,

Mr. Read well knows he [himself] examined [the accounts] when his lordship's brother passed them.

Received a letter from Mr. Griffith by Twiss about 16 April, saying Lord Herbert was willing the writer should come for England, bringing a rent-roll and his accounts. And Twiss brought a message from his lordship that if the writer came over "suddenly" well and good, otherwise he would stay at his peril—knows not what he meant by it, but next day he gave out that Mr. Edw. Kenny was to succeed the writer. Stayed till he received the answer from Mr. Kenny's brother and sister, then came out of the country, leaving a servant in the house and to look after the lands in hand—and if order came to any person to take the employment he was to deliver possession and dispose of the writer's few cattle to best advantage. Now a journey into Ireland will be a great charge; what it would signify to Lord Herbert's advantage he cannot imagine—rent received his accounts will show, profits of courts the bailiffs that gathered it will inform, and for waifs and estrays or felons' goods the chief serjeant can tell . . . Hopes he will excuse him that trouble.

Little Hem,
10 June.

Mr. Kenny understands the estate; his father lived upon it, and he himself for some time with his brother-in-law Mr. Thomas Herbert at Castle Island, and knows every man upon it of account. *HM*2.9/64.

1681

455. Edward Kenney to Mr. Robert Griffith at Mrs. Hodges' house at the sign of the Cross Keys in the Pallmall, London.

Received his of 26 July; one of 5 July he received about the 20th at Corke assizes. Came to Kerry with the judges. Was not willing to trouble his lordship until he returned the first fruits of his labours. Has near £400; will return it to London from Corke. This, with what is already paid, what Mr. Jones received and what is overcharged in the rent-roll, will nearly complete the half year's rent due 25 March. Will never be so backward again. Asks him to desire his lordship to sign the letter, as the other is not received. The lands he would take are Cragg, Ballifearin, Farinavaligh, Cilligan, Inchimore, [and] Inches, containing one plough-land and a half, with the same meres and bounds that Ann fitz Gerrald and her under-tenants enjoy; the lives to be his own, his son John, and John's son Thomas, the rent £16 per annum and £80 improvements. Got a verdict against Sullevan at the assizes. [Just] had news of Capt. Thomas Browne's death. Hopes, if he comes to Dublin, he will give the writer notice before he leaves London.

Castle Island,
10 August. *Armorial seal* 276.

1681

456. Charles Mason to Lord Herbert.

About nine years ago his late lordship commanded him to drain and enclose a parcel of ground belonging to the demesne at Castle Island; had to take in a piece in the possession of one Widow Garold. Mr.

Tho. Herbert, then agent, upon perusing the widow's lease, was of opinion it was not granted to her, and promised, if it appeared to be hers when Lord Herbert came over, to persuade him to give her allowance in her rent. Now she says the writer absolutely promised satisfaction, and has commenced a suit in the assizes. By a motion of Mr. Fittzherbert's the judges ordered a reference to Mr. Kenny. Entreats him to order Mr. Kenny to give her satisfaction that the writer may be freed from this trouble. She never mentioned a word while [the late Lord Herbert] was here. Begs that if Mr. Jones acknowledges the sums the writer charges him with his bond may be delivered to Robert Mason of Mountgomery.

Castle Island,
16 August. 98.

1681

457. Jo. Read to Lord Herbert at Mrs. Hodges' . . . London.

Attended Mr. Mathewes and compounded for the pro- and post-fines. He holds it at £50. Offered £40. He says he would not take under £100 for passing such an estate from any other. Supposes he'll take £45. Goes this day with the money to attend him at Llanvilling sessions; hopes to send a chirograph next post.

Sent a bill of exchange for £100 the beginning of this month. Mr. Ellis the drover promises to pay Lord Herbert what he can spare, the writer to supply him at his return. The tenants are very backward. Gives them time to make the best of their cattle at the fairs, will then use all severity.

The enclosed came from Mr. Fowlkes for a buck. Mr. Pryce of Parke has sent for one, Mr. Arthur Vaughan, Mr. Rees Lloyd, and others. Desires his pleasure in it. The judge and sheriff were supplied from Llyssyn, and Mr. Newport from Lymore. Hickman says here are fifteen brace of old does "extreame fatt" and will hardly live this winter if not killed. Mr. Newport intended to send for another buck to present [to] the Bishop.

Encloses another letter from Sir Richard Mason, who threatens the writer for the £100; was informed he intends to put the bond in suit next term. Desires Lord Herbert to tell him when he may expect payment.

Sent last post Mr. Herbert's return and his own, that Lord Herbert might prick the capital bailiff and signify his pleasure to the present bailiffs. Will expect word if he pitches on Mr. Pryce of Glanmahely.

Mountgo[mer]y,
29 August. *Armorial seal* *HM*2.23/37.

"Mr. Mathewes" is John Mathews, Chamberlain of cos. Denbigh and Montgomery. The £100 Sir Richard Mason was claiming is probably that borrowed by the 3rd Lord Herbert (see No. 442).

1681

458. Edward Kenney to Mr. Robt. Griffith at Mrs. Hodges' . . . London.

Received his with a copy of one from his lordship. Never received the one Griffith sent after his return from this place, nor his lordship's.

Has not been a slothful servant, for the account shows his lordship in his debt. There is above £100 of Ladyday rent not received, but since it is the report here that his lordship is to be married he may want money. Desires him again to transcribe the letter of 28 June—is confident his lordship will sign it. His lordship's instructions must be signed by himself.

Mr. Robt. Browne will sell his lordship the half plough-land of Killally, etc. Encloses a letter from Mr. Mason, also copy of a civil bill and order of reference thereon directed to the writer by Ann fitz Gerrald, which he is the unfittest person to decide, being his lordship's servant. What is ordered against Mr. Mason must light on his lordship. It will be contempt in him if he does not proceed to determination; desires his lordship to give him some scope whereby he may appear a just servant and fulfil the commands of the authority.

Hopes his two bills of exchange are come safe. If his lordship wants £100 about Michaelmas he will provide it himself at twenty-one days' notice, although no rent can be received so soon. Has written the utmost value of Cragg, and it will be a great favour if he will abate any. Means the £80 improvement to be laid out on Cragg and the [? demesne]. Duties are not payable Ladyday, but always at Michaelmas.

Curruragh,
30 August.

The detailed account of Ladyday rent follows.

[Sends this] to let his lordship know he must not expect any more on account of this half year. Desires to know how Capt. Browne came by his death, for malice will not let him alone in his grave. Wrote him already to enquire into Browne's estate in England, real and personal. Sent him a copy of Browne's will to let him know the writer's concerns with it.

Armorial seal 277.

Lord Herbert married in the following December. The Ladyday account shows expenses and allowances deducted from half of the gross total of the rent-roll (this total being £1,182 12s. 10d.).

[16]81

459. Ro. Jones to Lord Herbert at Mrs. Hodges' . . . London.

Pursuant to a letter from Mr. Griffith, he has delivered to Mr. Read to be sent to his lordship . . . (*a list of recent accounts, etc., follows*). Had they the counterparts of the Irish leases the last rent-roll might have been more perfect, but his letter of attorney did not empower him to sue the tenants and force them to show their titles, which many refused.

Mountgom[et]y,
2 September. 579.

1681

460. Charles Mason to Mr. Robert Greefith at Lord Herbert's lodgings in the Old Pallmall, London.

Hopes Mr. Kenny has reported the truth. Mr. Jones's objections are: 1. A half year's rent for Killgoram. *Ans.* Mr. Jones entering three months before the writer's time expired, and reaping the profits, he ought to pay the rent. 2. £6 for Currow More. *Ans.* It is for the year before the writer had possession. 3. The repair of Mr. Bastable's house. *Ans.* Had it not been done there would be no house standing. 4. The £17. *Ans.* Mr. Fittzherbert paid it to Jones for the writer, as he owned before Griffith in Dublin. 5. The exchange of the money returned after his late lordship's decease. *Ans.* The writer's commission extinguished with Lord Herbert's life, and he received the money by favour of the tenants and their trust in him; some gave him 12d. in the pound for forbearing May rent, but that did not answer the sixth part of the charge; did not receive one farthing of All Saint's rent. 6. Jones pretends part of the half year's salary is due to him because he received part of the rent. *Ans.* It was ready before he came, by the writer's diligence, and had been paid sooner if Lord Herbert's orders had been sent sooner; but Mr. Jones persuaded his lordship that the writer could collect by virtue of the old power, purposely to get the employment himself. Begs Griffith's assistance with Lord Herbert to get his discharge. Can, if required, give sufficient testimony by his lordship's empowering some indifferent gentlemen to hear witnesses—Mr. Fitzherbert or Mr. Willson joined with Mr. Kenny.

Noghovalls,
28 November. *Seal of a crest* 580.

The "objections" are, of course, to Mason's account.

[1681/2]

461. Jo. Edwards to Lord Herbert at Mrs. Hodges' . . . London.

Is joyful that Lord Herbert has made an end of wooing. Friday last Mr. Harris of Crinkton, the counsellor, kept a court baron at Dudston in Mr. Newton's name. On Monday "he himself" came to Chirbury and said he intended to call a court [only] to make enquiry for heriots; that perchance during his life he should not call it again, though his ancestors for many years kept courts there, the rolls whereof he can produce, and added abhorrence of the courses of some pretended lords the other end of the hundred. Mr. Read sent for the writer's advice. The only fundamental point is whether Dudston be a manor . . . As Lord Herbert's court at Chirbury is a manor court, putting up of little manors within the hundred may abridge its jurisdiction, but as a hundred court it will not. Dare not determine by how good advice the style of it was changed . . . One of the little lords, Mr. Gittings (related to him) came last leet save one purposely to dine with the writer, who, finding him in court, tendered him the juror's oath; which refusing, he fined him 40s. [Thus] made his kinsman's kindness a snare to him; but gratitude must give place to fidelity, meeting such an opportunity to assert Lord Herbert's right. Last week Gittings called him aside and made an offer to Lord Herbert of the purchase of his title as lord of Bromlow and Meadowtowne, two townships within the hundred, which title came to trial in a long suit between Gittings' ancestor and Lord Herbert's grandfather. Three persons have bid him money for it; he is needy. It would be wisdom to take it in, but [without] owning his right.

Rorington,
2 January.

Good New Year. Puts him in mind to favour his request that the little house in Chirbury be left out of the settlement. His wife's service to him and her ladyship, and hopes now to have them fixed here in the country. Thanks him for pardoning the fines he requested to be remitted; the offenders make thankful acknowledgement.

Endorsed: 1681/2. HM2.23/38.

Dudston, where Mr. Harris kept his court, is halfway between Montgomery and Chirbury, and thus on Lord Herbert's very door-step.

1681/2

462. [LORD HERBERT] TO MR. KENNEY. *Draft or copy.*

His servant Griffith received his of 6 December. The instrument confirming to him the common of mountain of Killmurry shall be sent . . . (*details follow*). Promised Kenney lease of the lands of Cragg before any other; but if the writer's interest be bettered by setting them in parcels to the townsmen as tenants-at-will, he sees it as no infringement of his promise. He shall have the abstracts of the leases this spring or summer. Cannot be positive about Killmurry till he has seen the lease, lest he might awake them to secure a thing that their sleepy neglect would forfeit. He shall have full power to grant a lease to the millers. Did signify that nothing that had not the writer's hand should be accepted as an order, but did not intend to exclude his agents' "distinguishing" the writer's interest upon emergent occasions, e.g., the late Irish fine. Cannot give his final resolution about Ballimac Adam till he has conferred with his sister Browne. Well approves his proposal about Moris Welsh—nurseries are not to be neglected upon an estate where there has been so much waste of timber; yet Welsh must not lop where he should prune, and his reward should not overpoise his deserts. Is concerned that those covenants of plough-boot and house-boot have crept into the leases; he is to interpret them as most agreeable to the writer's interest, otherwise these extravagances may [soon] leave the estate naked and uninhabitable. Allows him the clerk of the markets' court and its profits, anything in his bond to the contrary notwithstanding. Donnough Roe mc Phillip shall have preference to be tenant of the land he holds. Has heard nothing of the petition of John Cahane. Has not received Morris Fitz Gerald's letter. He is to act in Widow Fitzgerald's business as consistent with the writer's interest. Need not declare himself about the court until Kenney is resident upon the place; besides, he will expect account from the gentleman that now officiates, who, he is told, will be here in the spring.

17 January. 101a.

1681/2

463. [LORD HERBERT] TO MR. WILSON. *Draft.*

Is advised it is by no means his interest to grant a lease of Cragg to any, but rather to set it in parcels to the townsmen, who expect it and to whom it will be infinitely convenient. Is it really so? Is satisfied the writings left by his brother in Wilson's custody should continue so, without his agent should have occasion to use them. Service to Wilson's sister.

17 January. 101b.

1681/2

464. EDWARD KENNEY TO MR. ROBT. GRIFFITH AT MRS. HODGES' . . . LONDON.

Received a letter out of Kerry with an account that young Sullivan, "who, if he lives, will be ould Sullevan", was with "my Lord" in London, and what favours the latter conferred on him (but if they were such as he deserved it were the pillory). Prays a particular account of it, for the Sullevans are very high about it. What is become of Mrs. Browne?—heard no word of her since she went in quest of Utopia. Hopes he received the letter enclosed to Mr. Anthoney Saxbery of the Temple. Intends for Kerry in March, as soon as Corke assizes are over, to settle things against the removal of himself and family about May.

Curruragh,
24 January. *Seal of a crest* 278.

[1681/2]

465. EDWARD KENNEY TO MR. ROBERT GRIFFITH AT MRS. HODGES' . . . LONDON.

Received his lordship's answer to part of his letter; desires answer about Ballym[ac]Adam. Also has Sullevan's saucy letter to his lordship, a copy of Griffith's to Mr. FizHerbert, and one to be sent to Mr. Willson, all enclosed in one from Mr. Harris from Dublin. Never met such a heap of villainy and falsehood except the bill in Chancery. Will go to Corke on Friday to return money, but fears exchange will be ten per cent. Old Richard Twiss is dead, thereby escaping the severe chiding his lordship ordered him to give him. It is no small satisfaction to hear his lordship is married.

Curruragh,
7 February. *Seal of a crest* 279.

1681/2

466. [LORD] HERBERT TO MR. KENNEY. *Contemporary copy.*

Has examined Mr. Jones's accounts and Kenney's objections. Jones seems to have reason on his side, especially in the case of the arrears charged on O. Hea, Nell Hollis, and Jo[h]n mc David. The arrear for Currimore is recoverable only from Mason, the lessee, and not from Jones. The arrears of Killgoram are apparently due from Mason also. If Jones has made an entry as Mason alleges he might have indicted him. The writer is not to intermeddle, but to lay hold upon the most lawful and ready way for the recovery of his rents. Would have him narrowly enquire, in the case of Dr. Horance's arrears, whether he should relinquish them, the better to secure the advantage of setting a new lease. Jones says he is not liable for the arrears from Mr. Robt. Browne . . . Jones will come upon the place early this summer.

Kenney is to enquire into Browne's title to the lands he would sell. He should distrain for the arrears of Tullileage; Jones could not receive the rent due from the felons from the right owners of the cattle without making himself accessory to the felony. The charge of the suit against Dorney is £2 15s. 4d., which Kenney is to call for. Mr. Jones says Jo[h]n mc David ought to find out Dally of Com[m]anassig. Desires his opinion about Mr. Jones's bill of improvements and his claim for allowance for the boards. Mr. Mason should pay the £20 charged by him for half a year's salary. The charge for the return of moneys ought to be paid the writer also. Mr. Jones says there is £20 due from Mr. Hassett. Will not be concluded by his own opinion, and refers to him every particular in this letter, and the waifs and strays, felons' goods, fines, amercements, etc.

London,
15 February.

Almost forgot to direct him to enquire into Mr. Jones's purchase of Mr. Twisse's lease—whether he should have purchased it without the writer's privity, whether he used indirect measures to force Twiss to it, etc. 102.

1681/2

467. EDWARD KENNEY TO MR. ROBERT GRIFFITH AT MRS. HODGES' . . . LONDON.

Will have full information about Mr. Jones's account by the time Jones comes to Castle Island. Is sorry he ever writ one word of Cragg. Asks that, if [he cannot] have it all, he may have part, convenient to the demesnes. There is no living there without it. A small parcel must always be kept in his lordship's hand for grazing cattle distrained, sometimes a hundred at a time; the writer cannot spare grass to them, his holdings being too narrow. There will be more than sufficient for the town.

No man can find fault with his payments. Laid out and was overcharged a full half year's rent. Returned the Christmas gale before All Saints' in a bill from Alderman Newenham of £200 and one from Mr. Burrus for £100; so was out £400 before he received one penny. Has returned for next Ladyday gale in a bill from Mr. Smart for £177 10s. 6d., besides Mr. Harris's account, which he must clear at Corke assizes (which begin 20 March). Will thence return what is due of the whole year, although the tenants will be in arrears at least £150, some of which he will not receive till the Island fair.

His lordship intimated that his money lying in the writer's hands may be advantageous in London to the writer. It may be when in twenty-four hours a man may command in his money, but not in Kerry. Never wanted money or a friend to supply him. Exchange is oftener above ten than under nine [per cent]. If his lordship has friends in London that are merchants and would give the writer commissions to buy wool, beef, tallow, butter, hides, or leather, he would contrive exchange cheaper.

Immediately after Corke assizes he and his wife go to Kerry to repair the house and sow their garden, in order to a final removal in May. Is certain Mr. Harris gives from Dublin account of the suit with Sullevane. Will hear next Friday Capt. Meade's progress with the writ of possession; fears the sheriff, Mr. Hasset, will not be candid. Desires speedy answer about Bally mc Adam, about Morish Fitz Gerald's letter, and John Cahane's petition.

Curruragh,
28 February.

Jottings before sealing: Stephen Smith in rent-roll £32 per annum; his brother Josiah avers he never paid but £30. Wm. Perkinson £11 11s. in rent-roll; Josiah Smith [avers *omitted*] he paid but £11 2s., and that Mr. Wms. allowed all the taxes to Josiah.

Armorial seal 280.

1681/2

468. [LORD HERBERT] TO LORD BULKELEY, VISCOUNT CASHALLS, AT BARNEHILL, ANGLESEY. *Contemporary copy.*

Lord Willoughby will "suddenly" send a servant to Bewmaris with some conveyances to be executed by Mr. Owen Hughes (as one of Lady Wynne's executors) of Mr. Conningsby Williams' lands in Cherbury. This concerning the writer, he desires he would order some of his servants to be witnesses, that he be not at the charge of sending a servant of his own . . .

11 March. *HM*2.23/39.

"Barnehill" is, of course, Baron Hill, Beaumaris. Lord Willoughby was married to Mary, daughter of Sir Richard Wynn of Gwydir. Coningsby Williams, of Glan-y-Gors, Denbighshire, was an Anglesey landowner through his marriage to Margaret Owen, the direct descendant of the Penmynydd Tudors, by virtue of which he had the Penmynydd estate for life.

1682

469. EDWARD KENNEY TO MR. ROBERT GRIFFITH AT MRS. HODGE'S . . . LONDON.

Encloses his accounts for the year's rent due 29 September last. Has vouchers for every penny of the charge of Sullevan's suit. Charges £9 p.c. exchange for one bill; could exchange now for £7½ p.c., but his lordship wrote then for money. Desires immediate notice as soon as his bills come to hand, for the miscarriage of a bill may undo him. Hopes henceforward there will be no deductions since Sullevan's suit is at an end. Has got Mr. Henry Turner, nephew to the Lord Chancellor, as counsel for his lordship, who should advise [about inserting a clause] to make "the Dragon" give security for costs before admittance further; and [about depositing] the lease in Chancery to be forthcoming if Sullevan be indicted for the forgery. Has received about £24 more, but much is due of last year's arrears, of which he will receive what he can at Kerry. Desires to know of any want of method in his accounts.

Curruragh,
18 April. *Armorial seal* 281.

1682

470. Hen. Turner to Lord Herbert.

Begs pardon for not giving him more serviceable assistance; the reasonableness of his cause wanted but little aid to defend it. Hopes he will be quiet from any disturbance Mr. Sullivane can give him. Moved the Court of Chancery this day and informed them of Lord Herbert's obedience to their commands. Delivered the pretended lease to Mr. Sullivane into court, where it is to be kept in the hands of the register. Acknowledges his of 8 April.

Dublin,
9 "April".

Endorsed: Mr. Turner, counsellor in Dublin. Answered to Mr. Harries, 3 June. 99.

The correct date must be May, not April.

1682

471. [Lord Herbert] to Mr. Kenney. *Contemporary copy.*

Finds he received the sums charged in Kenney's account, and that he has paid those charged to the writer's servant Griffith. Expects the expenses of the lawsuit against Sullevane to be made out by acquittances, etc. Wonders—having been at so vast expense to dispossess Sullevane—how Kenney had not taken measures to receive the rent, and charged Anaghmore £18 2s. in arrears. Finds a difference between Kenney and Mr. Jones of £7 6s. 9d. in Ladyday gale; prays him rectify it while Jones is there and receive his reasons why the demesnes [etc.] were underset £15 12s. 6d. He should take a course agreeable to justice and the writer's interest over Bally mc Adam arrear; will not trouble his sister Browne in it. It is a mystery how Mr. Wm. Kenney, Mr. Crafts, and Don. Mc Phillip are without duties; prays him set it aright. Expects to find him punctual for the future.

London,
23 May.

Endorsed: Sent 6 June with letter of attorney to grant leases of the mills, the instrument confirming common of mountain, and order to pay Mr. Fitz Herbert's salary. 581.

A copy of the instrument confirming common of mountain is appended. The order to pay FitzHerbert's salary is the next letter.

1682

472. [Lord] Herbert to Edward Kenney, esq. *Contemporary copy.*

Formerly directed him to decline payment of the annuity and salary to the writer's cousin Francis Fitz-Herbert, esq., till the writer be saved harmless from a debt of Fitzherbert's in this kingdom; since when he has received by his order £20 towards indemnifying him from that debt. Therefore orders him to pay and continue paying the said annuity and salary.

23 May.

Endorsed: The original not returned; Kenney ought to return this. 103.

1682

473. EDWARD KENNEY TO MR. ROBERT GRIFFITH AT MRS. HODGES' . . . LONDON.

About Mr. Hasset's account he must consult Mr. Jones, who will stay in Kerry until the writer goes back towards midsummer. The sheriff of Kerry has a process to levy £54 on the estate for the post-fine. Could not raise so much after paying the crown rent, and was forced to "make all the friends I could" to get him to write to Mr. Harris, who, with Mr. Nethercot, his lordship's attorney in the Common Pleas, assures him it is really due, and that this is never paid or levied any other way but by the sheriff. Entered bond to pay midsummer day. Out of this first quarter's payment there are already that £54 and £20 10s. crown rent; but will endeavour to return £300.

Sent the whole year's account due Michaelmas last to his lordship and a copy to Griffith. Knows Annaghmore and Currymore will be charged in a note of arrears. The first must be recovered in Chancery; the other Mr. Mason has referred to his lordship—will distrain as soon as the note is returned. Has written his "result" about Cragg to Griffith; is told Mr. Jones has given large promises of it to one Anthony Palmer and other of his "Coronyes". Hopes his lordship will not dispose of his concerns here upon Mr. Jones's recommendation while the writer is agent. Mr. Jones is close in his business; he came armed with originals or copies of all the letters that mentioned him, which people in Kerry much admired at.

Jones will not part with the lease of Killbanavan under £100, which he says cost him £86—he says it is the least he can have for his journey into Ireland. Mr. Fitz Herbert has been very ill of the gout in co. Wicklow, near Dublin, since October, without hope of perfectly recovering, and has not written since; would have given this account sooner, but he might think the writer had some concern of his own in it. But the country is grown very disorderly for want of punishments in the courts and trials. Is sorry for his lordship's long disappointment in Smart's bill; the drawer dealt treacherously, for which he shall give a severe account.

Corke,
26 May. 282.

1682

474. EDWARD KENNEY TO MR. GRIFFITH.

Has this post sent Lord Herbert a bill of exchange for £300 payable at fourteen days' sight, drawn by Alderman Newenham of Corke on Mr. William Yate upon the Bridge, London. £54 to the sheriff of co. Kerry for the post-fine, £20 10s. crown rent long since paid, and £22 10s. exchange for this £300 at £7 10s. per cent is in all £397. But has not as yet, "as I am a Christian", received above £150 from the tenants. Will always, with God's assistance, keep the limit his lordship has appointed. Griffith is at least five letters in the writer's debt.

Corke,
13 June. 283.

[16]82

475. EDWARD KENNEY TO MR. ROBERT GRIFFITH AT MRS. HODGES' . . . LONDON.

Supposes Mr. Harris has given satisfaction as to the post-fine. Supposes the bills for £300 are come. A packet from Griffith by Mr. Harris is gone by to Tralee; will have it Sunday, for he, his wife, and family are just ready to mount for Kerry, and the woman all in tears to part from her friends—hopes time will wear off these troubles. Mr. Fitz Herbert's death has put an end to his annuity and salary. All things relating to Mr. Jones's accounts and Mr. Hassett's, etc., shall be answered before Jones leaves. Hardly had time to write this much, but from Kerry his epistles will try Griffith's wind, which Griffith never does to him—wisely, foreseeing the inconveniences to a man of his bulk.

Curruragh,
22 June. 284.

1682

476. [LORD] HERBERT TO MR. KENNEY. *Contemporary copy.*

Received the bill for £300. He will have received a discharge for his last year's agency with the order for common of mount[ain], power to set leases to the millers, and order about Mr. Fitz Herbert['s] annuity, which last he should remit back, for he hears the gentleman is dead. Will send him power to be seneschal of the courts. In a letter Mr. Wilson desires consent to a "Regall Union" of the writer's four parishes, which he says should be perfected by August, otherwise right of presentation, by virtue of a late act of Parliament, returns to the King. But Wilson's own interest is so concerned that he is to give satisfaction that the business is as he represents it. If the writer receives a pet[it]ionary certificate from Kenney, Mr. Wilson, and the tenants, which he will have registered in his court, then he empowers Kenney to deliver the enclosed parchment to Mr. Wilson. But if omitting the union does not appear dangerous or the tenants are dissatisfied or in danger of being prejudiced by it, then the enclosed is to be returned.

27 June. 104a.

1682

477. [LORD] HERBERT TO MR. WILSON. *Contemporary copy.*

His letter of 23 May put a great surprise upon the writer by telling him that his right of presentation to his parishes in Kerry is in danger of returning to the King—and this not till it is almost impossible to prevent it. He allows the writer no time to enquire into the necessity of such a consent as he desires, nor whether there be such an act of Parliament. Will not willingly act to the prejudice of his tenants, but they may suffer wrong and inconvenience by such a union, for his seigniory is large and well-peopled, and though the Protestants are not many yet, the government may in time think of measures to bring over the poor ignorants from their blindness. Cannot apprehend how he so lately came to the knowledge of a thing that so particularly concerns him, having lived so long upon the place, nor how he could promise himself the writer's consent without the advice of his agent and the pet[it]ionary consent of the most considerable tenants. However, he would not be too forward to doubt Wilson's integrity, so has enclosed his consent to Mr. Kenney, to be delivered if he be satisfied . . .

27 June. 104b.

[1682]

478. MARY MEADE TO [LORD HERBERT].

Her second son, John Herbert, is as likely a young man to make a scholar as any in those parts. He makes good verse in English and Latin, and has made progress in the Greek. His father's and her ambition was and is to make their children serviceable to his lordship's family. Requests he would receive him into his care and endeavour to get him a King's scholar's place at Westminister School. He shall have £20 per annum, if it be competent allowance, until he be better provided for Oxford. Youths in his condition are to be forwarded by the favour of noble persons, and his lordship, on many accounts, is entitled his patron. If he is pleased to condescend, he should send [to] her or her brother Kenney by post, and she will send him to London with all expedition

Tigsaxon,

1 July. 269.

1682

479. EDWARD KENNEY TO LORD HERBERTT AT MRS. HODGES' . . . LONDON.

Received the instrument for the common of mountains, [etc.] Could not avoid returning Annaghmor in arrear; could neither distrain nor sue while the suit with Sullevan depended. It can only be recovered in Chancery. Has execution for the costs at common law, but ordered Mr. Harris not to renew it until the long vacation—will have him then though it cost £5 of the writer's own money. Has Mr. Harris's acquittances; it is not customary to receive acquittances from counsel. Mr. Fitz H[er]b[er]tt engaged that if Lord Herbert did not allow his fee he would repay it. Took no receipts from those that gave bills of exchange. The difference between his account and Mr. Jones's about Ladyday 1681 is that Mr. Jones was tenant then to Celgorum for £5 10s. that gale; the remainder is Tullylegg, whereon the felon's goods were taken. He shall have from Mr. Jones his reasons why the demesnes, etc., were underset £15 12s. 6d. As to those charged without duties, Mr. Will Kenney first took Curranes for £44 rent and 13s. 4d. duties, but at the request of Capt. Browne and the others that then set the land he raised the rent to £46 and two capons. As to Mr. Croffts for Clashganiff, his duties are 2s. 6d. Donnough mac Phillip's is an old lease without duties. Will do what he thinks advisable about Ballyma Adam. Will send by the first conveniency a hundredweight of the black slat. It is the best in Ireland and much used for inward bruises. One of old Twisse's sons has served Mr. Jones with a subpoena about Killbanavan and thinks to oust him. It is best to let them try it out a little in the Chancery, then both will be weary of it. Encloses copy of young Richard Twisse's account of Killbanavan upon oath.

Castle Island,
1 July.

The account: How Mr. Jones got Killbanavan from Richard Twisse: He went several times upon Killenterrna with swords and pistols and commanded the said Richard with his wife and family to turn out of the lands. Notwithstanding, Ricd. kept in possession until all his and his tenants' corn was in stacks upon the fields. Then Jones "putt Crosses in all the Stackes", and would not permit Richd. nor his tenants to put the corn in one "Haggartt" to save it from stealing and from cattle. Whereupon twenty families were ready to famish if the said Richd. had not sold Jones the lands of Killbanavan to salve the poor peoples' lives. And all he had for it was gone in arrears of rent. The whole right title that he purchased belongs really to his lordship.

Present: Morish Conno[r] Richard Twisse his mark

288a.

Black Irish slate was known to the apothecaries as *lapis Hibernicus*.

1682

480. EDWARD KENNEY TO MR. ROBERTT GRIFFITH AT MRS. HODGES' . . . LONDON.

The post-fine was due the 24th instant (*sic*), but he has not received half the sum although he has distrained most of the estate. Has received several duns from the sheriff. Have not had a worse year these fifteen years. Two more, and such early payments will create a surrender of many of the late leases, eager as they were for them. Received the papers concerning Mr. Fiz Herbert (who died much in debt). The want of a seneschal sends good grist to the assizes now hasting. Has taken upon himself to be seneschal; hopes his lordship will confirm it, for it was absolutely necessary to keep the people from ruining one another.

As for Cragg, if it must go . . . But that part south of the river is absolutely necessary for the writer or whoever lives in this house and holds the demesnes. Will provide for Evan Jones's new house out of it; no other house of the town is near. Mr. Willson, as tenant to the widow, enjoys half the north part, the [only] part convenient to the inhabitants; if Mr. Willson has it it is but reasonable he should provide for three or four houses of the town on his land of Bohirnamalutt. For the remainder, he thinks Dr. Horan (a civilian, and a good benefactor to the town), Mr. Anthony Mulshnogg (a physician and a very necessary man to the town and country), and Tho. Mc Craith (recorder of his lordship's courts) are fittest to have it. The lease expires 25 March next. Will take all care to prevent law-suits, for one in an age is enough. His lordship's answer to Mr. Nagle shows his confidence in the writer. Can say nothing as to the deceased Lord's promise of the recordership to John Fitz Gerald; the person now employed behaves well enough. His lordship promised the lease of Canguilly to Donnogh mc Phillip, and no man can pay better; the full value is £20 rent, 13s. 4d. duties, and £3 heriot. The lease will be out 1 November 1683. Capt. Browne has a lease of Killmury for twenty-one years, many unexpired. Has often been solicited to set a lease of a tenement in town to Alice Fitz Gerald, but answered that he had no power; hears they are sending his lordship a petition about it. She is a good tenant and a civil woman; they promise "large matters of Buildeing".

Castle Island,
1 July. *Two armorial seals* 285.

[16]82

481. EDWARD KENNEY TO MR. ROBERT GRIFFITH AT MRS. HODGE'S . . . LONDON.

Hears from "my Lord" that he shall have power to be seneschal next post, also that he will do the writer all reasonable favours. But nothing can have the same gust as the one thing he is denied. Is the more troubled at its being given to another, who is now setting of it, as he (so he is told) cannot pretend to desert. If he had £400 per annum out of a family he would not thwart his lordship's agent in so inconsiderable a thing. Must take time to consider the business of the union of the four parishes, for a miscarriage would wholly reflect on him—his lordship has wholly referred it to him and strait-laced him in his instruction. Heard a murmur yesterday that the parish of Killinterne is impropriate and his lordship impropriator, and that Lord Baltinglass enjoyed it as such by his lease. Others say the then incumbent gave it to Lady Baltinglass to buy pins. The only prejudice the union may do is that his lordship or his heirs may have a mind to place two persons in it—after the country is better planted it may be a competent living for two. Mr. Wilson [suggests] it was his "bussiness" that put those scruples into his lordship. Wonders he does not give account of her ladyship being with child—heard it from others. Fears neither corn, firing, nor hay will be salved this year, and it is as bad in co. Corke.

Castle Island,
12 July. 286.

[16]82

482. THO. MEADE TO [EDWARD KENNEY]. *Copy on the dorse of No. 484.*

As to Mr. Willson's business, the uniting of those parishes may be a real convenience to him. Perhaps without it he will not be able to hold so many of that worth [unless], the parishioners requiring it, he set curates, and so be at more charge. It can't harm Lord Herbert's title. Thinks Mr. Willson suggested amiss to his lordship in saying he could not unite the livings unless by Michaelmas next. The parishioners cannot suffer unless it makes some come [far] to service, [so] that they stay at home and "jour" at their parson. Perceives Lord Herbert would not have it passed unless necessary to preserve his right to the presentation. Advises him to let him know his safety (the act empowering but not compelling) before he gives Mr. Wilson Lord Herbert's assent. His and his wife's service to him, his lady, and their little ones.

14 July.

'Tis the opinion of his brother Sir Jo. Meade that Lord Herbert's title cannot be impaired though there be no union. As to Mr. Willson's objection that unless his lordship forwards this union he will be forced to present four incumbents and the parishioners to build four churches, how did he himself get them all? If each parish be willing to raise and support a church, why should he force them to come to the church he thinks fit to erect unless equally convenient to all the parishes?

287b.

1682

483. ROBT. BROWNE TO MR. KENNEY. *Copy on the dorse of No. 484.*

Has made the following proposals to the now Lord Herbert rather than be at trouble at law, to justify the agreement made with Mr. John Blen[er] Hasset pursuant to the directions of the late Lord Ed. Herbert: Lord Herbert abating £10 a year out of the rent of Gortagh I Glynny and giving the writer a clause in his lease that as often as any life dies (paying a half year's rent as fine) he or his assigns should add another, and so for ever; and giving the writer up his deeds now in his lordship's or Mr. Roger Jones's custody; and abating the arrears (which he denies to be due) unless his chief-rent be £8 a year as in the deed. The writer will release to his lordship the commons of mountain for cattle without number, the sixteen acres in the east of West Meanus wood, Killaly Begg, and the part of Farrenybracke, Overdurtoge, now unjustly kept from the writer, and which upon wheedles by former agents he has neglected to sue for hitherto. Sent these proposals by Mr. Read and showed him Mr. Hasset's agreement, by virtue of which the writer released about £400 mean rate . . . If his lordship does not accept, the writer is to deliver the cattle which Mr. Jones took up for arrears . . . and take his course at law.

Meanus,
25 July. 287a

1682

484. EDWARD KENNEY TO MR. ROBT. GRIFFITH AT MRS. HODGES' . . . LONDON.

Sends copy of a letter from Mr. Robt. Brown, who has a right to most of the things he claims, but could never know it if some that were too near Lord Herbert had not "discovered" it. Would like an answer that he may take order about the arrear. Lord Herbert had better make some end with him than wage law . . . Mr. Brown has sold his interest in this last farm and got £50 by it. As to the union of the parishes, he refers him to Mr. Tho. Meade's letter and Sir John Meade's opinion—he is one of the greatest lawyers of this kingdom. Will keep Lord Herbert's assent until he receives his commands to give it to Mr. Willson. Has seldom seen one day of fair weather since he came here.

Castle Island,
28 July. 287c.

[16]82

485. EDWARD KENNEY TO LORD HERBERT AT MRS. HODGES' . . . LONDON.

Acknowledges the power for keeping the courts; will not spare pains or cost to recover their ancient lustre and authority. The disrespect to the courts may be seen in this: Of above sixty attachments returned in the two last court days there were not above five appearances, which Macraith says was more than have appeared these eight months. Hopes about 1 November to give a good account of [the business] of payment to the writer's father; desires order whether to pay the interest if he cannot pay the principal, and will take his orders in the strictest sense. Sent copy of a letter from Mr. Robert Browne; it were better to comply than wage law with so troublesome an antagonist.

Castle Island,
28 July. 289.

1682

486. [ROBERT GRIFFITH] TO MR. KENNEY. *Draft.*

Has commands to answer two letters of the 1st. The rent of An[n]aghmore should be recovered the speediest way with as little vexation as can be. His lordship does not expect acquittances for counsels' fees or exchange of money, and does not disallow Mr. Fitz Herbert's fees; he only desires everything as plain as possible. He approves that Jones and Twiss be for a while left to dispute their titles, and is assured Balli-mc Adam will be settled to his interest since it is left to Kenney, who knows the whole intrigue, whereas he, a stranger thereto, might act in his own wrong. Kenney's advice on the division of the Cragg seems reasonable. His lordship is satisfied with his information about Mr. John FitzGerald's demands, and will send his answer if he receives Alice Fitz Gerald's petition. He is pleased with his care in enquiring into the union of parishes, and would have him continue to enquire into the act which Mr. Wilson conceives to endanger his lordship's interest, and particularly whether Killinterne be impropriate. His lordship has received a letter from Madam Mead proposing that he has Mr. John Herbert admitted King's scholar; is sorry at present he cannot be serviceable in that respect, and knows Kenney can satisfy his sister of that. Yet it would be great satisfaction to him to find any of cousin Tho. Herbert's children qualified for anything in the donative of himself or any friend.

29 July.

Addition by Lord Herbert: "I approve of . . . this L're as writ by my Commands". Would have him keep the assent to the union till he [hears further]. 288b.

[c. 1682]

487. PETITION OF JANE, WIDOW OF RICHARD TWISS, TO LORD HERBERT.

He was pleased, in consideration of her husband's services and sufferings, to allow him £4 per annum abatement of his rent of Killinterna Farm, but he enjoyed it only for one year, his death happening soon after. Craves his kindness for her relief . . . 261.

Details of Lord Herbert's response to this petition will be found in No. 604.

[1682]

488. EDWARD KENNEY TO LORD HERBERT AT MRS. HODGES' . . . LONDON.

There is a small parcel of land in the tenure of Richd. Twiss called Inchiboy, which, with a garden in town, was demised for £2 6s. 8d. per annum. It has been in arrears ever since the garden was taken in by the late Lord Herbert for the convenience of this house. The lease is out 25 March next. Twiss's children do not concern themselves in it, but have left the poor tenants that "plowed on sheafe" in the lurch for the rent. There is no house or cabin. It lies most convenient to Jo[h]n Warren, an honest Englishman, and he is the fittest to be preferred to it. The outside rent is £3 and 3s. 4d. duties and 10s. heriot; went with two or three more to take an exact view of it.

Capt. Browne has been returned tenant at 6s. 8d. per annum to a small tenement in town, now waste and not one stick and hardly a stone standing on it; intends to re-enter at Michaelmas. One Tho. Fz Gerrald, a civil young man in this town, desires to be tenant to it. Asks power to set to farm these two, together with Cragg and Cangully.

[mid-September]. 2902.

This letter bears the London postmark of 25 September.

1682

489. RO. JONES TO LORD HERBERT AT HIS HOUSE OVER AGAINST THE CROSS KEYS IN THE OLD PALL MALL, LONDON.

Was served with a subpoena in the Chancery of the Exchequer of England to appear at Westmr. next Michaelmas at the suit of John, Lord Brereton, and others. Presumes it concerns his lordship. Sent to Mr. Fowle to order an attorney. Hopes to be in England before next term. Must attend a vexatious suit in Chancery here by George Twisse for the interest the writer purchased of his father, to whom he paid £86. With the charge he has been at it already amounts to £100, a sum too large to be cheated of. Is informed that Twiss designs for England to get money from Lord Herbert to carry on his suit; hopes he will not countenance him. Twiss says that hitherto Mr. Edward Kenny has supplied him with money—cannot imagine why. Has had troubles and tricks enough since he came hither, but does not question in a short time to put an end to them and leave. It will not be amiss to have some person by when Lord Herbert discourses Twiss, lest he proves "an affidavitt man", as well as his father and young Sullevane. Hears old Sullevane intends to proceed in his Chancery suit, and that Twiss is a creature of that family.

Castle Island,
7 October. 100.

1682

490. R. G. TO [EDWARD KENNEY]. *Draft.*

"My Lord" received his about setting Incheboy, etc., to Warren, Capt. Brown's tenement in town to Fitz Gerrald, and Canngully and Cragg to others. But his lordship has taken a resolution to execute leases himself, and would have him report what is most advantageous, with a draft of a lease most binding according to the customs of that country; he will then send leases to be executed. His lordship has received a bill of exchange of £200 on twenty days' sight. In respect it is so late and on so long a sight, he promises himself he will "suddenly" receive the remainder of that gale. Since Mr. Read has not sent [Kenney] an abstract of the leases, he will prepare one himself; is sensible he is at a great loss without such.

21 October. 290b

1682

491. CHARLES MASON TO MR. ROBERT GREEFITH AT LORD HERBERT'S LODGING.

Acknowledges his favours and entreats him to persuade his lordship to accept his answer to Mr. Jones, who designs no good to his lordship, and unjustly procured the writer's removal from his employment to advance himself to it.

Castle Island,
22 October. *Seal of a crest* 582.

1682

492. CHARLES MASON TO LORD HERBERT.

Troubles him in behalf of his poor sister. Entreats him to empower Mr. Kenny to set her a lease for two small tenements she holds in this town. Begs a favourable construction on his answer to Mr. Jones's objections to his accounts. There was malice in Jones procured by the writer's endeavour to defend Madam Browne from being forced to pay £60 unjustly. The case is: Mr. Wm. Browne enters into bond to pay one John Prichard £60 when the former recovers a parcel of land that Prichard pretended a right to; Browne never possessed the land and died before suing Prichard for the bond; Jones procured the bond from Prichard with a letter of attorney to sue Madam Browne as executrix to her husband, he to have half. This is the justice of that man that durst sue his master's sister upon such grounds. Will say nothing as to the wrong done old Twiss, lest it be thought malice.

Was sued the last two assizes by Widow Garold for a small parcel that he enclosed by his late lordship's command. Because Mr. Kenny could do nothing in it the judges ordered another reference to two gentlemen who will publish their award speedily, upon which the writer will be carried to prison, where he must remain unless his lordship orders Mr. Kenny to satisfy the widow. Mr. Jones told Lord Herbert the widow was fully satisfied, but made nothing out before the referees.

8 November. 583.

1682

493. EDWARD KENNEY TO MR. ROBERT GRIFFITH AT MRS. HODGE'S . . . LONDON.

Ordered Tom Macraith to tell him of the death of the writer's wife, who was buried at Castle Island the 24th of last month, leaving him seven sons and two daughters. Has now the greatest weight of business he ever had, for in September last a kinsman in Wexford died, leaving his whole estate (this year £600, in five or six years £1,000 per annum) to his only daughter Frances Kenney and the heirs male of her body provided she marry the writer's eldest son Edwd. Kenney; and if she refuse she is to have £2,000 portion, the estate going to the writer's son and his heirs male. He named one Mr. Hore overseer of the estate during her minority (she being but eleven and a half), and one Mr. Carew overseer of her education, desiring that it be with one of his sisters in Dublin—this to prevent her coming into the mother's hands, who is a dissenter, and has raised many rubs.

Cannot give account of the leases of Inchyboy, Caungully, Cragg, etc., until he is in the Castle Island in January. As to his lordship's expectation of the remainder of the Michaelmas payment, £100, it was paid thus: Post-fine £54, exchange of two bills £34 10s., King's rent £20. Would nevertheless have sent £100 had his letter overtaken him in Munster. Will endeavour to send £400 entire at Christmas. But merchants will seldom draw at less than twenty-one days for great sums. Mr. Harris sent letters from his lordship or Griffith, and one to Mr. Jones; missed them on the road. Has been troubled with a great cold and the gout since he came here. Wishes his lordship would come into Ireland next summer.

Dublin,
25 November. 292.

Kenney's kinsman in Wexford was Colonel Richard Kenney of Edermine, who had died on October 1st.

1682

494. Ro. Jones to Mr. Robert Griffith at Lord Herbert's house over against the Cross Keys in the Old Palmal, London.

Came last week into this country and shortly designs to see him. Hopes Mr. Kenny has told his lordship that all objections to the writer's Irish accounts are cleared; presumes he may have both his money from Mr. Fowle and a discharge. Mr. Read was gone for Monmouthsh'r, but his wife has sent by Floyd the carrier, now on the road, two pots of venison for Griffith and his lordship's coachman. Prays to be informed whether Lord Brereton makes the writer party to his bill against Lord Herbert. Lord Brereton puts him to trouble and charge; cannot yet tell how to be reimbursed. Thanks for all the pains he took to write to him in Irland.

Little Hem,
25 December. 584.

1682/3

495. [Robert Griffith] to Mr. Kenney. *Draft.*

"My Lord" is so wearied with the importunities of one Mr. Nagle in behalf of John Fitz Gerald that he refers it to Kenney; one Mr. Bateman is to discourse him in it. Nagle says Kenney denied to make any report in the business at the instance of John Fitz Gerald. Fitz

Gerald offers £5 per annum for the clerk of the markets' place, which his lordship has granted to Kenney without any account—though because he would not be ignorant of any profits arising out of his estate he desires a faithful particular of the profits the place yields *communibus annis*. His lordship desires an exact description of that part of the Cragg bordering on the town, with a particular of those houses that may be advantaged by having parcels of it, and, in case he should be disposed to live there, whether that tenement or part of it should be reserved to augment the demesnes; also whether some acres should be reserved for the building of new houses, as Lord Edward, by Jo[h]n Deelis's lease, provided. He should send account of Jo[h]n Fitz Gerald's condition in the world, and what improvements his father or he have made upon Cragg, Cawnguilly, Tulligibin, or other part of his lordship's estate (which his lordship mightily insists upon), and his ancestors' services to the family. He is to inform also how far the bargain the Deelises have had comes short of rewarding their services. How many years are unexpired of the lease of Kilcushney, etc.?

London,
2 January. 107.

1682/3

496. Rob. Griffith to [Roger Jones]. *Draft.*

His of 25 December came not till 10 January. Read it to "my Lord", who received no account of the business from Mr. Kenney, and cannot believe that [Jones] would, after so long in Ireland, have returned without some satisfaction under Mr. Kenney's hand—if he has not, he should not undertake a London journey for the purpose he mentions. His lordship does not understand how he can be at charges in Lord Breret[o]n's business; if he has, he cannot be at a loss how to be reimbursed. If the writer's Irish correspondence with him does not deserve thanks it hardly merits the contrary; does not fawn upon any, but nor does he intend any a prejudice.

London,
13 January. 585

1682/3

497. Edward Kenney to Mr. Robert Griffith at Mrs. Hodge's . . . London.

Left Dublin and steered to Wexford where he got possession of Capt. Kenney's estate. Got as far as his sister Supple's, near Youghall, by 20 December, when his journey and trouble of mind put him into a fever; is now in his journey home to Castle Island. Gave his nephew Herbert order to return Christmas gale's rent, but when the writer's back was turned the tenants would not pay; so he met at Corke but £80 instead of £300 or £400. Is ashamed to write without a bill enclosed. "Good mr. Griffith, bring me off this time, for if yow knew what a foot-ball fortune has made me of late . . ."

Corke,
16 January. 294.

1682/3

498. [LORD HERBERT] TO EDWARD KENNEY, ESQ., AT CASTLE ISLAND. *Draft.*

Directed him on 15 February 1681/2 to examine Mr. Roger Jones's answers to objections to his accounts . . . He is to make his report, deliver one part to Mr. Roger Jones, and send another to the writer, so that Mr. Jones has no more fruitless journeys.

London,
6 February.

Added is a copy of a note to John Read regarding money due from Jones. 105.

1682/3

499. EDWARD KENNEY TO MR. ROBERT GRIFFITH AT MRS. HODGE'S . . . LONDON.

Mr. Jones was so taken up with great company in this country that he was not at leisure to look after trifles, "as all his bussines with my Ld. Herbert was made"; he had not finished with Mr. Mason when the writer went to Dublin. It is reported Jones carried a budget-full of information against the writer; if he fails to make his charge good he will repent it.

Sends copy of the lease of Killcusney from Edward, Lord Herbert, to Morrish Fz Gerrald; has in his custody Fz Gerrald's assignment to Capt. Browne. Is advised that this instrument with possession is a good lease; but will try for it if his lordship be otherwise advised. Cannot deliver them up because they came into his possession by a trust he will not violate.

Would not have his lordship think he is so low that he would be so solicitous for a farm purely for the gain; looks after his conveniency, and none is so [convenient] to him but Cragg, etc. Does not doubt his lordship will set him the south part, for without it he can have neither bread nor beer, which if he is forced to buy as hitherto for his great charge of children and servants it will drain him of what little he has coming in. To be baffled by such a scoundrel as his opposer—never writes on it but is almost transported. Prays him use his interest—has not the face to beg from his lordship for himself. His improvements will be great on it; has laid out £40 already on the demesnes. Has often desired to know if Lady Herbert be with child (as they are informed).

Castle Island,
7 February.

An abstract of the lease to Morrish Fz Gerrald follows.
Note added: Mr. Willson is well recovered. 295.

1682/3

500. R. G. to MR. KENNEY. Enclosed to Mr. Harries. *Draft.*

He will receive a letter from his lordship with a protest upon his last bill of £300, which is much to his lordship's inconveniency . . . His lordship expects him to write oftener for the future. Mr. Jones is now in town. Hears Mr. Wilson has a patent from the faculty of the parishes for his own life. Kenney writes nothing of this, though his letter brings account of Mr. Wilson's sickness. His lordship times payments depending upon the punctuality of Kenney's returns, failure whereof will prejudice him.

10 February. 106a.

1682/3

501. [LORD HERBERT] TO MR. HARRYES. *Part only of a draft.*

. . . Sees no necessity of further concerning himself in the business of the union of the parishes, since Mr. Wilson is silent . . . Before he can do anything in Mr. Browne's proposals he wants a copy of the agreement between the writer's brother and Browne and an assurance of Browne's title, which seems to be in question by Mrs. Drew.

13 February. 106b.

[1683]

502. CHARLES MASON TO LORD HERBERT AT MRS. HODGE'S . . . LONDON.

Is now towards his latter end, and intends to return and spend the rest of his time in the place of his birth. When accepted as tenant to part of this seigniory he was obliged not to dispose of it without his consent. Entreats a line to that purpose. Will not dispose of it but to a good tenant and Protestant. 620A.

1683

503. EDWARD KENNEY TO [LORD HERBERT]. *Copy appended to No.* 504.

Encloses a list of those lands which best answer the intent of his lordship's letter of 12 June. The first parcel, marked "1", includes all the new-acquired estate, which will not sell as well as the old unless he warrants it. This will go off at ten years' purchase . . . It lies north-east of the town. The second parcel, marked "2", is next to Mr. Trant's concerns, and is the cream of the estate (except the demesnes) and is worth twelve years' purchase. This lies north-west of the town. The third parcel, marked "3", is what (if any) he would advise him to part from. Doubts whether it will come to ten years' purchase. It lies south of the town, three miles just.

It is a thousand pities to dismember this good manor, being now a circumference, and the manor-house the centre. If he is resolved to raise money out of this Irish estate for his convenience in England, the following proposal may do as well: His present rent is £1,200 per annum; crown rent is £40 11s; agency, sending the money to Corke, postages, etc., £50; exchanges at £7 per cent, £84. Remains clear but £1,025 9s. Now for a lease of the whole for thirty-one years he may have £500 fine and £1,000 per annum paid in London exchange-free. And if he has occasion for more money he may make it a fee-farm and receive £500 more at ten years' end . . . If this is not consistent with his inclinations, he humbly begs his pardon. His father can by Christmas have £2,000 or more ready, and if his lordship can stay so long he will willingly deal with him. Does not know a man in this county that can purchase £250 per annum, and the co. Corke men do not like this county.

Castle Island,
9 July.

		Present rate	Remainder of the full value at expiration	Unexpired
		£	£	
1.	*Bally ma Adam	38	22	2 lives
	*Tully Legg	21	59	7 years
	*Killmory	45	45	1 life ?
	Killcusny	42	3	13 years
	Ardnagragh	31	10	10 years
	Cordall	20	5	3 lives
	*Carker	50	—	3 lives

2.	West Meanus	53	7	7 years
	Curanes	46	4	3 lives
	East Meanus	8	—	fee farm
	Drom Trasny	31	14	7 years
	Tully Gibin	28	5	7 years
	Knockanahagilshy	16	4	7 years
	Killbanavan	6	25	2 lives
	Bohirna Malluff	28	4	2 lives
	Carhue	7	—	7 years
	Tully Legg	21	59	7 years

This parcel comes to the demesne in a semi-circle, except Tullylegg, which is here to make about the intended sum of £250 to be disposed of.

3.	*East Cark[e]r and part of Dromaltan	32	—	3 lives
	*Middle Cark[e]r and part of Drom[a]ltan	47	—	3 lives
	*West Cark[e]r and part of Dromaltan	32	—	3 lives
	Dirine	17	3	3 lives
	Killsarcon and Inchin Cumur	55	5	7 years
	Gortacapull	41	—	3 lives
	Mullen and * Adergovall	34	—	3 lives
	Caungnilly	14	7	½ year

This is all coarse mountain and not one limestone on it. What woods are left (not worth £50, all the tenants having house-boot, plough-boot, and other boot on it) it will be hard to keep from them. Here are all the bad paymasters, having bad bargains, except Mr. Sanders and Donnough ma Phillip. Mullen and Adergorvall are £4 per annum too dear; they will be surrendered next year. Dromaltan is of the old estate, though intermixed with Carker.

*The new interest.

296a.

The table has been simplified by reducing all the values to the nearest pound. This letter introduces for the first time the business of the sale of part of the Castle Island estate to Mr. (later Sir) Patrick Trant.

1683

504. Edward Kenney to Lord Herbertt at Mrs. Hodges' . . . London.

His lordship may accept Mr. Tho. Wills of Corke as tenant to Currymore in Mr. Mason's place. Wishes the rest of this seigniory were so well tenanted. Mr. Mason has other concerns in this manor that will answer any account. Has agreed to build a market-house for £60, which he hopes will be finished by November; will send a "draught" of it. Mr. Tho. Corbett has a lease of two lives of Cahargh, which bounds the demesnes and what the writer holds of Cragg, two-thirds round. As the rest of the estate is set for long leases he advises a letter to Mr. Tho. Corbett that his lordship is informed he intends to sell his interest, and desiring the preference of it. Will take a new lease of it, allowing for the purchase money a valuable consideration over and above the present rent. Or will buy Mr. Corbett's interest, and when his lordship has occasion to live here he will surrender it with this demesne upon reasonable terms. This is not to be omitted if he has thoughts of ever living here, and for his own part he wants it much.

Castle Island,
18 July.

Begs a good construction on this, for things of this nature are subject to have the worst sense put on them. 296b.

1683

505. Edward Kenney to Lord Herbert at Mrs. Hodgee's . . . London.

Answered his and wrote duplicates the four succeeding posts. Sent two bills of exchange from Corke, and the second bills by Mr. Griffith. Could not agree with Mr. Ambrose Moor upon the value at expiration, so the division of lands is sent to his lordship, Mr. Moore to send a duplicate to Mr. Trant. Mr. Griffith and this letter will expound some marginal notes on it. Division "1", present rent £243 1s., is improvable at expiration £191. Almost all the leases expiring in 1690 are in it, with one fee-farm, *viz*, East Meanus, Killally, and Farnibrack, set for £8 but worth £60 per annum—thinks it fit to try for them once more if his lordship's leisure admits of a suit. This division is all limestone, lying in the valley, "and fare-well Mannor of Castle Island if it be sould". This is the only parcel Mr. Trant's agent aims at.

Division "2", £270 13s. 4d. present rent, is improvable but £11. The three parcels marked * are promiscuously set with the three half plough-lands of Carker, which is part of the new acquisition, which Mr. Trant will by no means meddle with. Will never advise selling the Dromaltam without Carker, which Mr. Trant alleges was set first by itself by his lordship's late commissioners for £60. Adergovall, half a plough-land of Mullen, is "on the same account" as Cark[e]r, and is undervalued accordingly. Coggery mill, together with Callosoghty mill (which last is on Kill-Mory)—the rent of both being £25 4s.—is on Dromaltan, and Dromaltan mill the better of the two. If he must sell, this division is the fittest to be sold; the blame in aftertimes will be his lordship's if he parts with any other, having so exact information beforehand. It will cause many lawsuits with his tenants if the woods on these lands be not reserved, for plough-boot, house-boot, etc., will signify nothing in case of sale. But he prays he will take some other course than an absolute sale. His lordship having promised Donn. ma[c] Phillip a lease of Caunguilly, he has petitioned to be provided in case of sale. If a sale it must be, it is to be considered whether suit and service to the courts, etc., do pass; it must not without a large consideration, if at all—it will be a very ordinary manor without it be entire. Reservation of suit and service cannot be so proper [as] if a chief-rent of 3s. 4d. or some such a plough-land be reserved.

Division "3" was placed there at the importunity of Mr. Moore, and not at all consented to by Mr. Griffith or the writer, for these lands are as inconvenient to be parted with as the first division. Any sale to Mr. Trant is so great a disgust to all the English tenants and the best of the Irish, and so great a dump upon them, that they will all be gone. Fears if he says more he may give his lordship offence.

As to Bally ma[c] Adam, Lord Anglesy intends to administer for Capt. Browne to secure a large debt due from Browne. If Madam Browne, Lord Herbert's sister, by persuasion of Mr. Mason, insists upon the old lease and so avoids Capt. Browne's, the warranty must descend upon Lord Herbert, which may create suits between him and Lord Anglesy. In the late Lord Herbert's instructions to Capt. Browne dated July 1675 are these words:

> To send over the counterparts of Mr. Sander's lease and the lease of Bally ma[c] Adam to sister Browne (which he hears Mason has), and to deliver the standing order for payment of £22 per annum to her and her heirs during the continuance of her first grant. Considers it "varde" [? *void*] in that she did not defend the writer's title, but she being his sister he is willing to stand to it.

This is demonstration of an agreement between the late lord and Madam Browne, but Mr. Mason, taking advantage of the confusion, creates all this trouble. The thing will be very uneasy between Lord Herbert and Lord Anglesy, the latter's violent agent, Mr. Pierson, having an old grudge to Capt. Browne.

There has been a great feud between David Fz Gerrald of Cordall and Morish F[z] Gerrald of Killcusny about settling of bounds, the first being a new lease and the other an old. Mr. Willson and Mr. Jones have trod the bounds to the writer's satisfaction. Begs leave once for all to acquaint him that it will be very pernicious to dispose of any of this estate, which is the second or third best manor in this kingdom. Hopes he will see it next summer.

Castle Island,
17 August. 300.

There are a number of discrepancies between this letter and No. 503. Division '1' here was '2' in the earlier letter. '2' here was '3' before, while what is here called Division '3' was probably '1' before. Other discrepancies will be noticed. Ambrose Moor seems to have been agent for Patrick Trant.

1683

506. [LORD HERBERT] TO MR. MASON. *Contemporary copy.*

Upon his former letter praying consent to his assigning his lease, he ordered him to get the matter stated and recommended by Mr. Kenney; without which he will sign no consent, as deviating from the method he resolved upon. If Mr. Kenney represents the person he would assign to as sufficient, with name, vocation, and abode, and that consent is not only no prejudice to the writer but reasonable—he will take no pleasure in perplexing the concerns of his friends and tenants. If Mason suffers meantime, it is by his own irregularity . . .

30 October.

Endorsed: . . . To Mr. Willson and Charles Mason in Ireland.

*HM*2.22/20.

1683

507. EDWARD KENNEY TO LORD HERBERT. TO BE LEFT WITH MR. JOHN ROGERS, GOLDSMITH, AT TEMPLE BAR, LONDON.

Counsellor Longan gave small encouragement to oppose Sir Vallintine Browne's patent for fairs. Has agreed with Sir Vallintin after consulting Mr. Harris that it cannot be put to any other day than the enquiry *ad quod damnum* mentions. Another writ must be taken out newly naming the days for those new fairs; but the new enquiry must be at Lord Herbert's cost, which is not so genteel of the other part. Hopes to bring it under £6. Daily expects bills from his nephew Herbert, but money is scarce in Kerry. The hopes of seeing his lordship early next spring will hinder correspondency until then.

Dublin,
23 November. 291.

1683

508. EDWARD KENNEY'S AFFIDAVIT. *Copy appended to No. 509.*

Hearing there was a suit of *ad quod damnum* executed at the instance of Sir Valantine Browne to enquire what damage it would be to have new fairs and markets at Killarny and Arras Hill in the barony of Magonihy, the deponent told him it would be a great prejudice to the fairs of Castle Island belonging to Lord Herbert, being but about five days before. Sir Valintine promised to alter the time from five days to a month before the fair of Castle Island, but since refuses to comply. The fair of Castle Island is one of the ancientest of co. Kerry. Sir Valintine Browne has already two fairs yearly at Killarny within five miles, and one at Mullahiffe in the said county within seven miles of Castle Island.

27 November. *Juratum coram me*, Hen. Berkeley
True copy: Walter Bumbery, Dep. Cor.

293a.

1683

509. EDWARD KENNEY TO LORD HERBERT. TO BE LEFT WITH MR. JOHN ROGERS, GOLDSMITH . . . LONDON.

Sends copy of an affidavit he made before a Master in Chancery to put a stop to Sir Valentine Brown's new fairs, which was so stiffly opposed by four counsel that he fee'd Sir John Meade and Mr. Pine, two King's Counsels here. Upon a debate of two hours before the Lord Chancellor, he ordered a new writ and enquiry at Lord Herbert's cost, which is all they could expect—they would have gone without but for his agreement with Sir Valentine. Wrote formerly about Mr. Mason's assigning his lease of Currymore to Mr. Thomas Wills of Corke, merchant, a good tenant and a Protestant, who, by having that concern in Lord Herbert's manor, lays out considerable sums at their fairs. Such a tenant must not be slighted; his lordship should add in his consent. Is kept here by the hourly expectation of bills—hears the money is come to Corke.

Dublin,
1 December. 293b.

[1683]

510. J. Edwards to [Lord Herbert].

The names of the gentlemen who with the writer and Mr. Harding, [Lord Herbert's] chaplain, made expression of their joy to have him reside so nigh are Mr. Kerry of Weston, Mr. Middleton of Kinton, Mr. Bradeley of Stockton, Mr. Matthews of Wotherton, Mr. Prichard of Middleton, Mr. Bray of Marton, Mr. Georg Lloyd (his lordship's deputy recorder), Mr. Georg Penbury, and Mr. Thomas Bowdler of Marton, who present their service, and will wait upon him next week—which day, shall be signified to Willm. Lateward, his bailiff.

21 December.

Hopes the wine is very good; used all interest he could to the vintner and by friends in Salop, particularly by Mr. Scholfeild, her ladyship's neighbour in Shropsheir, who was very zealous when he knew where it went.

Endorsed: Mr. Edwards of Rorington's letter of the names of those that present Mr. Wynne, 21 Dec., 1683. *HM*2.21/7.

All the places named, including Rorrington, are within the hundred of Chirbury.

[1683-4]

511. [Lord Herbert] to Mr. Wilson. *Contemporary copy.*

Thanks for his of the 13th. Will in a day or two have perfected the conveyances to Mr. Traunt; has reserved all that the nature of such bargains admits of. [Agrees] that the lands he parts with are most improvable, yet being all (Killsarcon excepted) set for three lives, the profit after so long a term in such a country is uncertain, especially [compared] to other leases improvable in six years. Wished all the woods might have been reserved, but they must make the best of Caunguilly. The sale no way touches upon the presentations.

His marginal notes in the returned papers give great satisfaction, "and shall be a Rule unto me". Will be tender of Mr. Browne's conveniency. Minds him to repeat the writer's services to Lord Kerry and Capt. St. Leager. Has no advice from Mr. Kenney or his nephew of their Welsh journey. Gathered from his servant Griffith that Wilson [comes to] Lymore, where he shall be welcome, and not likely to return alone to Castle Island. He should direct letters at Mr. John Rogers's ..... "My Service to your Sister".

[? October - April]. *HM*2.22/54.

[16]84

512. Rob. Griffith to [Lord Herbert].

Mr. Forbus says there is no news and therefore will not write till next week. Waited on Lord Newport; Mr. Andrew Newport was there. Lady Newport was abroad; purposes to wait on her about Monday. Saw Mr. Thomas Newport, who longs to write to [Lord Herbert], but will not venture it by post. Mr. Wms. will write next week; hopes to bring Trant and him together to settle "that matter". Mr. Wms.'s opinion of [Lord Herbert's] Irish patent agrees with the instructions sent Mr. Kenney. Wonders no Irish letters have come. Mr. Oliver wrote about Salter's business by post and by Mr. Moses Reynald. Will, since till next term is allowed to plead, have Mr. Wms.'s opinion upon the particulars of debts paid. Mr. Coningsby Wms. sends his service. Prays that the note on the back (*missing*) be hastened to Mr. Edwards, that they lose not the opportunity of Mr. Wms.'s being in town. [Lord Herbert's] correspondent has turned over his shop to his servant and goes for quietness' sake [to France *deleted*] beyond sea. Mr. Forbus says Mr. Charleton will be in town next week; will then take care about his commands. Cannot give a fuller account till the Thursday post.

London,
17 May. *HM*2.23/42.

"Mr. Wms." is William (later Sir William) Williams, the ex-Speaker. If by Lord Herbert's "correspondent" Rogers, the goldsmith, is meant, he did not stay long abroad, for he seems to have been back at his business in July (see No. 523).

1684

513. Edward Kenney to Lord Herbert. To be left with Mr. John Rogers . . . London.

Is troubled that at this time he must send without a bill to pay off the year's rent due Ladyday and 1 May. The country is so poor after last winter that money is not to be had until the fairs. Has no more of his own lying by. Could have borrowed if he had been in condition to go abroad—[going] to Wexford in March his horse threw him and broke two of his ribs . . .

Before he knew of the reservation in Mr. Trant's deeds for distraining for Michaelmas rent he took bonds from those tenants; hopes they will not put him to suing them. Hears of a *nisi prius* in this county next assizes between the Duke of Ormond and one Mr. Gun of this county about chief-rents. Lord Herbert shall have as little trouble in this business as any; will write more if occasion be.

Cannot join with Mr. Moore in any report about Coggery Mills; cannot consent to abate anything of the purchase money at £14 per annum *pro rata* as the land was sold. When the mill comes to Mr. Trant it will be worth double, and yields Lord Herbert's tenant Falvey not much less now. Hears the mill will be reconveyed to Lord Herbert by Mr. Trant, who will build a mill elsewhere on his estate and bind his tenants to it. The thing aimed at is to give Lord Herbert no more for the mill than it is now valued at. They value it at £20, the writer at £40—and in time Mr. Trant will make £20 per annum of it.

Mr. Robert Brown's wife is dying, so that he cannot mind businesses. Mr. Willson went yesterday to see her. The collector daily sends for the crown rent due 25 March, and neither Mr. Moore nor the writer knows how much Mr. Trant's land is to pay. Fears to be distrained daily. Hopes all the crown rent is not on his lordship's part.

His nephew Herbert, tenant to Clidane, has been served with a lease of ejectment by one Carthy that pretends to be the ancient proprietor. This thing is not new—all the great men of this province have been solicited by this fellow to assist him in it, but it never went so far before. It will blow off, for the Act of Settlement renders him incapable to sue. Will instruct Mr. Harris to appear.

Mr. Worth, Second Baron of the Exchequer here, lately brought over a commission which takes up all discourse; it is called a Commission of Grace for the Remedy of Defective Titles. (*The greater part of the commission follows verbatim here.*) It was opened and read at the Primate's house in Dublin about fifteen days since. The commissioners resolved to take time what method to proceed in. Public proclamation will be made for all parties to come in when further instructions come from His Majesty. Lord Herbert is highly concerned in it as to part of his estate—the lands the writer gave account of on another occasion, and to be added is this parcel the ejectment is brought for. He should write to London for further intelligence and the soundest advice to be had. If he understands it aright it will be a great settlement to this kingdom. He must come over or employ some person out of England, or the writer, to attend it in Dublin. [Sends] next post a copy of this for fear of miscarriage.

Castle Island,
17 May. *HM*2.22/22.

1684

514. [Lord Herbert] to Mr. Wm. Williams. *Contemporary copy.*

Has writ to Mr. Trant that on his part he refers to Williams the settling between them the value of the mills sold to him, which upon sealing were left to examination in Ireland, where their agents could not agree . . . What he does shall be conclusive to the writer. His servant is to wait for Williams's directions in his other concerns. *HM*2.22/51a.

1684

515. [Lord Herbert] to Mr. Trant. *Contemporary copy.*

Finds "our friends" in Ireland not like to agree the value of the mills, therefore desires him to name some person in London to whom he will refer it. Refers it on his part to Mr. Wms. Desires an end of it while his servant stays in town, and the money paid to Mr. John Rogers, goldsmith. His servant will inform him of some complaints of Trant's agents from the writer's tenants. Will not believe he countenances such . . . Nor agents nor tenants can make them misunderstand one another. *HM*2.22/51b.

1684

516. John Oliver to Lord Herbert at Lymore Lodge.

Encloses a *dedimus* and warrant of attorney for him to sign before two of the commissioners named, for Mr. Coningsby Williams to suffer a recovery. Mentions many more acres than, by a letter from Mr. Edwards, the estate is—Mr. Griffith could not exactly say what it was. Being an error on the right side it can do Lord Herbert no prejudice; the greater sum for the composition will not be above 3s. 4d., and altering the *dedimus* would cost 7s. 2d., besides [delay]. Begs it be sent the following post, for fear Mr. Coningsby Williams be gone out of town and his lordship lose the benefit of this term. Lord Herbert [signs] the warrant, and the commissioners under *capt. and cogn.*, and endorsing their names on the *dedimus*; the commissioners should fill up the blank when the warrant is taken. There needs no oath, as in a fine, so any two commissioners may do it.

Luxemburgh was taken by the French yesterday sennight; and the report today is that Genoa is also taken, but of this no certainty. Prays his direction about Mr. Salter.

31 May.

The commissioners are: Sir John Prise, bart., Sir Humfrey Mackworth, Mathew Prise, esq., John Edwards, esq., John Read, gent., and Moses Reynolds, gent. *HM*2.23/41.

1684

517. P. Trant to Lord Herbert at Lyme-more.

Waited with Mr. Griffith [on] Mr. Williams, and they showed him what was writ to him and to Lord Herbert about the mill, by which it was plain their agents did not intend they should agree. Therefore, as Lord Herbert does, so he leaves it solely to Mr. Williams to put a rate upon it equal and indifferent. Has not only not encouraged his agents to be disobliging to any that relates to Lord Herbert, but has desired both agents and friends in that country to behave themselves other[wise].

The cause of difference was that some gentlemen would cut what timber they pleased in the woods Lord Herbert sold him, and when restrained to the boots reserved upon Canguilly they took it ill. They have [now] accommodated the matter. But to do his agent some right: the latter told Mr. Kenny that if he would show anything from Lord Herbert, he would acquiesce in it; but he had nothing to show to warrant what he insisted upon.

A commission is lately gone for Ireland called a Commission of Defective Titles, by which it is intended to raise some money. It will be of use where one doubts his title is not very good: for a small composition he shall have as strong a grant as the King can make, and it will put by all commissions of enquiry and pleading deficiencies, etc., which of late have much disturbed people in their possessions. Grants thus made it is believed will be confirmed by act of Parliament. Has some lands he thinks to take a new patent for. It is worth Lord Herbert's consideration whether it be not fit to [thus] fortify his title to all the lands he holds by the same title as those he sold the writer, for which Lord Herbert gave a general warranty—doubts in unfavourable times he may be in some danger.

London,
3 June.

Endorsed: Mr. Patrick Traunt's letter. *HM*2.22/23.

1684

518. ROB. GRIFFITH TO LORD HERBERT AT LIMORE.

Finds nothing in the enclosed that requires immediate answer. Started a division of the crown rent, which Mr. Trant would not agree to. Does not understand the lease of ejectment about Clydane, without it be a thing created among themselves to expose a deficiency in Lord Herbert's title to the new-acquired lands; has writ to Mr. Harris and Mr. Kenney. Mr. Trant told him of this Commission of Grace. Mr. Wms. advises following Mr. Trant's opinion and accepting the "use" he can do in this; believes he will do for him as for himself. Trant has ordered his tenants to pay suits and services to Lord Herbert till he finds cause to the contrary—which is an obliging intent. Trant can serve Lord Herbert more in this than any friend he has. Fears his title to some lands there is questionable; if so he would, were it his [own], refer settling it wholly to Mr. Trant. Says this not by way of advice—his lordship knows best.

On Saturday Mr. Wms., Mr. Trant, and he met to settle the mill; thinks there will be no necessity of a Dublin attendance. Suspects the trust of some persons in Ireland. Will not now trouble him with it—but would not have him hereafter set a foot of land in Ireland by letters of attorney. Will observe every tittle in his yesterday's letter.

London.
5 June.

Seal of a monogram and motto (in Welsh)

*HM*2.22/24.

[16]84

519. [ELIZABETH, DOWAGER LADY] HERBERT, TO [LORD HERBERT].

He has given her sufficient testimony to conclude her happiness in having one of the best brothers-in-law. Is sure the world cannot tax her with ingratitude. But thinks it fit to acquaint him that if he does not speedily order her payments of her £30 a year arrears on Llyssyn, which he has assured her should never be disputable, she is advised by counsel, and is resolved, to take the first opportunity of the law and be no longer deferred by Read's persuasions.

London.
20 June. 110.

Lady Herbert was writing again in similar vein on July 18th (*Montgomeryshire Collections*, Vol. XX, p. 52); another letter from her on the same matter is dated 23 June, 1685 (*ibid.*, p. 55). The earlier letter make it clear that Lord Herbert had written a placatory reply on June 30th, 1684.

[1684]

520. JHO. READ TO LORD HERBERT AT LYMORE.

Has not been unjust to him or his tenants. Mr. Lateward knows that Smith says he will sue the writer. When he saw Lord Herbert in that passion, taking the writer as a party concerned for Smith, he told Smith he would have nothing to say or do for his concern. Will not intercede for any of them.

Armorial seal

Endorsed: 1684. 109.

[1678-91]

521. PETITION OF PHILLIP HORAN TO LORD HERBERT.

Became indebted to Mr. Redmond fz Gerald for tithes, who sent to the parish pound one large beef, price 25s., and ordered the constable to deliver it to him in satisfaction. Redmond's brother, John fz Gerald, took the said beef, not lawfully appraised, pretending he and his brother sustained more cost of court than the cow was worth, notwithstanding that Mr. Thomas ma Craith detains the price of a milch cow from the petitioner as cost of court for the same suit. Asks him to take Redmond and his brother before him to show cause, [etc., etc.].

Endorsed and initialed by Lord Herbert: To be strictly examined and redressed if Tho. Mc Craith has wronged the petitioner. 264.

1684

522. WILLIAM MATHEWS TO LORD HERBERT AT LYMORE PARK.

Long expected to receive the money due on account of Lord Herbert's brother. The reality of the debt is known to Mr. Read. Is much "at a stand" that he has so small regard to his brother's memory as to offer a composition. Is not afraid to wage law. As for the common defence of having no assets to pay—knows how to prove [otherwise]. If others have been menaced into a composition, he will not. Intends to have Mr. Serjeant Powell's advice. But hopes Lord Herbert will prevent further trouble.

Strand, at the Pewter Platter
without Temple Bar,
12 July.

Seal of a crest

Endorsed: Wm. Mathew, pewterer . . . *HM*2.23/43.

1684

523. ROB. GRIFFITH TO LORD HERBERT AT LYMORE.

Could not get the pictures till yesterday, though he has been ten times to Nello's for them. He pretends he is not paid for one frame and the case; Mr. Charlton is of another opinion. Had them too late for Montgomery carrier; sent them this day by Rogers, Ludlow carrier, to Madam Arabella at Oakeley Park, where they will be this day sevennight. At Nello's he found Mr. Howard sitting for his picture, and Madam Howard with him; their service to him and his lady. They are both for Tunbridge; if there be any news there she will write to her sister. The cuts at Lord Macklesfield's are three without frames, without which he conceives them useless . . .

Mr. Con. Wms. will suffer the recovery at Shrewsbury assizes; ordered Mr. Oliver to give the warrant of attorney to Mr. Moses Reynalds and has directed him in it. Enclosed is Mr. Williams's determination in his own hand. Much insisted to have half a year more, but no better could be obtained.

If he sends a receipt for £91 in full of the purchase money of Coggery Mill to Mr. Rogers, he will receive the money upon sight. Mr. Trant refers the following to his consideration, whether they ought not to be paid by Lord Herbert: The interest of the £2,000 Trant advanced from 25 September to 1 November, the day the deeds were executed, £12 3s. 8d. to the stationer for engrossing the deed of revocation and four skins and a half of parchment, £2 18s. 6d.; to Mr. Rice for examination of the title . . . for drawing the revocation, etc., 5 guineas; in all £20 9s. 8d. Recommends answering that he had the £2,000 pending a treaty that took effect, and part of the consideration money; that Trant had Lord Herbert at a disadvantage in the rating of the mill, and might have had a favourable bargain, besides the interest of the purchase money from sealing to this time. Can say nothing to the business of Mr. Rice; always said he deserved at least five guineas, and Lord Herbert sent him two, which he returned. "If your Lordship can gentilely wipe off this, you may." He would do well to take notice of these things in a letter to Mr. Trant [per] Mr. Rogers. Knows he will do it friendly—his pen carries "a powerfull prevalency".

Wonders what world Mr. Kenney is in. Writ to him and Mr. Harries for a speedy state of the case of such deficiency in Lord Herbert's title to any of his estate as might [need] the Commission of Grace, and "a method persons in that kingdome take" in that business. Hears nothing, so can only procure Mr. Trant's reasons under his hand, and send them by the time Mr. Wms. will be at Limore, a week hence. Mr. Trant would observe what method others take and endeavour to do better.

Mr. Wms. and he dined at cousin Hooke's. Williams drank Lord Herbert's health, and said he would trespass upon him for a great deal of venison this summer to entertain the "visitants" of the new-married people at Glascoed; he will be with Lord Herbert from Gloucester assizes and be sworn burgess of Montgomery, and talked of spending £40 or £50 there. Has waited upon him often from Lord Herbert, but still empty-handed. He should give him a fee of five guineas, for though he is Lord Herbert's friend, yet fees are the friends of business. And if Lord Herbert is disposed to see him at Glascoed to wish the young couple joy, Williams would not be a little proud—"but this I speake without booke". He should advise with Williams about everything material, especially about Lady Herbert, who, Mr. Read said, was about to sue. The law is chargeable, and the event nowadays very uncertain.

Lord Herbert has so often inculcated thoughts of matrimony to him that he resolves to pursue it in earnest—not that he is fond of such a change, but circumstances require it. Will continue some time in town.

19 July.

This day letters say that the D. of Lorraine pursued the Turks that deserted Pest so close that he entered with them the lower town of Buda, and that the mines were ready to be sprung under the walls of the upper town. It is by all hands believed to be taken.

*HM*2.22/25.

"Nello" must presumably be Kneller. "Madam Arabella" is, of course, Lord Herbert's sister. Lord Herbert's receipt for the payment for Coggery mill is the next document in the bundle. In the sum referred by Trant to Lord Herbert's consideration it will be noticed that the guineas are reckoned not at 21s. but at 21s. 6d., that being the value then of the golden guinea in terms of England's silver currency. Glascoed, near Llansilin, had been the inheritance of William Williams's wife, who was a daughter and co-heiress of Watkin Kyffin of Glascoed. The assumption that the capture of Budapest was completed was two years too soon.

[1678-91]

524. [LORD HERBERT] TO ————————. *Draft.*

Would not trouble to write to such a gentleman, but is obliged to tell him his thoughts of the usage he had from him [over] the hair he sent up to Edwards to be made into a periwig. "You have dealt with mee like a very greate Rascall." To demand £8 besides the hair for such a wig as he sent—not worth £5—is "a true tast of such a sparke". He said he could not [use] the writer's hair ("I say you had worked most of it in") and that he would have nothing to do with the wig sent up six weeks or a month ago, and supposedly in his custody, though he does not own it. "You are much mistaken if you thinke thus to impose upon me." He shall allow the writer the price (£10) that one of his own trade put upon the parcel of hair, in either a good wig or money, and very soon. Experiences more of his dealing—the two last bobs, especially the last, is the worst of bleached hair that ever he saw. Expects a troublesome reckoning with such a blade. Only wishes he could see him to give a personal reprimand in the method he deserves. *HM*2.23/85b.

1684

525. JOHN WOODHOUSE TO LADY HERBERT. LEFT WITH MR. BALL AT MRS. CORBETT'S IN SALOP TO BE DIRECTED. POST PAID 2D.

Has been solicitous to accomplish her pleasure. Knows but three persons [suitable], and they are in good employment. The master of the first would not part with him for his advancement—charity dwelt much at home. The other is Mr. Vaughan, late agent for Mr. Henry Herbert of Worcest[e]rshire, who is "falne into a soliciteing way" in Sim[m]ons Inn, London, and cannot be diverted, though fit for her purpose. The last is the eldest son of Mr. Richard Avenant of Shelsly, "great agent" of the last Mr. Fowley and (in weighty matters) of the present three Fowleys. His son is not thirty, but has been a man of business under his father ten or twelve years—his father has managed husbandry, orchards, hops, ironworks, purchased lands, let leases, dealt in wood, etc. He is a comely plain man; his parts and learning look no higher than business. Has the young man's consent, and hopes to prevail with his father. She needs a man of greater experience, but whoever she has must learn something at her charge. If he can prevail, she shall see him in a month or five weeks . . .

Sheriff Hales,
24 July. *HM*2.23/44.

Lord Herbert was at this time seeking a new agent for his Irish estates. The Henry Herbert here referred to later became the 1st Lord Herbert of the second creation. Thomas Foley of Witley Court, Worcestershire, a successful ironmaster, had died in 1677, leaving three sons, Thomas (father of the 1st Lord Foley of Kidderminster), Paul (Speaker of the House of Commons), and Philip (of Prestwood, Staffordshire).

[1684]

526. [Lord] Herbert to [John Woodhouse of Sheriff Hales]. *Holograph copy.*

The first of the persons he recommends he finds too difficult to be purchased. Knew the second himself, but he is not to be weaned from the gain and practice of the law. The third has nothing to struggle with but a father's consent. It would be better had he more years and law; but can superstruct in a short time on the groundworks of judgement, sobriety, [etc.]. If he has no hopes of the first man, he prays him continue so that the writer may see the last as soon as he can, for his Irish affairs grow out of order and want a manager more versed in law than himself, one he may entrust over [there]. Desires occasion to return him thanks—begs him to throw away a day or two at Lymore.

[late July or early August]. *HM*2.23/77.

1684

527. [Edward Kenney] to Lord Herbert. To be left with Mr. John Rogers . . . London.

He has cause of complaint that money has not been sent long before, but the country is miserably poor . . . Under are written copies of two bills of exchange, one of £150 drawn by Alderman Newenham on Mr. William Yale, another of £50 drawn by the same on Mr. Peter Vansittart; exchange £11. Could not get bills in Corke for London for more money; has taken bills for Dublin, where he goes on Monday, whence more money shall be remitted. Will overtake Mr. Harri[s] in Dublin before he begins the circuit; will consult together about the new Commission and the *nisi prius*, and take out records, etc., for the trial next assizes in Kerry. The first bill is sent to Mr. Rogers.

Corke,
1 August.

Copies of the bills follow. *HM*2.22/27.

The letter is unsigned. According to the copy of the bill, William Yale lived "upon the bridge in London".

1684

528. THE DUKE OF ORMOND'S JOURNEY FROM WINDSOR. *Addressed to*: [LORD HERBERT OF] CHERBURY AT LYM[ORE].

August 5, Tuesday night at Alebury, 24 m., [from] London 35; 6th, to Col. Vernon's, thence to Banbury, 23; 7th, dinner and supper [at] Warrick, 16; 8th, Bermindgham, 14, [and] to Wolverhamton, 24; 9th, Shiftnall, 8, [and] to Sherwbury, 12, 20; 10th, Sunday, to continue there; 11th, to Cherk Castle.

Endorsed: Lord Worster's journey. *HM*2.23/75.

The paper is torn, but the postmark, August 5, suggests that this is an actual missive despatched at the time from London, not a note jotted down on the back of an old letter. The miles would appear to be Irish miles throughout—traditionally eleven Irish miles equal fourteen English ones. Col. Edward Vernon's house was at North Aston, about ten miles south of Banbury. In W. M. Myddelton's *Chirk Castle Accounts*, 1666-1753, pp. 180 ff., a number of disbursements relating to the Duke's visit are recorded.

1684

529. PHILL. HARRYES TO LORD HERBERT.

Mr. Kenney and he waited on counsel, whose advice is to have a petition or claim speedily entered before the Commissioners for Remedy of Defective Titles, in order to having a patent passed for the lands in the schedule, which were decreed in 1657 by the Court of Exchequer to Edward, Lord Herbert; but do not think it proper to progress until his "result" be had. Intends to set out for the Munster circuit Monday next, and be at Traleey at Kerry assizes to be held there 10 September, when a trial will be had by *nisi prius* between one Carthy and Lord Herbert for Cleydane; has good hopes to cast him.

Dublin,
14 August.

Mr. Kenney [must] continue here lest prejudice redound to Lord Herbert's estate in this new-created court. The instructions to the Commissioners and their method of proceedings are herewith.

The schedule: Killmory, etc., 3 plough-lands; Bally mc Adam, etc., 3 plough-lands; Tulyleeg and Knocknaneanagh, 2 plough-lands; Clidane, ½ plough-land; Inchyboy, ½ plough-land. *HM*2.22/28.

The instructions to the Commissioners are No. 21 in this bundle; the "method" is set out at length, in ten paragraphs, following this letter.

1684

530. EDWARD KENNEY TO LORD HERBERT. TO BE LEFT WITH MR. JOHN ROGERS . . . LONDON.

Thought he had satisfied him of the necessity of passing some of his estate upon this new Commission for Remedy of Defective Titles, [and] that he knew which lands by the lists sent in Mr. Trant's business. But a list is in Mr. Harry's hereinclosed. His lordship's ancestors, at least since the commencement of Baltinglass's lease, were never seized or possessed of them until the late Lord Herbert, by the writer's brother Herbert, got the decree in 1657, and a patent afterwards, which not being granted pursuant to the uses of the Act of Settlement and Explanation (for those lands were never seized or sequestered), consequently they are still vested in the King—which His Majesty will grant to all possessors if they take hold of his present commission.

There is a neighbour in Kerry who put up his old title (though a forfeiting person) and recovered from Sir William Petty last assizes some of his estate [and] got possession, and it is now decreed to him in this Court of Claims, for no other reason but because the lands were not seized nor sequestered, and now because he is in present possession.

There are so many "whipsters" about this court, he durst not stir out of this city until he secures this business; entreats him hasten his orders. Two plough-lands sold to Mr. Trant are on the same score, Carker and Adergovall; is told his lordship gave a general warranty. He is out of possession, but Mr. Trant may pass it.

Encloses copy of a bill of exchange for £100 endorsed by Alderman Ram of this city payable by Mr. Thomas Jeve at the Peacock in Milk Street, London. Hopes he thinks the tenants' money is not in the writer's hands. This is a very dead year, and impossible to get money until Michaelmas or All Saints.

Dublin,
16 August. *HM*2.22/29a.

The bill of exchange is drawn by Andr. Moore of Drogheda in favour of Samuell Clarridge, and endorsed by Able Ram.

[16]84

531. THO. NEWPORT TO LORD HERBERT AT LIMER PARK.

A gentleman, one Mr. Freake, has been with him, who has some concerns nigh Lord Herbert's estate in Ireland, and desires to know whether he would part with anything more there. He extols mightily Mr. Trant's bargain, and will give as many years' purchase as he, and deal for what quantity of land Lord Herbert will dispose of. Has neglected writing two posts to enquire into his abilities. Finds him very sufficient, and like to be a good chapman. Understands he is now upon sale of an estate in Norfolke of £500 per annum, and intends to purchase in Ireland. Desires instructions how he shall proceed—to his chamber in Tanfeild Court, Inner Temple.

26 August.

Service to his sister. Lord Radnor is turned out from being President of the Council, and Lord Rochester is made President in his place; Mr. Sidney Godolphin is put in to the Treasury First Commissioner, and Lord Midleton Secretary of State in his room.

Armorial seal *HM*2.22/30.

The writer is Lord Herbert's brother-in-law, later Lord Torrington. "Mr. Freake" is presumably the Piercy Freke, esq., who is mentioned in Burke's *Extinct and Dormant Baronetcies*, p. 210, as enjoying a fair estate in co. Cork.

1684

532. John Woodhouse to Lord Herbert at "his Lymer", near Salop.

This week was designed for attendance upon him with Mr. Avenant, who was as far as the writer's house. But being informed that his father's affairs are managed without the methods of law, that he [knows] little of law, and that friends are hard upon the father to marry him, the writer durst not bring him; for wooing or marrying would render him incapable of Lord Herbert's service. Has not confidence to come till he has forgiven this disappointment.

Sheriff Hales,
28 August. *HM2.23/45.*

1684

533. [Lord] H[erbert] to Mr. Traunt. *Holograph copy.*

One Mr. Freak has sent to know whether he would sell any new lands in Ireland, and would be chapman at a better rate than Trant purchased—"and stuffe of this kind". Made a former promise that Trant should have the refusal of [such]. Desires a line. Will not conclude a further sale till he has leisure to come up to London to follow it.

Prays advice touching this new "act of grace" in Ireland. His last patent contains the names of all his lands, as fully conveyed as word can grant. Therefore thinks it unnecessary to take notice of it, being, he fears, a commission rather to enrich the commissioners, and perhaps a great grievance to the nation. It resembles the common auction by inch of candle [to] "who can sweare best for an Estate". Their method is to post the estate for a fortnight to bring in all that can be said against it, which is exposing an inheritance to the utmost hazard, and putting up a mark for enemies to smite at. His lawyers think it needless; but he subscribes to Trant's judgement. But no patent can be fuller than his, that grants an estate absolute from the Crown or any claiming thereby.

Has ordered Mr. John Rogers, his goldsmith, to wait on him for the remaining moneys awarded by Mr. Wm. Williams for Coggery Mills. Will be obliged by speedy payment.

Was surprised by false news reporting Trant's death. Knows nobody whose loss would have disordered his mind so much—nor was it occasioned by the state of money matters between them.

4 September. *HM2.22/31.*

1684

534. [Lord] H[erbert] to Mr. Kenney. *Holograph copy.*

Received his of 16 August, and with his counsel considered Kenney's reasons for running Kilmurrey. Ballimacadam, Tullileag and Knocknaneenagh, Clidane, and Insheboy under the shelter of this new "act of Grace". They think it unnecessary to struggle much for it, because these names are recited at large in his patent and the crown rights thereto as fully granted to Edwd., Lord Herbert, and his heirs as words can express. Sends a transcript of the patent, dated 26 February 1667; in the conclusion is a clause as comprehensive for interpretation to his advantage as can be. Nevertheless, he is to advise with the best counsel for knowledge and honesty and accordingly proceed. Does not bind him to opinions this side the water, but trusts to his affection, etc. Cannot conceal his mistrust of this "act of Grace". [Is confident it will prove at last a cheat, only to enrich the commissioners. *The sentence deleted.*]

The bill of exchange by Mr. Andrew Moore is accepted. Requests a rental full and perfect. Is assured Kenney posts the other returns as speedily as he can. Need not trouble him with unnecessary advices; is confident he will lay out his best vigilancy to intercept any malicious designs. Nor need he charm Kenney with fair words, who [knows] there is nothing in the writer's power he is not sure of whenever he commands it.

7 September.

He should urge the writer's estate to his counsel as old Queen Elizabeth established estate, not on the same foot with newer titles, and enquire whether it be advisable to shake this old foundation with new pillars.

*HM*2.22/29b.

[16]84

535. ROB. GRIFFITH TO LORD HERBERT AT LYMORE.

Returned this day sennight from Conway sessions. Lord Bulkeley, Mr. Thomas Bulkeley, and Mr. Mostyn gave him their services. The latter was just recovered of a violent fever; this post brought account of his relapse. Went with Mr. Rogers to Mr. Traunt, who paid the £91. He seemed to expect some notice by Lord Herbert of Mr. Rice [etc.]. Trant said he knew no Mr. Freake, but when Lord Herbert resolved to sell part of the Irish estate he [himself] would be as fair a bidder as any. Trant still apprehends a necessity of Lord Herbert's laying hold of the Commission of Grace. If his grant from the crown is good, he [does not need] the aid of the Commission. Recommends reviewing both his patents, to examine whether the particulars suspected to be defective are in the first; if not, how they are granted by the latter—if as lands of the crown without taking notice of late possessors, his title is unquestionable, but if as the late lands of Lord Herbert or the Earl of Desmond, he questions the validity of the title (those lands being possessed by others at the breaking-out of the late rebellion, and never the inheritance of the Earl of Desmond or the Herberts). Those persons, 'tis true, were concerned in the rebellion and their estates forfeited. Nevertheless the possessors at the time of the forfeiture ought to be named or nobody. If passed under any other disguise the crown is deceived and the grant defective. This ought to be narrowly examined, that if there be occasion he may lay hold of the opportunity. Though this Commission is set on foot to bring money into a great lady's purse, yet it will be of infinite advantage to that kingdom and perfect its settlement.

Mr. Traunt says Mr. Kenney has no orders to permit the tenants of the purchased lands to dig limestone. If he will enclose a letter to that purpose, Mr. Traunt will send it to his agent to be delivered. Will call at Lord Macklesfield for the pictures and give them Mr. Rogers.

London,
16 September.

Will open no more Irish letters without fresh orders. Met Mr. Mathew Price—was surprised to see him in town. *HM*2.23/46.

"Mr. Mostyn" is probably either Thomas, who became the 2nd baronet, or his younger brother Richard. Sir Roger Mostyn, 1st baronet, was married to Lord Bulkeley's sister. Thomas Bulkeley, of Dinas, was Lord Bulkeley's brother.

1684

536. EDWARD KENNEY TO LORD HERBERT. TO BE LEFT WITH MR. JOHN ROGERS . . . LONDON.

Has with great impatience expected his answer to several of his. Mr. Rogers gives account of bills received and of sending his letters to Lord Herbert—but not one syllable from him. Cannot express his trouble when daily he expects part of his estate to be in a condition to be inched from him, and the remedy in his [own] hands, and will not order the prevention of it. All men in Lord Herbert's condition in Ireland pass patent now. Must wait until Mr. Harris returns from the circuit; but has been often advised by good counsel to post Lord Herbert's claim without "expecting" any more—which he durst not do. No man knows how long this Commission will hold; doubts not, upon dissolution of it, narrow enquiries will be made into such estates as have not secured its protection. Does his part in informing him of it.

Dublin,
23 September. *HM*2.22/33.

[1684]

537. [LORD HERBERT] TO MR. GRIFFITH. *Draft.*

Is in none of his letters positive against the Commission of Grace, but ever [wished] him to proceed as Mr. Traunt and Mr. Kenney upon counsel shall think meet. Meets with none here but thinks it dangerous, but has not bound Mr. Keny to this advice. Appointed him to take out a copy of the last patent for Griffith to peruse . . . Cannot do more. Since he says he will manage this business, he should take this for orders to open the writer's letters from Ireland and answer them. His meaning is not to [act] out of obstinateness, nor would he draw unnecessary charge that will shake the foundations of his Irish estate; but will not spare the charge of securing it. Sends Mr. Rogers orders to deliver Irish letters to him; he is to send them to the writer after answering them. Relies much upon his judgement and honesty, and much commends his modesty. Would fain reward his affections if he knew how—"in that only bate of your modesty . . . May I yet give you joy of matrimony". 618.

[1684]

538. [LORD HERBERT] TO MR. ROGERS. *Holograph copy.*

Cannot imagine what makes him thus silent. If he has wronged him, he desires to know in what, that he may excuse himself. Directs his Irish letters to him to be sent over to Mr. Kenney, who receives none. The matter now is the "Act of Grace" in Ireland, wherein he is "mighty concernd". In his last, about 10 September, he gave Kenney full instructions, but 'tis not received by him. Prays him for the future acknowledge receipt of his letters to Kenney.

[7 October]. *HM*2.22/34b.

1684

539. [LORD HERBERT] TO MR. KENNEY. *Holograph copy.*

Receives his letters, "and admire you doe not receive mine"—is confident Mr. Rogers does his part in sending them to the post-house. As to the great question of the Commission of Grace: Finds no counsel here, who has viewed his patent, but thinks it needless. Nevertheless gives him authority to take the best advice, and if he finds it necessary to "come in" upon examination of his patent, "in gods Name doe it". Has said this often in letters, but they all miscarry, it seems.

7 October. *HM*2.22/34a.

1684

540. ROB. GRIFFITH TO LORD HERBERT AT LYMORE.

Delivered his [enclosure] to Mr. Traunt, who lately wrote Lord Herbert his sentiment of the Commission of Grace in Ireland; a necessity of Lord Herbert's laying hold of it sticks still with the writer. Hopes his counsel considered the writer's reasons. If the business prove otherwise than his lordship promises, the fault is not the writer's. The £91 was paid. Thinks he forgot to give his reasons against opening [more] Irish letters without fresh orders; some came while he was at Carnarvonshire . . . Hears Lord Brandon is in town; will wait upon him about the pictures.

7 October. 586.

1684

541. EDWARD KENNEY TO LORD HERBERT. TO BE LEFT WITH MR. JOHN ROGERS . . . LONDON.

Wrote to Kerry to nephew Herbert a little before the assizes; also to Carthy, who brought the ejectment, whom he advised to let fall his suit, and he would solicit his lordship in his behalf—which was so well seconded by nephew Herbert that the man did not go on with the *nisi prius* but relies on that proposal.

Mr. Harris is returned from the circuit, and admires they have not received one word in answer to letters sent eight weeks past. There is no man in Ireland in Lord Herbert's case but has or will pass patent on this Commission of Grace. Is resolved, without further advice from him, to post up Lord Herbert's claim with all speed; and if he does not approve, he can stop proceedings if answer comes in thirty days. Has posted himself, to the use of his son, to the value of £500 per annum, much of it the same [title] as Lord Herbert's. Mr. Rogers wrote word he received the bill of £100 sent with a packet of letters to his lordship.

Dublin,

11 October. *HM*2.22/35.

1684

542. James Gallwey to Lord Herbert at Leimors Lodge in Mongumerie shire.

Showed his petition, with Lord Herbert's reference, to Ed. Kenney, esq., upon whose report Lord Herbert would consider [it]. Last winter, with much trouble and charges, he proved his right and "Lawfull challeng of my deere Lord Ed.". Is satisfied Ed. Kenney, esq., made his report of the true allegations in his petition. Left Ireland above three months since; and being at great charges by sickness in Bristole and the time here (always expecting him), and his money spent, and no other shift but his dependence on Lord Herbert, he prays him order £5 here for him, and advise when he will come, or when he would have the writer come to his house—for he is resolved, though it be winter, to go thither if he does not come soon, to give a just account of his challenge and get satisfaction according to Lord Herbert's promise. Expects answer by next post to Mr. Rogers.

London,

19 October.

Endorsed: James Galloway . . . *HM*2.22/36.

1684

543. Rob. Griffith to Mr. Kenney. *Contemporary copy.*

Has several times desired a particular of the lands he apprehends might be defective in title and wanting the aid of the Commission of Grace; and a full state of the case—how they come to be under a more defect than the rest, what methods others take to remedy like defects, at what rates they compound, what contingent charges *pro quanto*, who to be applied to for favour, and in general what he advises for preventing the consequences of neglect of this opportunity. Gathers his letters have fallen into other hands, since it is not to be imagined Kenney would [fail] in a matter of this concern. Therefore sends this under the protection of Mr. Moore, whose letters possibly are not so familiarly fingered.

Without the particulars his lordship cannot give positive directions. If there is a necessity of supplying the title there must be composition, if composition, then an undeniable necessity of using friends and interest (the first step in the case); and the gaining thereof must be his lordship's own work, not to be attempted by another without recommendations. Kenney's diligence and "privacy" are necessary ingredients. It ought to "take noe aire but what my Lord allowes", nor any act or art used beyond his directions, for fear of a miscarriage.

23 October.

Received his of the 11th since writing. Much wonders he and Mr. Harries have received no letters. The putting of Carthy's business by was well done. But wishes he had spared his forwardness in posting his lordship's claim. If he has not done it, prays him stop his hand. And fail not since he is in Dublin to write "postly".

*HM*2.22/37b.

[1684]

544. P. TRANT TO LORD HERBERT AT LYMORE.

Mr. Griffith says Lord Herbert did not receive the writer's letter. It was to lay his thoughts before him as to passing patent under the Commission of Grace for some of his lands. Takes the original title of all his estate to be by grant from the Crown upon the attainder of Lord Desmond, and that the lands were before the late rebellion claimed by his ancestors, and sued for as part of that estate. But the parties whose these lands were recovered and enjoyed them until the late rebellion. And these proprietors were parties to the late rebellion, by which they forfeited their estates, which then vested in the King. Lord Herbert claimed these lands as of right, and they were accordingly granted to him. The question is whether they were forfeited by Lord Desmond's attainder, and granted to him. If so he cannot mend his title by any new grant. But if they truly belonged to others, not to Lord Desmond, and those persons possessed and enjoyed them until the late rebellion, and did then and not before forfeit them, and Lord Herbert has them by virtue of his old right and not by any new grant from the Crown, then it will be at best a disputable title. And there are those that offer to make out the title to be absolutely in the King. Whether they can do it is a question . . .

[*postmarked* 23 October]. *HM*2.22/32.

1684

545. ROB. GRIFFITH TO LORD HERBERT AT LYMORE.

Will with integrity discharge his Irish affairs, so far as recommended to him, and punctually regard his directions about letters, when a west wind blows any this way. Supposes Mr. Trant's letter brought reasons "convincive" of the necessity of what the writer often represented. Recommends using Mr. Trant's interest—through him only can Lord Herbert without hazard effect it. Many would be glad to discover this flaw, out of prejudice to him or advantage to themselves (which they would easily make could they once smell it out). Therefore his own name should be used only in the fiat and patent. Mr. Trant is forward to be his friend beyond what many a near relation would venture "at this time of day".

Sent the enclosed to Mr. Kenney, who cannot without prejudice act further in this. Advises him not to afford Kenney great latitude after undervaluing Caunguilly £8 in the sale to Mr. Trant (with intention doubtless to serve his own or friends' designs). He will remember his importunate letters about having a lease of it to the old tenant at £20 a year, affirming it would be well set at that. Now Mr. Trant's agent has set it to the same tenant at £28, and gained the old man's displeasure for refusing a reward. Mr. Trant showed him Mr. Moore's letters. Lord Herbert should not grant power to make leases or promise preference till upon the place himself. It will be no advantage to take notice of this till there, yet it serves to alarum him.

Berry the stationer is come to town. Mentions this because Mr. Rogers said Lord Herbert was at a loss for an intelligencer. It would be easy and cheap to have some person of the Post Office send Gazettes and a weekly letter (frank, which they have privilege to do). Will go with Mr. Rogers if desired, and bargain as if for himself.

Condoled with Lord Brandon on his brother-in-law's unhappy death. He said he will send Lord Herbert the pictures. Mr. Wms. is well; Mr. Mat. Price and he sat with him the night before term. Is sorry Williams and Lord Herbert had no interview in the country. Did not touch him upon the Irish business. If he thinks fit to order Mr. Rogers to attend Sir Edward Herbert with a letter and a fee, he is the best able to advise, being so familiar with the constitution of that kingdom.

25 October.

Received the enclosed since writing. Will advise with Mr. Trant tomorrow. Does not approve of Mr. Kenney's posting up Lord Herbert's claim. If he can serve in this, Lord Herbert should send him next post letters to Kenney and Harryes (open) giving them positive orders to move as directed by the writer; and another to Mr. Trant to desire assistance, and a letter [of authority] to himself. Kenney has given it too much air already, there's no more sleeping on it—the ice is broke. Mr. Trant has lately married a daughter to Lord Slane near Dublin. Lord Herbert [might] wish him joy of it. He should take no notice of any proposal of Carthy's—when his patent is passed all such pretenders are excluded. *HM*2.22/37a.

The first enclosure is Griffith's copy of his letter of 23 October to Kenney, written below this. The second enclosure is no doubt Kenney's of 11 October, transmitted to Griffith by Rogers in accordance with the standing arrangement.

1684

546. Rob. Griffith to Lord Herbert at Lymore.

Mr. Trant agrees the claim ought not to have been posted up before some of the Commissioners had been prepared; he offers to write to some of them that are his friends to use Lord Herbert as if it were his own business (giving the writer the letters to be sent to Kenney), and will advise of anything he thinks useful for guiding Lord Herbert's agents. Writ to Mr. Kenney this post stirring him up . . . Absolutely wants a particular of the lands to be passed, with the denomination of each plough-land and rent. If Kenney fails him, Lord Herbert may give him this—with all haste, that Mr. Trant may recommend them to the Commissioners.

On Sunday morning about five Lord Powys's house in Lincolne's Inn Fields was burnt to the ground. His "Gent of the horse" and a friend's child were burnt, the Lord, Lady, and the rest narrowly escaping. Nothing was saved, and the loss is computed at least £30,000.

Sent this day sennight a commission to Anglesey to take cousin Con. Williams' recovery.

28 October.

Writ to Lord Herbert's butler this post desiring to have his trunk and box sent up. *HM*2.22/38.

Lord Powis's house, and the fire that destroyed it, are referred to in E. Beresford Chancellor's *The Private Palaces of London*, p. 132, but (citing Narcissus Luttrell) the date of the fire is wrongly given as November 26 instead of October 26. The October date is confirmed by the postscript to No. 548.

1684

547. [LORD HERBERT] TO MR. KENNEY. *Holograph copy.*

It is a miracle that none of his letters to the writer miscarry and all his to Kenney are drowned in passage. Has resolved upon a shorter cut—to put the whole managing of his affairs touching the Commission of Grace into the care of his former servant Mr. Robert Griffith . . . (*The authority and instructions given to Griffith are here explained*). [Hopes] to find him compliant to these orders. He has already stepped out of the way by not waiting for his orders and posting up his estate, involving him in troubles God knows how intricate.

Lymore.

28 [October].

A letter in the same strain to Mr. Harries follows. *HM*2.22/40b.

In the details given here of Lord Herbert's instructions to Griffith (see No. 550) Patrick Trant is not referred to by name.

[16]84

548. MEREDITH LLOYD TO LORD HERBERT AT LYMORE LODGE.

Mr. Mathew Price promised to give him the writer's thanks for his lovingly charitable invitation (he being in a mournful condition in these —to him—calamitous times). Gratefully accepts his offers, and will, as soon as he can after the term, wait upon him at Lymore Lodge. In the interim he begs him to speak not of his coming to anybody lest it obstruct his intention. Cousin David Lloyd cannot without loss wait upon him till after the term, but if he will write his commands by the next post he will readily obey them; he is capable of serving him in any employ—he should write to him at Mr. Jenings's chamber in the Inner Temple. Respects to his lady.

28 October.

On Sunday morning last Lord Powys's house in Linconlne's Inn Fields by accident was burnt to the ground. The loss is reckoned to be £20,000 at least. All his writings were destroyed.

Armorial seal 111.

[1684]

549. [LORD] H[ERBERT] TO MR. TRAUNT. *Holograph copy.*

Received last post a letter without date but so full of courtesies it could be none but his. Finds an instinct to fly to him for assistance whenever occasions call—who knows they are made to serve each other . . . By an over-hasty action, Mr. Kenney, his agent in Ireland, has posted part of his estate . . . Takes his title to be as Trant stated it . . . Is himself no expert, and, which is worse, remote. Entrusts his former servant, Mr. Robert Griffith, who is enjoined to wait on Trant continuously, and do whatever he commands. Hopes to prevail with him to direct him. Has a great opinion of this Griffith's honesty . . . Wishes him all joy of his new matrimony.

[28 *or* 29 October]. *HM*2.22/40d.

1684

550. [Lord] Herbert to Mr. Griffith. *Holograph copy.*

Approves well his answers to Mr. Ed. Kenney. And since he requires words more authentic: These therefore empower him to open all letters from Ireland, if need be to advise with counsel, after which he is to report thereof to Mr. Patrick Traunt, who will advise what answers to make and put him into the best method for passing a new patent. Mr. Kenney and Mr. Harris have orders not to proceed without Griffith's directions, and orders positive to do as he directs . . . . . .

29 October.

Will subscribe Griffith's own form if [he wishes]. Since letters miscarry so frequently, would fain prevail with him to make a step over and see an end of this distraction. If he is so inclined, lest they lose more time, he has ordered Mr. Jo. Rogers to furnish him with any sum within [£]20 for his charges . . .

Likes his advice [to visit] Sir Ed. Herbert (taking Mr. John Rogers) and discourse at large his case with him, beginning or concluding with a fee. Griffith knows his title. Takes it to be by grant from the Crown upon the attainder of the Earl of Desmound; and that the lands in dispute were wrested out of his ancestors' possession by the late rebellion, for which reason they were returned to his family by the Court of Claims in Ireland and confirmed by the Act of Settlement and his new patent. How Sanky or army officers' titles can evade this he knows not. But oaths can batter down the strongest rampart of right, especially in that country.

Is much dissatisfied about Caungully, but will pick no quarrels at this time. He must find a course of directing letters to some honest third body in Dublin who is to distribute them to the agents. It is not unusual for malicious [persons] to take up letters and prevent them coming to their proper agents. Warrants Mr. Traunt will furnish an honest man in Dublin to see letters delivered, being well paid quarterly. Desires to hear whether this proposition of sending him over takes—"it is ten to one you have not time for matrimoney".

Lymore Lodge,
29 October.

May [soon] answer whether Griffith shall procure him Gazette[s] and news from some[one] of the Post Office. *HM*2.22/39.

The next document in the bundle commences with a slightly different and somewhat shorter version of this letter, presumably a discarded draft.

[1684]

551. [LORD HERBERT] TO MR. JOHN ROGERS. *Holograph copy.*

Prays him accompany Mr. Rob. Griffith, if he has leisure, to Sir Edward Herbert, Chief Justice of Chester, and give him a fee, and Mr. Griffith and he are to advise with Sir Edward about this new "act of grace" in Ireland. If Griffith has occasion for more money on the like occasion, he is to furnish him. Refers it to his discretion—"keep within decent bounds".

[29 October]. *HM*2.22/40a.

1684

552. ROB. GRIFFITH TO LORD HERBERT AT LYMORE LODGE.

Received this evening his of the 29th, with letters to Mr. Trant, Kenney, and Harries. If Mr. Trant gives reason why he should go over, nor the late storms at sea nor the illness of the roads shall [prevent] him. But if the business may be perfected by directions from hence it will save the charges. Will give account of this and Lady Herbert's business by Tuesday's post. Ought to have received his letter a week sooner. Three of his letters came together—a shameful abuse, done at Poole, possibly by some great neighbour's influence. Lord Herbert's interest with Lord Castlemaine may perhaps remove this roguery.

Lord Rochester is made Lord Lieutenant of Ireland and the D. of Ormond called over. Col. Kirke goes Governor for New England. Mr. Williams's service.

8 November. *HM*2.22/41.

Lady Herbert's business is referred to in the next letter.

1684

553. ROB. GRIFFITH TO LORD HERBERT AT LYMORE.

Will make no proceeding without sound advice. Waited upon Sir Edwd. Herbert [with] Mr. Rogers, and [explained why] Mr. Trant judges a necessity of a patent, and [why] Lord Herbert hopes the contrary. He answered that none can make his title too secure, especially in that kingdom, and since the design is to raise money for the Crown, or those the Crown thinks fit, care will be taken to inspect the titles of all estates, and all advantages taken of defects, therefore recommends passing patent where any doubt remains, the composition being not excessive. But he advised Lord Herbert's agent should attend some able person in Dublin, where recourse may be had to all records, and his opinion under his hand be sent before further proceedings ; he much blamed the hasty posting his claim. Asked him if he knew Mr. Rice of Dublin, who managed Mr. Trant's patent of the lands bought from Lord Herbert ; he said he knew him well, and there could be none abler and honester. Went to Mr. Trant and desired his letter to Mr. Rice . . . . .

Sir Edward is very angry that Lady Herbert or her counsel should suspect him of partiality, and says he cannot be Lord Herbert's counsel if it be a Montgomeryshire lawsuit ; but wishes him a happy riddance of her. Advises that Mr. Edwards draw the case, which may be sent hither for further advice. Looks upon the £30 a year as a plain case.

If there be such a deed by his brother she may produce it before counsel; whether he had power to make it the writings [will show]. If counsel agree she has a right to it, Lord Herbert's judgement will tell him whether it be for his honour and advantage to stand trial when sure to be worsted. The embezzlement he speaks of will serve little, since he might have taken remedy another way, and no man may right himself otherwise than by law. The world will clamour (as in the case of Lord Brereton), and [say] he sets up the embezzlement to colour wronging her.

If the case were his own, if counsel [say] the £30 a year would be recovered, he would by some friend compound the arrears and continue payment or buy it out, which might be had at easy terms. Would then bring a bill in Chancery against her to discover the goods embezzled, and for relief against the deed of pin-money (which she is most unreasonable not to cancel). Thus no judge or jury could have any room to favour her.

Mr. Trant says Lord Rochester often talks very kindly of Lord Herbert. He may give services to Lord Rochester in a letter to Mr. Trant, with congratulation for his new government, wherein he may upon occasions be Lord Herbert's friend.

12 November. *HM*2.22/43a.

[1684]

554. [Robt. Griffith] to Mr. Harries. *Contemporary copy.*

Sir Edward Herbert advises Mr. Stephen Rice be retained and instructed . . . Pray be assisting to him . . . and care should be taken if Mr. Kenney be not in town that Mr. Rice has his fee. Writ twice of late to him with letters to Mr. Kenney; wishes he would return answers.

[12 November]. *HM*2.22/43e.

1684

555. P. Trant to Mr. Rice. *Contemporary copy.*

"Deare Cousen". There is a concern of Lord Herbert's in Kerry, which some are of opinion he ought to pass patent for in the present Court of Grace. He desires no unnecessary expense, but will be at any necessary charge to secure his title. He is the writer's very good friend. Therefore recommends Rice to enquire diligently into it, and advise what should be done, concerning himself in it for him as for the writer.

London,
12 November.

His attorney and agent have orders to attend him. *HM*2.22/43b.

[16]84

556. Matthew Scollard to Lord Herbert at the Lodge near Mongomery.

His promise when the writer waited on him lately in Mongomeryshire makes him bold to beg that, since John fitz Gerald, his serjeant in the manor of Castle Island, is certainly dead (as he has already informed him), he would direct Mr. Ken[n]y to place him in that employment.

Dublin,
12 November.

Begs he will order his secretary to send answer to Castle Island. Will give sufficient security.

Armorial seal *HM2.22/42.*

[1684]

557. [ROBT. GRIFFITH] TO MR. RICE. *Contemporary copy.*

The matter wherein Lord Herbert desires his advice is "soe pathetically comprehended" in the enclosed, he has nothing to add . . . He should enclose his opinion to Mr. Trant, whose letters have a better passage than his lordship's. Mr. Kenney and Mr. Phillip Harries have orders to gratify his advice and trouble . . .

[12 November]. *HM2.22/43c.*

1684

558. EDWARD KENNEY TO MR. ROBERT GRIFFITH. TO BE LEFT WITH MR. JOHN ROGERS . . . LONDON.

Has often and largely given account to Lord Herbert of the business of a new patent for the three plough-lands of Killmory, the three plough-lands of Bally mc Adam, the two plough-lands of Tully Leage and Knocknaneanagh, the half plough-land of Cludane, and half plough-land of Inchiboy on this new Commission of Grace. None of those lands were Lord Herbert's before the Rebellion of Ireland; but when the spoils were dividing Mr. Thomas Herbert, then agent, thought his employer should put in for a share, and so put up some old pretended title, and interest being made and the people not so curious, those lands were adjudged in the Court of Exchequer, in the usurper's time, to Lord Herbert. So those lands were not seized nor sequestered; and [thus] not forfeited to the King; if not forfeited, the late patent is "out of doores", for they were granted as such, and the King deceived in his grant. Now the King is pleased to quiet the possession whether their title be right or wrong . . . .

Had gone home the beginning of September, but durst not leave until some end to this. Had proceeded on it, for he had his lordship's order; but received Griffith's, which put another stop to it. Has lost his time and labour, neglected business at home, spent £100, "and now goe home with my finger in my mouth". Will stay for answers from his lordship. If he goes he must come again, for none can swear his lordship in possession but he, who receives the rents. The composition money is but the sixth of one year's rent. 'Tis true the patent will be more chargeable than others because it goes through more offices than formerly. Has done his part as friend and servant. If his lordship will leave a gap in his estate it is certain there are those that will enter.

Dublin,
18 November. *HM2.22/44a.*

1684

559. [LORD HERBERT] TO ANDREW NEWPORT. *Draft.*

To conclude abundance of trouble this year came news that his agent in Ireland has posted part of his estate; which will yet cost a considerable sum . . . This his agent thrust him upon contrary to directions. Must [now] go through with it. Sir Edw. Herbert and Mr. Traunt advise he must get the Commissioners' fiat, and a new patent if he can . . . Has made his former servant, Robert Griffith, solicitor to this business. This is to beg him to call Mr. Rob. Griffith often to account, and to entreat his counsel—his niece's jointure is involved. His own circumstances are "such aboveforth", his own attending would plunge him into deeper difficulties. [Yet] to rely absolutely on the virtue of an Irishman or a discarded servant is not the wisest thing. Therefore endeavours to prevail with him to supervise both their actions . . . Has ordered Rob. Griffith to wait on him. Prays him give Lord Newport a hint of this—he may help the writer out of these briars—Lord Rochester, with whom they have both great interest, could sway the Irish Commissioners to do him reason at a reasonable rate.

21 November. *HM*2.22/45.

[16]84

560. AND. NEWPORT TO LORD HERBERT AT LYMORE.

His sister Newport is fully satisfied with what Lord Herbert says concerning the cabinet plate. Has been all about the town for furniture for "poore woman's" dressing-room and closet, but has not found what pleased him. Has bought an Indian silk (one piece) for her closet. Would have sent a pattern but was hurried away to supper in a strange house, where he now writes. The piece cost but 32s. Lord Herbert's sister Lyttelton likes it, and Mrs. Lacon also. Has seen some hanging like that in the withdrawing-room at Eyton, but not the same pattern, though as good, and very lively; it may serve for her dressing-room. Would be glad of her positive orders lest it be disposed of. Must know whether he is to provide fringes for the furniture he buys, whether by furniture is intended cushions or chairs or both, and what nature and sizes. Will get him the best wine he can, but the carrier (in Wood Street) will not be in town this fortnight.

Lond.,
22 November. 108.

"Sister Newport" is Lady Newport, wife of Francis, Viscount Newport—Andrew Newport's brother. Andrew Newport almost invariably referred to his niece, Lord Herbert's wife, as "poor woman"—though he wrote to her as "dear child"!

1684

561. [LORD HERBERT] TO MR. GRIFFITH. *Draft.*

Has left the enclosed unsealed that he may peruse them, as well that to the Duke Monmouth and to Mr. Kenney. Would have answered sooner, but was deterred t'other day by a fire in his library, where if he had not been the instant it showed itself it might have burnt his library and writings and all that was anything worth to him—perhaps the whole house. It burnt within an inch of a shelf of books before it discovered itself.

26 November. *HM*2.22/46b.

1684

562. [Lord Herbert] to Mr. Kenney. *Draft.*

Received his of 1 [*recte* 18] November . . . Has now taken a shorter course, their communication being so uncertain through bad winds, [? worse] postmasters, or negligence not calling for [letters] from the post-house in due time "and soe have gone the circle". Has appointed Mr. Rob. Griffith correspondent in this, whose advice he is positively to follow—he is to transact "the great intreage" of this matter. Will be glad his composition prove but the sixth part of a year's rent, but doubts Kenney calculates amiss. If he is discharged from this court as to his brother Mead's and his son's estates, the writer will not press him to stay in a town where the air does not agree with him. But prays him leave Mr. Harries fully instructed . . .

Since he goes into the country, he gives him further instructions touching the yarn Lady Herbert expects. She designs it "third", for linen, one half as formerly bespoke (the £20 worth) to be the finest sort of "third" yarn. Desires them in long hanks, the bottoms being faulty often.

Has a letter from one Mathew Scollard desiring to be serjeant in the manor of Castle Islands. Has nothing to say for him if he be a native—designs to engraft as many English in the seigniory as he can get.

Lymore Lodge,
26 November. *HM*2.22/46a.

"Bottoms" are balls (of yarn, etc.).

1684

563. Rob. Griffith to Mr. Kenney. *Contemporary copy.*

His of the 18th gives the fullest, and if true the most rational, state of Lord Herbert's case, and very convincive of the necessity of passing a patent. This is the first exact account from him he has seen. His lordship manages all his affairs with advice and weighty consideration, whereby he may not blame himself or be blamed by posterity. 'Tis therefore his lordship insists to have this case truly stated and able advice taken, that it might be carried down with the patent to his heirs, for his honour and their satisfaction. Could well agree to proceeding, upon his last letter; but would receive Mr. Rice's opinion for justification.

He cannot in reason be expected to wait longer in Dublin. Is advised that if he makes affidavit of his lordship's possession before any of the Commissioners and leaves it with Mr. Harries, he need not stay (which would increase his own troubles and his lordship's charge and prejudice his interest in Kerry). Without doubt his friendship and service will be rewarded by his lordship . . .

London,
4 "November" [*recte* December]. *HM*2.22/44b.

1684

564. Rob. Griffith to Lord Herbert at Lymore Lodge.

Received his with [one] to Mr. Kenney; answered this from him as on the back. He will observe how far Kenney would insinuate this Dublin journey; yet thinks it best he defer taking notice of it, and could wish there had been less vinegar in the ink Lord Herbert writ his last with. Is fully convinced of the necessity of this patent, therefore will next week set out for Dublin with commendatory letters from Mr. Trant to his friends the Commissioners; and having put the wheels a going, will return to keep Christmas at Carnarvonshire. When the patent is conveyed to him there he will send it to Lymore by the mountain way, or be himself the bearer. Will account for his charges from Carnarvonshire to and in Dublin and back to Carnarvonshire only. Cannot allow it proper to trouble Mr. And. Newport: Lord Rochester will not go over till spring, before which his patent will be passed, and Mr. Newport's interest thrown away (which he may reserve for another occasion); secondly, Mr. An. Newport is "nice and timerous" in appearing for any, though a friend, that he suspects under displeasure. Repeats that a letter to Mr. Trant about Lord Rochester to the purpose formerly mentioned will not hurt him. Congratulates the delivery of his library. His recommendation of the writer's kinsmen shall never be [forgotten]—the brother will offer thanks by letter.

6 December.

Supposes Mr. Oliver has sent the recovery from cousin Con. Wms.

*HM*2.22/47.

1684

565. Phill. Harryes to Mr. Robert Griffith.

Received Lord Herbert's of 29 October and Griffith's of 12 November thereunder written. Mr. Kenney and he attended Mr. Rice, who has promised by this night's post to send Griffith his opinion. Much admires that any person should possess Lord Herbert that Mr. Kenney or he had so far proceeded that part of his estate was posted up in order to a hearing and composition. Prays him acquaint Lord Herbert that in August they told him they thought it requisite to pass this new court for certain lands which were returned in the Civil Survey in 1640 (*sic*) to have been the propriety of sundry forfeiting persons; since when no prosecution or transaction has been made relating to a foot of his estate, nor intended to be [without] his commands. [Awaits] further direction.

Dublin,
13 December. *HM*2.22/48a.

1684

566. Edward Kenney to Lord Herbert. To be left with Mr. John Rogers . . . London.

Mr. Stephen Rice, counsel appointed by Mr. Griffith to give opinion in the business of the Court of Grace, will this night give [it] Mr. Trant; by Mr. Griffith's orders he would not give it to the writer or Mr. Harryes, but [said] they might tell Lord Herbert that a patent must be passed. This, with some late passages, makes him suspect Lord Herbert has conceived some opinion of him not so candid . . . No man has been more just and willing to advance his affairs . . .

Dublin,
13 December.

Begins his journey to Corke on Monday, whence before Christmas he will send money, and twelve days after for Kerry, whence he shall have a rent-roll and account. *HM*2.22/49a.

1684

567. EDWARD KENNEY TO MR. ROBERT GRIFFITH. TO BE LEFT WITH MR. JOHN ROGERS . . . LONDON.

Mr. Rice will give Mr. Trant his opinion this night. Thinks it hard he could not have it. Rice says a new patent must be passed if his lordship's lands were posted . . . If [there be] any miscarriage in this affair he washes his hands of it; did what was necessary in all serious judgements here—Sir John Temple, Sir John Meade, Mr. Whitfield, and now Mr. Rice (a very ingenious man, but does not much exceed those mentioned) . . .

Dublin,
13 December. *HM*2.22/50.

1684

568. EDWARD KENNEY TO LORD HERBERT. TO BE LEFT WITH MR. JOHN ROGERS . . . LONDON.

His last gave account of leaving Dublin. Thought to have a good sum ready here, but it does not exceed £200, and exchange high at £7 10s. per cent. Underwritten is a copy of the original bill to Mr. Rogers. Expected directions about the yarn, but it must be expressed by the name of linen or woollen, according to the use intended.

Corke,
23 December.

The underwritten bill has been removed. *HM*2.22/52a.

[1678-1691]

569. [LORD HERBERT] TO——— ———. *Holograph copy.*

"The electuary youle receive by the bearer . . . I hope youle have the benefit of . . . I'me apprehensive your sisters don't use you well, and that may perplex your thoughts, which . . . disturbe[s] the whole Fabricke of the Body . . . If soe, you shall commande what can make you easy . . .
Dear Cosen, your most humble servant" *HM*2.23/85a.

1684/5

570. [LORD] H[ERBERT] TO MR. KENNEY. *Holograph copy.*

Cannot blame his resentments, nor could avoid giving occasion—so many letters have miscarried. Suspects his [own] hand was too well known, and [so] busy knaves [could] molest his patent concern. For which reason, and that the counsel he trusted most was in London, he put the managing of all into his former servant Robert Griffith's hands, who was also to go over and see all settled. No trusting uncertain postage was the controlling reason he took this way. Let this satisfy his mind. Nor should he imagine the writer takes it well that Mr. Stephen Rice refused to show him his opinion; this shall be intimated to him. There's hardly anything of this nature done but imprudent overdoing it gives offence never intended by the "Primier Agent". It is the fashion of the world, where they conjecture men begin to fall, to add to their misfortunes. These are tokens of that general plague that infests the morals of this age. Assures him it lies not in the power of any man to undermine him in the writer's friendship.

5 January. *HM*2.22/49b.

1684/5

571. [Lord] H[erbert] to Mr. Phil. Harris. *Draft.*

Finds his of 13 December to Griffith very satisfactory—a truer state of the question, and fuller, than any he remembers. Robert Griffith is now sent over to prevent miscarriage, etc., by sending by post, and personally to see this whole business settled, that there may be no more confusion—it has been a continuous comedy of errors.

5 January. *HM*2.22/48b.

1684/5

572. Jno. Rogers to Lord Herbert at Lymore Lodge.

Has this day paid Lord Brereton £200 and has a discharge from him according to Lord Herbert's copy—only it is not [yet] the 37th year of the reign.

8 January. 587a.

1684/5

573. [Lord Herbert] to [Edward Kenney]. *Holograph copy.*

Finds enclosed in his of 23 December his first bill for £200 (his second not paid). By that same post Mr. John Rogers gave no notice he had received any from Kenney, [so] sent it him. Supposes next post will tell it is accepted; he shall have advice. His wife would have linen yarn. Explained this in a former letter, with "a great deale more stuffe" . . . Also she would have them in skeins—the bottoms, it seems, have lost credit amongst the housewives.

Lymore Lodge,
12 January. *HM*2.23/52b.

1684/5

574. [Lord] H[erbert] to Mr. Rogers. *Holograph copy.*

His of the 8th gave advice he had paid Lord Breerton the £200 due last Christmas. Sent his lordship in return for his present two pots of venison by Lloyd the carrier. In Rogers's letter was one from Mr.

Kenney enclosing a bill of £200; [returns] the bill for him to get it accepted. Service to Mr. Fra. Child. "Your affectionate".

Lymore,
8 (*sic*) January. 587b.

Francis Child was Rogers's partner.

1684/5

575. ROB. GRIFFITH TO MR. KENNEY. *Autograph copy.*

Formerly wrote that if he left town he should leave an affidavit of the possession and all necessary instructions with Mr. Harries. Thinks [Lord Herbert] writ much to that effect. Doubts he has not received those letters, since he finds nothing done. He is with all imaginable expedition to send his servant or some other that can make affidavit, and a particular of the lands to be passed. Mr. Rice and Mr. Harries agree an affidavit from such a person will be sufficient if he has no concerns of his own wherewith "this small affaire of his lordships" may be mingled: but his [own] coming purposely is absolutely unnecessary.

Dublin,
24 January. *HM*2.22/53d.

1684/5

576. ROB. GRIFFITH TO MR. HARRIES AT DUBLIN. *Autograph copy.*

Recommends to him, by Lord Herbert's orders, passing a patent in the Commission of Grace of such parcels in Kerry as to Stephen Rice, esq., his counsel, seems necessary, whose advice he is to go by. If difficulty arise, application is to be made to Mr. Baron Harstonge or Mr. Baron Worth, who will be assisting to remove any obstacle. He is desired to lay out the charges of this patent, which Edwd. Kenney, esq. (whose instruction he is to call for) is to reimburse. The patent when passed he is to enclose in a box and send by the master of any of the three doggers to the writer at Mr. Richard Owen's house at Holyhead [or] at Mr. John Rogers's house within Temple Bar, London.

28 January.

Underwritten is an order to Kenney to pay the charges. *HM*2.22/53e.

1684/5

577. ROB. GRIFFITH TO LORD HERBERT AT LYMORE.

Upon coming to Dublin (where the late surprising news found him) he waited upon the two barons (the leading men in that Commission) with Mr. Traunt's letters . . . Received from both a warm assurance of [assistance]. Resolved to proceed to passing the patent, not doubting but that Mr. Kenney had made affidavit of the possession and left all instructions with Mr. Harries. But [nothing was] left, without which he could not enter upon the business; which notwithstanding fell out luckily, for he would certainly have proceeded a great way to no purpose, the Commission being determined by the King's death, and Lord Herbert would have been in the same case with hundreds that had paid composition money whose patents perhaps never will be passed, unless his present

Majesty revives the Commission, whereof is yet no appearance—has laid out for timely notice if there should be . . .

London,
17 March.

Appended are copies of Trant's letters to Mr. Baron Worth and Sir Standish Hartstonge. *HM*2.22/53a.

[16]85

578. Jo. Read to Lord Herbert at Lymore.

Attended Mr. Mathew Pryce at Parke; when he read Lord Herbert's letter he gave the writer liberty to argue the whole matter. Finds if Mr. Wms. had writ at first he had been well satisfied. He seems willing to comply, and says that all the writings concerning the difference betwixt the borough of Mountgomry and the out-corporations are in London. Pryce will be there himself Wednesday the 20th, and give Mr. Williams full account. Lord Herbert should write Mr. Williams to discourse Mr. Pryce before he sees "our" judge. Saw in a newsletter to Mr. Pryce that Sir John Trevor will be Speaker, and that "our representative" should not continue long there. Some gentlemen of this country speak big words about it, but the most considerable thing reflecting on Mr. Wms. in their petition is his being Recorder of Llanvilling, and in taking the right of Mountgo[mer]y they conceive violated his oath. They'll not leave a stone unturned, and talk of great friends that will see them righted.

Penryddlan,
12 May.

Desires he will order his groom to let the writer's mare have a leap of Lord Herbert's largest horse. *HM*2.9/65a.

The point at issue was whether the burgesses of Llanidloes, Llanfyllin, and Welshpool had the right to participate in the election of a member of Parliament for Montgomery Borough. "Our representative," William (later Sir William) Williams, M.P. for Montgomery, was petitioned against by Col. Charles Herbert of Aston (son of Sir Edward Herbert the Attorney-General) apparently on the grounds that they had been prevented from doing so.

1685

579. [Lord Herbert] to Mr. Wm. Williams. *Holograph copy.*

Has writ to Mr. Mathew Price touching such writings as concern "our" corporation affairs at Montgomery; finds he'll deliver such as he has. Mr. Price will be in town the 20th, where those writings are, and desires Williams to find him out and speak with him before Price speaks with Sir Edw. Herbert. He expected only a little courtship, and missing it stirred his choler. Encloses a true list of "our" burgesses as the recorder gave [it], by which Williams may challenge the false burgesses that signed Mr. Ch. Herbert's petition.

16 May. *HM*2.9/65b.

1685

580. EDWARD KENNEY TO LORD HERBERT. TO BE LEFT WITH MR. JOHN ROGERS . . . LONDON.

This city and no other place in Ireland can furnish that sort of yarn. Will buy it before he leaves; desires directions for sending. There is little talk now of the Court of Grace, only a late letter from His Majesty to the Lords Justices to suffer those that paid their composition money to pass patent—[of whom] the writer makes one and wishes his lordship made another. Advises him, if by any means he can, to pass those lands in patent, for he is frequently alarmed about them. Sent a bill of £200 on 3 April from Corke enclosed to Mr. Rogers and a duplicate to his lordship, but never received one syllable. Cannot send a rental until he goes to Kerry, nor money till July—the county is "abominable poor", having little trade of late. But the fairs come in. His lordship's money does not stop in the writer's hands but the tenants'. One cannot destroy them with too much severity. His frequent being here is no disadvantage to his lordship's concerns.

Dublin,
19 May. 297.

1685

581. EDWARD KENNEY TO LORD HERBERT. TO BE LEFT WITH MR. JOHN ROGERS, GOLDSMITH, NEAR TEMPLE BAR, LONDON.

Received his mentioning receipt of £200 bill from Corke. Told him in his last he would provide the linen yarn. Re-entered on Capt. Thomas Browne's lease of Bally ma Adam for arrears of rent. The under-tenant, one David Rouch, a kind of counsel-at-law, has subpoena'd the bailiffs into Chancery. Often desired his directions which he should stick to, Madam Browne, his lordship's sister's, interest, or Capt. Thomas Brown's. Imagines there was an agreement between Edward, Lord Herbert, and Madam Frances Browne, or he would not be so "overseen" as to grant the second lease to Capt. Brown whilst the first was in being. Lord Anglesye's agent is now taking out letters of administration of the goods of Capt. Brown as principal creditor; apprehends more danger from him than from his lordship's sister, she being secured her part of the rent during her lease (which he has seen under Edwd., Lord Herbert's, hand). This is not fit to be left to the writer's discretion.

Dublin,
26 May. 298.

1685

582. [EDWARD KENNEY] TO LORD HERBERT. TO BE LEFT WITH MR. JOHN ROGERS . . . LONDON.

Begins his journey for Kerry on Friday, though but three weeks married. Will be at Castle Island (God willing) before the 22nd, which is their fair, and a great expectation of money. Will thence send bills of exchange, a full account, and a perfect rent-roll. Will do what is safest in the business of Bally ma Adam.

Dublin,
7 July. 299.

[16]85

583. Somersett Fox to Lord Herbert at Limore Park.

Was indisposed with his old distemper when he received Lord Herbert's fat buck, for which he returns thanks. As to the other part of his letter, he neither knew nor heard of any such debt. Waited on Lord Herbert's brother a day or two before he died, when he complained how expensive his journey to London had been, and said his lady was following to pin up the basket, and yet he never mentioned any debt due from the writer. Knows not what writing Lord Herbert has found, being well assured he never owed any such.

Cayneham,
1 September. 416.

To "pin up the basket" is to bring things to a conclusion.

1685

584. Humfrey Owen to the Hon. Madam Browne. *Holograph copy.*

It is "my Lords" pleasure that for the better managing of her affairs she should sign and seal the enclosed letter of attorney before some of the supreme officers of the town, as the mayor and town clerk, that it may be of greater repute if transmitted to Ireland; and that she give authority to his lordship to act in the business of her estate in the possession of John Bray. It remains only that Mr. Browne's will be sent with directions how the writer shall order her affairs here and in Ireland (in case he goes thither). Asks also for such deeds and papers as concern the trust. The bond of Mr. Tho. Browne is in the writer's custody to be used for her advantage.

Lymor Lodge,
17 September. 118.

1685

585. Edward Kenney to Lord Herbert. To be left with Mr. John Rogers . . . London.

Sends copy of a bill of exchange for £300 drawn by Mr. Thomas Willes of Corke on Mr. Anthony Ball, merchant, in Abchurch Lane, London. Sent the original to Mr. John Rogers. Will stay here a full month.

Dublin,
19 September.

The "first bill" is appended. 302.

[16]85

586. Richard Old to Lord Herbert at Lymer Lodge.

Esteems his letter by Mr. Herbert's servant, yet should look upon it as a rebuke for this long delay in giving an account of his charge. It would be impertinent to express to him so evident a truth that frequent and long intermissions have been a great prejudice to Mr. Herbert's progress. Assures him that since his last return hither he has applied himself so as considerably to improve his knowledge, but his industry has not yet wrought that pitch which the writer desired. But can declare without reserve that he continues in all virtuous courses, without inclination to vice. Since his last coming to Oxford they have gone through with an entire body of moral philosophy and have made considerable progress in geography and the rudiments of practical astronomy, and are now entering upon the study of the civil law, beginning with Justinian's *Institutes*.

Ch. Ch., Oxon.,
30 September. 119.

Richard Old's pupil was Francis Herbert of Dolguog and Oakly Park—Lord Herbert's nephew.

[1685]

587. J. EDWARDS TO LORD HERBERT AT LYMORE LODGE.

He may send his commands to be left with Mr. Harrison, stationer in Lincoln's Inn Gate. Will wait on Mr. Newport about the trees—he came not to town till last night, Mr. Hosier says, and Lloyd the carrier will not be up till next week. This morning Aylif and Nelthrop received sentence of death upon their outlawry at the King's Bench, one of the first judgements of death that ever came from his merciful kinsman Sir Edwd. H.—for though the second judge pronounces sentence 'tis the act of all. Service to his lady.

London,
"28" October (*postmarked* 27th). *HM*2.23/74.

Ayloffe and Nelthorpe were executed on the 30th for complicity in the Rye House Plot. Sir Edward Herbert was the newly-appointed Chief Justice.

[16]85

588. AND. NEWPORT TO LADY HERBERT AT LYMORE LODGE.

"D. child". Only yesterday Mr. Edwards came about the fruit trees, yet must have them on Thursday to be sent by Lloyd the carrier. Must know the length of each wall and its position. They are to have ten foot betwixt each tree, and the ground must be made very good. Those were the orders he received from Sir Harry Capell and followed for the trees sent to Eyton. Will get the names of the choicest fruits from Sir Harry and have them sent next week by a Shrewesbury carrier to sister Corbett, whence Lady Herbert may fetch them on a couple of Welsh tits.

Yesterday Parliament met. Encloses the King's speech. The House of Commons took till Thursday next to consider it, and adjourned till then. The Turk loses daily by the Emperor, the King of Poland, and the Venetians. Teckely, going for help to relieve Caschaw, was siezed by a bashaw and sent to the Grand Signior to satisfy with his head for occasioning the breach of truce. Most of Teckely's forces have taken pay under the Emperor and Caschaw has surrendered. Will Harbord went into France lately without leave granted, if not denied. They are very angry for it at Court and talk of summoning him by privy seal. The reason of his going—pretended [to be] to place his daughters there for their health—is variously discoursed. A long debate in the Lords about sending for Lord Delamere because [he was] not indicted; it was said an indictment had been sent into Cheshire, and the King sent word he should be tried as soon as by course of law he could. The debate was adjourned to Monday. Hears the House of Lords is very thin and that summons is sent for all the lords to appear, there being sixty or seventy wanting.

Mr. Astly, the "Apholster", has sent 8½ yards of the mat to the carrier's inn. He will have half a crown a yard for it and sixpence for the canvas it is in—21s. 9d.

Lond.,
10 November. 115B.

"Sister Corbett" must be Newport's sister Anne, widow of Edward Corbet of Leighton, eldest son of Sir Edward Corbet, 1st Bart.—he had died as long ago as 1653. "Teckely" is Count Tököli. The charge against Lord Delamere was that of complicity in Monmouth's rebellion.

1685

589. [LORD HERBERT] TO MR. E. KENNEY. *Holograph copy.*

Has long threatened coming over to Ireland, but is forced to think of another way to clear accounts with him. Has sent Mr. Humfrey Owen, "a gentleman that belongs to me", to visit Castle Island. Desires he will acquaint him with all particulars—he is likely for the future to transact the writer's affairs with Kenney. Has given Owen a note of all bills returned to the writer or his goldsmith since Kenney's agency began. Desires the adjusting of waifs and strays, heriots, and such royalties. Owen is empowered by letter of attorney for inquisition into the writer's concerns. Is well assured in Kenney's management, but it is fit once in three or four years that the tenants should have the writer's ear. He will find Owen a very discreet, just, and tender person, who will avoid so much as shading Kenney's authority among the tenants, but will rather preach up observance, and thank him (for the writer) for his good methods, fair accounts, and upright justice. He should discourse at large the late Commission of Grace. Owen should stay five or six weeks. Kenney will find the inward man as much a gentleman as the outward.

24 November.

Endorsed: By Mr. Hum. Owens. 116.

[1685]

590. ——————TO LORD HARBART AT MOUNTGOMRY. FRANK.

The E. of Radnor has preferred his petition for a grant of Ranger of the Forest of Snowden, etc., enjoyed by Lord Herbert's ancestors and granted to him [though patent was stopped in passing. *Deleted*]. Thinks the Earl will have [it] without Lord Herbert, by interest in some person or other, can stop it. Had it yesterday [from] friends of the petitioner. He may judge the Admiral capable of serving him herein.

Added in another hand: Received his last post; cannot possibly answer it so soon—"pray make my peace with your Spous".

[*postmarked* 5 December]. *HM*2.21/19.

The addition is perhaps by the writer's wife, though the identity of both is unknown, the letter being unsigned. The admiral referred to is, of course, Lord Herbert's kinsman, Arthur Herbert, later Earl of Torrington.

1685

591. JOHN OLIVER TO MR. HUMFREY OWEN AT LORD HERBERT'S AT LYMORE LODGE.

Consulted Mr. Lewis Lewis about the business he was concerned in for the town of Mountgomery; he says it was upon a bill in the Excheque-er Chamber, and that the papers were delivered to Mr. Rice Morgan of Stallo, his client therein. This suit was about Flossam Common belonging to Mountgomery. There was another suit prosecuted by Lord Powys. Has, by direction of Mr. Richard Mason, delivered a copy of the information upon the *quo warranto* to Mr. Williams, who will be in the country before Christmas, where some of the corporation should attend him about drawing their plea for next term. Prays him give the enclosed bill to Lord Herbert and humbly requests payment. This sessions at the Old Bayly one Bateman, a chirurgeon, was found guilty of high treason for conspiring the death of his late Majesty. This day sennight Mr. Hamden is to be tried there.

12 December.

Mr. Lewis thinks the name was Flossam Common. 'Tis above twenty years ago. 113.

1685

592. JOHN OLIVER TO MR. HUMFREY OWEN AT LORD HERBERT'S AT LYMORE LODGE.

Mr. Newport attended him yesterday morning. Newport received a letter from "my Lord" and immediately went to the Lord Treasurer, the writer staying for him in the privy garden. The Lord Treasurer told him that Lord Radnor had petitioned the King for these places, which was referred to the Lord Treasurer, and so he directed Mr. Newport that a caveat might be entered on Lord Herbert's behalf against any such patent. Went with Mr. Newport to the office, but "my Lord" does not sit on Fridays. Went this morning and gave in a note for a caveat; on Monday it will be entered. Has not delivered the letter to Lord Radnor, on the Lord Treasurer's advice. [Lord Herbert] should send up a petition to His Majesty for these places, setting forth their being enjoyed by his ancestors, and the warrant from his late Majesty for the same. Finding the warrant would be of great service.

19 December.

Mr. Hambden is to be tried Wednesday sennight. Service to Mr. Bailiff Morgan.

Endorsed: 24 February [16]80, news by Mr. Henry Guyse that the Board of Treasury refused to pass his lordship's patent because it was desired for life; during pleasure was offered. April 1680, the King promised to renew the patent. 112.

1685

593. John Oliver to Mr. Humfrey Owen at Lord Herbert's at Lymore Lodge.

Prays him acquaint Lord Herbert that the caveat is entered. Thanks his lordship for his letter and bill of exchange. Mr. Williams went home this morning.

22 December. 114.

1685

594. [Lord Herbert] to Capt. St. Leger. *Holograph copy.*

Thinks it a great while since he heard from him. Has appointed the bearer, Mr. Owen, to call, presenting this and the writer's service. Would renew the league of friendship and continue the correspondence begun in a double glass, which distilled itself into a double letter, since which he has not heard from him nor Parson Wilson. Prays him begin again.

[? December]. 117.

1685

595. [Lord Herbert] to Mr. Wilson in Ireland. *Holograph copy.*

Holds it proper sometimes in the concerns of a remote estate to send a person of his family to visit it. Doubts not Mr. Kenny manages it with a great deal of prudence on the landlord's part and a competency of tenderness to the tenants. Nevertheless, he will not be so wanting to his tenants as not to send over sometimes, that if there be abuses they may be redressed in time. This, and to acquaint himself with the business of the estate, is the principal task of the bearer, Mr. Humfrey Owen. Prays him enter into familiarity with him and instruct him, and help him to good "Aucthors" to converse with. Purposes "I" [*recte* he] shall stay six weeks. Entreats him give him all the countenance he can.

[? December]. 115A.

1685/6

596. [Lord] Herbert to Mr. Humfrey Owen at Castle Island.

Since Owen left, the bearer, Mr. John Gerald Delis, came "in a Complaining Condition". It seems he was formerly recorder to the writer's courts. He now "pretends" to be tenant to Bally mac Adam. Is not certain whether it be set by Mr. Kenney or Owen, so cannot write but "recomendatory". Prays him do what may be kind to him and secure for the writer. Is unwilling he should depart the seigniory.

Lymore Lodge,
27 January.

Endorsed with notes about Ternygoote, Bally mc Adam, and Dissert apparently relating to rents. 120.

1685/6

597. NEWS-LETTER TO LORD HERBERT AT MONTGOMERY. *Unsigned.*

A French minister [expelled from] Holland addressed himself to the Bishop of London and the ministers of the Savoye, who, informed of his ill life, refused to admit him. He petitioned the King, and after examination the King told him he was an idle person, and that what he said of the Bishop was false (the fellow thought he pleased the King by railing against him). The ministers of Savoy were commended for their discreet deportment. M. Claud is writing a history of persecution of the French Protestants. There was a noise that the brief was stopped at the Great Seal, but it was on this account, that only French Protestants that conform to the Church of England shall enjoy the benefit of it.

On the 11th three vessels were cast away on the coast of Wicklowe, [one *omitted*] with wool for England, another with provision for France, and one from Chester. Also a ship (one Mason, master) with thirty passengers, coming from Nasson on the 18th, was cast away—two saved. With her went the *Charles* (Capt. Ryder, master) with above forty passengers and all the Lord Lieutenant's horses, but is not heard of, as also the *Elizabeth* of London, that went last month with the Lord Lieutenant's goods.

Lord Digby dead after a short sickness, and much lamented. On Monday morning died Lord Arran of the spotted fever; he will be interred in Westminster Abbey till the Duke of Ormand can convey him to Ireland. The Duke has but one of his children alive, the Countess of Devonshire, and two grandsons, Lord Ossery and his brother Lord Butler. It's said Lord Devonshire lost £60,000 by the burning of Montague's House, and that he was bound in £22,000 to deliver it up in good repair. It's also said he intends to go to Holland—knows not for what reason. On Friday the Earl of Castlemaine parted for Rome by way of France, £8,000 being allowed him. Madam Sidley, being made Countess of Dorsetshire, and the Queen somewhat displeased, is removed from Whitehall to St. James' Square, where she has purchased a house. The King has commanded the Archbishops to order the clergy not to preach controversies of religion, and has prohibited the priest any more to endeavour to persuade him to anything contrary to his promise to the nation.

28 January. 417.

Jean Claude's *Les Plaintes des Protestans cruellement opprimés dans le royaume de France* was published in 1686. The brief here referred to was that authorizing a subscription for the relief of Huguenot refugees. "Nasson" is Neston, in the Wirral. There is an account of Montagu House, Bloomsbury, in Chancellor's *The Private Palaces of London*, pp. 82-83, and of its destruction in Ellis's *Original Letters*, 2nd Series, Vol. IV, pp. 89-90. The news given here of Castlemaine's departure conflicts with the account in the *Dictionary of National Biography* (Vol. XLIII, p. 149), which says that he embarked at Greenwich on 15 February.

[16]85/6

598. A. NEWPORT TO LORD HERBERT AT LYMORE-LODGE.

Gave him or "poore Woman" a post or so since Lady Churchill's answer concerning the picture of the Princess, who could not get the painter to come to her and finish it by reason of the great quantity of work he has for others. But if she will have a great one, she thinks it may be sooner despatched. Mr. Beaver told him the bracelet was finished, but he cannot get it from him, so lost the opportunity of sending it by Mr. Hosier, who left this morning in the Shrewesbury coach. His brother and sister Newport are apprehensive "poore Woman" may be in danger of losing her eye by its continuing so long out of order and for want of proper remedies, wherefore they desire he would let her come hither, whether they will have her own chamber ready, and thereby prevent the objection of charge. Cannot meet with the French cook, and presumes he is employed by some other; is in quest of another. If he succeeds not, will he have an English cook, and upon what terms?

The King of France has given no satisfactory answer to the King's third memorial for the restitution of Orange, according to the Treaty of Nimeguen. He says he will have no sovereignty in his dominions but his own. He will not remove his dragoons hence nor release the ministers of Orange in Languedoc and Provence. He makes great preparations for land and sea service, both in the south and [north] of France. What and where he will attempt is not known. His sea commanders are not to open their instructions till under sail two days. The brief for the relief of the French fugitives here is in the press; 'tis believed the contribution will be very great. Lord Tyrconell is made a lieutenant-general in Ireland. Lord Dover's regiment of horse is to be turned into a fourth troop of guards, Lord Colchester and Jack Darcy the two lieutenants.

Lond.,
9 March.

Sends the writs to Mr. Hughes for keeping the Easter quarter sessions at Mountgomery. There is a report that Lady Sunderland will be Groom of Stool to the Queen. 140.

I am much indebted to Mr. Oliver Millar for giving me his views on the opening passage of this letter, regarding the portrait of Princess Anne; he suggests that the painter in question is most likely to be Willem Wissing.

[16]86

599. J., [Lord] Brackley, to Lord Herbertt at Lymore Lodge.

Has always been an ill newsmonger. Sir Richard Midleton is suddenly to be married to the widow Whittmore, and Lord Northampton is to have Sir Stephen Foxe's daughter (£20,000 down and £5,000 at her father's death). The Duke of Northumberland still keeps his wife in a monastery. The Duke of Allbemarle goes Governor of Jamaica and Viceroy over all the islands there. There is talk of five judges to be removed. Lord Willtshire is in town and presents his service.

London,
20 April. 121.

Sir Richard Myddelton's marriage had actually taken place the day before.

1686

600. EDWARD KENNEY TO LORD HERBERT. TO BE LEFT WITH MR. JOHN ROGERS . . . LONDON.

What he so much dreaded is come to a head. Mr. Thomas Fz Gerrald, after three years' close and private management of his business, has served the terre-tenants of the three plough-lands of Killmorry, the plough-land and a half of Carkir, and the half plough-land of Adergovall with a summons in ejectment. This business is carried on with all the violence and malice imaginable. Has written to Mr. Phillip Harryes to appear for his lordship, for the ejectment is from the King's Bench. Mr. Trant is concerned in two plough-lands of the five; if he be staunch, his interest joined with his lordship's will do much. Is sorry they did not appear in this before Mr. Owen left. Will go to Dublin next term if necessary.

Castle Island,
3 May.

Copies of the summons and of the notice by Laurence Keng, the casual ejector, to Donnogh O Daniell, are appended. 588.

1686

601. [SIR] J. CHARLTON TO LORD HERBERT AT MONTGOMERY.

Received this day by Robert Mason his letter in behalf of Montgomery for next assizes. Was before importuned and engaged for Pool, as most indifferent for the whole county, which he cannot retract.

London,
7 May. *Armorial seal* *HM*2.23/49.

Sir Job, having been deprived of his position as a Judge of the Common Pleas, had been re-appointed Chief Justice of Chester eight days before the date of this letter.

[16]86

602. A. NEWPORT TO LORD HERBERT AT LYMORE LODGE.

Must now contradict what he told "Poore Woman" by his last, for sister Newport, going farther than Chiswick yesterday with Lady Sunderland, was in such pain by the gravel stirred by the coach that she made bloody water. Fearing the long journey into Lord Herbert's parts, and the want of remedies in a like case upon the road, she has resolved to lay aside thoughts of a visit to her children this season. So he must expect no further trouble than will be given by the writer. Brother and sister Newport nevertheless desire him to promote "Poore Womans" going to the Bath after taking the Clee-hill waters, and he asks notice what time Lady Herbert goes to the waters at the Clee Hills; intends to move towards Shropshire on 7 June, and would make Ludlow his way from Worcester if she will be [there] when he is at Worcester about June 7th [? *recte* 9th], 10th, or 11th.

Lond.,
27 May. 122.

This discussion of Lady Herbert's taking the waters is continued in two further letters from Andrew Newport dated 1 and 12 June ("Old Herbert Papers", *Montgomeryshire Collections*, Vol. XX, pp. 61-2). There are several other letters from him in the same volume, pp. 53 ff.

[16]86

603. J., [Lord] Brackley, to Lord Herbert at Lymore Lodge.

Is glad his lady has lost her ague and finds no inconvenience by the powder, but fears "we shall all, by these declarations". Great talk of the abbey lands, but nothing begun. The camp is now on Hounslow Heath, and the King has sent for his subjects from out of foreign armies. So many weddings he has forgotten most of their names. Mr. Thomas Pellum has married Lord Clare's youngest daughter. Sir Edward Mansill's son is married to a great fortune. Arthur Herbert has Sir William Cliffton's regiment.

London,
29 May. 123.

[c. 1686]

604. Petition of Jane, widow of Richard Twiss of Killinterna, to Lord Herbert.

Subsequent [to] a former address four years past, immediately after the decease of Richard Twiss, it was his pleasure to allow her £5 yearly to be paid by his agent. Now though his orders for payment are come (if she be not misinformed) to Edward Kenney, esq., his agent, she has not received any part of it. Moreover, her husband had set the farm of Killinterna according to the rent of £26 yearly, and the farm's being now raised to £38 renders her son, Richard Twiss (with whom in a mesne estate she is cohabitant) incapable to maintain her. Her husband had waited on him in England, and the tediousness of the journey home to Kerry, with old age, brought him into a sickness whereof he died. Is now in her ninetieth year. 263.

1686

605. John Cadwalader to [Lord Herbert].

Desires him to order a tenant in this neighbourhood to pay the man that made the hay in the Bridge meadow. People being scarce, he had to give 12d. every day's "math or moweing"; which comes to 14s.

Llyssyn,
29 July. *HM*2.24/2.

[16]86

606. [Sir] Stand. Hartstonge to Lord Herbert.

Has his abstract of his case by the bearer, who seems well to understand it. Has given his opinion as faithfully as his skill will reach. Cannot subscribe him wholly secure, but believes him in no present danger. Lord Herbert will as soon find friends as his enemy to better his title. The last sitting of the late Commission for Defective Titles had assuredly made it good. Hopes to wait on him at his home; if not, as soon as he is in capacity in Ireland to serve him it shall be readily sought.

Trewerne,
21 August.

Endorsed: Touching the Irish land questioned by Thomas fitz-Gerald in ejectment. 589.

1686

607. ARTHUR DEVEREUX TO LORD HERBERT.

Is startled to find by his letter that the boring irons have not been all delivered. Sent them by Richard Phillipps the carpenter this six months to be delivered to Mr. Lateword; thought they had been faithfully restored. Will enquire into it as soon as his servants return from the coal pits. Thanks for thinking him worthy of being bailiff of Lord Herbert's town. But would be excused this year, for there are clouds which will grow into storms between Sir Godfrey Copely and himself about encumbrances upon the writer's estate—he and his lady are arrived in London, where the writer must attend them next term.

Nantcribba,
23 August. *Armorial seal* *HM*2.23/50.

Sir Godfrey's wife was Katherine, daughter of John Purcell of Nantcribau, now Devereux's seat.

1686

608. JOHN OLIVER TO MR. OWEN.

Received his yesterday with Mr. Newport's letter, which this morning he delivered to the Lord Treasurer, who ordered the writer to enter a caveat, which he did. If anything happens he will be sure to give "my Lord" an account thereof. This day the Bishop of London's cause was argued before the Lords Commissioners . . . Mr. Williams ordered him to send a copy of the *quo warranto* and plea against the town of Mountgomery to peruse in the country. Conceives it very proper for Mr Robert Mason to wait on Williams to answer any matter. Service to Williams and the rest of the corporation. Presumes his lordship has the *Gazette*, else he would have sent it. It is said there was a skipper on the Exchange today lately from Hamburgh who said the Danish army had thrown bombs into Hamburgh.

31 August. 125.

[16]86

609. R. B. TO LORD HARBUTT AT LYMOR LODGE.

Spoke with a gardener near Kingsinton and saw his cypress plants. His highest are but 2½ foot. They are two summers' growth. It's rare to find any higher or older, for the last frost destroyed it all. He will bate nothing of 5d. apiece. He serves a great many gentlemen in Shropshere. This is the season to remove them because of taking root before hard weather, but the spring is safest. Spoke with another gardener who would bate little of 12d. apiece and yet [his] are no better.

Haymarket,
23 September. 124.

1686

610. JOHN OLIVER TO MR. HUMFREY OWEN AT LORD HERBERT'S, LYMORE LODGE.

Received his and "my Lords" commands about the caveat. Consulted several about entering it. To make sure, he has entered two more in the two Secretaries of State's offices, so that no patent can pass for any estate in Ireland but must come to the Lord Treasurer or one of the Secretaries and notice given to the writer. The way a patentee must go (as he is informed by one Mr. Cooke, a clerk in the Secretary's office these thirty years) is by the King's commands to one of the Secretaries to write a letter to the Lord Lieutenant of Ireland or the chief commander there to grant such a thing to such a person, which letter must be sent by the Secretary to the Signet and there entered, and thence transmitted to Ireland. But if the estate be of value, as this is, the Secretary first acquaints the Lord Treasurer, who reports the matter to the King, and if the King thinks fit to grant it, then the letter is sent to the Signet. His lordship need not enter any caveat in Ireland. Will call often at those several offices to endeavour that no surprise may happen. Begs word if Mr. Robt. Mason has been with Mr. Williams about the *quo warranto*.

28 September. 126.

1686

611. [LORD] ROCHESTER TO LORD HERBERT, NEAR OAKLY PARK, MONTGOMERYSHEIR.

He was formerly acquainted that Thomas Knatchbull, esq., appointed by the peers receiver of money assessed on them by virtue of the Poll Act, had set him *insuper* £20 1s.; which by some mistake or neglect is not yet paid. Desires payment before 20 January, thereby preventing process of the Court of Exchequer for recovering the same; which the writer can in no wise hinder, the money being appropriated by Act of Parliament to particular uses.

Treasury Chambers, Whitehall,
6 December. *Armorial seal* *HM*2.23/51.

The address by which this letter was directed is misleading. Oakley Park, Montgomeryshire, is two miles north-east of Llanidloes, and a long way from either of Lord Herbert's seats. Oakly Park, near Ludlow, belonged to the Herbert's of Dolguog. The term *insuper*, peculiar to the Exchequer, signifies 'in debit'.

[16]86/7

612. ANNE BROWNE TO LORD HERBERT AT LYMOR LODGE.

Is not twenty-one yet, and as her father by his will desires Lord Herbert's care of her, so she chooses him for her guardian.

10 January. "Your . . . neece".

Her mother's service to him, his lady, and Aunt Alice.

*HM*2.23/52.

1686/7

613. E. CARLOS TO MR. HUMPHREY OWEN, LIVING WITH LORD HERBERT AT CHIRBURY

Has sent per "your Keeper" what letters are for Owen's family, and will keep his promise, God willing.

Salop.,
11 January. 127.

1686/7

614. T. TALBOT TO LORD HERBERT AT LYMER LODGE.

Received his dated 9 December relating to one Mr. Price who rides in the Earl of Peterborow's own troop. 'Tis but within a few days past that he knew whom it came from. Remembered the name Lymer Lodge, but thought it might be in the forest of Deane, from one Mr. FitzHerbert, and that the flourish at the beginning was the abbreviation of his name. But producing the letter at Lady Newport's he was better instructed. Does not know at present of any opportunity of advancing him, but will not fail to recommend him to the kindness of his officers, and to use his interest in his colonel to prefer him. Will do this to show Lord Herbert that it is not only those that live in the sunshine have an influence upon the writer.

London,
25 January. *Seal of a crest* 138.

[? 1686/7]

615. WI. WILLIAMS TO LORD HERBERT.

Perused the papers relating to Montgomery; has directed such searches and proceedings as [may be] useful for the defence of their borough in the *quo warranto*. Thinks they have an honest sufficient legal defence, and that the rights of the borough cannot be taken away by judgement in the *quo warranto*; the corporation ought not to be dissolved, though they cannot, it may be, as things are, maintain all their royalties claimed and sometimes used.

It is neither his short stay [here], the weather, nor the deep ways hinder his waiting on Lord Herbert. Neither can he write what it is. Hopes as the days lengthen the tempest will be allayed. May [see] him next spring. Intends for Gray's Inn Wednesday next week.

[? January or February]. *HM*2.9/82.

[? 1686/7]

616. [LORD] BRERETON TO LORD HERBERT AT LYMORE LODGE. FIRST TO LONDON.

Gives him this second trouble to request answer in a post or two whether he will admit those releases the writer signed when he signed that for Lord Herbert's last Christmas payment, and which are witnessed by Mr. Child's messenger. These being first showed Mr. Rodgers and he certifying Lord Herbert they are authentic, then (they being dated according to the time the money is payable) hereafter Mr. Rodgers may pay upon receipt of the said acquittances if the writer is not in to[wn].

25 February. 180.

[16]86/7

617. AND. NEWPORT TO LORD HERBERT AT LYMORE LODGE.

Finds Lord Herbert did not receive the box with the red serge, etc., for his libraries. The writer's niece Powle sent a box the same day by the same carrier, either to him or to "poore Woman", with linen, crewels, etc. The carrier, Nathaniell Jones, undertook to deliver at Mountgomery. He should appoint somebody in Shrewesbury to enquire after him at Wm. Jewson's. Always sends by Wm. Lloyd when he is in town, but he comes only once in three weeks.

The King of France declares he will give no disturbance to Germany this summer. 'Tis a jest about town that if one asked the King of France who is to be thanked for his being quiet, he would "sell him a Bargaine", for some say he begins to be ill again. Yesterday Harry Savill and cousin Arthur Herbert (Rear-Admiral) were discharged of their employments upon the same account as others of late. Lord Culpepper some time since married his daughter by Mrs. Willis to one Inglefield, for whom he has lately recovered an estate of £2,000 a year, and more depends upon the same title. Few now think Parliament will sit; a fortnight will clear that question. Fears Lady Rochester will die in a few days.

Having of late had some dealings in plate upon occasion of his executorship he was put in mind of their discourse at Lymore concerning the "Stye (as I thinke you calld it)" which Lord Herbert bought for "poore Woman" for a dessert of fruit and sweetmeats, but sent back. The writer pressing him to send for it again, Lord Herbert said that if the writer would give her the "Stye" he would give her dishes and a cistern of silver. If Lord Herbert will make good that promise the writer will send her down a silver "Stye". 'Twould be a favour to have the money he has laid out for Lord Herbert paid here, because he is out "a pretty deale of money, besides for my Nephew, &c . . . ."

James Porter is to be Vice-Chamberlain. Has not yet [heard] who is to succeed Arthur Herbert as Master of the Robes.

London,
8 March. 147.

"Inglefield" is Sir Charles Englefield, bart., of Englefield, Berkshire, and Wootton Bassett.

1686/7

618. JOHN OLIVER TO MR. HUMFREY OWEN AT LYMORE LODGE.

Desires him to acquaint "my Lord" that yesterday he and Mr. Rogers paid the £21 1s. at the Exchequer for Lord Edward Herbert's poll money, and have a tally. Delayed paying it in hopes it might have been saved, but upon enquiring at the Pipe, etc., he found that processes have gone out into several counties, especially Midds., for levying what is unpaid.

17 March. 139.

1687

619. JOHN OLIVER TO MR. HUMFREY OWEN AT LORD HERBERT'S AT LYMORE LODGE.

Enclosed is "my Lords" writ. Mr. Rice Foulkes tells him the Marquess of Powys is preparing a replication to the Corporation of Mountgomery's plea; he will be pressing for a rejoinder presently. Thinks Mr. Robert Mason would do well to come up that he may be ready to give full instructions. [Will move for prohibition but doubts it will not be granted. *Deleted*]. Service to the Corporation.

7 April. 134.

Lord Powis's activities in the *quo warranto* proceedings against Montgomery are seen, from the opposite side, in No. 34.

1687

620. M., [LADY] BRERETON, TO LORD HERBERT AT HIS LODGING IN WHITHALL.

Could have heartily wished he had paid her without moving the court. But if he cannot waive it she has appointed Mr. Apleton of Lincol's Inn to move the court tomorrow, and prays there be no interruption. He cannot but be sensible the Chancery decree her Lord got for Lord Herbert to pay him will indemnify him if he pays her.

18 April. 179.

1687

621. [LORD HERBERT] TO WM., BISHOP OF ST. ASSAPH. *Draft.*

Has information from the par[ishioners] of Llandyssell that he continues to suspend Mr. Petter Edwards (till it please God "to reduce him to his former abilities") and orders him a coadjutor meantime. Having abundant experience of Mr. Vaughan's ability, they are not desirous of anyone else, and request that, according to their former application, he will continue Vaughan amongst them. Has heard Mr. Vaughan, and he answers the character the gentlemen of Llandyssell give him. He deserves countenance and encouragement; and if resident he shall not want what books the writer has to promote his studies.

29 April. *HM*2.23/53.

Llandyssil is barely three miles from Lymore.

1687

622. JOHN OLIVER TO MR. HUMFREY OWEN AT LYMORE LODGE. *Small part only.*

. . . The Marquess of Powys has not replied to the *quo warranto* that they talk much of. Service to "my Lord".

2 May. 135.

[16]87

623. W., [Bishop of St.] Asaph, to Lord Herbert.

Will the more cheerfully obey his request in behalf of young Mr. Vaughan upon Lord Herbert's assurance of his being a worthy person. Has ordered his continuance at Llandyssel as coadjutor to Mr. Edwards during his unfitness. Lord Herbert's influence over him will be of great advantage to his ministry in that place, and the benefit of his good library will fit him for a better. Thanks him for these favours to a poor churchman, and trusts Vaughan will do it many years after the writer is gone. Much desires to kiss his hands ; meanwhile will not be wanting in his duty to pray for his health and prosperity.

4 May. *HM2.23/54.*

1687

624. John Oliver to Mr. Humfrey Owen at Lymore Lodge. To be left at Mr. Thomas Seys' at Bishop's Castle.

This afternoon Capt. Herbert sent for the writer to give an account of the Marquess of Powys's proceedings in the *quo warranto*. When replication comes the Captain will go to the Marquess to endeavour to stop proceedings, but he does not think it fit to put the Marquess in mind of it ; will give Lord Herbert an account. Capt. Herbert has had but an indifferent welcome to London, being last night discharged from his captainship ; he was at Whitehall [earlier] and some questions were asked, to which he did not give satisfactory answer, as is supposed. [Wrote] Tuesday last that the prohibition was denied.

7 May. *Armorial seal* 137.

1687

625. John Oliver to Mr. Humfrey Owen at Lymore Lodge. To be left at Mr. Thomas Seys' at Bishop's Castle.

Yesterday received his dated the 2nd. "Where your letters and mine stay I cannot imagine." Searched at the Statute Office in 1674, 1675, and 1676, but cannot find any statute acknowledged by Lord Edward Herbert. The Marquess of Powys has not yet given replication. Hopes he received his letter about Capt. Herbert and the other acquainting him that the court would not grant prohibition.

14 May. 132.

1687

626. Hum. Owen to Mr. Oliver. *Copy in Lord Herbert's hand.*

There is a cause depending in the Court of the King's Bench, holden at a place called "lez Kings Courts" in Dublin, by Mr. Maurice fitz. Gerald, lessee of Tho. fitz Gerald, esq., against Lord Herbert in ejectment for lands in co. Kerry, to be tried Michaelmas term (which begins 6 November, though all the others [are as] in England). His lordship is willing, if the cause miscarry, to have a writ of error returnable at the

King's Bench at Westmr., which he must send to be left at the post-house in Cork, by way of Dublin.

Castle Islands,
28 August.

The panel of *venire* makes Hen., Lord Herbert, defendant, without any addition. Lest a letter with such a writ miscarries he should sue out two writs and send one to Mr. Richard Owens, postmaster at Holy head, to send to the writer at Dublin at the Goat in Copper Alley, Mr. Rees Davies's house, by one of them of the packet-boat or honest seamen. Owens has done the writer greater service.

By the rule of counsel there should be ten [writs] if cheap at test—five according to the enclosed. Advice of counsel [is that] they should have three or four writs of error, the first with a test 17 November . . . 148.

1687

627. JHO. JERVIS TO MR. HUMPHREY OWEN AT CASTLE ISLAND.

Sent away his letters for England and gave Sir Jno. Meade and Mr. Longan their fees. Met with Mr. [? Pyne]; finds [Lord Herbert] may command his money in England when he pleases. Met the Earl of Inchyquin, and finds great expectations of [Lord Herbert's] coming hither, and a room furnished on purpose for him. Told him he thought his lordship intended to be as private as he could, but Lord Inchyquin will press hard to have him lodge at his house. Mr. Crofts presents his service, and is mightily thankful that his lordship will accept of his offer.

Corke,
1 September. 149.

Lord Inchiquin was Lord Herbert's brother-in-law by his marriage to the dowager Lady Herbert.

[16]87

628. ———————— TO MR. HUMFRE OWEN AT MR. MALLYBOURN'S IN CORKE. *Torn.*

Prays two lines, when he is quiet at the Island, to let him know his thoughts concerning "my Lds." claim to Mr. Kency . . . . . and what will satisfy "my lord", [that] the writer may be prepared against the next meeting with Mr. Keney, that things may be composed. "This to your selfe".

11 October.

Fragmentary notes and accounts in Humphrey Owen's hand on the dorse : . . . wolf £4; soldiers £1 10s.; prisoners £14 14s. 3d.; wolf cubs £1 10s.; Cler. pac. £10; 2 bitch wolves £8; "Strand Polls" 5s. Island parish £20 8s. Foxes 9s. Assess £24 5s. County total £42 1s., seigniory near the third part of the barony. 590.

The notes on the dorse look like the jottings of a high sheriff or some other county official.

1687

629. JOHN OLIVER TO MR. HUMFREY OWEN. TO BE LEFT AT MR. REES DAVIES'S AT THE GOAT IN . . . DUBLIN.

Received a letter from "my Lord" to send a writ of error, Maurice Fitz Gerald plaintiff and his lordship defendant, but he does not say in what court. Bespake the writ; it is made out as if the cause were in the King's Bench in Ireland, for the cursitor says that if it be in the Common Pleas or Exchequer there a writ must be had out of the King's Bench there to remove it thither, and then a writ here to remove it to the King's Bench here. Received no other letter than that upon Wednesday from his lordship from Chester, who intended thence for London, but the coaches were all taken up for a fortnight.

15 October.

Although the writ came to the cursitor at 11 on Saturday night from the Lord Chancellor, it came not till yesterday. Encloses it and hopes it will prove right. Owen's counsel and attorney will give him directions, for they see these things often there.

18 October. 128.

1687

630. JOHN OLIVER TO [LORD HERBERT].

Seeing his lordship has the convenience of sending a letter by a safe hand to Mr. Owen, he thought it best to send the two writs of error, that he may send them [that way], which is far securer than post, for the messenger will deliver them to Mr. Owen whether at Corke or Dublin. The trial is the 17th of next month. Designs to send two others of other dates on Thursday to Mr. Owen at Mr. Rees Davies' at the Goat in Dublin. Hopes he will remove the cause into England if it go against him in Ireland. Consulted Mr. Moses Reynolds, who is now here, and they thought it best to send this to Reynolds's clerk in Shrewsbury, who is to wait upon his lordship as soon as it comes. Hears nothing of the Marquess's proceedings against Mountgomery. Has no news, but supposes Mr. M. Lloyd has written.

25 October.

Moses and the writer are now drinking his lordship's health and her ladyship's. 146.

1687

631. JOHN OLIVER TO MR. REES DAVIES AT THE GOAT IN . . . DUBLIN.

Sends him the enclosed by command of Lord Henry Herb[ert], who desires him to deliver it with all speed to Mr. Humfrey Owen, his lordship's agent, who should now be with him from Corke.

Clifford's Inn, London,
27 October. 129.

1687

632. JOHN OLIVER TO MR. HUMFREY OWEN AT MR. REES DAVIES'S IN . . . DUBLIN.

Sent him Tuesday sennight a writ of error returnable *quindena Martini*. Has since received his letter for three or four writs, and [another] for ten writs. But the charge for each being 16s. 6d. he has only sent four, returnable *octavis Pur[ificationis]*. His lordship will send two by an Irish tenant he has with him. The writs are tested 17, 22, and 25 November, and 27 October. The cursitor makes a doubt whether he can justify making a writ before the *teste* day, but unless they will allow a writ tested before the trial it is impossible to have a writ from England before execution. The cursitor says they commonly test writs before trial. One is made Fz gerald, the others Fitzgerald. Four days must be allowed to move for a new trial or writs of error, as here in England. The return of the first writ is so short he cannot have the record certified in time, and then they will have *executionem judicii*.

27 October. 130.

1687

633. JOHN OLIVER TO MR. HUMFREY OWEN AT MR. REES DAVIES'S AT THE GOAT IN . . . DUBLIN.

Sent this night a letter to Mr. Rees Davies wherein he has sent Owen a large letter with two writs of error. Sent it to Davies lest it be interrupted.

27 October. 133.

1687

634. JHO. JERVIS TO MR. HUMPHREY OWEN AT CASTLE ISLAND.

It is the opinion of all counsel concerned that the challenge, either against the sheriff, "or, for want of hundreders, either of them", must stand good. One living in any part of the county and having a freehold within the barony is a good hundreder, or one living in the barony and having a freehold anywhere in the county. So he must be very cautious how he relies upon that challenge . . . It has cost him time and money in the Rolls Office. Finds only those lands granted to Garret Fitz James by patent of defective titles in the time of Charles I. Finds Sir Jerom Sankey's certificate, wherein are Bally mc Adam and Tulligg Edmond but none of the other lands. If there be a patent he will find it before Owen comes to town; so he must not fail to bring proof of the seizure and sequestration. But they will be undone unless he makes good one of the challenges, for things are very much altered, as he will perceive by the next news letters—the King now sending the Lord Lieutenant into every county to see who will consent to the abolishing of penal laws, that he may know his friends from his foes. He is most earnest to have a parliament to abolish those statutes [and] to pass an act for naturalizing all foreigners, both Jews and gentiles; so in all probability "my Lord" will be privileged by next term—if not, Mr. Fitz Gerald's courage will be much abated. The Civil Survey was not authentic, so he has got another. Capt. Shaw acknowledges the bond but says he has performed the condition; Sir Jerom, as he says, in his lifetime conveyed those lands to Capt. Browne in "my Lords" name. Sir Jno. Temple is expected; will secure him on their side. Nugent is made Lord Chief Justice, Justice Martin removed out of the Common Pleas into his place, and Sir Bryan O Neale brought into his. So if Sir Collins comes over he thrusts out Lyndon or Worth. Has sweetened Mr. Lyndon. Service to Mr. Wilson. Remembrance from Mr. Davis and his wife.

Dublin,
29 [October *omitted*].

The words of Fitz Gerald's patent are . . . (*the wording follows*). Hears Mr. Harris is well; Sam Tench is gone to persuade him over, but he is not expected till spring. Mr. Fagan lives very well here. Sends him a subpoena, for they must be well prepared in everything. He must bring Mr. Saunders up to give account of his holdings. Reeves is a good freeholder.

On the outside: Furnished the bearer with 4s. 9d.; prays him stop it out of his pay. *Armorial seal* 150.

1687

635. John Oliver to Mr. Humfrey Owen.

Begins with a copy of No. 634. Sent him another letter dated 29 October with this very letter transcribed, for fear that sent the 27th with the two writs should miscarry. Received his from Mr. Rogers dated 16 October. Has now sent him two writs more, one tested 19 November, the other 26 November, both made Fz gerald, not Fitz gerald. He should erase the mark of the *teste's* upon the label, for the cursitor thinks it not fit that should be seen.

8 November. 131.

The 'other' letter is no doubt No. 91 in the Appendix; it is dated 1 November, not 29 October.

1687

636. John Oliver to Lord Herbert at Lymore Lodge.

Sheriffs for England were pricked last night: Shropshire, Robt. Leighton, esq. Hereford, Herbert Masters, esq., old sheriff; Glouc., Henry Hall, esq.; Cheshire, Thomas Lee, esq.; Worcester, Sir Walter Blount; Monmouth, Phillipp Jones, esq.

3 December. *HM2.24/4.*

[16]87/8

637. James Sloane to Robert Rochford, esq., at Dublin. *Copy on dorse of the next letter.*

A gentleman has retained him for Lord Herbert, and desires to know how to bring his cause in Chancery here, as Lord Killdare did [by *omitted*] Sir Maur. Eustace . . . *An explanation of the method follows.* But what should be the grounds of equity God knows, for the gentleman is a stranger to the title. In Lord Kildare's case the Lord Chancellor offered a feigned issue—whether George Fitzgerald, the person attainted, was the *cestui que trust*—but would not let them try it in Ireland; and because they would not try it here made a decree against the verdicts and judgements in Ireland. [Understands] he is counsel for Lord Herbert.

London,
16 January. 592b.

1687/8

638. JOHN OLIVER TO MR. OWEN.

Retained Mr. Sloane yesterday; on the other side [is his letter] designed for Mr. Rochford (which Owen himself can as well answer). Sloane has ordered him to take out a subpoena, which he will send, that Owen may convey it to Holy head and so to Ireland. Prays him draw the bill himself and send it, and to bring the writ of error betimes, so that *executio judicii* may not go out. Service to "my good Lord"— Mr. Lloyd sent him a parcel by Lloyd the carrier, and therewith come some seeds he was commanded to buy.

17 January. 592a.

1687/8

639. JHO. JERVIS TO MR. HUMPHREY OWENS AT MR. JNO. OLIVER'S CHAMBER IN CLIFFORD INN, LONDON.

Is glad to hear things are well at the Lodge. No money is received yet; the tenants, not seeing "us" drive, believed there were no orders to receive, and seemed as if they thought there was no rent due. Owen's giving orders not to distrain was the reason of his forbearance. But receiving his letter yesterday, he has sent abroad, and does not question but in two or three weeks to send the £200. Has no account of any horses but what he brought down himself, they being lamed and killed in Mr. Walsh's journey through co. Wicklow. Walsh had the impudence to come to him the other day for money that it cost his son in endeavouring to cure one of them. Parted with none, but gave him an account of his treachery to "my Lord", he being servant to the commissioners when Killmurry was sequestered . . . There is no danger of anyone stirring till after Easter term. Received a letter from cousin Fleming that the record is enrolled *capiator*. Now everyone cries that if they had known sequestration was the matter to be proved [there was] nothing so easy. Duty to his lordship.

Castle Island,
25 January. *Armorial seal* 151.

1687/8

640. [LORD] HERBERT TO MR. HUMFREY OWEN.

On Wednesday last Mr. Moses Reynolds sent him a subpoena to be served in Ireland upon the two Fitz Geralds, Moris and Thomas. Despatches his groom for Ireland to see them executed on their persons in Dublin or in Kerry. Directed him to Mr. Rice Davis of Copper Alley.

26 January.

Notes on the dorse in a contemporary hand: £76 18s. 8d. interest of £440 left by Madam Vaughain received by "Esqr. Herbert". £39 9s. 4d. to the poor of the parish, *sed quaere.* 154.

1687/8

641. [LORD] HERBERT TO MR. JOHN OLIVER, ATTORNEY, AT CLIFFORD-INN, LONDON.

By good luck he opened the letter to Mr. Humfrey Owen from Mr. Moses Reynolds and Oliver, and found the subpoena returnable 13 February. Sent his servant immediately with it for Ireland to see it executed. Hopes Mr. Humfrey Owen is with Oliver before this. If possible he is to procure the seeds he sent for. Received the bundle of papers and seeds from Meredith Loyd; service to him.

Limore Lodge,
26 January.

For the future he should direct all things [to . . . . . *the name deleted and illegible*] lest others be absent. 172.

1687/8

642. [LORD] HERBERT TO MR. JOHN OLIVER, ATTORNEY, AT CLIFFORD'S INN, LONDON.

The subpoena was sent for Ireland express by the writer's servant to see it executed, that he may make affidavit thereof before some Master of the Chancery. Remember the seeds.

Limore Lodge,
29 January. 155.

1687/8

643. [LORD] HERBERT TO MR. HUMFREY OWEN AT LONDON.

Told him he had sent the subpoena for Ireland . . . Would have him consider the safest and best "for me to fall into the road" of paying Lord Brererton the annuity now suspended by his lunacy. Lord Ranalagh says he'll get a deputation from His Majesty to receive it. Does not like these high "abretrary" methods. The most legal and safest way is to have that court that decreed him to pay it to Lord Brererton to order, the writer consenting, that Lord Ranelagh should receive it during Lord Brererton's indisposition. His design is only to do things secure and not to delay payment. When it is resolved, [will] order payment by Mr. John Rogers.

"Let the little Bagnett I bespok of you to buy for me, the crose bar and thing a top be Iron guilt, so the Knife and bodkin and belt to it". There is a book of his grandfather's writing which he has not in his library. Desires him to procure it in Dark Lane, the likeliest place for such things. 'Tis called *De Religione Gentilium*—cannot answer for his Latin, whether 'tis *Gentilum* or *Gentilium.*

29 January. 156.

[16]87/8

644. Ed. Lloyd to Humphry Owen. Leave at Mr. Oliver's chamber in Clifford's Inn, London.

The two casks of usquebaugh are come and will be sent forward per next trow without fail, together with some wine for which he received order lately in the country.

15 February. 152.

1687/8

645. Jho. Jervis to Mr. Humphrey Owen. To be left at the Goat in . . . Dublin.

When David Adeney came over "my Lord" wrote to Mr. Wilson that Owen would be here immediately; last night Mr. Mason came with the same news. There is no money to be had in the country; people deal here altogether by paper, which it is thought will soon grow scarce. There was never such a loss of cattle for many years, many dying fat and no one knowing their distemper. Tom Corbett's are all dead, cutting two inches of fat upon the brisket, so that no man can persuade him but that his were bewitched. There are small hopes of money till the island fair unless Mr. Kenny assists, who sends word he is now raising money in co. Wexford to that end; will go to Corke [just] before the assizes to press him forward. Kenney has yielded possession of demesnes but not one penny of rent. Hears Carthy is admitted *in forma paup*[*eris*]. *A passage follows too torn to be intelligible.* Service to Mr. Davis and his family.

Castle Island,
21 March. 153.

1688

646. Jho. Jervis to Mr. Humphrey Owen.

Received a letter which he is certain he did not deserve. A few days after coming into this country Mr. Herbert showed him a letter from Mr. Bollard that the bill was not come to hand, but as soon as it came it should be paid. He afterwards showed the writer Mr. Davis's letter—knows Mr. Davis's hand—giving an account of the good advice he had given his brother-in-law, and that the bill was paid. If things fell out otherwise he heard no more of it. Hopes to see him "suddenly". Service to Mrs. Wilson.

Castle Island,
22 May.

Mr. Herbert has shown him a letter from Mr. Bollard that the bill was gone back protested upon a mistake. 157.

1688

647. Jho. Jervis to Mr. Humphrey Owen. To be left at the Goat in . . . Dublin.

Is sorry his anger continues. Wrote an account by those that came to meet Mrs. Wilson, but gives this account . . . *Repeats the substance of No. 646.* The subpoena was desired by Mr. Herbert, who says the only evidence Carthy has against "my Lord" is an acquittance by Mr. Herbert's father to Carthy's father for 20s. rent out of the lands of Cluddane, whereas it should have been for his proportion of it, he holding but a fifth or sixth—it was set to so many tenants, everyone a gneeve. Carthy believes he has evidence to satisfy a Lord Chancellor, though it may not satisfy a jury. He may not do amiss to send down another [subpoena] against the lessee and lessor of the two plough-lands on the mountain, for if he relies on those lands being seized and sequestered he his mistaken. Those who know best say all the rest of Roche's estate was seized—that where Mr. Moor lives, Currens which Mr. Hassett has, and other places in the valley—but no man thought those two ploughlands, being mountain, worth the taking, though any might have had them for the asking. So unless he can by an entail or other way "invalid" Mr. Gyles Herbert's sale, if it comes to a trial his lordship must lose it. He should consider whether he may do better in Chancery. Goes this week to Lytter to discourse Mr. Thomas Hassett concerning it.

There is not like to be any money before the Island fair. Mr. Kenny has been three weeks in the country, has not raised 20s., and is forced to borrow money to carry him home. Owen may have cattle distrained, but then the people cry they are ruined because their cattle have barely strength to be driven. Sir Jerom Sankey's deed must be in the hands of Gunter. Can get no papers out of Mr. Fitzmoris's hand—he says Owen promised him security. Sent the horse he rode hither along with those that came to meet Mrs. Wilson. There are two in George Twisse's hands. All well here, only many are as envious as the "divelo".

Castle Island,
27 May. 158.

1688

648. Jho. Jervis to Mr. Humphrey Owens at the Goat in . . . Dublin.

Cludane is no vill, but is in the constablewick of Killinterna. It is where Mr. Herbert built two cabins for his ploughmen, and they are all the inhabitants. There never was anyone in that place known to serve as constable, only Mr. Thomas Herbert once appointed one Owen Dawly that lived there as his servant. Has this from Mr. Edward Herbert. As to the other, it is the general opinion that unless it be compounded, "my Lord" will be cast. Goes on Friday to Lytter, and then will give a further account. Patricke Pierce now comes with all his forces against Bally mac Addam, so he must consider what defence to make. Mr. Kenny has agreed with Mr. Fitz Gerald to enter into possession of Killcusney; gave him notice of the arrear upon it—does not believe his lordship's distraining for his rent can prejudice Madam Browne's action. "He" is dissatisfied about Tubbermange, and to secure it is earnest to take the next half plough-land of Bally mac addam adjoining. Gave Mr. Mason reasons why he should not be very forward in it. He said Owen gave the same reasons last year, which was much to his loss; he is making a large provision there for one of his sons. Mr. Fitz Gerald and his tenants could no longer agree, so they are all fled, which is the reason he now deals with Mr. Kenney. Hopes he is satisfied about

Mr. Herbert's bill. Has not sent Owen's horse, knowing he cannot come as yet. Travelled in vain to Kilkenny with Mr. Wilson's horses, who is now forced to send fresh ones. Takes no notice of the later part of his letter because there is malice enough in that place, but he has "her" letter by him, wherein she gives account of Mr. Fagan's kindness, and of what money she had of him, and desiring the writer to pay him, which he did. Owens was the first to give him notice of her death. If she wanted anything she was to blame for not letting the writer know.

Castle Island,
29 May. 159.

1688

649. JHO. JERVIS TO MR. HUMPHREY OWEN AT THE GOAT IN . . . DUBLIN.

Much admires that Mr. Drew so misinforms Owen as to the arrears; he has not paid—Mr. Wilson took it upon himself. Neither is Mr. Sanders like to receive sixpence before the Island fair—such a thing as money is not known here. The tenants' hope is that one cow will give [as] much this year as two last, and that they all [will be] bought into co. Corke to repair the dairies there—only they are loath to part with them before they have recovered themselves. The loss of cattle has been as great in co. Corke as in co. Kerry, and that being the place for cows is all the hope this county has. Above a hundred families are gone a begging out of the seigniory and as many more are starving; abundance are turned to thieving. The head tenants will stand, and never were people more thankful to "my Lord" for his long forbearance. They desire patience till the Island fair, and then if they fail to clear Michaelmas and all arrears they desire no mercy.

Mr. Kenny has got possession of Kilcussny and is gone home without receiving £5. Mr. Fitz Gerald is gone to live at a part of Killmurry with Maurice Fitz Gerald, his lessee. But he is in a very low condition and the people all forsake him and complain they have paid him their rent beforehand; he assures them of his recovering that land in a short time.

As to the writer's coming to Dublin, he cannot imagine why Owen mentions it, for if Madam Browne's cause be at issue he supposes it is his lordship's business. If Owen has occasion for money he should send orders to distrain, and there will soon be as much as will serve. All things are alike to do well [except] those plough-lands on the mountain, which must be Owen's care. As to the other, there is evidence found that will serve without going into Chancery. Does not yet hear from Mr. Pierce.

Castle Island,
4 June. 160.

1688

650. JHO. JERVIS TO MR. HUMPHREY OWEN AT THE GOAT IN . . . DUBLIN.

The subpoena[s] shall be served upon all save Gunter. Mr. Fitz Morris has sent a bundle of papers to Dr. Anthony to deliver to the writer. Tullileagh and Kave Knyveag never had constable or other officer in the memory of any, save the constable of this place, they being in this parish. Cannot tell what he means by "the Rocke of Seazin and Sequestration", but cannot find by any person that ever this was seized or sequestered. Intends to wait upon Mr. Bateman, who has the mountains of Brasnagh adjoining, which were also the estate of Roch . . . . As to familiarity with "that family", it has been no more than could not be avoided, and no ways prejudicial to "my Lord". Mr. Kenny, Capt. Meade, Mr. Herbert, and all their families are in co. Corke. Although "he" seems forward to pay his lordship's money, the writer is satisfied it will come to a suit. Mr. Patricke Pierce has done nothing as to Bally mc Adam to their knowledge, but lest he should have gone privately and sworn service of the tenants (who are great rogues) it would not do amiss to search into it. Hopes the money is paid Mr. Davis.

Castle Island,
12 June.

On Thursday sennight at noon, Mr. Trant having bought Mr. Kenny's corn and employing people to burn some, the straw burnt his lordship's barn to the ground in half or quarter of an hour. 171.

1688

651. Hum. Owen to Lord Herbert.

The bearer coming in company with Lord Kerrye's second son (bound for London and thence for Oxford), he renews his request for the sending over of his lordship's patent, etc. As to his estate here, all care is taking to save that which it is feared the tide will carry down, for on the last day of the term a motion was made before Sir Stephen Rice on behalf of Esquire Denny of Tralee, alleging lands now questioned were in his possession very long in "the time of the Claymor" and his ancestors' without suit, and that he might plead the Statute of Limitations, to which the court consented. Then was another made for Lord Herbert to have the same rule, which so awakened the Chief Baron that he ordered it be moved this term. In this case is Lord Orrery for £1,000 a year, and Mr. Bateman of Kerry. And it is so general a case that it is thought to be too good a bar to pretenders not seized or possessed this twenty years, and that it is too good a piece of law to be admitted by three judges against their friends. It is of so general a concern to the English interest that if it be denied no art here on this side can stop the present current. Cannot determine what a petition to His Majesty, attended by persons of greater concern than Lord Herbert, may produce. It is to be hoped he would not so much reject it but agree to hear counsel . . . *Details and effect of the statute follow.*

Dublin,
15 June. 161.

1688

652. Jho. Jervis to Mr. Humphrey Owen at Dublin.

Sent Murphy into co. Corke to show Gunter the subpoena . . . Mr. Fitzmorris sent some papers, of no value . . . Has given instructions for serving Roch and his lessee. Carthy's subpoena was out of date before he could be served, but he wishes the other was as secure . . . Mr. Bateman is in Dublin.

Sends Owen's bay nag. Got the white one not long since by much entreaty. He will much admire at the condition of the saddle, and that it was left to the writer to ride on from Dublin. But [the horse] was thought too good for him to look at till Mrs. Wilson brought Owen's orders for them. As for the bridle, Mr. Nicholls suffered it to come into the hands of Theodor Mason. Hopes that by this their civility to Owen he can guess at their behaviour towards the writer. Lt. FitzMaurice's service.

Castle Island,
20 June. 162.

1688

653. JHO. JERVIS TO MR. HUMPHREY OWEN AT THE GOAT IN . . . DUBLIN.

Is concerned that he cannot receive one kind letter from him. Perhaps some that cannot govern all with the applause they expect have been busy. When Mr. Herbert left two or three weeks since he showed him a letter from Mr. Bollard owning the mistake in the bill of exchange and saying he had ordered it to be paid. If these be fallacies they will fall hard upon Mr. Herbert, who averred he would satisfy to the utmost farthing any damage in charges or interest; he is not yet returned.

Was lately in Mr. Carthy More's company. There being a great difference betwixt him and Capt. Sullivan about some lands, it seems they study revenge, and he swore that if the writer would get this writ against him removed, his castle should not secure him, though forced to turn bailiff himself. Sends to have it removed; does not question getting the money.

Mrs. Fagan is this day gone to Killarny fair. Received a submissive letter from Mr. Gunter desiring to meet him at Killarny. As to the writer's boy, it is no other than he expected, though there was no need of anything of that on brother Hughes's side . . . This morning after Murphy went Twisse sent Owen's bay nag, but miserably poor—"which is an argument that he need not demand Graseing". Wrote that Clydane was no vill nor had constable or tithing-man; [observes] Owen says the contrary.

Castle Island,
24 June. 163.

[16]88

654. W. [LLOYD, BISHOP OF ST.] ASAPH, TO LORD HERBERT AT LIMORE PARK.

Is ashamed he has not answered his two letters. But Lord Herbert will excuse him when he knows how his thoughts have been employed—has now more of that employment than ever. His first letter recommended a young man of Newtowne for the vicarage of Llanllwchaiarn, if he found him fit. Found him yet in deacon's orders, and so raw that he would not venture to put him in priest's orders ; was therefore not sorry he had disposed of that vicarage before he came. His other letter was in behalf of young Mr. Vaughan, whom (as Lord Herbert desired) upon his father's voluntary cession he instituted to the rectory of Mallwyd.

The bearer has been his chaplain two or three years, and was with him in the Tower during his imprisonment. Not knowing how His Majesty may deal with the writer, he hastens the bearer away to the rectory of Newtown, to which he has instituted him; he will acquaint Lord Herbert with all he would know.

24 June. *HM*2.23/57.

[? 1688]

655. [LORD HERBERT] TO THE BAILIFFS, ALDERMEN, AND BURGESSES OF MOUNTGOMRY. *Holograph copy.*

His propositions touching the dispose of their free-land to a more profitable use relished ill with them. Is discouraged to make further motions, or acquaint them of what reputation they are abroad. Their piercing eyesight detects a design to convert the free-land to his own use, under pretence of prevailing with the burgesses to invest it in trustees for ever for the poorest inhabitants for buying a stock of wool yearly to put them on work (the stock to increase yearly as much as the land will yield), for setting out of which money to undertakers who are to repay the principal every year and find money of their own to [pay] wages for working up the raw wool or whatever it be for the market, the bailiffs or trustees setting a fitting rate upon the labour that the undertakers may carry on to their profit . . . The trustees accountable to the poor . . .

Then this divesting the corporation and investing [the] poor [secures] the free-land for ever . . . Whether the overthrowing of the corporation does not overthrow their right to the free-land—happen it will fall to the King or to whom he conveys the lordship of Mountgom[er]y; which his proposition prevents, and a unanimous action of theirs with quiet possession will be good against all claims. Will, if they apply to him, say much more for their better satisfaction, and will come to a treaty on it as counsel advises. Is not ambitious of handling their money or anything in their trust. Seeks no benefit of them, unless by enriching them he enables them to pay rents for his own freehold, which lies unfortunately about a town wilfully poor, when they have it in their power to enrich themselves honestly.

To which end, for a second means, they ought to invite able shopkeepers and give them the freedom of the town. And those of the town that have not stock to set up shop or repair their houses ought to set their houses to work . . . . . . to carry on the trade of the town in their station as workmen, workwomen, and workchildren. Then will houses be fitted to receive judges, counsel, and gentry; want of which is what hinders the Great Sessions from the town, and will drive away quarter sessions and other meetings. If judges, counsel, and gentry would have assurance of good accommodation, he could procure the latter Great Sessions for this year; and in time, if the town betters, it may be held there constantly, as shire town.

The town hall is found fault with as too cold and out of repair; which must be mended by stopping the window at the end, and wainscotting or hanging it for sessions time, and making two large "doormant" windows each end of the table. Then to procure Mr. Mason and Mr. Thomas Francis to build, repair, and furnish houses. Then will judges and lawyers have no objection, and the rest of the town will accommodate the gentry very well.

Proposes that those who wilfully withstand the good of the town be disfranchised for years or for ever; and that they sit in council to advise about bye-laws for better regulating their under-members, [and] how to increase their markets and fairs, which suffer by miscarriage. They must produce their patents, grants, and custom-book, and instruct counsel, to keep them within their liberties ...... Hopes these propositions will savour with them, and that they will out of hand call in all their members to consider them. Will give assistance freely if they please to take it. And to ease their minds of their groundless jealousy of him, he declares once more he has no design on their free-land but to order it so that it yields profit to the parish in spite of any disaster to their corporation; which, though granted for ever, is forfeitable if the condition of the grant be not observed ...

Their way of proceeding first [should be by] consent under hand and seal of every member that is a burgess, to be procured at the bottom of a parchment containing their free will to refer conclusion of the whole matter relating to the good of the corporation and securing the free-land to the parish (after it is alienated from the corporation) to eleven or thirteen of the wisest and ablest of the corporation, aldermen and burgesses, to be chosen in common hall by major vote of the whole corporation. Those chosen to agree upon a place of meeting to consider the matter and adjourn from day to day till they have perfected it ('tis matter to be decided by major vote, making seven a "Coram"), to choose an able clerk to "method" and record their orders, who may be their Recorder—and if he be one of the thirteen he may vote likewise—and "the lawyer" to sit with them as assistant to resolve in point of law. And those not consenting to election of the select number for concluding all things ... ought to be esteemed enemies and to have forfeited their privileges and broken their oaths; and so they may legally proceed by major vote to disfranchising them as refractory and wilful persons. Will nominate the great plebeian Mr. Edward Price of the Genyefin one of the eleven or thirteen, who, when convinced to the reason of these proposals, will prove a main pillar for the ... lasting good of Mountgomery town and parish; which is much wished by the writer, though wanting that sound judgement many of them are endued with. *HM*2.9/84.

By the "freeland" of the borough is meant certain town lands in the revenues from which all the freemen of the borough enjoyed a share.

1688

656. JHO. JERVIS TO MR. HUMPHREY OWEN AT THE GOAT IN ... DUBLIN.

When they parted at Lazy Hill, Owen ordered him to deliver those papers to Mr. Davies, which he did into his own hands at the foot of his stairs; he carried them into his room, but may have forgotten where he laid them. The copy of the attainder is but a small paper, but there he will certainly find it. Mr. Berry and his master could not agree to divide stakes; delivered the four cobs to Berry ..... Carthy of Clydane is not yet come into this country. Is glad to receive a letter without mention of that unlucky bill. Mr. Herbert came home an hour since. Mr. Wm. Kenny and his lady are now on the sea bound for the Bath, and will go to Lymor Lodge to get a lease from "my Lord" of Tullygibbeene and Fayhudeffe, he having bought Michael Fitz Gerald's interest therein; Thomas is much concerned, and swears he never shall buy his. He may acquaint his lordship if he thinks fit.

Castle Island,
1 July. 164.

"Cobs" might be horses, but are more probably coins—a cob being a Spanish dollar.

1688

657. HUM. OWEN TO LORD HERBERT. TO BE LEFT AT THE POST-HOUSE IN SALOP.

Encloses copy of the Articles of Plantation of Munster in the Rolls Office, which makes all differences determinable before the Council in England for want of a President and Council in Munster; which, dated at Westmr. by Queen Elizabeth, and being in nature of a covenant between her and the undertakers (whereof his great-grandfather was one), seems to ascertain where all undertakers should have determination of matters between them and the Irish. Requests him to petition His Majesty in Council alleging this, and that he is sued for part of these plantation lands by Maurice Fz Gerald and Thomas Fz Gerald, Wm. Foly, Dominick Roch, Callaghane Mc Callaghane, and Owen Mc Carthy—part of the grand seigniory of Mount Eagle Loyal, erected in pursuance of the said articles; that these lands were gained from the usurpers in 1657, and he ever since possessed peaceably of them till these two last years; that by the depositions of witnesses (most Irish) it has been part of the seigniory for many years, some speaking to more than sixty years' knowledge. Requests this way because he fears not only that the land in question will be given from his lordship, but when Sir Patrick Traunt comes to make his election all will be disjointed; and last of all the whole will be in danger. There is time to do it at the assizes at Kilarney on 4 September. It will be easier followed in England than here, and better success may be expected upon rational grounds. If this fails he knows not what will become of the whole plantation. Here are many instances every day of favours to the Irish and disaffection to the English. Will mention Lord Corke and Burlington's case because he is coming over. Sir Christopher Hatton was an undertaker in Waterford; he sold to one who sold to Lord Corke's ancestor, who has had possession 88 years till the tenants were served in ejectment in May or June last. The assizes being there twice a year, and his lordship in England, time was with much ado given for the long vacation. This is for £1,000 per annum, claimed by one whose estate of £2,000 per annum has all this time joined to it. Any who has land in this kingdom can give an account of such and worse things. Knows of no other way but a patent from this King to some great person, as Lord Dartmouth, of all escheated lands in the barony of Trughanackmy in Kerry or in co. Kerry at large. It would be good employment for Madam Bromley to solicit. Can think of no other way. Has used all ways imaginable to stay the trial against his lordship, but it will not do. Is foretold the cause will go against him, and no writ of error will delay it anything worth the cost. All causes left to law here against the old or new interest are in danger, since the Act of Settlement is called a law against Magna Charta, and not to be taken favourably, as Mr. Attorney has declared.

Lord Herbert's house in the seigniory is delivered up by Mr. Kenney, who is in possession of Kilcushney, where Thomas Fitz Gerald, his lordship's adversary, lived. Fitz Gerald's hopes of the estate have broken him and all his tenants, and they are all run away, he himself to his father-in-law in co. Corke. Several tenants have quitted the Island, some [from] lands near to Mr. Wm. Kenney because of his ill neighbourhood. Wm. Kenney and his wife are going to the Bath, with an intention to wait on Lord Herbert for a lease of Tulligibine and Fahaduffe. This is to be said against it: He has built and settled in a small parcel recovered out of the seigniory, pretends it to be "ought of the seigniory" and [that] he may prevent the taking of distresses there; Lord Herbert by his book can tell the arrears of what he holds already. But £10 2s. 8½d. was paid of last year's rent of what he desires at Fahaduffe and Tulligibine, which was £27 13s. 4d., and this last half year is £13 10s. Yet he made a bargain for one of the brothers Fz Gerald's interest and designs to weary out the other. Mr. Crofts has not sent, nor can he hear from Mr. Kenney's man here what is done about his arrear. If Lord Burlington comes to stay here longer than next winter it is to encourage his tenants, assuring himself all will be well here now the Prince of Wales is born.

Dublin,
6 July. 593.

[16]88

658. W., [Bishop of St.] Asaph, to Lord Herbert.

Is now upon his way to Poole, where he is to preach on Sunday next, and hopes to wait on him. Sends this bearer to [learn] whether he dines at home tomorrow, that he may wait on him then; or what other time he may enjoy that happiness.

27 July. *Armorial seal* *HM*2.23/55.

1688

659. John Oliver to Mr. Humfrey Owen at Mr. Rice Davies' at the Goat in . . . Dublin.

Their proceedings on the writ have been managed so well by Mr. Turbill that the adverse party has not done anything towards affirming their judgement in Ireland. "My Lord" is safe till next term upon the writ of error, notwithstanding their alarm of a writ of possession. But they are resolved to break through all laws, which if they do the Court of King's Bench here will be able to make them pay dear . . . Now sends a special injunction to use if they bring any other action. Received his letter with the piece of the Act of Plantation, and attended Mr. Solicitor-General with it for his opinion from hour to hour, but could get nothing from him before he went to town last Wednesday afternoon, except a promise he should have it from Oxford. Is heartily sorry matters are like to be so bad with his lordship in Ireland. Several of the persons Owen arrested appeared, and Dick Price wants instructions to declare.

The charter of Mountgomery is gone; the Attorney-General replied and the writer rejoined, and they gave notice of trial at the bar, countermanded it, and then gave notice of trial at the assizes in Salop. But the corporation not being too rich, and taking the example of Bishop's Castle (who withdrew their rejoinder after the expense of £60 or £80 in pleading, etc.) they sent the writer an instrument to withdraw and so judgement is entered against them.

Spoke to Mr. Church about Owen's own business; he has not yet proceeded to outlawry. Sent Owen's letter to his lordship and acquainted him that the matter was before Sir Wm. Williams. Will endeavour to do as he desires with Mr. Blenerhassett. Service from his wife.

31 July. 165.

The Solicitor-General now was Sir William Williams.

[16]88

660. Ja. Knight, junr., to Mr. Humphry Owen at Castle Island.

Has taken a *constat* of the patent. Searched the books in the Surveyor-General's office and can't find that ever Owen the now lessor, or Dennis the father, or Cormock the grandfather, took out a final settlement or so much as claimed at Athloane. Thus they were not transplanted, as he imagines. Got Mr. Shea to find that book; will take a copy attested under Mr. Grace's hand—the copy Owen left is not under Mr. Sands's hand. Got him to take 9s. to search for it. The copy will cost about a ducat more. This day Mr. Donovan Carthy, attorney, give notice of a trial for Cludane next assizes. Service to Mr. Mason.

Dubl.,
ult. July. 594.

The ducat was worth 9s. at the official rate of exchange in 1661 (*Cal. of State Papers, Ireland*, 1660-62, p. 197), but it would appear from No. 662 that in 1688 it was worth only about two-thirds of that sum. This is the first appearance in these letters of James Knight, jr., who about this time seems to have become Lord Herbert's attorney in Dublin.

1688

661. Pat. Fagan to Mr. Humprey Owen at Castle Island.

Is glad the troublesome bill is paid. Does not doubt the bill on Mr. Croftes will be paid. What does he mean by saying many of the writer's actions will eat a great sum at 6s. 8d. apiece? Is willing to pay the rent of the house proportionable to what he holds—would pay that without any suit. Had he known Mr. Mc Craith and Mr. Kenny would not allow it out of what they owed him—Mr. Mc Craith once said he would take it on himself—. . . . . . (*sentence not completed*). Is not inclined to pay the cost of the actions against him for that rent, though it should cost more in the superior court, nor can he believe any besides Mr. Jarvis would admit such actions into a court . . . The old woman has been troublesome expecting account of what Owen did for her. Prays him secure the offer he made the writer of the land and fairs. Respects to Mr. and Madam Wilson.

31 July. *Armorial seal* 756.

1688

662. CHID. BROOKES TO MR. HUM. OWENS AT CASTLE-ISLAND.

In Owen's bag left here to discharge Lord Herbert's crown rents he found 68 ducats weight, one plate cob, and one piece called a "dogg-doller", which last he returns, it being not current money. The crown rent due is £20 10s., and the collector usually has 5s. Has received but £20 12s. 9d. Is sorry not to have met him. Had Mr. Wilson let him know when they would have been here his last jaunt should have been deferred.

Tralee,
8 August.

Endorsed: Chidtley Brookes. 166.

1688

663. JOHN OLIVER TO MR. HUMFREY OWEN AT MR. REES DAVIES' AT THE GOAT IN . . . DUBLIN.

Believes Owen hears no more of the writ of possession. He should make no use of the injunction against Fz Gerald till occasion [arises], for they are safe until next term upon the writ of error. Cannot yet find Mr. Blanerhassett. Enclosed is Owen's case and two regulations. Both Mr. Solicitor's and Sjt. Pemberton's came too late for a petition, Mr. Solicitor being at the circuit, which began yesterday at Shrewsbury. Consulted Mr. Sloane, who better knows the constitution of the place; he thinks it better not to petition till the trial [is ov]er [and to get] Mr. Solicitor and other friends to back it. There may be irregularity of the trial, which, "strenghtd" by affidavits in Ireland, may be ground for a petition. He should be sure to give above twenty years' peaceable possession in evidence. But for fear of an Irish jury he sends two subpoenas to be served upon the plaintiffs and their lessors, whose names he hopes are right—Fitz-geralds being already served and in contempt. They should be served personally if possible as soon as the trials are over, if against "my Lord", and affidavits made here in England before 23 October; then doubts not but to send an injunction to stay execution before the Irish term. But for safety he should procure a writ of error in Ireland if in any court but the King's Bench—if there, the writer will send one. Service to Mr. Rees Davies.

21 August. 167.

1688

664. THE GENTLEMEN OF MONTGOMERYSHIRE TO LORD HERBERT.

Upon a public meeting at this time of the Great Sessions of all the gentlemen of the county here present, choice is made of Mr. Pugh of

Mathaverne for knight of the shire and Capt. Charles Herbert for burgess, to serve in this approaching parliament. They give him notice thereof as a person of great figure in their country, and request his approbation.

23 September.	Robert Mathewes	Eduard Vaughan
	J. Edwards	Pryce Devereux
	Rich. Mytton	Evan Glynne
	Arthur Vaughan	Nath. Maurice
	Ga. Wynne	Elis Juckes
	Edw. Jones	Gilbert Jones
	Rees Mondy	Sydd. Bynner

Added after folding: Mr. Edmund Lloyd consents but could not be met with till after it was sealed. *HM*2.9/66.

Charles Herbert was duly elected for the borough, but the knight of the shire was Edward Vaughan of Llwydiarth.

[16]88

665. JA. KNIGHT, JUNR., TO MR. HUM. OWEN AT CASTLE ISLAND.

Received his by Mr. Twisse last night. Encloses copy of the bill [etc.]. Gave Twisse two cobs for serving Madam Hassett, and he is gone over in the packet-boat. Encloses the subpoena against Owen Carthy; it's returnable 3 November—if he can get here by the 1st he may do it. Mr. Davis made difficulty to accept the £20 bill, but paid it. Presumes he has heard all the news. The last packet told them that Magdelen College was restored by His Majesty, who is now in a good posture of defence (in case the Dutch be so hardy [as] to attempt invasion) having 40,000 men in arms besides the trained bands, above forty good ships of war and twenty fireships ready; hopes they need not fear the Dutch this winter. Prays him, seeing Carboy Egan does not execute the decree, to employ any he thinks fit, assuring him 40s. out of the first money got by it; and to send the decree to Lt. Browne to get a warrant upon it. Prays him not forget the little bill on Mr. Jo[h]n Hassett, also the Twisses' money.

Dubl.,
18 October.

20 October. Since the above, a packet came in that tells them the Dutch were seen between the Dogger Sands and New Castle this day sennight, so it's to be feared they are landed by this. Do not hear that "our" fleet has engaged them. The King goes in person to quell this invasion. 595.

In fact, of course, the Prince of Orange had not yet set sail for the first time.

[16]88

666. JA. KNIGHT, JUNR., TO MR. HUM[PHREY OWEN AT] CASTLE ISLAND.

Hopes he is safe returned to the Island. Wishes him a Merry Christmas. Has a rule Roch shall pay 40s. costs before he proceeds, [and] a proclamation of rebellion against him and his lessee for not answering—they promise to give answer next term. Has Fitz Gerrald's execution returned by the sheriffs of this city. Shall he proceed against the bail or send a *testat*[*um*] *ca. sa.*? Mr. Donovan says Mr. Kenny the elder has ordered him to give an appearance; but nothing of Kenny the younger. Knows he'll mind the writer's little concern of Ro. Browne's decree to get the money; presumes he has Jack Hassett's.

Dubl.,
4 December.

Two packets due. Though the wind has been fair these two days "and two bowles at the head, yett wee have [them] not". The last packet brought much strange news, which he [will] have heard.

Armorial seal 596.

"Ca. sa." is presumably *capias ad satisfaciendum*.

[1688]

667. ANSWER OF THE GENTLEMEN OF CO. SALOP TO THE P. OF ORANGE'S PROPOSITION OF A VOLUNTARY LOAN TO DEFRAY HIS EXTRAORDINARY EXPENSES. *Copy in Lord Herbert's hand.*

Since last night there seems some alteration in affairs, whereupon they have consulted together and think it expedient to respite their thoughts of those proposals then made to them till they have seen precedents from other counties; then will follow the best examples. Will send answer up by some gentlemen of their own county.

Endorsed: Touching the loan the P. [of] O. proposed in his letter.

*HM*2.15/2.

1688/9

668. JOHN OLIVER TO MR. HUMFREY OWEN AT MR. REES DAVIES' AT THE GOAT IN . . . DUBLIN.

"My Lord" came hither on Thursday, and the first question he asked was if the writer had had any letters from Owen. Told him none since the end of October, at which he is strangely disturbed; he has not heard from Owen these five months. He should send him a letter by the first post with bills for what money he can get. The enclosed *Gazette* will give the news. Happy New Year.

1 January. 169.

[16]88/9

669. JO. READ TO LORD HERBERT.

St. Julian's house is in the same order as he has known it this fifteen years; it's dry overhead. Mr. Young will procure of the Earl of Pembrock's agent a copy of the lease for Newport Castle. Is informed there is in it but the castle and the moat. This piece where the cinders were taken up is a waste piece enjoyed by the corporation of Newport; Lord Pembrock's agent will not suffer workmen to dig there. Mr. Jenckins, being steward of the lordships of Llybeneth and Llyswerie, had the keeping of all writings concerning them; demanded them of Mrs. Jones, his administratrix, who promised they should be laid aside. Will attend Lord Herbert as soon as he can go abroad. His and his wife's prayers.

2 January *Armorial seal* *HM*2.23/56.

[16]88/9

670. Rees Davis to Mr. Humphry Owen at Castle Island.

Received the enclosed. The postman w[ould have] had two shillings, but they cost eighteen pence. The Lord Deputy has sent Lord Mun Joye and the Lord Chief Baron Rice into France to our King to know his will concerning Eierland. Several families have gone for England.

8 January. 170b.

1688/9

671. Ja. Knight to [Humphrey Owen].

Deferred taking out *scir. fa.* on the writ of error in Carthy's business, but fears a discontinuance, for the Lord Chancellor with the Chief Justices will sit on errors, they being all in town, and Lord Mountjoye and the Lord Chief Baron being this day sent to France to wait on His Majesty. It is expected all will remain quiet till their return. He should be here by the beginning of term. Prays him call upon Mr. Robt. Crompton, giving him and his lady the writer's service, and ask him to send the £3 3s. 6d. Money runs at a very low ebb in this town. Hopes something is done in Browne's decree and Mr. Jo[h]n Hassett's small sum.

Dubl.,
12 January.

Yesterday brought news that five or six Protest[ant] captains and lieutenants of Sir Thos. Newcomin's regiment in the north went off, sending their com[missio]ns sealed up to Sir Tho. Several of the Protest[ant] soldiers, with sergeants and drums, went with them, and, 'tis said, carried double arms. 'Tis said they have disarmed the Lord of Antrim's regiment of new-raised men. 'Tis said Lord Kingstone, Coote, and others are up at Sligoe and have declared for the Pr[ince]. Col. Richd. Hamilton came lately from Lond.; 'tis said he had a pass from the P[rince] and is to return in ten days; his business was to acquaint His Excellency here with the condition of the Roman Catholics in Eng[lan]d. Presumes he heard the King escaped the second time and got safe in France, that the Lords have desired the Pr[ince] to take the government and call a convention the 22nd instant, and that he has done accordingly. 268.

[16]88/9

672. Ja. Knight, junr., to Mr. Hum. Owen at Castle Island.

Is glad he has recovered from his late indisposition. Encloses the *testat. cap.*; can't proceed against the bail till it be returned. Fancies the captains that are so brisk now to muster "sans Com'n" will soon be quiet and cool. Is told Tralee and Ballybegin Castles have "shut upp for Engl. Garrisons", fortifying themselves and succouring the English; has no account thereof from Owen. Prays him, if he goes to Tralee before coming here, to tell Madam Eliz. Hassett that if she has any money to send the writer, she should send it by him. Sent her a bill protested, which she sent him. If he has any idle minutes he may throw them away reading the annexed. Will take care of his writ of error, etc.

Dubl.,
15 January. 597.

Ballybeggan is close to Tralee, two miles to the north-east.

[16]88/9

673. [MRS.] E. HASSETT TO MR. OWENS AT CASTLE ISLAND.

Had a protested bill come down last post, payable to Mr. Knight. Mr. Peirce Rice, who drew it, immediately sent another, which she is confident will be paid, or she will make Rice pay Owen.

Traly,
21 January. 598.

1688/9

674. ROBT. CROMPTON TO MR. HUMPHREY OWNES AT CASTLE ISLAND.

Mr. Knight should have [had] his money long ago, but, being desperate[ly] ill and under the doctor's hands, he has been at a vast charge. The last letter from Mr. Knight ordered him to pay Alderman Myagh of Corke, which he will in a fortnight; owes him £3 3s. 6d. The "dismisse" Knight got again[st] one Fokeman in Killarney, which "he" paid 14s. 6d. [for], his attorney notwithstanding carried to Corke and served Mr. Hawkins, who paid the 14s. 6d. . . . Cannot get Fokeman with the decree—he stands in defiance, as does Batten. Is £6 out of purse. Prays him deliver this to Mr. Knight; it will tell him he is pretty well, but his wife is sick.

Traly,
21 January. 599.

1688/9

675. JNO. HUSSEY TO MR. HUMPHRY OWNES AT CORKE.

Encloses his account, according to Mr. Twish's orders. Desires that, if he intends for England, he will order payment by Dr. Daly or another. Is to pay a sum of money on 25 March to Mr. Jame[s] Trant.

Castle Island,
14 February.

Understands he has the disposal of Mr. Mason's two colts. Pheoder was very free that the writer should have them for £4. Will pass bond to pay the money to Mr. Mason . . . or allow it in what Owens owes.

754.

The account is No. 98 in the Appendix—a bill for groceries, hardware, spirits, etc. "Pheoder" is probably Theodore.

1688/9

676. C.D. to Mr. Humphrey Owen at Alderman Field's house without South Gate, Corke.

Showed the letters to the persons they were for and encloses their answers. Owns the receipt of the malt from Mr. Trant—had intelligence that Doune Falvey intended to take all along with him without paying "my Lords" rent. He and Owen's aunt would also have some of the meal, but cannot have it from Mr. MaCraith. The fellow entrusted by Mr. Corbett made over his corn to others, and offers the land to Mr. David fitz Gerald of Cordal. If the writer had anything under Tho. Corbett's hand of the like date with his mother's covenant, he would endeavour to secure the land and get back his goods. The fittest man here to be seneschal is James Trant, for if they put in a distressed man he will bring what part of the county yields to any of "your" courts' order to the last extremity of poverty. Nor will any be able to mind it as well as Mr. Trant, who lives in town and is well friended and esteemed in the county. He should endeavour to discourse with Sir Val. Browne in Corke, whence he has not yet returned. Resolved to plough Cahirnanhards lands and use for it the oats remaining. Could take up malt and meal elsewhere [than] from those unwilling to deal honestly with his lordship. Gave ten shillings for his wage to Richard Jones, which George Twisse thought enough; the poor man is more indebted to Roger Hollis, Ter. Shanaghane, and John Hussey (besides small sums to Wm. Holli and others) than what he left is worth. Heard Richard Jones sent hither a garron by the man that brought Mr. Wilson's mare, but the fellow disowns it. If he will order Tho. MaCraith to deliver the colts and come upon Mr. Mason's concerns at Bally mc Adam, the writer will keep them; [otherwise] better let them lie in Mr. MaCraith's stable.

16 February. 173.

The writer is possibly the Dr. Daly of the preceding letter.

1688/9

677. Jno. Hussey to Mr. Humphry Ownes.

Mr. James Trant will pay no money, for what rent he owed he paid to the mills' rent, and that he cannot have from Falvey or Tho. mc Craith.

Castle Island,
16 February. 755.

1689

678. [Lord] Brandon and F. Gerard to the High Constables of co. Montgomary. *Contemporary copy.*

By virtue of a commission from the Earl of Macklesfield, Ld. President of Wales, to them his Deputy Lieutenants for summoning the militia, these are to require them to summon the militia to appear the 25th of this instant at Walch Poole with horse, arms, and ammunition, according to the Act of 14 Chas. II for ordering the forces, to come with pay and ammunition for three days. And the horse are to bring one shilling a man for the muster-master, and the foot sixpence.

14 September. *HM*2.15/6.

1689

679. JNO. BRADSHAWE TO MR. RICHARD STEDMAN OF DREVOR.

Is ordered to acquaint him that Lord Maclesfeild has ordered him a commission for Deputy Lieutenant of co. Mountgomary, if he will accept. Lord Brandon will be at a general meeting of the militia at Welch Poole on Wednesday next, with his commission, and desires his company to assist in settling the militia.

Poole, "Your servant Unknowne".
21 September. *Armorial seal* *HM*2.9/67.

1689

680. JHO. JERVIS TO MR. HUMPHREY OWEN AT CASTLE ISLAND. MR. RICE, POSTMASTER OF TRALEE, IS DESIRED TO HASTEN THIS.

Received a letter from Jno. Purcell, and finds one here to Owen which he guesses is from Mr. Oliver with the writs of error . . . Carthy of Castleloch has a lease from Mr. Denny within "that barony", but whether for lives is questioned. If he be no freeholder the challenge will stand good, for there must be two. Cannot understand what "my Ld. did [with *omitted*] Sr. Patr.", but Mr. Davies says his lordship went away very pleasant. Cannot get any idea who is like to be sheriff; it is fancied [it will be] Buckrose Moore or one of the Skiddeyes, so by all means this jury must be put by, and then the cause may go as well as if managed by others. His lordship left the Coventry letter and answer, and rule for the regulation of the kingdom (which he borrowed) with Mr. Davies to be copied and delivered to Owen; has paid for it. It is a pleasant regulation. Jno. Purcell shall hear from him. Service to Mr. Wilson.

Dublin,
22 October. *Armorial seal*

Notes on the dorse: Paid Mr. Connor £69 [in] 6s. 8d. pieces. The possession: O.D., C.Tho., and Thos. B. H. The pedigree: C. Tho., etc. The challenge, etc.: O.D., Tho.McC., Charles Thomas. The seiz[ure] etc.: T. McShane, Tho.Liddy, Charles Connor. 168.

"Carthy of Castleloch" is presumably Denis MacCarthy, first cousin to Florence MacCarthy, who was grandson of the great Florence MacCarthy. According to Butler's *Gleanings from Irish History* (p. 70) the second Florence had granted Castlelough to Denis. The persons listed in the notes are apparently witnesses to the various aspects of the case, possession, pedigree, etc.

1689

681. JA. KNIGHT, JUNR., TO MR. HUM. OWENS AT LYMA LODGE.

Arriving in this kingdom in May he repaired to London in July, hoping to meet him and other friends there. Wanted money, yet would not call to Lord Herbart for his account, £13 14s. 7d., because Owen might have accounted with his lordship. Was in hopes of visiting Ireld. again. Entreats him to take course to send part or the whole or to recommend it effectually to his lordship, that he may get a little to subsist on. Was in hopes upon "our" armies going over that he [need] not have troubled Owen on this account till their meeting in Ireld. Lodges at Mr. Poole's house at the upper end of Peppard Street, near Newgate in Chester.

Chester,
9 December. 600.

"1690" [1689/90]

682. [LORD] HERBERT TO MR. HUMFREY OWENS, BAILIFF OF MOUNTGOMERY.

In the writer's news last letter he gave notice of the dissolution of this parliament and that another was to be called on 20th March, and asked him to engage their friends and the burgesses of Mountgomery to stand to their old member, Capt. Charles Herbert (who is expected "suddainly" out of Ireland), Lord Torrington having desired the writer not to forsake him. Desires him to write to the gentlemen of their country. Has himself written to the chief of the gentry, *viz*, Jho. Price, Mr. Vaughan of Loydiarth, Mr. Devereux of Vaynor, Mr. Pugh of Mathavan, and Mr. Loyd of Berthloyd.

8 February.

Knows not when the election day will be. Supposes Mr. Ch. Herbert's agent will give the burgesses a dinner, which it will be Mr. Thomas Mason's care to manage. Service to Mr. Mason and his son. 181.

1689/90

683. [LORD] HERBERT TO "MR. BAYLEIFES AND MY BROTHER BURGESSES" OF THE TOWN OF MOUNTGOMERY. *Addrressed:* MR. HUMFREY OWENS, BAILIFF OF MOUNTGOMERY.

The King thinking it fit to dissolve Parliament and call a new one to meet him 20th March, the writer recommends Col. Charles Herbert once more to be returned as member of Parliament for their borough. In doing which they not only discharge themselves worthily but oblige the Colonel, the Earl of Torrington his brother, and the writer, who is never wanting in doing their corporation in general and themselves in particular all the good he can. The Colonel has the King's leave to come over, and they expect him every day.

15 February. 174.

[1689/90]

684. [LORD] HERBERT TO MR. HUMFREY OWENS, BAILIFF OF MOUNTGOMERY.

Thanks him and their brother burgesses for returning Col. Charles Herbert. Wrote a more formal letter last week. But between themselves—"and let it not goe from amongst the Brethren"—might they not assume their old custom of returning from the town, excluding the foreign burgesses from signing with them? Or, to keep up their old privilege, might not one return be made from the town and out-burgesses and another from the town alone? All corporations will this parliament assume their old customs of election and returning. Would know whether he has the writ yet, and the day of election.

Would have taken it kindly if he had acquainted him what happens in the country, as the writer does what happens in town. Hears out [of] Shropshire that Tho. Price of Lanvillin is secured and imprisoned by Sir John Price. But he hears not a word from his Clerk of the Peace; is this as it should be? Prays him acquaint Roger Jones that his letter wherein Mr. Nightinghall desired his good word to the Bishop of St. Asap was three weeks missing and the gift disposed of long before it came.

[*postmarked* 18 February].

Hears Col. Herbert is landed; believes he will see his election over before he comes for London. Is told his sister Brown is selling her time in Weston Farm; prays him advise [her] to give Mr. Edward Price first refusal. It is just she should do so. 274.

"1690" [1689/90]

685. [Lord] Herbert to Mr. Humfrey Owens, Bailiff of Mountgomery.

Mr. Devereux will be answered by the Colonel himself, thus: 1. He is in London; 2. He stands; 3. He will attend the parliament. Is not sorry men show themselves; it is a return for standing for the out-boroughs against the town and the writer not many years ago. Mr. Tho. Mason sent word Mr. Devereux would not molest the Colonel. Would have been well enough pleased if the Colonel had directed Mr. Devereux be returned, yet will take it very ill of those that quit the Colonel while the writer is engaged for him. The town of Pool were so civil as to send by Capt. Mostyn to know whom the writer would declare for. Took it very well at their hands, and pursued a complaint of theirs against Wm. Lloyd, who had done ill things in their neighbourhood; if the good intelligence between them is already broken, he should let the writer know, that he may behave himself accordingly. Is confident Mr. Tho. Mason will manage both his son's and Col. Herbert's concerns. If need be (wishes he were driven to the necessity) Owen must leave off his indifferency or return from the town alone without the out-burgesses. Ever expected a fickleness.

The town is obliged to the writer that the next assizes are fixed at Mountgomery, also the winter assizes, and it will be the last of the circuit, as Littleton Powis told him on going for Ludlow (where he now is, striving for parliament man).

Mr. Daniell Whittingham must know the writer cannot spare freestone. Has a great deal to do with it in his garden. Owen must not suffer any to be taken away, and is to let Roger Jones know as much. Would know whether Owen pays postage for news that the writer puts "Frank" upon. If so, 'tis supererogation, "and since you like it, pray continue it. And when you are a-weary, let me know".

27 February. *Armorial seal* 176.

This letter is franked by Lord Herbert.

[1689/90]

686. [LORD] HERBERT TO [MR.] HUMFREY OWENS, BAILIFF OF MOUNTGOMERY. *Badly torn.*

He tells of the writer's letter going out of the way to Oswestry, but not whether it was broke open. Does not forget his purpose of changing the post road, but the world is so busy in elections . . . Approves of the Colonel's resolution and Owens's of returning by the home burgesses. The Colonel's being a sworn burgess signifies not one straw in a committee of election; but will use it as an argument to send him down to look after his business and spend some moneys in town among their poor neighbours. Does not approve of Owens's project of Frank Herbert—it will be much better the Colonel be returned, because it will be "direct crosing the former proceedings and by the same person". But the out-b[urgesses] are ungrateful to put him up . . . Owens [? will know how] to manage matters for the town's advantage in recovering their ancient rights. The sheriff must confine his . . . .(*torn*) . . . . of war within the law or Mr. Read will find his blind side and recover damages. Col. Herbert is now in town; he wrote that he resolves positively for Mountgomery and says he has written to all the gentlemen of the county to be for him. Moreover, he is willing that anything be done in this election that advances the writer's and the town's interest most, so all is referred to Owen's "Courage and Conduct". Colonel Herbert cannot come down to the election, but entrusts Mr. Mason and Owens with the care of it.

We have had a mighty victory against the Irish, the part commanded by Capt. Ousley. "The second part go miles of[f] from the first, by Lanier who command[s]. They are in a strange consternation. If they [will bu]t follow their . . . . (*illegible*) . . . . the busness is done".

. . . . Street,
[*postmarked* 1 March].

Armorial seal 275.

"Frank Herbert" is Francis Herbert of Dolguog. The High Sheriff at this time was Edward Lloyd of Berth Lwyd.

1689/90

687. WOLFRAN SMYTH TO RICHARD HERBERT, ESQ., AT DOLGEOG.

Hopes the rheum will not so much trouble his lady now the blood is taken away. Has sent an unguent to annoint the lower part of her back with, night and morning, only forbearing at the time of her courses. Is glad her teeth are neither black nor loose, which seldom escape one in her condition. If she loves sweetmeats, she should forbear them as much as she can. Desires she will brew her[self] some scurvy-grass drink with wormwood in it. Many thanks for his token.

Salop.,
2 March. 421.

"1690" [1689/90]

688. [LORD] HERBERT TO MR. HUMFREY OWENS, BAILIFF OF MOUNTGOMERY.

Received his of 28 February. Col. Herbert is resolved to stand, makes no doubt of the King's leave to attend the parliament, and thanks the gentlemen for their consent; he will discharge the trust most faithfully. If they expect the writer's private opinion, he must say he believes Col. Herbert has, besides public, private concerns that will necessitate him to attend a longer time than next session, which Owen is to communicate to those most concerned, as Mr. Devereux, etc. Hears no opposition against Mr. Edw. Vaughan as their knight; is well enough satisfied with him. In the enclosed, Owen has Mr. Charles Herbert's consent to do what is best for the town's and the writer's interests. Owen can best judge how to retrieve their lost privileges. There must be art and secrecy and judgement—of which Owen is enough master. "You have your Cue. Letters may miscarry".

5 March. 184.

[1689/90]

689. [LORD] HERBERT TO MR. HUMFREY OWENS, BAILIFF OF MOUNTGOMERY.

Received his account of the election and the manner of Owen's return. The affair must wait till they have fitter materials; there is no haste. 'Twas happy there was "no necessity for it". Is glad of the good accord between parties. Owen did not tell him who were the chiefs in the regiment of ale-houses, who treated and who were treated, what was spent, and whether the spending in town has enabled the writer's tenants to pay their rents—"a very considerable matter, but not worth mentioning". He is to acquaint sister Brown—"I mean Mr. Edward Price"—with her propositions. But intends no close bargaining for himself, therefore she must look out elsewhere.

[c. mid-March]. 182

[16]90

690. ROB. GRIFFITH TO MR. HUMPHREY OWEN, HEAD BAILIFF OF MONTGOMERY.

Mr. John Hasset, a person unknown to the writer, is pressing for renewal of Killmurry lease. It is "my Lords" pleasure that Owen and Mr. Jones report what they conceive fittest and safest to be done. Has discoursed Mr. Wilson on this.

29 March.

Had he not known Mr. Hum. Owen's handwriting, he would not have believed the parable of the prodigal son so strange to him that he expresses no gratitude to a brother who has acted nothing to the dishonour of his friends; if it lies in his way he will serve him out of abhorrence to unnaturalness. 175.

[? 1690]

691. [LORD] HERBERT TO MR. HUMFREY OWENS, BAILIFF OF MOUNTGOMERY.

Received his of the 6th with the writs for the quarter sessions. Would have them kept at Mountgomery for this time. Nobody has spoken to him that it should be anywhere else, so knows no reason why the poor town should not have the advantage the others do not desire. None has been so much a sufferer as Mountgomery. While the writer's interest lasts (God knows how long, "considering the last turne upon the Toe—I will not explaine") they shall find the benefit.

Believes he has settled their two assizes for this year with Sir John Trenchard, who has promised that this spring and next winter sessions shall be at Mountgomery, and that from next spring he will give the spring assizes to Pool or Llanvilling and the winter assizes to Mountgomery constantly. If 20s. spent will not enable tenants, assizes and quarter sessions may have the same objection, and then it is no purpose to endeavour the enriching so slothful a generation, and a new method must be taken to improve those more worthy of improvement, or at least capable. "Your Loveing freind".

12 April. 183.

1690

692. [LORD] HERBERT TO MR. HUMFREY OWENS, BAILIFF OF MOUNTGOMERY.

Last night came David Adney with the white horse and colts, a letter from Owen, and a project in parchment which the writer does not understand, perhaps never will—but he will shortly come into the country and receive his meaning more at large. Would be glad to hear that Owens' slow neighbour Mat Morgan had done the business so long threatened.

15 April. 177.

1690

693. [LORD] HERBERT TO MR. HUMFREY OWENS, BAILIFF OF MOUNTGOMERY.

Blames him for uncertainties. Men in London can't be so particular in their times of going out [of] town. Would have the quarter sessions held this time at Llanvillin. Are [so] busy listening after news that they have no leisure to write any. There's good news from Ireland. K. James has quitted Ardee and "wee" pursue and encamp at night whence they marched in the morning. K. W. expects to be in Dublin ere this, having got his army between the enemy and Dublin. News from the fleet not so good and Lord Torrington much blamed, but how guilty none knows yet; Lord Devonshire and Lord Pembrock are gone down to examine where the fault lies.

5 July. 178.

[late 17th C.]

694. GA. WYNNE TO ———.

Is confident there is a long time unexpired in the bearer's lease. Cannot determine whether he or the bearer has it, for the writer's key is at Plasse Newydd. Would willingly burst the door open, but his study is within his tenant's apartment. Begs him to deal as favourably as he can with the bearer till the writer can search his "custody", which shall be immediately after 5 November.

Endorsed : Gabriell Wynn's letter for Edwd. ap David's lease.

471.

APPENDIX

LIST OF DOCUMENTS OMITTED FROM THE CALENDAR

NOTE: This list does not include documents which by date or provenance would be excluded from the Calendar itself (see *Introduction*, p. 3). Nor does it include mere copies of calendared documents.

Part I - HERBERT OF POWIS CASTLE

1. Notes on the authority of [Catholic] Bishop Richard Smith, to satisfy the scruples of "Mr. Hor." [? 1629]. 389.
2. Conditions for giving the present [Catholic] Jubilee. 11 July, 1636. *HM*2.12/13.
3. The State of the Case of Sir Percy Herbert . . . submitted to the . . . House of Parliament. [? 1651]. *Printed.* *HM*2.12/55.
4. Order of the House of Lords taking sequestration off Lord Powis's estates. 18 July, 1660. *HM*2.14/2.
5. Note of Lord Danby's demand for rents. [1683 or later]. 426.
6. The same. [1686 or later]. 428.
7. State of the case touching the improvement of Sedgmoore. [1685-1688]. *HM*2.9/81.
8. Reasons against a late patent of Mr. Keck and Mr. Heyton offered to the Lords of the Admiralty by the City of London. [? 1683-1688]. 766.
9. Orders by the Lord Mayor and Aldermen of London concerning a patent to Keck and Heyton for incroachments in the Thames. 13 September and 19 December, 1687. *Contemporary copies.* 418.
10. Rentroll and survey of the manor and farm of Acton Burnell, Acton Pigott, Ruckley, Langley, Burrington, Rusbury, and East Wall. [? 1688]. 771.
11. Receipt, John Evans to Mr. Richard Hughes, by order of Viscount Mountgom[er]y, to the use of the Marquess of Carmarthen. 22 January, 1689/90. 440.
12. Ral. Mylott to Mr. Richard Hughes at Welsh Poole. London, 8 April, 1690. *HM*2.23/67.
13. Inventory of Lord Powis's muniments, writings, etc. [c. 1690]. *HM*2.23/48.
14. Blank commission for a major in the Marquess of Mountgomery's regiment of horse. St. Germaines, 10 March, 1691 [N.S.]. *HM*2.15/10.
15. Receipt, John Evans to Mr. Richard Hughes to the use of the Marquess of Carmarthen. 8 August, 1692. 443.
16. The same. 9 August, 1692. 441.
17. Receipt, Rees Thomas to Mr. Richard Hughes to the use of the Marquess of Carm[ar]then. 11 August, 1692. 442.
18. Receipt, Rees Thomas to Mr. Hughes. 21 June 1693. 438.
19. Receipt, Rees Thomas to Mr. Hughes of Llanlligan, to the use of the Marquess of Carmarthen. 21 June, 1693. 439.
20. Edwd. Partner to———————. 2 July, 1695. *Partly in code.* *HM*2.23/71.

Part II - HERBERT OF MONTGOMERY and HERBERT OF DOLGUOG

21. Commission of the peace for [? Shropshire]. [1453-9]. *Copy, late 16th C., defective.* 482.

22. Speciall Orders and directions set foorth by the Queenes Maiesties commandement, to all Justices of Peace, and all Maiors, Shiriffes, and all principall Officers of Citties, Boroughs, and Townes corporate, for stay and redresse of dearth of Graine. London, 1600. *Printed.* *HM*2.9/45.
23. Cessment of 10s. on the town and liberties of Mountgom[er]y for provision of His Majesty's house for "Sturks", and 5s. towards relief of the poor prisoners in the county gaol. 29 May, 1609. *HM*2.9/48.
24. Cessment of 10s. on the borough of Mountgom[er]y for provision of "Sturkes". 29 May, 1611. *HM*2.9/47.
25. Poem upon the death of Mr. Hugh Broughton. August, 1612. By W. Primeros. *HM*2.21/4.
26. Sir Edward Herbert's expenses at Ambois and Tours. 1619. 320.
27. The same, at Tours. June 1619. 323.
28. The same, at Tours, and between Tours and Amboys and Paris. [1619]. 321.
29. The same. November, 1619—February, 1619/20. 322.
30. Recipe "for intolerable heat of the urine". [? early 17th C.]. 762.
31. Receipt, Lord Herbert to Tho. Roper. 14 June, 1627. 328.
32. Richarde Thompson's account, Monmothshire. 1629. 802B.
33. Inquisition relating to Ryston, Mountgom[er]y, Wititree, Tuneburt, Stocton, Woderton, Marinton, the church of Churburye, and warren in the manor of Worthin. [early to mid 17th C.]. *Copy, part only.* *HM*2.9/85.
34. Poem, *The Storm*, by Capt. T. Herbert. [? c. 1620-1640]. 476.
35. [Lord Herbert's] notes on the modern French discipline of war. 1638. *HM*2.12/16.
36. Note of Richard Owen's dealings [with Lord Herbert's tenants in Anglesey, Caernarvonshire, and Montgomeryshire]. [? c. 1640]. 800.
37. An Alderman of New-castle to his Friend in London. 8 September, 1640. *Copy; substantially the same as the version printed in* Cal. of State Papers, Domestic, 1640/41, *pp*. 28-9. *HM*2.12/20.
38. The King's licence to Lord Herbert to be absent from Parliament. 10 August, 17th year [1641]. *HM*2.12/34
39. Blank certificate by commissioners in co. Salop for levying money for disbanding the armies, etc. [1641]. 765.
40. Mr. Davenant's Remonstrance to the Commons House of Parliament. [July, 1641]. 475.
41. Draft of motion in House of Commons based upon Lord Herbert's petition (No. 186). *Endorsed:* "1644" [*recte* 1646]. *HM*2.9/0.
42. Particulars of the estate of Richd. Herbert of St. Julian's, esq., for which he desires to compound. [c. 1647]. *HM*2.21/22.
43. Detailed estimate of the cost of building the new castle at Montgomery. 23 June, 1649. *HM*2.9/23.
44. Council of State to the Committee for Compounding ordering that Lord Herbert have allowance of the remainder of his fine. 22 January, 1649/50. *Contemporary copy.* *HM*2.9/32.
45. Answer of Wm. Basill, esq., His Highness's Attorney General, to Lord Herbert's bill of complaint. 25 November, 1650. *Office copy.* *HM*2.22/9.
46. Petition of Lady Mary Herbert and Lord Herbert to the Commissioners of the Treasury. [December, 1655]. (See No. 237). *HM*2.12/47.
47 Order by the Commissioners of the Treasury discharging Lord Herbert's heirs from further question as to his fine for delinquency. 2 January, 1655/6. *HM*2.12/48.
48. Notes in preparation for a law-suit, compiled by Lord Herbert's servant or solicitor. 1 October, 1658. *HM*2.12/50.
49. Lord Herbert's acceptance of the general pardon. 7 June, 1660. *HM*2.14/1.
50. The King's Instructions for the Earl of Carbery on his appointment as Lieutenant of Southwales and Northwales. 1 October, 1660. *Copy in Richard Herbert's letter-book.* *HM*2.14/3/5
51. Form of a warrant to issue from Deputy Lieutenants [in South and North Wales] to high constables. [1660-61]. *Copy in Richard Herbert's letter-book.* (See No. 277). *HM*2.14/3/9.

52. Summons to the high constables of the Montgomeryshire hundreds to meet at Poole on 6 February. 23 January [1660/61]. *Copy in Richard Herbert's letter-book.* *HM*2.14/3/10.
53. Lord Herbert's account with Thomas Herbert, his agent in Ireland. 1663. 94.
54. Receipt for King's rent and fees paid into the Irish Exchequer. 10 July, 1664. *HM*2.22/15.
55. Interrogatories and depositions in a suit between the Earl of Orrery and Lord Herbert as to boundaries in Culcow, Cluddane, and Ballimacruttery. 1667. *HM*2.22/17.
56. Lord Herbert to Rece Morgan. [? 1660-73]. *Jotted notes for a draft only.* *HM*2.23/82.
57. Collection of Proceedings in the House of Commons about impeaching the Earl of Clarendon . . . 1667. *HM*2.14/5.
58. List of those in the Commission of the Peace for co. Salop (with quorum indicated). 15 November, 1670. *HM*2.9/49.
59. Receipt, Tho. Freckleton to Sir Hen. Herbert, for £50 for the use of Capt. Hen. Herbert. 29 February, 1671/2. *HM*2.23/16b.
60. Order signed by Louis XIV for the march through France of the English cavalry (with related papers). *Endorsement in the hand of Capt. Henry Herbert.* [1671/2]. *HM*2.14/7c.
61. Capt. Henry Herbert's narrative of his journey through France with his regiment. 1671-3. *Includes also three poems, one by Vavasar Powell on the late K. Charles.* *HM*2.14/7a,b.
62. ——————— to [? Lord Herbert]. Mountgom[er]y, 25 March, 1673. *Fragment only.* 407.
63. Record of soldiers aboard H.M.S. *St. George* under the command of Capt. Henry Herbert. 1673. *HM*2.14/9.
64. Lord Herbert's appointment of Richard Herbert of Dolgiog as his deputy *Custos Rotulorum* for co. Mountgomery on his going to Ireland. 3 June, 1673. *Armorial seal.* *HM*2.9/51.
65. Note on preparing antimony for chickens. [? late 17th C.]. 763.
66. Reasons offered by the London merchants against a public insurance office. [? late 17th C.]. *HM*2.15/19.
67. Draft by Lord Herbert for 4 gns. on Thomas Fowles, with receipt appended. 4 May, 1677. *HM*2.23/27.
68. The Commons address to the King. 25 May, 1677. *Copy.* 767.
69. List of commissioners for co. Mountgomery for raising £600,000 for 30 ships. 1677. *HM*2.9/56.
70. Order from the Lords Commissioners for Assessing the Peers to the Poll Tax to Lord Herbert at Llyssin to signify his income and estate. Westminster, 11 April, 1678. 413.
71. Serjeant Maynard's arguments [in a case of privilege]. 1678. *HM*2.14/6.
72. Fr. Fitzherbert's account of legal expenses. Michaelmas 1678. 574.
73. E.W. to ———————, about money due from one Durrant. 14 February, [16]78/9. 414.
74. Account of the descent of the family of Herbert. [c. 1680]. *Fragmentary.* *HM*2.21/26.
75. Return of Popish recusants, hundred of Dythur. [c. 1680]. 477.
76. Poem, [? *The Tr*]*ue English* [? *Man*]. (A political satire). [c. 1680]. 478.
77. 2 poems, *To M.M., esq., Chief B*[*ailiff*] *of our B*[*orough*] *of M*[*ontgomery*], and *Mr. Recorder's Charge to the Serjeants.* [October, 1680]. *HM*2.9/59.
78. Poem, *To a Grand Jury at a Great Court for the Borough of Mountgom*[*er*]*y.* October, 1680. *HM*2.9/60.
79. Ed. Whittingham's narrative of the election of the second bailiff of Mountgom[er]y. October, 1680. *HM*.2.9/57.
80. Draft of a bill for limiting pro- and post-fines in Wales, "given Mr. Andr. Newport". 1681. *HM*2.9/63.
81. [Lord Herbert's] propositions to Mr. Firth and Mr. Thomas for "finishing a house for me" in Soe Hoe Square. *Jottings of necessary improvements.* 1681/2. *HM*2.21/6.

82. Security by John Muckleston, butcher, Holborn, and Robert Lloyd, glover, Aldersgate Street, for William Davies, admitted into Lord Herbert's service as a footman. 24 October, 1682. *HM*2.23/40.
83. The King's Instructions for the Commissioners for Remedy of Defective Titles in Ireland. 13 May, 1684. *Contemporary copy.* *HM*2.22/21.
84. Receipt, Lord Herbert to Patrick Trant, esq., for £91 for Coggery Mills. 29 July, 1684. *Holograph copy.* *HM*2.22/26.
85. [Lord Herbert] to Mr. Harries. Lymore, 28 [October], 1684. *Holograph copy.* (See No. 547). *HM*2.22/40c.
86. [Robt. Griffith] to Mr. Kenney. [12 November, 1684]. *Holograph copy.* (See Nos. 554 and 557). *HM*2.22/43d.
87. P. Trant to Mr. Baron Worth in Dublin. London, 31 December, [16]84. *Contemporary copy.* (See No. 577). *HM*2.22/53b.
88. P. Trant to Sir Standidge Hartstonge, one of the Barons of the Exchequer of Ireland, in Dublin. London, 31 December, 1684. *Contemporary copy.* *HM*2.22/53c.
89. Reasons (with answers) against excepting persons of £20 per annum or £500 stock from the intended general pardon for the Western Rebellion. [1685]. 768.
90. [Lord Herbert] to——————. *Brief note requesting a certain ring and a letter.* [c. 1682-1691]. *HM*2.23/76.
91. John Oliver to Mr. Humfrey Owen at Dublin. 1 November, [16]87. (See No. 635). 136.
92. Jno. Hussey's account to Mr. Humpry Owen for miscellaneous goods. June-September, 1688. 753.
93. The same. November-December, [? 1688]. 752.
94. The same. December-January, 1688-1688/9. 751.
95. Mr. Humphry Owen's debt to James Fitz Gerald, mainly for ale and brandy. [1688/9]. 656.
96. John Oliver to Mr. Rees Davies at Dublin. 1 January, 1688/9. *Forwarding No.* 668. 170a.
97. Patrick Fagan's account to Mr. Owen for brandy, etc. 16 January, 1688/9. 749.
98. [John Hussey's] account to Humphry Owen for miscellaneous goods. 16 January—11 February, 1688/9. 748.
99. Warrant for Lord Herbert's salary at £1,500 per annum for October-December, 1689, and his receipt to the Treasurer of the Household, 12, June, 1690. *Copies.* *HM*2.15/9.
100. The same, for salary January-March, 1690, and receipt, 12 June, 1690. *Copies.* *HM*2.15/8.

INDEX

INDEX

References generally are to Letters, as serially numbered in the foregoing pages; references prefixed by the letter A are to the Letters listed in the Appendix; references to the Introduction are by page numbers, and these are given in italics. Abbreviations used in entries of Irish place-names are: t—townland, p—parish, b—barony, E—England, I—Ireland.